Law in the Metaverse

Law in the Metaverse

When two worlds collide

Jacqueline Watts

Contributors

Gareth Hall
Courtney L'homme
Mann Matharu
Azhar Sadique

Bloomsbury Professional

LONDON • DUBLIN • EDINBURGH • NEW YORK • NEW DELHI • SYDNEY

BLOOMSBURY PROFESSIONAL

Bloomsbury Publishing Plc
50 Bedford Square, London, WC1B 3DP, UK
1385 Broadway, New York, 10018, USA

Bloomsbury Publishing Ireland Ltd
29 Earlsfort Terrace, Dublin 2, D02 AY28, Ireland

BLOOMSBURY and the Diana logo are trademarks of Bloomsbury Publishing Plc

First published in Great Britain 2025

1

British Library Cataloguing-in-Publication Data

A catalogue record for this book is available from the British Library.

ISBN:	PB:	978 1 52653 075 2
	Epdf:	978 1 52653 077 6
	Epub:	978 1 52653 076 9

Typeset by Evolution Design and Digital (Kent)
Printed and bound by CPI Group (UK) Ltd, Croydon, CR0 4YY

MIX
Paper | Supporting responsible forestry
FSC® C013604

Dedication

'The true sign of intelligence is not knowledge but imagination.'

Einstein

To my amazing son, Matthew, whose curiosity reminds me of the boundless possibilities ahead; To my husband, for your love, support and belief in me; To my mum and dad, for your love and encouragement that has guided me every step of the way; And to all my family, whose love has always been a source of strength.

This book is dedicated to you all, with gratitude for your faith in me.

Preface

'What is now proved was once only imagined.'

William Blake

The metaverse represents a new chapter in the evolution of human interaction, commerce, and culture. Virtual worlds, Web3 and other emerging technologies, are rapidly redefining the boundaries of our social, economic, and legal frameworks. As this space grows, so too does the need to examine its relationship with the law. Can traditional legal principles adapt to this new world, or do we need to develop entirely new laws, regulations and principles?

My fascination with the intersection of law and technology began during my studies at King's College, London. In 2005, I had the privilege of taking a jurisprudence class with Professor Brownsword and it was his pioneering insights into the relationship between the law and technology which sparked my enduring interest in this field. Over the years I have had the opportunity to work with many technology clients who have been pushing the boundaries with their innovations and emerging technologies. This has deepened my understanding of how innovation challenges existing legal systems and creates opportunities for fresh perspectives. Innovation does not wait for the law to have the answers, it just demands a solution. Clients need advice and support regardless of whether or not the law is clear, established or certain. Legal professionals need to dig deep, often into first principles and analogous situations to try and forge a decisive path forward for their clients.

This book explores the legal implications of a virtual world, examining how traditional legal principles hold up in this novel context and identifying areas where they fall short. It is my hope that this work contributes to the dialogue about the role of law in shaping the new digital world, fostering a framework that promotes innovation while still protecting fundamental rights and values. It offers a consideration of fundamental underlying jurisprudential principles, as well as providing practical guidance for practitioners seeking to navigate this space right now on how they can guide and support their clients in this new terrain and also looks to the ongoing future development in this space.

I invite you to join me on this journey through the legal landscapes of the metaverse, as we consider the challenges, opportunities, and possibilities that await us in this new frontier.

Jacqueline Watts
January 2025

Preface

Contributors

GENERAL EDITOR AND CONTRIBUTOR

Jacqueline Watts

Jacqueline is an experienced Solicitor who specialises in acting for clients with cutting-edge innovations in the emerging technologies space. She is the director of a boutique law firm in the City of London and heads up its busy Corporate and Commercial Team.

Jacqueline advises a range of innovative clients across a multitude of sectors and disciplines, each at varying stages of funding, expansion and exits. She is an expert in emerging technologies and has a busy practice supporting pioneering clients in blockchain, cryptoassets, Web3, artificial intelligence, quantum computing, IoT and autonomous vehicles.

She has a keen eye for emerging trends, is an active member of the IEEE Spatial Computing for Metaverse Initiative, was shortlisted in the Women Leaders in Tech Law for the Women, Influence & Power in Law UK Awards 2024 and regularly speaks at industry events including Tech Summit London, Zebu Live and the Global Intellectual Property ConfEx in London.

Jacqueline completed her Law Degree and Masters in Law at Kings College, London. She started her legal career focusing on Criminal and International Criminal Law, having interned on the Charles Taylor Defence Team at the Special Court for Sierra Leone then working at a specialist Criminal Law, Criminal Appeals and Prison Law Firm in Mayfair, London before moving into Corporate and Commercial Law in the City of London.

Comments about Jacqueline:

'A go-to resource for me to get support and guidance on legal questions related to all things web3.'

McVal Osborne, CEO Gro3.io (former Chief Data Officer for Flight Story)

'Her heart is on the side of innovators looking to change the world for the better. She knows obstacles will likely be placed in their way, and her motives are always to safeguard and protect her clients to keep their dreams alive.'

Benjamin Ayres, Co-Founder of Raze

'One of the very few lawyers who are doing great things in this [blockchains and web3] fast moving sector.'

Mann Matharu, CEO Qi Digital

CONTRIBUTORS

Gareth Hall – contribution towards Chapters 14 & 15

Gareth is a Senior Associate at DAC Beachcroft LLP. His specialisms include complex, financial and white-collar criminal defence and he acts for both individuals and multi-national corporate entities throughout criminal and regulatory investigations and litigation instigated and investigated by the National Crime Agency (NCA), Serious Fraud Office (SFO), the Financial Conduct Authority (FCA), the Competition and Markets Authority (CMA) and His Majesty's Revenue and Customs (HMRC). Gareth routinely advises both regulated and non-regulated businesses on anti-money laundering, bribery and sanctions issues and he is experienced in handling complex internal investigations and regulatory and criminal self-reporting in these areas.

Gareth's key criminal and investigations experience includes:

- Being part of the team that acted in *R (on the application of KBR, Inc) (Appellant) v Director of the Serious Fraud Office (Respondent)* UKSC 2018/0215, a successful Supreme Court Appeal on the extraterritorial application of the SFO's powers to compel the production of documents under the Criminal Justice Act 1987;
- Conducting wide-ranging internal investigations for financial services institutions arising out of potential sanctions breaches, and for non-regulated entities following whistleblower allegations of internal fraud, committed by senior managers; and
- Acting for multiple individual clients during compelled and 'caution' interviews during the SFO's long running investigations into allegations of bribery and corruption at a major UK-based engineering and energy company.

In addition to his criminal and regulatory investigations and litigation experience, Gareth has a burgeoning commercial litigation practice, where his focus is on assisting both regulated and non-regulated clients to investigate instances of internal fraud, including push payment and business email compromise. Gareth is increasingly engaged to advise on strategy for both investigating such situations and seeking the recovery of funds, whether from fraudulent account operators or via the relevant financial institutions including utilising the Court's *Norwich Pharmacal* and *Bankers Trust* jurisdiction to provide victims of fraud with access to information held by relevant third parties via Orders to compel its production. Where such matters – and others Gareth is involved in – proceed to settlements, he has gained substantial experience in drafting and negotiating such agreements.

Gareth's key commercial litigation experience includes:

- Representing a multinational financial services company, following a cyber breach leading to the company falling victim to a 'Change of Payee' fraud. The matter concluded with successful recovery of funds, including cryptocurrency, from fraudulent accounts and via a negotiated settlement with involved parties following long running litigation;

- Advising a major company in the construction industry to investigate an incident of 'Authorised Push Payment' fraud including advising on strategy for recovery and information gathering from relevant financial institutions; and
- Advising a UK-based financial services company to investigate an incident of fraud following a cyber breach, leading to the successful return of the entirety of the stolen funds, in excess of £1.5m.

Courtney L'homme – contribution towards Chapter 13

Courtney is a private client solicitor who specialises in providing legal advice and services tailored to individuals, with a particular focus on personal and intergenerational estate planning. Her work encompasses drafting Wills and Lasting Powers of Attorney, advising on intricate trust arrangements, and creating comprehensive estate plans, all with the goal of protecting assets and ensuring effective succession planning for her clients.

In addition to estate planning, Courtney offers expert guidance on taxation matters, including inheritance tax and related obligations. She primarily works with high net worth individuals, helping them navigate complex legal structures that safeguard both their immediate interests and long-term objectives. Her role is essential in addressing the intricacies of family dynamics and dependencies.

Courtney is a full member of the Society of Trust and Estate Practitioners (STEP) and The Association of Lifetime Lawyers.

Mann Matharu – contribution towards Chapter 7

Mann Matharu is a renowned British technology entrepreneur, early-stage investor, award-winning author, and a leading voice in the realms of Blockchain and Cryptocurrency. Driven by a mission to transform the dynamics of monetary flow, he is pioneering revolutionary changes in payment processing.

As the founder and CEO of Qi Digital®, Mann helms one of the most influential Web3 payment gateways in the world. This company reflects his deep-rooted belief in the power of advanced internet technologies like blockchain and Ai to foster entrepreneurship globally and make it accessible to all.

A true visionary, Mann's entrepreneurial journey is marked by a series of groundbreaking ventures. He established 'Brilliant' in 2002, one of the UK's pioneering web development agencies, showcasing his foresight in recognising the internet's potential long before it became mainstream. His 2012 venture, 'Cartway', emerged as a leading white-label e-commerce solutions provider, catering exclusively to Payment Service Providers.

As a Futurist, Mann is a regular Guest Lecturer at Brunel University London, Imperial College London and Dauphine University Paris, where he discusses future technologies whilst inspiring young minds and academics across multiple faculties.

He sits as an Advisor at the Brunel Business School and is a registered Mentor with the Association of Business Mentors. He also advises startups and scaling businesses with brand, marketing and global product positioning.

Mann's literary prowess was celebrated in 2017 when his debut novella, 'The Monk of Lantau' (published 2015), garnered The Book Excellence Award in Philosophy. The book, lauded for its outstanding design and appeal to readers, was compared to Paulo Coelho's 'The Alchemist' and Hermann Hesse's 'Siddhartha' during a live BBC radio interview in 2018.

Beyond his professional achievements, Mann is equally passionate about humanitarian causes. He has been a mentor with The Prince's Trust, guiding young entrepreneurs at the cusp of their business journeys. His commitment to social causes has led him to 10 Downing Street for discussions with the former UK Prime Minister, David Cameron, and to the House of Lords to engage in talks on various UK and International charitable initiatives.

Mann Matharu's life and work stand as a testament to the power of visionary thinking and the impact it can have on the world.

Azhar Sadique – contribution towards Chapter 5

Azhar Sadique is a Partner and Director of Brand Innovation at Abion, with a prominent role in shaping the future of intellectual property (IP) and brand strategy. He serves as an Advisory Board panellist for various tech providers within the intellectual property industry and chairs the AI Task Force for CITMA (Chartered Institute of Trade Mark Attorneys) Counsel. His influence extends to academia, where he lectures for CITMA, CIPA (Chartered Institute of Patent Attorneys), and INTA (International Trademark Association), while also contributing as a committee member of the Brands and Innovation Committee.

With over 15 years of experience in the IP industry, Azhar is noted for his serious interest in the Metaverse. His investment in several pioneering companies that transitioned to the Metaverse highlights his focus on technical advancements rather than just promotional opportunities. As an author, he has contributed to leading publications on IP technology (IPTech) and is a passionate advocate for driving transformative change in the IP and branding sectors.

Contents

Table of Statutes

[*All references are to paragraph numbers*]

Table of Statutory Instruments

[*All references are to paragraph numbers*]

Table of International Material

[All references are to paragraph numbers]

Table of Cases

[*All references are to paragraph numbers*]

Chapter 1

Introduction

'The metaverse is here, and it's not only transforming how we see the world but how we participate in it – from the factory floor to the meeting room.'

Satya Nadella, Microsoft CEO

WHAT IS THE METAVERSE?

1.01 The metaverse means different things to different people. There is currently no single accepted definition of the term metaverse. The Oxford English Dictionary still reflects the science fiction roots of the term, which was coined in the Neal Stephenson book *Snow Crash* from 1992, and states that the metaverse is:

> 'A (hypothetical) virtual reality environment in which users interact with one another's avatars and their surroundings in an immersive way, sometimes posited as a potential extension of or replacement for the internet, World Wide Web, social media, etc'[1]

1.02 Today the concept of the metaverse is far from science fiction. Top brands such as Nike, Adidas, Gucci, Disney, Hyundai and JP Morgan have a presence in the metaverse in one form or another. It is estimated that the metaverse will be worth $5 trillion by 2030 and is set to become the biggest new opportunity for many industries.[2] Large online platform games with millions of users, such as Roblox and Fortnite, are considered to form part of the metaverse, or at least what some are coining a form of 'proto-metaverse'.[3]

1.03 The metaverse is looking to redefine how we interact with each other in both work and play. In 2022 75% of American children aged 9–12 were regularly playing Roblox.[4] In 2021 a Gucci bag was sold in the Roblox metaverse for more than a Gucci bag costs in real life.[5] In 2022 the MTV Video Music Awards introduced an awards category for best metaverse performance. In 2023 there was a Metaverse Fashion Week held in Decentraland with brands such as Adidas, Vogue and DKNY represented, as well as a music festival in the Fortnite

1 https://www.oed.com/dictionary/metaverse_n?tab=meaning_and_use#130112796.
2 Value Creation in the Metaverse – the real business of the virtual world, June 2022, McKinsey & Company.
3 http://www.cam.ac.uk/stories/metaverse.
4 http://www.cam.ac.uk/stories/metaverse.
5 http://amp.scmp.com/magazines/style/news-trends/article/3136325/digital-gucci-bag-sold-us4000-gaming-platform-roblox.

metaverse at 'Coachella Island' to coincide with the real-life Coachella festival. Eminem, Lady GaGa, Ariana Grande and Travis Scott have all played concerts in the metaverse. There are even plans to build replica virtual cities of Dubai and Adu Dhabi in the metaverse, where you will be able to make real-life visa applications and real-life licence applications digitally via the metaverse.[6] In May 2024 Wales became the first part of the UK to have a virtual metaverse presence having launched as a destination on the metaverse platform Spatial and 'Visit Wales' started advertising using virtual billboards in Roblox.[7]

1.04 For many, however, the idea of the metaverse is intrinsically linked with the decision of Facebook in October 2021 to rebrand as Meta and build its own form of the metaverse – an immersive virtual reality technology. The metaverse is described by Meta as:

> 'the next evolution in social connection and the successor to the mobile internet. Imagine a set of digital spaces that you can move seamlessly between. Like the Internet, the metaverse will help you connect with people when you aren't physically in the same place and get us even closer to that feeling of being together in person.... the metaverse will include familiar 2D experiences, as well as ones projected into the physical world and fully immersive 3D ones too... the metaverse isn't just for gamers or developers, it will be for everyone. And our hope is that in the next decade it will reach a billion people.'[8]

1.05 McKinsey and Co have prepared an extensive report into the potential of the metaverse and believe that 'the metaverse seems to be whatever people's imaginations dream it to be...[however] beyond the hype, the metaverse is real, potentially revolutionary, and has the makings of a significant opportunity'.[9]

1.06 Nick Clegg, former Deputy Prime Minister of the UK and President of Global Affairs for Meta describes the idea of the metaverse as a patchwork quilt of different technologies and platforms.[10] At its core the concept of the metaverse is an immersive digital realm where interactions take place virtually in real-time, typically via avatars. The technology is a mix of virtual reality, augmented reality and mixed reality (often referred to as extended reality or XR) and typically, but not exclusively, uses some form of blockchain technology.[11] For many the idea of

6 https://thefintechtimes.com/abu-dhabi-and-dubai-are-the-worlds-first-metarverse-cities/.
7 http://www.gov.wales/croeso-i-gymru-wales-becomes-first-uk-nation-launch-metaverse-experience.
8 https://about.meta.com/uk/what-is-the-metaverse.
9 Value Creation in the Metaverse – the real business of the virtual world, June 2022, McKinsey & Company.
10 https://nickclegg.medium.com/making-the-metaverse-what-it-is-how-it-will-be-built-and-why-it-matters-3710f7570b04.
11 Blockchain is perhaps best known as the technology which underpins cryptocurrency; however, its application is much wider than this. At its most basic the blockchain is a digital database or 'ledger' which automatically records everything that happens within its code. Each new record (interaction etc) forms a new block. The technology linking the blocks together uses a very secure type of cryptographic encryption which minimises the risk of these records being altered. This means that the data recorded on a blockchain can, on the whole, be trusted.

the metaverse is synonymous with Web3 and the next revolution of the internet. Currently it is the gaming industry that is leading the way in forging the idea of the metaverse but its expansion is likely to transcend many traditional industries from being able to virtually train surgeons to holding virtual conferences; visiting historic landmarks to educating students; re-experiencing memories to working within virtual office spaces. The metaverse also encompasses the concept of digital twins,[12] which is a rapidly growing area in the industrial metaverse.[13]

1.07 Whilst recent focus has been on the revolution brought about by artificial intelligence, the metaverse is continuing to take shape with the involvement of major international organisations, across a range of different industries.[14] The EU considers that it is likely that it will take a further 10–15 years until the potential of the metaverse is achieved; until that time, we expect to see a growth in the use and sophistication of the technology until peak optimisation and widescale adoption. In December 2024 the Leadership in Immersive Technology Act of 2024 was introduced in the US into the House of Representatives and Senate. The Bill, which is seeking to establish an Immersive Technology Advisory Panel, recognises immersive technologies as a 'critical technology' for the USA and notes it is 'widely expected to function as the next major computing platform'

1.08 Many of the barriers at this stage are put down to issues with the XR hardware capabilities and costs. That said, XR hardware providers are making great strides in developing ever advancing virtual reality headsets to try and enable a seamless journey from real life into the metaverse and to create other form of AR wearables like branded smart glasses.[15] In January 2024 the Tech Giant Apple entered the race with its Vision Pro. This is felt by many to be the pivotal turning point for virtual reality hardware and caused the term 'spatial computing' to become one of the buzz words of 2024. In mid-2024 it was announced that Apple would be focusing on its next generation of Vision Pro with a lower and more competitive price point. It is thought that the next generation of Vision Pro will be sold by Apple for around the same price as its iPhones.[16]

LAW IN THE METAVERSE

1.09 The metaverse will impact almost all aspects of real life ('IRL'); accordingly, the law will be called upon to determine issues both in the metaverse and where those issues spill into real life. Both the law, and legal practitioners,

12 A digital twin is where an identical replica of a physical asset or location is created in an XR format.

13 https://ec.europa.eu/info/law/better-regulation/have-your-say/initiatives/13757-Virtual-worlds-metaverses-a-vision-for-openness-safety-and-respect/F3409320_en.

14 In 2024 we have seen collaborations between Sony and Siemens in the metaverse, Disney invest $1.5b into the metaverse and McDonalds launch 'My Happy Place' amongst others.

15 Such as the Ray-Ban Meta smart glasses https://www.ray-ban.com/uk/ray-ban-meta-smart-glasses.

16 https://9to5mac.com/2024/06/18/apple-vision-cheaper-halts-work-pro-model-headset/.

need to understand the intersect between real-life laws and the metaverse. This book seeks to explore this intersect. It considers key real-life issues which will present themselves in the metaverse, as well as novel concepts in the metaverse which need to be dealt with in real life. It examines how these issues should be interpreted within not only a domestic legal framework but also from a multi-jurisdiction perspective and using possible technological solutions.

1.10 There is currently no one single piece of legislation, or even regulation, which covers all the issues concerning the metaverse. Whilst many law-makers are closely watching the development of the metaverse and Web3, it is still likely to be some time before we see any specific metaverse law. Perhaps making the greatest strides in exploring the legal impact of the metaverse is the European Union. The EU Parliament considered the impact of the development of virtual worlds on civil, company, commercial and intellectual property law issues in January 2024[17] and in its response the EU Commission[18] emphasised that it was closely monitoring the metaverse to ensure that existing legal and regulatory framework would be sufficient. The EU Commission has confirmed that irrespective of whether or not they implement a dedicated EU metaverse regulatory framework at this time, they are developing a virtual world toolbox on the key issues affecting the metaverse.

1.11 This book is based largely on the law in England and Wales but given the metaverse itself is not constrained by traditional geographical or geopolitical boundaries there are multi-jurisdiction and cross border considerations in most metaverse matters. In addition, many consider that the technology itself, and the use of smart contracts, can help to govern the metaverse and regulate its users. The question remains as to how far this is possible given the numerous legal issues at play when you are trying to build a new world, albeit virtual in nature. Technological controls and regulatory/legislative controls are not necessarily mutually exclusive and the answer may in fact lay in a combination of both.

1.12 There are many fascinating legal issues involved in the metaverse; this truly is a new frontier. There are also many competing issues in the metaverse including those between a centralised governance and the decentralised philosophy of the blockchain. You also cannot think about the metaverse without also looking at artificial intelligence and its meteoric uptake in adoption in society, as well as 5G infrastructure and internet of things (IoT). The metaverse is intrinsically linked with digital assets, cryptocurrencies and digital twins. Pioneering BCI (Brain-Computer Interface) technology is currently also being explored to try and create a seamless experience, where brain activity could be used to control your activity in the metaverse.

1.13 Many real-life laws and regulations will still apply in the metaverse, but there are also new challenges that will need new laws. It is not however, always just simply a case of extrapolating issues from the metaverse into real life and then judging conduct by traditional real-life standards rooted in reality, when it

17 resolution 2023/2062(INI).
18 (SP(2024) 299).

is known to be virtual reality. At least for now, however, real-life rules, laws and precedents will play a significant role. Until the time that there are new laws and regulations in place, legal professionals advising clients in the metaverse need to carefully consider the different harms to which their clients are exposed and the third parties for which they may be responsible. Where possible these risks should be addressed in a pragmatic fashion, whether that is for now only in contracts or via technological solutions or otherwise.

Chapter 2

The rule of law, principles of justice and the metaverse

"This metaverse is going to be far more pervasive and powerful than anything else. If one central company gains control of this, they will become more powerful than any government and be a god on Earth."

Tim Sweeney, Epic Games

2.01 The Rule of Law has long been the object of discussion by legal theorists. With the advent of the metaverse, with its new concepts and ideas, it begs the question as to whether the metaverse fits into the traditional idea of the Rule of Law and traditional principles of justice. To understand this question, we need to look at the concepts underpinning traditional societies in real life and the creation of modern legal systems. The issue of the Rule of Law and justice in the metaverse are not simply academic considerations given there is a dark side to the metaverse, with the risk that it could be used as a weapon or an intelligence system to spy on other states or to carry out corporate espionage.[1]

2.02 The metaverse is not in the conventional sense a 'state', but it does bear many of the hallmarks of being a 'society', and therefore requires proper regulation and governance. To understand the principles behind the governance of the metaverse one can look to legal philosophers and jurists who have for centuries considered why there has been a need for laws and regulation when people live together in societies and interact with each other. It is important to consider socio-legal considerations, and why societies have developed legal governance, as well as considering whether laws even remain relevant and appropriate in this new frontier. In their analysis of the law in the metaverse Caballero and Balbuena noted that it is often in fact technology that changes the law and the law has to react to technological advancements.[2] Technology usually advances much faster than the law is able to and therefore the law is often having to try and catch up. The law in this area is typically therefore reactive to social and technological changes as opposed to proactively causing changes. We have seen this in particular with the changes to laws that are being driven by digital

1 https://www.europarl.europa.eu/RegData/etudes/STUD/2023/751222/IPOL_STU(2023)751222_EN.pdf.

2 Joxerramon Bengoetxea Caballero and Roberto Leopoldo Cruz Balbuena 'Institutions of law in the metaverse' Oñati Socio-Legal Series (ISSN: 2079-5971), Oñati International Institute for the Sociology of Law.

assets such as the Property (Digital Assets etc) Bill and the case of *D'Aloia v Persons Unknown Category A & Ors*.[3]

2.03 Humans have for generations built their communities on a form of law and order. One of the key functions of law is that of social control. Citizens have grown used to the existence of laws and rules governing their behaviour. All modern societies have some form of laws and, as Sir Henry Maine emphasised, most primitive societies had some form of law and order, even if these do not appear to have been uniform.[4] To understand why we have laws we can look at anthropological and sociological research.[5] The metaverse is its own society with different communities within it. Users are coming together, working together, living together, and playing together in the metaverse. Users of the metaverse need to determine what behaviour should be punished and how. There is therefore a need for some form of law and order in the metaverse.

WHAT IS THE RULE OF LAW?

2.04 This is not a straightforward question, and has been debated for centuries. Many theorists and their philosophies are representative of the religious and social constructs at the time of their writings. Although the concept of the metaverse was a far cry from any of the classical jurisprudential philosophers' minds when writing their theories, many of these still remain relevant today when we explore the extent to which the Rule of Law applies in the metaverse landscape. Although in the metaverse humans are represented through avatars, humans still on the whole control those avatars and the underlying motivation behind their actions largely remain the same as in real life. Users still exhibit the same emotions and concerns, whether this is manifested in the metaverse or in real life. In some respects, therefore it is only the technology, and the way people can now interact, that has changed and not so much the people themselves. People now choose to join together for a quest in the metaverse rather than embark on a crusade in real life, attend a concert together in the metaverse, work together in a virtual office, buy metaverse real estate or play virtual sports together. The underlying behaviour therefore largely remains the same as in real life. The question is the extent to which the shift in the way people can interact with each other via the metaverse impacts the underlying rule and need for law. How much does it matter that the harm caused in the metaverse is different to that in real life, and does it matter that you can take off the virtual reality headset and leave the metaverse? What if in the future the interaction is so seamless you can step into and out of the metaverse instantaneously and with the development of haptic suits users can now physically feel sensations derived from interactions within the metaverse. What if BCI technology is deployed to access the metaverse?

3 [2024] EWHC 2342 (Ch) (12 September 2024).

4 Sir Henry Sumner Maine, 'Ancient Law' (1901) London.

5 In 'Towards anthropologies of the metaverse' (2023) Journal of the American Ethnological Society Tom Boellstorff believes it is essential to consider the metaverse from an anthropological perspective.

NATURAL LAW AND THE METAVERSE

2.05 The Classical Greek theorists Aristotle and Plato first developed the concept of Natural Law and the idea that there is an innate sense of right and wrong which governs behaviour. John Locke promoted the idea of Natural Law in his 1689 *Two Treatises of Government*, in which he considered that morality underpinned laws. Fuller in the 1960s felt there was an inner morality of law and concluded that laws had a utility of purpose with a shared rationale, which he termed "principles of legality". The idea of Natural Law is an interesting concept in respect of the metaverse and whether there is an inner morality which governs behaviour and exerts control over right from wrong. If humans have an inner morality, then we would expect to see virtuous acts being exhibited in the metaverse and communities start to be developed with rules underpinned with virtue.

2.06 It will be interesting to see whether the same moral issues are as important in the metaverse as in real life. Is killing someone's avatar as morally abhorrent in the metaverse as killing someone in real life? Whilst the current gamified use of the metaverse may not mean that there is much concern over the death of an avatar, since in games avatars are often killed and regenerated, we would expect to see condemnation where there is interoperability between platforms, or say where a business user kills someone's avatar in say the industrial metaverse or workspace – especially if this was to lose the user access to certain materials or causes an unreasonable delay.

2.07 This is likely in fact to be a non-issue in the metaverse, since we expect the technology itself to prevent really abhorrent acts from being able to take place in such scenarios. The interesting cases are likely however to border on those areas where morality and law collide such as adultery. Adultery is still illegal in some countries, although not in the UK, and it will be interesting to see whether and to what extent more morality-based laws are translated into the metaverse. Could we in fact start to see other forms of morality come to light which are of relevance only really in the metaverse?

2.08 If there is an inner morality which then guides the Rule of Law then this may, however, be skewed in the metaverse. This is because the nature of the technology makes people feel that they are able to behave in a manner that they would not normally in real life.[6] In the metaverse users are physically in a different place from those that they are interacting with, they are wearing a VR headset, the metaverse landscape may be fantastical and their avatar may not even look human. As a result it may actually be very hard to try and apply real-life laws in the metaverse and in fact law in the metaverse may not necessarily

6 This is highlighted by Brookings, a US think tank who discuss the idea of the "online disinhibition effect' that causes people to behave differently online than they would in the real world' https://www.brookings.edu/articles/ai-makes-rules-for-the-metaverse-even-more-important/.

be respected just by virtue of it being the law.[7] This is similar to the idea of 'mob rule' in which humans behave differently from the way they usually would as a result of a feeling of being 'faceless' and not identifiable.

2.09 Rather than the law reflecting an inherent morality, Thomas Hobbes in his 1651 book, *Leviathan* believed that humans are inherently cruel and selfish and therefore there is a need for rules and laws as a form of social contract to control such behaviour. He considered that without laws and rules humans would descend into a chaotic state. To some extent this has been seen with some of the crimes which have already been reported in the metaverse.[8] It is however, difficult to test this theory in the metaverse since users still remain citizens in real life and are subject to real-life laws and controls. Where it can more readily be considered, however, is where there is a lacuna of real-life laws but the harm being suffered in the metaverse could still be considered as selfish and cruel such as wrongfully imprisoning or trapping someone's avatar against their will. This is unlikely to fall under any existing real-life laws but has the ability to cause harm and suffering to the other metaverse user. If one takes the Hobbesian approach, then there is a need to make sure that the metaverse is properly governed with laws and controls to protect avatars against each other especially when the harm is not governed by real-life laws.

AUTHORITY AND THE METAVERSE

2.10 Many theorists have emphasised the importance of having an adequate system of governance to achieve the Rule of Law. Raz[9] stressed that there was the need for clear rules and set out key features of laws including being stable, prospective and the requirement of an independent judiciary. Montesquieu[10] emphasised the importance of a distinction between the separation of judicial power and legislative power, namely a separation between the law-makers and those who make determination on cases. It is important therefore that there are proper checks and measures implemented in the metaverse which properly separate the administrative governing function of the metaverse platforms and its powers. At this stage, as set out below, there is no proper separation of powers in the metaverse; there is no independent judiciary or accountable separate final judicial decision-maker. Ultimate decision-making remains with the platform owners, who typically 'police' the space via moderators and then enforce contractual breaches of the terms of use via suspension and expulsion. Users often have very little ability to respond to allegations made. This will need to be addressed should the metaverse want to reach its full potential.

7 https://jcli-bi.org/index.php/jcli/article/download/25/15/135 (9/12/2023).
8 There have been reports of sexual assaults and grooming in the metaverse on numerous occasions.
9 Joseph Raz,*The Authority of Law* (Oxford University Press, 1979).
10 In M. De Secondat, Baron De Montesquieu, *The Spirit of Laws*, (1794), London.

2.11 The metaverse itself is not a democracy; the different platforms are controlled by the owners of the platforms, effectively with an authoritarian rule. We have seen from history that citizens throughout the ages have sought to revolt against such rulers in real life, but it remains to be seen what type of political landscape users of the metaverse desire, and if there is any such desire at all for change. This is likely to come to prominence only once we start to see the merging of metaverse platforms, the ability to move between different metaverses (interoperability) or if we start to see the formation of just one all-encompassing metaverse. For now, users can effectively vote with their (digital) wallets and move from one platform to another if they do not like the way it is being run. In the future, this will not likely be the case. If we reach the vision of a true metaverse, one where users can seamlessly enter and move around between platforms, states, lands and activities then the issue of governance and rule will have to be addressed. At that stage serious consideration needs to be had as to how the metaverse should be ruled, which in turn will drive how it is governed and users are controlled.

2.12 Dicey[11] considered that the key to the Rule of Law was equality. He felt that everyone should be subject to the law and that no one should be higher than the law. This is very important when considering the metaverse. Consideration must be had as to what systems can be implemented to ensure that there is equality in this new landscape. One must consider what equality would mean in the metaverse. Would this relate to access to the internet, speed of internet or restrictions which may be implemented by traditional states depending on where you live or what your avatar looks like or where it lives within the metaverse? The disadvantages caused as a result of access to poor technology and internet is often terms the 'digital divide' and it is a central concern that needs to be addressed for many who are looking for the widescale adoption of the metaverse.

2.13 In more modern times the idea of the Rule of Law as a balance between the individual and the state, where both accept that compromises are required to enable society to function, is highlighted by Lord Bingham in the Sixth Sir David Williams Lecture on the Rule of Law. He eloquently said 'the individual living in society implicitly accepts that he or she cannot exercise the unbridled freedom enjoyed by Adam in the Garden of Eden, before the creation of Eve, and accept the constraints imposed by laws properly made because of the benefits which, on balance, they confer.'[12] In the metaverse users therefore need to accept some constraints to ensure that the metaverse is not a lawless terrain without fear of consequences. This is often at odds with some purist advocating for full decentralisation without any oversight from governments or centralised regulated organisations.

11 A.V. Dicey, *The Law of the Constitution* (Oxford University Press, 2013).

12 https://www.cpl.law.cam.ac.uk/sir-david-williams-lectures2006-rule-law/rule-law-text-transcript (8/12/23).

2.14 The United Nations highlight that one of the principles of the Rule of Law is that it holds the state accountable with publicly declared rules and principles used to independently judge standards.[13] This should also translate into the metaverse, which should implement suitable rules as well as underpinning principles to ensure that the metaverse is designed with the Rule of Law at its core.

UTILITARIANISM AND THE METAVERSE

2.15 Jeremy Bentham is often considered to be the father of utilitarianism. This is the concept of being able to assess the utility of an action by its impact on pleasure and pain. Bentham's form of utilitarianism only views the impact on the collective rights of society as opposed to considering everyone's individual needs. The Rule of Law for Bentham therefore is based on what maximises happiness and minimises harm. For him the law should reflect and uphold the greatest good for the greatest number. Adopting the utilitarian philosophy and applying this to the metaverse one must first consider the concept of what is good, or what Bentham termed hedonism in the context of the metaverse; what causes pleasure in the metaverse. This may not necessarily be the same as in real life, but is likely to be positive human interactions and a sense of well-being. Negative feelings in the metaverse are likely to flow from bad interactions between users, a user feeling deceived or cheated or harmed.

2.16 In contrast to Bentham's ideology Mill's theory of utilitarianism instead focuses on the impact of something on an individual. He believed that impeding someone's liberty can only be justified if it is to prevent a harm. Hadziselimovic[14] in his 2023 article seeks to apply Mill's concept of utilitarianism to the metaverse and balance a user's freedom of speech against a wider right to privacy. Many pioneers of the metaverse prefer the ideology of a 'free metaverse', one of liberty and the ability to freely interact. Mill's theory seeks to balance liberty and harm. Although, at this stage it is likely that we do not really understand the extent and levels of harm from the metaverse. It is a new technology and a new way of interaction. We do not know whether some people will be affected by harm in the metaverse more than others or whether this will mirror the traditional vulnerabilities in society in real life or other factors.

13 The United Nations state the Rule of Law includes a requirement 'to ensure adherence to the principles of supremacy of the law, equality before the law, accountability to the law, fairness in the application of the law, separation of powers, participation in decision-making, legal certainty, avoidance of arbitrariness and procedural and legal transparency' https://www.un.org/ruleoflaw/what-is-the-rule-of-law/#:~:text=It%20includes%20prevention%20of%20serious, protect%20their%20fundamental%20human%20rights. (8/12/2023).

14 Adnan Hadziselimovic (2023): Open justice transformations impacting extended reality (XR) environments. International Journal of Performance Arts and Digital Media.

KANT

2.17 In his moral theory on the Rule of Law, Kant considered that humans have an internal freedom of choice in respect of their moral actions. He devised the concept of the categorical imperative, being the methodology to identify universal moral duty which should be considered as law. Kant sought to challenge the utilitarian view and instead focused on the idea that there was a moral underpinning of law connected to something being right and wrong.

2.18 In the metaverse the idea of Kant's categorical imperative is however difficult to apply because not everyone involved in the metaverse is actually human; instead some avatars are being controlled autonomously via technology or by corporations.[15] It is interesting to consider how the interplay of real-life people interacting with both other real-life people via avatars as well as with autonomous avatars controlled by smart contract or other forms of technology will impact on the Rule of Law in the metaverse. The more complicating factor being that users are unlikely to know which is which when they are interacting in the metaverse behind the shield of an avatar. This could be addressed by the technology itself, with a form of identification of who is controlling the avatar. In real life the law, and the Rule of Law, have been able to adequately adjust to corporate entities and even technological advancements in artificial intelligence.

NORMATIVITY AND THE METAVERSE

2.19 Kelsen and Hart in their theories on the Rule of Law both explored the idea of norms within society. Kelsen believed that a legal system was a collection of norms with a superior norm, which he termed the '*Grundnorm*'. The *Grundnorm* is an objective legal authority on the way something ought to happen and the consequences when this is not done. The *Grundnorm* is the root from which the legal authority for an obligation is derived.

2.20 At this stage it is probably too early to determine whether there is a *Grundnorm* in the metaverse and if so, what this may be. An important place to start however, is to consider the feedback the European Commission received from industry stakeholders in respect of the metaverse, a majority of whom highlighted the importance of privacy and protection against harm, especially for children. Further, the JURI Committee study on the metaverse conducted by the European Parliament's Policy Department for Citizens' Rights and Constitutional Affairs, which was requested by the European Parliament's Committee on Legal Affairs,[16] explored ethical issues in the metaverse. They consider that the underpinning issues that have been identified in respect of regulating and

15 https://doi.org/10.1007/s11569-022-00426-x Grinbaum and Adomaitis, Moral Equivalence in the Metaverse (2022), Springer Nature B.V. 2022.

16 https://www.europarl.europa.eu/RegData/etudes/STUD/2023/751222/IPOL_STU(2023)751222_EN.pdf

controlling artificial intelligence should also apply to governing the metaverse.[17] Whilst these are certainly key issues which will go towards the *Grundnorm* of the metaverse, however this must ultimately come from the users themselves and therefore may take some time to identify.

2.21 Whilst the idea of the *Grundnorm* is an interesting concept in respect of the metaverse, Kelsen's theory is however, premised on the idea of the existence of centralised governance, which is itself at odds with blockchain, which is decentralised. It will therefore be interesting to see whether, with a decentralised forms of the metaverse whether the idea of general societal norms will be relevant at all. It may instead be that groups with shared norms group together and establish their own form of *Grundnorm.*

2.22 Hart's theory on the Rule of Law explored why citizens accepted rules. He believed that it was the 'internal point of view' which was the reason why citizens followed rules and behaved in a certain way. The 'internal point of view' was based on normative behaviour and centred on the idea that there is a common understanding of what is acceptable behaviour, and what is morally objectionable. He believed that there was something inside everyone guiding behaviour. The concept of an 'internal point of view' is an important theory in respect of the metaverse because it considers whether there are shared inner moralities that drive what is right and wrong in the metaverse. The internalisation of a rule in the metaverse may not happen immediately and may take some time to evolve as a majority of users have to accept the rules.

LAW AND MORALITY IN THE METAVERSE

2.23 Kelsen with his concept of the 'Basic Norm' looked at the idea of the connection of law to a moral standard, which in turn justifies a legal order. Telefonica, in its 2022 report on social and ethical challenges of the metaverse, emphasised the need to consider values and ethics in the metaverse.[18] They felt that the UNESCO recommendation in respect of the ethics of artificial intelligence should be used as a starting point. The report looks at the idea of liberty in the metaverse and the risk that the technology could blur reality and mixed reality to the extent that a user is unable to properly distinguish these. They further identify the potential issue of dissociation from the real world as a result of excessive time in the metaverse.

17 The European Parliament considers that the metaverse should 'be built on the principles of 1) universal fundamental rights, not exceptions, 2) innovation, not exploitation, 2) cooperation, not confrontation.' https://www.europarl.europa.eu/RegData/etudes/STUD/2023/751222/IPOL_STU(2023)751222_EN.pdf.

18 These are 'respect, protection and promotion of human rights and fundamental freedoms and human dignity; Environment and ecosystems flourishing; Ensuring diversity and inclusiveness; Living in peaceful, just and interconnected societies' http://www.telefonica.com/en/wp-content/uploads/sites/5/2022/05/social-and-ethical-challenges-metaverse-EN.pdf.

'VOLKSGEIST' AND THE METAVERSE

2.24 It is vital to understand that users of the metaverse come from multiple different backgrounds, with different legal systems, morals, beliefs and faiths. It is not for one particular state to try and impose its morality on everyone else. Whilst the metaverse is a new dimension, ultimately it is still a sum of its parts. A rich tapestry of people interacting in a new space. The metaverse citizens bring with them their own views, moralities, and expectations. Learning can be taken from legal history in respect of the evolution of societies and their justice systems. The German romantic movement stressed the importance of customs and history as the bedrock of a society. For Savigny the roots of the law were considered embodied within its citizens and this represented the moral underpinnings of the law, what they termed as *Volksgeist* or 'spirit of the people'. On this basis each user of the metaverse would embody their own roots of law, bring these into the metaverse and this would determine how they interact with each other and the resulting laws and governance of the system.

2.25 The question remains of the importance of where someone lives, or originates from, in real life when determining how they will behave in the metaverse or how they should be governed. Will we see clusters of users with similar morals joining together and regulating the metaverse, or their part of the metaverse, regardless of where they live in real life or will we see similar territorial lines being drawn in the metaverse mimicking real-life territories?

LEGAL PLURALISM AND THE METAVERSE

2.26 The concept of legal pluralism is the idea that there can be multiple different legal systems within one society, whereas legal centralism focuses solely on the law of the state. Traditionally the study of legal pluralism has focused on the interactions between state law and religious or tribal laws. The idea of legal pluralism is often examined within sports clubs, trade unions or organisations.

2.27 Legal pluralism is important in the context of the metaverse because any rules or governance of the metaverse will inevitability sit (at least for now) within existing state laws and legal systems. Initially theorists believed that the internet had the potential to sit outside the scope of traditional state jurisdictions, but it is now largely accepted that it instead sits within plural systems online and offline.[19] When considering legal pluralism in the metaverse Caballero and Balbuena felt that it could be best described as a 'public place of private ownership'[20] with a combination of both public law and private law.

19 Michael Anthony C. Dizon: Law and Networks: Legal pluralism in information and communications technology

20 Joxerramon Bengoetxea Caballero and Roberto Leopoldo Cruz Balbuena 'Institutions of law in the metaverse' Oñati Socio-Legal Series (ISSN: 2079-5971), Oñati International Institute for the Sociology of Law.

SHOULD THE METAVERSE BE GOVERNED BY PRIVATE ENTITIES?

2.28 Currently each metaverse is governed in the first instance by the platform owner itself. There are contractual terms of use and licensing agreements which are mandatory for those who want to access, use, and engage within a particular metaverse. For example, Meta has created a Code of Conduct for Virtual Experiences,[21] which is a private user agreement to cover the development and use of its platforms. The metaverse therefore is still largely considered to fall under private law. As the number of users and use cases of the metaverse increases, however, the topics that transpire will transcend into public law and should be subject to public policy. If we take the idea of one global metaverse, an idea that there will become one interlinked virtual realm that enables users to flow between different spaces and platforms in all aspects of their life, then this must move past the idea of private law.

2.29 Even though virtual communities are privately governed they should still take into consideration the principles of public governance and the Rule of Law.[22] It is incorrect to believe that regulation and liberty are mutually exclusive in the context of virtual communities and at the very least underlying human right principles should be taken into consideration when resolving issues within virtual communities.[23] Decision making within virtual communities is not always transparent and ultimate power lies with the owner of that community or platform, who then can simply remove a dissenting participant and exercise ultimate and unfettered control.[24] In real life public bodies are held to account by way of judicial review which is underpinned by the idea of reasonableness and fairness principles.

2.30 As the metaverse evolves there is a strong need for proper governance. This should be distinct from the private law rules established by the platform owners because the interests of the platform owners will not necessarily always be aligned with what is beneficial to be able regulate the metaverse. A macro-level framework of rules, expectations and laws should be established to deal with the key principles of the metaverse and its control. Dworkin emphasised the need for laws to 'follow from the principles of justice, fairness and procedural due process'.[25] There is a fundamental need for equality before the law in the metaverse. The law in the metaverse therefore must be based on principles which enable equality and do not unfairly favour one user over another user based on arbitrary standards determined by a private profit-making entity. This is not

21 https://www.meta.com/en-gb/help/quest/articles/accounts/privacy-information-and-settings/code-of-conduct-for-virtual-experiences/?utm_source=www.google.com&utm_medium=oculusredirect.

22 Berkeley Technology Law Journal [Vol. 25:1817] pp1818 – 1885.

23 Nicolas Suzor, *Rule of Law in Virtual Communities,* Berkeley Technology Law Journal v25:1817 *(2010).*

24 Nicolas Suzor, *Rule of Law in Virtual Communities,* Berkeley Technology Law Journal v25:1817 *(2010).*

25 R Dworkin, Law's Empire (Fontana, 1986).

dissimilar to the concept behind the need for the Digital Services Act package regulations in the EU which effectively set out the expectations on Tech Giants in respect of their qualifying technology platforms. As discussed in the next chapter this regulation will apply in respect of the metaverse platforms and is an indication that oversight of Tech Giants is clearly on the radar of law-makers.

THE CHALLENGES OF THE RULE OF LAW IN THE METAVERSE

2.31 In its 2024 report on the metaverse and its impact on human rights, the rule of law and democracy the Council of Europe highlight that one of the main challenges of the metaverse is going to be balancing human rights and democracy against other competing stakeholder interests.[26] The report calls for human rights, the rule of law and democracy to be embedded into the metaverse by its design and argues that the metaverse should be built around these principles. Further to protect the Rule of Law in the metaverse it would be imperative to reflect 'principles of legality, legal certainty, prevention of abuse of powers, equality and access to justice'.[27] This is clearly a positive move; the challenge, however, will be trying to ascertain what the Rule of Law actually means in the metaverse especially, as outlined earlier in the chapter, there is not just one accepted idea of what is the Rule of Law.

2.32 Whilst there are numerous theories upon which to try and base the concept of the Rule of Law in the metaverse, the task is trying to reconcile these not only with themselves but with the diverging views of metaverse citizens. The number of users is likely to grow exponentially within a technologically advanced landscape – which itself enables avatars to act in a way which could never be possible in real life. The challenges are many, but what is clear is that proper consideration of the Rule of Law in the metaverse is needed now, whilst there is still the unique opportunity to design the metaverse around the same.

2.33 The issues with the Rule of Law in the metaverse are however much deeper rooted since all users of the metaverse sit not only within the virtual metaverse community but also sit within traditional communities. A user's behaviour in the metaverse may therefore not only impact on other users within the metaverse but also have an impact outside the metaverse. The concept of governance, what is the Rule of Law and justice are not universal. We must be careful not to impose a form of Rule of Law, justice or governance in the metaverse which is entirely western-centric or suited only to serve the Tech Giants or favour one type of legal system over another. This is important if the metaverse is to become truly borderless and revolutionise the internet as we know it. There are very different laws, governance, attitudes and tolerances between different states.

26 http://rm.coe.int/the-metaverse-impact-on-and-its-impact-on-human-rights-the-rule-of-law/1680ae6bce.

27 http://rm.coe.int/the-metaverse-impact-on-and-its-impact-on-human-rights-the-rule-of-law/1680ae6bce.

2.34 The global nature of the metaverse means that it will be very difficult to apply one universal way of governance, law and control[28] and instead it may be necessary to take a more global view and see where there may be alignment and common viewpoints.[29] It may be better suited to try and achieve a collective unification of as many different countries as possible to try and ratify an international treaty on how to govern the metaverse, rather than it being dealt with state-by-state. Trying to achieve some form of international consensus is itself not easy. The metaverse crosses not only traditional state boundaries but will include users of different faiths, who may have grown up with different customs and beliefs so there must also be consideration of religious laws which will also impact the metaverse. For centuries leading politicians and diplomats have been unable to find solutions for disagreements between states which may itself manifest in the metaverse itself. We may see international political divisions spill out into the metaverse.

WHAT ARE THE FUNDAMENTALS OF GOOD GOVERNANCE IN THE METAVERSE?

2.35 It is important to identify what would be the basis of good governance in the metaverse and who should then be responsible for enforcing and reinforcing the same. It must be asked whether this should be the responsibility of the technology platforms, individual governments, or supranational organisations.

2.36 Many key stakeholders in the metaverse have set out their view about what is important in respect of the governance of the metaverse. TikTok highlighted the importance of not ignoring societal issues and ensuring that the metaverse provides for diversity, equality, and inclusion.[30] TikTok stressed that there should be responsible practices supported by suitable regulations to protect against the harm that are likely to manifest, given the types of existing online harms between users in other interactions such as cyberbullying.[31] The Lego Group emphasised the importance of protecting children and designing the metaverse to actively promote well-being in children.[32] Mastercard stressed there was a requirement to

28 Garon cautions that 'governance of the internet and operation of domestic law varies considerably from country to country, and the metaverse will exacerbate rather than flatten this trend' Jon M. Garon, *Legal Implications of a Ubiquitous Metaverse and Web3 Future, 106 Marq. L. Rev 1963 (2022).*

29 The European Parliament's Policy Department for Citizens' Rights and Constitutional Affairs report that 'due to global character of metaverse the discussion on its ethics should embrace a globally representative range of participants, which aim to reach a broad consensus rather than impose a standard of any particular jurisdiction.' https://www.europarl.europa.eu/RegData/etudes/STUD/2023/751222/IPOL_STU(2023)751222_EN.pdf.

30 https://ec.europa.eu/info/law/better-regulation/have-your-say/initiatives/13757-Virtual-worlds-metaverses-a-vision-for-openness-safety-and-respect/F3410937_en.

31 https://ec.europa.eu/info/law/better-regulation/have-your-say/initiatives/13757-Virtual-worlds-metaverses-a-vision-for-openness-safety-and-respect/F3410937_en.

32 https://ec.europa.eu/info/law/better-regulation/have-your-say/initiatives/13757-Virtual-worlds-metaverses-a-vision-for-openness-safety-and-respect/F3411869_en.

ensure that the metaverse has suitable security and protected privacy.[33] Vodafone felt that metaverse platforms must 'tackle illegal and harmful material'.[34] Siemens distinguished the industrial metaverse and the distinction between business to consumer and business to business relationships[35]. Sky stressed the importance of the protection of intellectual property rights.[36]

DOES LAW ACTUALLY MATTER IN THE METAVERSE?

2.37 At its root the metaverse involves multiple human interactions. Whilst it may be avatars who are interacting, these are on the whole simply manifestations of the human personalities behind them. In addition, the technology itself enables interactions like never before. To date there has been no viable alternative to having laws and rules to achieve some form of consensus and harmony between human interactions. Cyber law theorists originally argued that cyberspace presented the opportunity to depart from traditional state-made laws and instead implement its own rules and self-governance but later acknowledged that this was a fallacy and recognised that cyberspace was already covered by existing regulations albeit that commercialisation and private corporations using market forces could direct and guide rules in this space.[37] We have seen this over the years with the emergence of the Tech Giants, yet it remains to be seen how this will apply in the metaverse.

2.38 This is not to say that there is not scope for some form of evolution of law and governance in the metaverse to reflect the new technological landscape. Working with jurists it is possible that technologists can help to construct the technological environments and platforms to reflect the Rule of Law, thereby setting constraints and boundaries within the metaverse itself. For example, you could set up systems within the metaverse to prevent a monopoly or to prevent territorial domination. Some academics consider that eventually real-life laws and courts may not be required to govern virtual worlds and that the users could self-regulate and control the virtual worlds themselves without interference from the real world.[38] This wave of thinking is often termed 'cyberlibertarian'.

33 https://ec.europa.eu/info/law/better-regulation/have-your-say/initiatives/13757-Virtual-worlds-metaverses-a-vision-for-openness-safety-and-respect/F3411848_en.

34 https://ec.europa.eu/info/law/better-regulation/have-your-say/initiatives/13757-Virtual-worlds-metaverses-a-vision-for-openness-safety-and-respect/F3411662_en.

35 https://ec.europa.eu/info/law/better-regulation/have-your-say/initiatives/13757-Virtual-worlds-metaverses-a-vision-for-openness-safety-and-respect/F3409320_en.

36 https://ec.europa.eu/info/law/better-regulation/have-your-say/initiatives/13757-Virtual-worlds-metaverses-a-vision-for-openness-safety-and-respect/F3411621_en.

37 Nicolas Suzor, *Rule of Law in Virtual Communities,* Berkeley Technology Law Journal v25:1817 *(2010).*

38 Gregory Lastowka and Dan Hunter, *The Laws of the Virtual Worlds,* 92 CALIF. I REV 1, (2004).

2.39 Brownsword supports a move towards governance by technology itself.[39] He believes that there are three stages of disruption. The first stage, which he considers equates to systems like the metaverse, is where there is general discontent with the use of the law to govern. This he believes comes about as people start the question the validity of traditional laws to govern online environments. The initial stage still sees an interaction between traditional laws and norms and technologies. People, however start to challenge not only the traditional concepts around the conflict of laws but instead look at whether specific laws themselves should be governing the technologies or whether the technology should be self-governing. The second stage is where there is a shift to governance by technologies but still a human-centric approach. At this stage he believes that there are questions as to the authority and rule of law itself but the technologies effectively govern human-centric laws. In the context of the metaverse this is likely to encompass the idea of smart contracts which may automatically enact specific transactions or actions, but ultimately have been designed and implemented from a human-centric perspective. The third stage takes this further and sees control exerted by the technology. At this stage specific actions are prevented by the technology. He considers this to be 'human-protective' but not 'human-centric'.

2.40 With the metaverse, and Web3 in particular, we are going through what many consider to be a digital revolution, akin to the seismic changes caused by the industrial revolution. Brownsword[40] explains that we have already seen authority and respect for laws being challenged.[41] In his consideration of the third wave of disruption Brownsword goes further to examine whether the key concepts of the Rule of Law would be applicable in a landscape where there is governance by machine or whether our idea of justice would be relevant or necessary where there is governance by technology. This is an interesting concept in the metaverse since the technology itself may prevent a user from doing anything against the rules but wider issues then need to be considered as to what is considered to be right and wrong, whose decision this would be and how this is updated, changed and who is held to account.

SMART CONTRACTS AND THE RULE OF LAW

2.41 Smart contracts could be used to implement the Rule of Law. For example, the smart contract could be designed from a utilitarian viewpoint to prevent the

39 Roger Brownsword, *Law, authority, and respect: three waves of technological disruption,* Law, Innovation and Technology (2022) v14 no, 5-40.

40 Roger Brownsword, *Law, authority, and respect: three waves of technological disruption,* Law, Innovation and Technology (2022) v14 no, 5-40.

41 The question is: why should we recognise the authority of your rules simply because they are presented as 'the Law'; why should we respect the requirements and prohibitions of your rules simply because they are presented as 'the Law'?' Roger Brownsword, *Law, authority, and respect: three waves of technological disruption,* Law, Innovation and Technology (2022) v14 no, 5-40.

greatest harm for the greatest number of users by preventing something from happening. A smart contract could incorporate moral parameters. The issue, however, with imposing and enforcing a Rule of Law with smart contracts is that, as above, there is no one universally accepted view on the Rule of Law and how this should be upheld. The smart contracts have to be programmed and designed by humans. Smart contracts are not able to make moral decisions themselves. Therefore, it goes back to the same dilemma as to whose idea of the Rule of Law should be imposed. It would also be somewhat at odds with the concept of decentralisation to impose smart contracts prohibiting behaviour based on arbitrary concepts of the Rule of Law which are likely to evolve as society itself changes.

2.42 It may be that smart contracts could instead be used to control behaviour in the metaverse to ensure that behaviour is in line with the Rule of Law and preventing behaviour which is not in line with this, termed by some *lex informatica* – where technology can be used to resolve legal issues.[42]

WHAT IS THE IMPACT OF DECENTRALISATION ON THE RULE OF LAW?

2.43 Decentralisation is an important feature of the metaverse. Whilst this may not necessarily be the case in many of the current metaverse platforms, it will be an important evolution of the metaverse. In such circumstances there would be no central organisation tasked with governing behaviour and interactions will be peer-to-peer. Given the lack of centralised control important safeguards will need to be factored into the metaverse. This could be affected by way of smart contracts, which could embed features representing a form of the Rule of Law as above.

2.44 The Rule of Law may not work in the same way when you introduce peer-to-peer relationships.[43] This is because under a centralised system the law is what puts the rights, responsibilities and obligations on individuals. The law is imposed by a centralised body and then this is then monitored, controlled and enforced by a centralised body. By moving to a decentralised system there is a need to reconsider some legal issues, given there will no longer be any state-controlled body.

2.45 Certain cyber law theorists believe that cyberspace should be a utopia where a collective of users should be able to create their own rules and norms and should a user not want to participate in that part of the internet then they should move to a different part of the internet with different rules or grow a

42 Michael Anthony C. Dizon 'Law and Networks: Legal Pluralism in Information and Communications Technology (undated).

43 Melanie Dulong de Rosnay, Peer-to-peer as a design principle for law: distribute the law. Journal of Peer Production, 2015, Disruption and the Law, Issue 6, pp1-9.

new community themselves.[44] This theory, whilst dismissed in part by other academics[45] may have more relevance in the metaverse, especially a decentralised metaverse. Whilst it is likely there will be the need for wider governance in the metaverse, it is also highly probable that specific clubs or communities will also form in the metaverse with their own rules and regulations. One of the challenges will be dealing with how these interrelate and interact.

WHAT IS JUSTICE IN THE METAVERSE?

2.46 There is a distinction between law and justice. This is because not all laws are just or fair. John Rawls coined the 'justice as fairness' concept.[46] He later evolved this concept to stress that the concept of justice as fairness was aimed at the political construction of justice in constitutional democracies where the citizens are free and equal.[47] Rawls considered that the fundamental question was how a citizen could be considered free and have equality within a society where there is a fair system of cooperation.[48]

2.47 The metaverse is not a society based on free and equal people. Currently users of most metaverse platforms do not have the ability to vote on the governance of the platform. The rules of each metaverse's society are based on the different platforms and implemented by the owners of the platform. There is little to no democracy in respect of either the substance of these rules or how they are applied. There is no political liberty, a key tenant of justice as coined by Rawls. The principles of justice as set out by Rawls are therefore unlikely to be achieved in the metaverse at this stage. Whilst there may be the pursuit of some sense of fairness it will not be possible to achieve proper justice within the metaverse until there is a separation of ownership and rule.

2.48 There is a risk with online platforms generally, since these are ruled by all powerful Tech Giants, that we are reverting back to antiquated totalitarian rule.[49] This applies as much to the metaverse today as it did to the internet generally back in 2006. At this stage Rawls' 'social contract' is unlikely to be achieved unless there are true controls over bargaining powers behind a veil of ignorance.

44 David R Johnson & David G Post, *Law and Borders – The Rise of Law in Cyberspace* 48 Stan L. Rev 1367 (1995).

45 Nicolas Suzor, *Rule of Law in Virtual Communities,* Berkeley Technology Law Journal v25:1817 *(2010).*

46 A Theory of Justice, J. Rawls, (Cambridge, Mass.: Harvard University Press, 1971; rev.ed.,1999).

47 Justice as Fairness: a Restatement, J. Rawls (Cambridge, Mass.: Harvard University Press, 2001).

48 Justice as Fairness: Political not Metaphysical, J. Rawls (Princeton University Press, Philosophy and Public Affairs, v14, no3 (1985) (pp223-251).

49 Alistair S. Duff: Neo-Rawlsian Co-ordinates: Notes on A Theory of Justice for the Information Age, International Review of Information Ethics vol. 6 (12/2006).

2.49 The current iteration of the metaverse fails to have proper dispute resolution mechanisms that are distinct from the owners of the specific platform. At this stage most platform terms enable the owners of the platform to act however they please, in their discretion, to suspend or remove a user from the platform.[50] Currently one of the issues is that there are not effective mechanisms in place to properly test or challenge a determination by the platform owner.[51] This is something that needs to be examined before the metaverse can truly be capable of offering some sense of justice. If there is to be one metaverse or at least an ability to seamlessly journey between the different metaverse platforms there must be more thought as to how rules and law can be uniformly applied across the different platforms and whether it is possible to create an independent judicial arm – the independence of the judiciary being a key requirement of Hayek in respect of the Rule of Law.

2.50 There is the need to reconsider the idea of liberty in the internet age.[52] This remains important, if not more important, in the context of the metaverse and whether there should be a right for everyone to be able to access the metaverse and concerns around the digital divide. People may be unable to access their workplace or access specific public services if they do not have the necessary infrastructure to access to the metaverse. This is similar to complaints that have been raised as society has moved from analogue to digital but depending on the use and integration of the metaverse into real life this divide is likely to manifest itself to a greater degree.

USE OF THE METAVERSE TO ACHIEVE JUSTICE

2.51 There is scope for the metaverse itself being used to foster principles of justice. Virtual reality can be used for restorative justice, for example it can be used to transport convicts into a virtual situation where they could see and experience the harms that they have caused.[53]

50 Roblox terms state 'if you violate these User Terms or any of the Roblox Terms including the Roblox Community Standards, Roblox reserves the right, in its sole discretion, to terminate or suspend (i) your Account and (ii) your right to use and access the Roblox Services, including by suspending or terminating any alternate account(s) you create or have created.' http://en.help.roblox.com/hc/en-us/articles/115004647846-Roblox-Terms-of-Use Decentraland terms state 'In the event of your breach of these Terms or any suspected fraudulent, abusive or illegal activity, the DAO and/or the Foundation may, without limitation, suspend your Account, block any infringing Content and adopt any other action deemed necessary to prevent future breaches' http://decentraland.org/terms/#:~:text=By_using_or_otherwise_accessing,and_the_Site_pursuant_to.

51 This was examined in respect of the game Second Life in the US case of *Bragg v Linden Research, Inc* where the owners of Second Life sought to ban a user under its licensing terms.

52 Alistair S. Duff: Neo-Rawlsian Co-ordinates: Notes on A Theory of Justice for the Information Age, International Review of Information Ethics vol. 6 (12/2006).

53 Kate E. Bloch, 'Virtual Reality: Prospective Catalyst for Restorative Justice' University of California, Hastings College of the Law UC Hastings Scholarship Repository (2021).

2.52 Further, academics[54] consider that virtual reality could actually be used to create a veil of ignorance[55] since the human behind the avatar would be unknown, one such example given would be having criminal trials using avatars because the jury would then not know the appearance, race or physical appearance of the defendant and thus eliminating bias associated with this.

CONCLUSION

2.53 This chapter considers the Rule of Law, principles of justice and the metaverse. The key takeaway points are:

- Despite being a new frontier traditional theory of the Rule of Law and Justice are still important to understanding how to govern the metaverse.
- Traditional theories however need to be considered against the new possibilities created by the technological advancements of the metaverse and changes in society caused as a result.
- The multicultural and cross border nature of the metaverse means that great care is needed to ensure that law, order, justice and governance of the metaverse reflect different cultural, faith and ethical considerations that underpin these systems. The regulation of the metaverse should not be dictated by the Tech Giants or even just by western-centric ideals and values.
- The metaverse sits within existing real-life legal infrastructures and is an example of legal pluralism. Legislators need to dissect the interplay between such systems and set clear boundaries over where cross-over is appropriate. At what stage is it appropriate to deal with matters in the metaverse and where are real-life sanctions and redress appropriate?
- Technology can be used to control behaviour but thought is needed to ensure that there are safeguards. Attention is needed as to whose values, beliefs, principles of justice and law and order are reflected in the technological solutions.

54 Mary Anne Franks, The Desert of the Unreal: Inequality in Virtual and Augmented Reality, University of Miami School of Law Institutional Repository (2017) vol:51:499.

55 Rawls considered that to achieve principles which are true and fair there is a need to apply the veil of ignorance to make fair decisions.

Chapter 3

The legal framework and jurisdiction in the metaverse

'The Metaverse is not magic, it is a new world created by aliens from planet Earth to give an infinite experience of the existing world'.

Anuj Jasani

3.01 Some believe that there is currently a legal vacuum in the metaverse given there are no specific metaverse laws, punishments and consequences yet in existence.[1] There are, however a myriad of domestic laws, international laws and regulations which will still govern interactions in the metaverse as well as contractual and licensing terms governing behaviour on the different platforms.

3.02 The current iteration of the metaverse is seen by many as an evolution of social media and gaming. As the metaverse starts to be used for different interactions, typically traditionally carried out in real life, it is likely that the basic principles and key issues relating to these interactions will still be based on existing real-life laws and regulations but there are likely to be some gaps which will require further consideration and over time specific laws and regulations to be implemented[2]. There are many positive opportunities for the metaverse but, as highlighted by the World Economic Forum, steps still must be taken so that potential harms and dangerous environments are mitigated.[3]

LEGAL FRAMEWORK OF THE METAVERSE: INTERNATIONAL LEGISLATORS' PERSPECTIVE

3.03 Governance of the metaverse is already on the agenda of many international legislators. The US have flagged immersive technology as one of their most important emerging technologies[4]. The Leadership in Immersive Technology Act of 2024, introduced in December 2024, establishes the role of a principal advisor on immersive technology[5] who is to be responsible for the development of immersive technology in the USA and the coordination

1 Arian Dizaji and Ali Dizaji 'Metaverse and its legal challenges' Synesis, V15, 2023, ISSN 1984 – 6754 (30 January 2023) http://seer.ucp.br/seer/index.php/synesis/article/download/2395/3402
2 Such as the necessity to legislation on cryptoassets being considered a form of property.
3 http://www.weforum.org/agenda/2021/10/what-is-the-metaverse-why-care/
4 As reflected in 10387(c)(6) of Research and Development, Competition, and Innovation Act 42 U.S.C. 19107(c) and the Leadership in Immersive Technology Act of 2024 introduced in December 2024..
5 Section 4 Leadership in Immersive Technology Act of 2024.

of the different Government agencies on using immersive technologies. It also establishes a wider advisory panel, which is to include people from key Government departments, to look at the impact of immersive technologies on key areas such as consumers and the economy, as well as to advise on other important areas such as cybersecurity safeguards, data protection and international collaborations. The Act also requires that an in-depth study is undertaken within two years on key issues relating to immersive technologies and its impact on society together with recommendations on best practice and guidelines.[6] We do not yet know how much, if any, of this regulation will remain with the new Donald Trump Administration but it does follow on from the US Congressional Research Services report for the Members and Committees of US Congress in August 2022[7] in which it was confirmed that Members of US Congress are interested in the issues affecting existing online platforms and would like to explore issues further with the metaverse. This report highlights that the key areas of concerns for the US Congress include content moderation, data privacy, market power, competition and the digital divide. With the election of Donald Trump as the 47th President of America, the involvement of 'Tech Billionaire' Elon Musk and the wider support of the other Tech Giants as seen at his inauguration in January 2025, we can expect to see a greater legislative focus on technology generally in the US, including virtual worlds, immersive technologies, the metaverse and cryptoassets.

3.04 Significant work has been done by the EU in respect of the metaverse, which they term 'virtual worlds'. The EU Commission sent out a call for evidence in spring 2023 for its initiative to 'develop a vision for emerging virtual worlds (eg metaverses) based on respect for digital rights and EU laws and values.'[8] In his 2023 opinion on Virtual Worlds Oliver Röpke[9] emphasised the importance of legislators working with those in industry to try and build a safe and responsible metaverse.[10] The European Parliament held a hearing on the regulatory challenges in respect of the metaverse in April 2023[11] and on 17 January 2024 adopted resolution 2023/2062(INI) on the policy issues relating to the development of virtual worlds from the perspective of civil, company, commercial and intellectual property law issues. Under this resolution they stressed that it is importance that the metaverse is built on 'ethical, sustainable and human-centric' principles and preserves fundamental EU values as reflected in the Charter of Fundamental Rights of the European Union.[12] The European Parliament affirms that existing

6 Section 6 Leadership in Immersive Technology Act of 2024.
7 https://sgp-fas.org/crs/misc/R47224.pdf.
8 https://ec.europa.eu/info/law/better-regulation/have-your-say/initiatives/13757-Virtual-worlds-metaverses-a-vision-for-openness-safety-and-respect_en
9 the President of the European Economic and Social Committee
10 https://eur-lex.europa.eu/legal-content/EN/TXT/PDF/?uri=CELEX:52023AE0888
11 https://www.europarl.europa.eu/committees/en/hearing-on-regulatory-challenges-of-the-/product-details/20230420CHE11607
12 https://www.europarl.europa.eu/doceo/document/TA-9-2024-0029_EN.html

EU regulations will continue to apply in the metaverse[13] but the EU Commission is considering whether it is necessary to implement an EU-wide framework on the metaverse.

3.05 In September 2023 China confirmed its three-year action plan to accelerate development in the metaverse. The plan includes creating governance systems and a standard regulatory framework. In January 2024 the Ministry of Industry and Information Technology for the People's Republic of China formed a working group for metaverse standardisation to work with key stakeholders such as Huawei and Chinese universities. This is being seen as an intense focus from China on the metaverse, in particular on the industrial metaverse.

3.06 The United Arab Emirates is taking great strides to establish itself as a leader in Web3 and the metaverse. Dubai has pledged its intention to become one of the top ten metaverse economies in the world and is quickly establishing itself as a hub for metaverse and blockchain businesses. Dubai has created the Dubai Virtual Asset Regulatory Authority and passed the Virtual Assets and Related Activities Regulations 2023[14] which regulates virtual assets in Dubai. The Dubai Metaverse Strategy stresses that their aim is to develop 'global standards in building safe and secure platforms for users and develop metaverse infrastructure and regulations to accelerate the adoption of these technologies'.[15] The Dubai International Arbitration Centre (DIAC) has even established a metaverse arbitration centre with its own laws[16] where hearings themselves can be held in the metaverse.[17] The UAE Emirate of Ras Al Khaimah's Digital Assets Oasis (RAK DAO) is aimed at Web3 companies and includes specific regulations for DAOs.[18]

3.07 Finland has also specifically developed its Metaverse Initiative as a way to achieve its 'Metaverse Vision' by 2035.[19] They consider that the metaverse must uphold the pillars of inclusion accessibility, ethical and sustainability.

13 The resolution highlights the importance of the following pieces of regulation that will apply in the metaverse : the Digital Services Act; the Digital Markets Act; the Data Governance Act; the Data Act; the AI Act; the General Data Protection Regulation (GDPR); the General Product Safety Regulation; the Unfair Commercial Practices Directive; the Markets in Crypto-Assets Regulation; European Digital Identity; the Directive on Copyright in the Digital Single Market; the Regulation on the EU Trade Mark; the Directive on the Protection of Trade Secrets; the European Accessibility Act; and the Web Accessibility Directive

14 https://media.umbraco.io/dwtc/ogdex1ok/virtual_assets_and_related_activities_regulations_2023_jun5.pdf

15 http://u.ae/en/about-the-uae/strategies-initiatives-and-awards/strategies-plans-and-visions/government-services-and-digital-transformation/dubai-metaverse-strategy

16 https://www.diac.com/en/about-diac/

17 https://campaignme.com/dubai-international-arbitration-centre-diac-unveils-its-metaverse-platform/

18 https://www.rakdao.com/our-story/.

19 https://www.digitalfinland.org

LEGAL FRAMEWORK OF THE METAVERSE: UK REGULATORS' PERSPECTIVE

3.08 The Digital Regulation Cooperation Forum (DRCF) is a multi-regulatory body comprising of the Competition and Market Authority (CMA), Information Commissioners Office (ICO), Office of Communications (Ofcom) and the Financial Conduct Authority (FCA). It was formed by way of a cooperation between different regulators in respect of online platforms since they acknowledge that these platforms raise novel issues, questions and challenges for regulators.[20] In May 2022 the DRCF held a 'Metaverse Symposium'. The Department for Digital Culture and the Department for Business, Energy and Industrial Strategy were also in attendance at the Symposium. The Symposium highlighted the need for regulators to ensure that there is consistency between the regulators in respect of the metaverse and the collective aim to protect consumer rights and rights of UK citizens.[21] It was confirmed that regulators are looking at where current regulations and current regulators are able to adequately govern the metaverse and where there may be a need for new regulations or even new bodies to govern specific metaverse related issues.[22]

3.09 In December 2023 the DRCF published its Immersive Technologies Foresight Paper which looked at regulatory issues in respect of immersive technologies and the metaverse. They identified that there are several areas that regulators will need to consider in respect of the metaverse and that they need to remain alert to specific risks associated with new types of fraud and the distortion caused to a user's use of the metaverse. The DRCF position on the regulation of the metaverse is that:

> '[w]hilst immersive technologies and environments develop and use cases evolve, existing regulation will continue to apply. However, the technology may raise novel issues, some of which might require regulators to think in new ways or take new, innovative approaches.'[23]

3.10 In March 2024 the Intellectual Property Office published its report on intellectual property in the metaverse since they consider that the legal issues relating to intellectual property law in the metaverse had not been properly considered.[24] This report again highlights the adaptability and innovation of current regulators to take on the challenges presented by the metaverse.

20 https://www.gov.uk/government/collections/the-digital-regulation-cooperation-forum

21 https://competitionandmarkets.blog.gov.uk/2022/06/22/the-metaverse-and-immersive-technologies-a-regulatory-perspective/

22 https://www.digicatapult.org.uk/expertise/blogs/post/the-meteoric-rise-of-the-metaverse-how-can-government-and-industry-regulate-it/

23 https://www.drcf.org.uk/__data/assets/pdf_file/0027/273195/DRCF-Immersive-Technologies-Foresight-Paper.pdf

24 https://www.gov.uk/government/publications/an-analysis-of-the-metaverse-ip-landscape/an-analysis-of-the-metaverse-ip-landscape-html

3.11 We expect that, rather than the metaverse causing the UK to have to reinvent its regulatory framework, the existing regulators will, at least for some time, seek to absorb many of the key risks identified within the metaverse. Rather than see a new regulator being created for the metaverse itself we will expect to see the purpose-based approach to regulation continue, demarked by the underlying harms rather than the technology itself.

INDUSTRIES' VIEW ON THE LEGAL FRAMEWORK IN THE METAVERSE

3.12 There is a significant interest in the governance and regulation of the metaverse from key industry stakeholders. There was feedback from 169 organisations on the EU Commission's call for evidence on the governance and regulation of the metaverse. This came from key industry leaders, trade bodies, and interest groups. The overwhelming theme was a need to protect the vulnerable and safeguard against the inevitable harms that will manifest in the metaverse. The volume of detailed feedback to the EU Commission itself shows how much interest there is from a significant range of different stakeholders, all wanting to get involved in the development and regulation of the metaverse. Each contributor had their own viewpoint and specific points of interest but collectively these were illuminating and built a picture of what key stakeholders wanted in terms of governance of the metaverse. Notwithstanding the complexities which have been caused by not having one universally accepted viewpoint of the metaverse itself, the feedback shows the breadth of issues that need to be considered and the impact of the metaverse in all its incarnations.

3.13 Interestingly Meta acknowledges that the metaverse is already subject to existing laws such as GDPR and the Data Protection Act 2018 but where there are new issues which relate uniquely to the metaverse then they believe that the regulators should include all stakeholders in any decision making.[25] They believe that it should be a collaborative process with proper participation from industry stakeholders like themselves.[26] This should be not only on specific regulation but also on policy. Whilst there is without doubt the risk that these requests are ultimately self-serving given the pace at which the metaverse technologies are evolving however, and the interaction between Big Tech and traditional national and international governance, this should not be simply dismissed as a point of conflict without further consideration.

3.14 As part of its feedback Vodafone felt that it was still too early in the adoption of the technology to need binding legislation specifically in respect of the metaverse but welcomed the approach of the Commission to make its recommendations in respect of the metaverse.[27] Epic Games, the creators of

25 https://ec.europa.eu/info/law/better-regulation/have-your-say/initiatives/13757-Virtual-worlds-metaverses-a-vision-for-openness-safety-and-respect/F3411487_en

26 https://ec.europa.eu/info/law/better-regulation/have-your-say/initiatives/13757-Virtual-worlds-metaverses-a-vision-for-openness-safety-and-respect/F3411487_en

27 https://ec.europa.eu/info/law/better-regulation/have-your-say/initiatives/13757-Virtual-worlds-metaverses-a-vision-for-openness-safety-and-respect/F3411662_en

Fortnight, felt that the focus in the EU should be on enforcing the existing Digital Services Act[28] and therefore applying existing laws and regulations to the new technology. The European Lotteries believed that where something is illegal offline it should still be illegal in the metaverse especially in respect of gambling and advertising laws.[29] The European Union Intellectual Property Office (EUIPO) considered that intellectual property rights should still be upheld, protected and capable of being enforced in the metaverse.[30] Finally, TikTok raised the issue of jurisdiction in the metaverse, especially if the metaverse is decentralised.[31] If the metaverse is truly to become decentralised then exploration is needed to determine how to govern and regulate interactions without a governing body.

EXISTING LEGAL FRAMEWORKS

3.15 Despite there being no one unified law of the metaverse there are a number of existing laws both in the UK and EU which will be useful in starting to build up a legal framework for the metaverse. Many current laws across the UK and EU deal with the governance of the platform owners, such as the Data Protection Act 2018, General Data Protection Regulation (2016/679) (GDPR), the Digital Services Act,[32] the Digital Markets Act (DMA)[33] and the Digital Markets, Competition and Consumers Act 2024 as opposed to only dealing with interactions between individuals in the metaverse.

3.16 Under the law of England and Wales the common law should be able to piece together a jigsaw of different relevant laws, precedents and underlying legal principles to determine cases prior to any legislative framework specifically on the metaverse coming into effect. As highlighted by the Law Commission this is not however always an easy feat given new technology often creates unique situations. Some do believe that there is a need for new laws and ways of dealing with disputes in the metaverse. HHJ Pelling KC in his 2023 speech confirmed that he would expect some legislative reform to accommodate these emerging

28 https://ec.europa.eu/info/law/better-regulation/have-your-say/initiatives/13757-Virtual-worlds-metaverses-a-vision-for-openness-safety-and-respect/F3411575_en

29 https://ec.europa.eu/info/law/better-regulation/have-your-say/initiatives/13757-Virtual-worlds-metaverses-a-vision-for-openness-safety-and-respect/F3410769_en

30 https://ec.europa.eu/info/law/better-regulation/have-your-say/initiatives/13757-Virtual-worlds-metaverses-a-vision-for-openness-safety-and-respect/F3411618_en

31 https://ec.europa.eu/info/law/better-regulation/have-your-say/initiatives/13757-Virtual-worlds-metaverses-a-vision-for-openness-safety-and-respect/F3410937_en

32 Regulation (EU) 2022/2065 of the European Parliament and of the Council of 19 October 2022 on a Single Market For Digital Services and whilst this does not have effect in the UK per se most metaverse platforms are international in nature and therefore EU regulation is important in building up an idea of the underpinning legal framework for the metaverse generally.

33 Regulation (EU) 2022/1925 again applies in the EU only but is a key part of the legal framework for digital platforms.

technologies.[34] In September 2024 it was confirmed that the UK Jurisdiction Taskforce, an expert group led by the Master of the Rolls had been tasked to consider issues relating to digital assets.[35]

ONLINE SAFETY ACT 2023

3.17 The Online Safety Act 2023 deals with the regulation of online services, content and platform owners in the UK. It came into force on 26 October 2023 and is regulated by Ofcom who are in the process of preparing various codes of conduct and rules.[36] The Act describes its purpose and intention under its introduction under Part 1 [**my emphasis**]:

> **PART 1 Introduction**
>
> **1 Introduction**
>
> (1) This Act provides for a new regulatory framework which has the general purpose of **making the use of internet services regulated by this Act safer for individuals in the United Kingdom**.
>
> (2) To achieve that purpose, this Act (among other things)—
>
> (a) imposes duties which, in broad terms, require providers of services regulated by this Act to identify, mitigate and manage the risks of harm (including risks which particularly affect individuals with a certain characteristic) from—
>
> (i) illegal content and activity, and
>
> (ii) content and activity that is harmful to children, and
>
> (b) confers new functions and powers on the regulator, OFCOM.
>
> (3) Duties imposed on providers by this Act seek to secure (among other things) that services regulated by this Act are—
>
> (a) safe by design, and
>
> (b) designed and operated in such a way that—
>
> (i) a higher standard of protection is provided for children than for adults,
>
> (ii) users' rights to freedom of expression and privacy are protected, and
>
> (iii) transparency and accountability are provided in relation to those services.

3.18 We can see from discussions on the Act in Parliament that it was intended that the metaverse would be covered by the Act. When discussing the Act[37] Nadine Dorries, Secretary of State for Digital, Culture, Media and Sport said:

> 'The metaverse is included in the Bill. Not only is it included, but, moving forward, the provisions in the Bill will allow us to move swiftly with the metaverse and other things'.[38]

34 https://www.judiciary.uk/speech-by-hhj-pelling-kc-issues-in-crypto-currency-claims/

35 https://questions-statements.parliament.uk/written-statements/detail/2024-09-11/hcws84

36 The first draft code is the Children's Safety Codes published in May 2024

37 when it was a Bill during a reading in Parliament

38 https://hansard.parliament.uk/commons/2022-04-19/debates/F88B42D3-BFC4-4612-B166-8D2C15FA3E4E/OnlineSafetyBill

3.19 The Act[39] however currently does not apply to one-to-one live aural communications which is defined at s 55(5) as:

> 'content—
>
> (a) consisting of speech or other sounds conveyed in real time between two users of the service by means of the service,
>
> (b) that is not a recording, and
>
> (c) that is not accompanied by user-generated content of any other kind, except identifying content.'

3.20 Interactions between avatars in the metaverse, where there are only user-to-user aural communications, may therefore strictly speaking fall outside the Act. What is important for the metaverse, however is understanding sub-section (c) of the above definition. Chris Philp the Parliamentary Under-Secretary of State for Digital, Culture, Media and Sport in the ninth reading of the Bill considered that the metaverse would not be generally exempt under s 55(5) despite its prima facia exclusion for one-to-one live aural communications since:

> 'The actions of a physical avatar in the metaverse do constitute user-generated content of any other description'.[40]

3.21 It is still far from clear how a judge would interpret this provision should it become necessary in court. It remains to be seen whether there is any interest in testing what was meant by content which is 'not accompanied by user-generated content of any other kind, except identifying content'. Despite the view of Chris Philp, it is unclear how far simply creating an avatar falls within the remit of only being 'identifying content', since in the metaverse you are identified as your avatar and therefore by its nature the avatar would be the identifying content. Further, the other exceptions listed under s 55(2) are existing forms of communication methods – email, SMS and MMS. If the use of the metaverse, or at least some part of the metaverse, is purely as a form of communication tool, albeit virtually and in real-time there is certainly an argument to be had that such embodiment falls within the same categories of the other exceptions.

3.22 It seems clear that the intention of Parliament was to broadly cover the metaverse – albeit the exclusion of aural communications does mean that there are certainly still some unknowns. It is therefore prudent for platform owners to design their metaverses, including controls around avatar-to-avatar interactions, with safety by design in the forefront of their minds.

3.23 Despite the above uncertainty we would still expect Ofcom to include the metaverse within its codes and failures to comply will almost certainly result in sanctions. Depending on the uptake in adoption and use of the metaverse it

39 Section 5(2)(i)

40 https://hansard.parliament.uk/commons/2022-06-14/debates/ecfe5eda-bf86-4f7c-9225-18c4aa625dfc/OnlineSafetyBill (Ninth Sitting)

is likely that the exclusion will be repealed in any event under section 220,[41] especially if there is a successful argument run in court that avatar-to-avatar communications are exempt or at least if there is considered to be sufficient confusion over the intention of Parliament on this point.

Children

3.24 Insofar as the Act does apply to metaverse platform owners or those providing a service in the metaverse then they must comply with the Online Safety Act 2023, s 12 in respect of children unless there are adequate safeguards in place that deny access to their platform by children. Under s 12 there is the duty to protect children where the services are likely to be accessed by children. This includes the way that the services are designed, operated and used, as well as the content on the platform.[42] In the metaverse children will be able to access parts of the platform which would not comply with the Act, such as space that would have something which is harmful for children.[43] Therefore, it is expected that additional safeguards will be required by the metaverse platforms to be able to properly comply with this Act and the Ofcom Codes.

3.25 It will be difficult for the metaverse platforms to effectively monitor and enforce what children are doing in the metaverse given its global nature, and there may be a disconnect between the avatar and the underlying users details if there is a move towards decentralisation, much like the concerns with wallets in cryptocurrency transactions the platform owners may not be fully aware of the ages of some users. Metaverse platform owners should still, however, look to build their platforms with safety by design. Section 12(6) requires that any age verification or age estimation technique must be highly effective. With blockchain technology it would be possible to create a technological solution with smart contracts to prevent access to parts of the metaverse which are not suitable for children.

DIGITAL MARKETS ACT AND DIGITAL SERVICES ACT

3.26 Probably the most important pieces of legislation impacting the metaverse today, albeit is EU law and not domestic English Law, is the Digital Markets Act (DMA), which required compliance in the EU by March 2024, and the Digital Services Act (DSA)[44] which came into force in the EU for all platforms on 17 February 2024. These are together referred to as the Digital Services Act Package and form a set of rules for digital services in the European Union. This

41 Section 220 provides the Secretary of State the right to amend or repeal the exclusion for one-to-one live aural communications where it is felt necessary because of 'the risk of harm to individuals in the United Kingdom presented by one-to-one live aural communications'

42 Under section 12(8)

43 Content is harmful to children is categorised under section 60

44 Regulation (EU) 2022/2065 of the European Parliament and of the Council of 19 October 2022 on a Single Market For Digital Services.

is one of the first comprehensive frameworks for the all-encompassing regulation of digital services and focuses on the role and responsibility of the Tech Giants in respect of the same.

3.27 The EU Commission state that the goal of the DSA is to:

> 'protect…consumers and their fundamental rights online by setting clear and proportionate rules. It fosters innovation, growth and competitiveness, and facilitates the scaling up of smaller platforms, SMEs and start-ups. The roles of users, platforms, and public authorities are rebalanced according to European values, placing citizens at the centre.'[45]

3.28 Under the DMA comprehensive rules have been put in place for 'gatekeepers', who currently include Meta, Apple, Alphabet, Microsoft and ByteDance.[46] Most current metaverse platforms will come under the remit of the DMA and there are significant fines for non-compliance – up to 10% of worldwide annual turnover or up to 20% if there are repeated infringements. Whilst this will not have effect in the United Kingdom it is still important to consider in the context of the metaverse's legal framework, especially given the multinational nature of the metaverse it is inconceivable to imagine a metaverse without an EU presence.

3.29 The DSA is monitored and supervised by the European Commission and National Digital Service Coordinators will be designated in each EU country.

RELEVANT LEGAL FRAMEWORKS FOR OTHER TECHNOLOGIES

3.30 Regulatory frameworks for other technologies such as artificial intelligence, IoT and cryptocurrencies are important in the context of the metaverse insofar as compliance with these regulations will be necessary where such technology is included within the metaverse,[47] but it also can be used as a foundation for other emerging technologies with similar risks and concerns.

3.31 The EU AI Act[48] is the first international legislation governing artificial intelligence. The Act introduces different levels of risk of artificial intelligence. It is likely that any AI used as part of the industrial metaverse and made for autonomous decision making in the metaverse will be categorised as high risk given it will typically use to some extent real-time biometric data.

45 https://commission.europa.eu/strategy-and-policy/priorities-2019-2024/europe-fit-digital-age/digital-services-act_en#:~:text=Digital%20Services%20Act%20(DSA)%20overview,online%20travel%20and%20accommodation%20platforms.

46 https://digital-markets-act.ec.europa.eu/designated-gatekeepers-must-now-comply-all-obligations-under-digital-markets-act-2024-03-07_en

47 For example digital twin technology, which make up much of the industrial metaverse includes virtual reality, IoT devices and artificial intelligence.

48 Regulation (EU) 2024/1689

3.32 To guide decision making in respect of the metaverse, regulators in the UK are already looking to how AI is starting to be regulated elsewhere and the ethical issues related to this.

HOW SHOULD WE GOVERN THE METAVERSE?

3.33 The metaverse transcends multiple traditional jurisdictions which make it difficult to govern. There may be several solutions to this, one being to develop new real-life laws and regulations specifically for the metaverse and the other being to develop a clear framework for the metaverse for internally dealing with disputes itself.

3.34 There is the need to work with all stakeholders involved in the metaverse to develop a governance structure for the metaverse which may even eventually enable self-regulation.[49] It is all too early to know for sure how this will transpire; however, as the metaverse evolves and matures what is important is that there are in place proper safeguards and protections until such time as there is either self-regulation or specific legislation and framework.

3.35 It is likely that what we will actually see is a combination of both specific real-life laws, virtual metaverse rules and platform terms to resolve issues in the metaverse. In most cases the platforms themselves should be able to regulate behaviour and take action as necessary, however, where the harm is so serious that this crosses into harm in real life or the remedies in the metaverse are not suitable for the harm caused then we expect to see real-life action being taken.[50]

LEGAL PERSONALITIES

3.36 In the metaverse users are typically represented as avatars. In most cases there will always be a human personality behind that avatar. Complexity, however, arises where there is no human personality and the avatar is being controlled with artificial intelligence or via a corporation.[51] Avatars used commercially should be considered distinct from their developers as the avatar becomes more like a tool

49 As discussed in Journal of Metaverse – Navigating the Metaverse Business and Legal Challenges: Intellectual Property. Privacy and Jurisdiction, Maria Kalyvaki, 2023, v3. Issue 1 pages 87 – 92 http://dergipark.org.tr/en/download/article-file/2901353

50 David Assalone, Law in the Virtual World: Should the Surreal World of Online Communities be Brought Back to Earth by Real World Laws, 16 Jeffrey S. Moorad Sports L.J. 163 (2009).

51 The idea of the responsibility for loss caused by software using AI was considered by the Courts in Singapore in *B2C2 Ltd v Quoine Pte Ltd [2019] 4 SLR 17,* who found that it is the knowledge of the underlying developer that should be used. This was considered by Cheong in Avatars in the metaverse: potential legal issues and remedies (2022) Int. Cybersecur. Law Rev 3:467 – 494 who raised concern about whether the Court would come to the same conclusion once artificial intelligence is capable of deep learning.

of the trade rather than something representing its human controller.[52] There are legal commentators who consider that eventually all avatars will have their own legal personality, akin to the corporate veil, especially where artificial intelligence is involved in the evolution of the avatar and therefore, we could eventually see avatar v avatar legal actions.[53]

3.37 The issue of the legal personality of avatars was briefly considered by the European Parliament in resolution 2023/2062(INI). The door was left open to avatars getting status as a legal personality in the future as the EU Parliament believe that further thought is required as to whether a distinct legal status should be created for avatars.[54] Consideration is definitely needed as to where the blame for certain actions should lie, for example for the most heinous of offences committed by corporate bodies in real life the corporate veil can be pierced. As a minimum the European Parliament feels that there should be suitable know-your-client (KYC) processes in place to deal with identifying the underlying controller of the avatar. Some have even advocated that avatars should be registered in a form of central registry and their regulation should take its lead from company law.[55]

JURISDICTION IN THE METAVERSE

3.38 Jurisdiction is the extent to which a state can legislate, apply and enforce its laws. The issue of jurisdiction in the metaverse is not straightforward, especially when we do not yet have a definitive definition of a metaverse. What we have today is a series of metaverse platforms (or proto-metaverse platforms) and these platforms operate primarily as online platforms governed by contractual terms of use. As such each platform has subjected its users to a jurisdiction of their choosing, as typically contained within their terms of use. The complexities arise however where we have to consider interactions between users who may be based in different territories and in certain circumstances where specific jurisdictions will apply.

3.39 If we take the future iteration of the metaverse, where the metaverse is more than simply a series of detached platforms and there is full interoperability, one will have to consider principles applicable to the conflict of laws to determine jurisdiction and where there is legal standing.

52 https://www.orfonline.org/research/crime-and-punishment-in-the-metaverse-a-primer

53 Cheong, Int. Cybersecur. Law Rev. (2022) 3:467–494 – https://link.springer.com/content/pdf/10.1365/s43439-022-00056-9.pdf and Tiffany Day Tiffany Day, *Avatar Rights in a Constitutionless World*, 32 UC Law SF Comm. & Ent. L.J. 137 (2009). Available at: https://repository.uclawsf.edu/hastings_comm_ent_law_journal/vol32/iss1/5

54 European Parliament resolution 2023/2062(INI) para 21

55 Cheong in Avatars in the metaverse: potential legal issues and remedies (2022) Int. Cybersecur. Law Rev 3:467 – 494

Public v private law

3.40 Just as in real life the metaverse requires consideration from both the private law and public law perspective. In the first instance private law considerations are likely to centre on the contractual terms in place on the different platforms, and any contractual terms agreed between individuals.

3.41 As the metaverse increases in size, scope and application we would expect an increased focus on public law considerations. Whilst the metaverse is not in itself a state, given its composition and potential in terms of size and disparity between the individual users and the platform owners, public law considerations should be seriously considered as a priority in the metaverse.

PRIVATE INTERNATIONAL LAW, CONFLICT OF LAWS AND THE METAVERSE

3.42 The law of England and Wales can assert sovereignty of jurisdiction over anyone who is actually physically within England and Wales. To assert jurisdiction in the courts of England and Wales over someone based outside England and Wales in most cases (other than specific rules around consumers domiciled in the UK) you have to meet at least one of the gateways in the Civil Procedure Rules 1998, SI 1998/3132, PD6B. You must show that there is a serious issue that needs to be decided and that England and Wales is the most appropriate place for this to be done. In accordance with the Civil Procedure Rules 1998 civil court claims can only be served outside the jurisdiction of England and Wales with the permission of the court.

3.43 On the issue of jurisdiction for European Union members under EU law all EU members are subject to Brussels I Regulation (recast) (EU) No 1215/2012. This Regulation provides that EU members must only be sued in the state in which they are domiciled. This means that where there is a private international law dispute in the metaverse between persons whom are both domiciled in EU member states the jurisdiction for bringing a claim will be based on the domicile of the respondents. This principle still applies to consumers and employees in the UK despite the end of the transition period of the UK coming out of the EU due to the amendments to the Civil Jurisdiction and Judgments Act 1982. In all other cases the common law will apply, which includes the Civil Procedure Rules 1998 as above.

3.44 England and Wales remain subject to the Rome I[56] and Rome II[57] Regulations which were incorporated under English law under The Law Applicable to Contractual Obligations and Non- Contractual Obligations (Amendment etc) (EU Exit) Regulations 2019, SI 2019/834. These regulations will apply to disputes pertaining to contractual issues[58] and non-contractual matters[59] such as torts and product liability in the metaverse.

56 (593/2008)
57 (864/2007)
58 Rome I
59 Rome II

3.45 Under Rome I the guiding principle[60] for jurisdiction where there is a choice of law under a contract is that the law of choice will be chosen by the parties except in consumer contracts[61] where in most cases the applicable law shall be where the consumer resides.

3.46 Rome I is important for users of the metaverse specifically when dealing with the platform owners. Most metaverse platforms contain a 'choice of law' clause but many users will also be consumers. Users may decide to contract with each other in the metaverse and these interactions would be governed not only by any contractual terms of the specific metaverse but may also be implemented by smart contract. Care is required to check what may have been contractually agreed.

3.47 Under Rome II the general rule determining jurisdiction in respect of torts is where the damage occurred. The general rule for product liability[62] is that the jurisdiction should be where the person who suffered the damage lives, or where the product was brought or law where the damage occurred.

3.48 The Hague Principles deal with conflict of laws in respect of commercial contracts.[63] It is non-binding on its members but upholds the principle of autonomy and that where a choice of law has been selected by the parties this should take priority. There are currently 91 members of the Hague Conference on Private International Law including the UK, the USA and the EU. This is important for the metaverse since some certainty can be obtained through ensuring that there is a choice of law clause in any contract entered into on the metaverse.

3.49 One of the key issues in the metaverse, however, is that as an individual user you may not be able to readily identify where the other party is domiciled. In the metaverse you may not know their real namc or physical location. As such this makes determining jurisdiction complicated not only from a legal perspective but from a practical perspective.

Issues with private international law and the metaverse

3.50 In 2024 the Law Commission put out a call for evidence in 'Digital assets and ETDs in private international law: which court, which law?'.[64] In this call for evidence the Law Commission state:

> 'Our review of the rules of jurisdiction indicated that the difficulty in ascribing real-world locations to digital actions and digital assets is a significant challenge which private international law will have to overcome.'[65]

60 Article 3(1)
61 Article 6
62 Article 5
63 https://www.hcch.net/en/instruments/conventions/full-text/?cid=135
64 https://cloud-platform-e218f50a4812967ba1215eaecede923f.s3.amazonaws.com/uploads/sites/30/2024/02/Conflicts-full-document-FINAL-pdf-1.pdf
65 https://cloud-platform-e218f50a4812967ba1215eaecede923f.s3.amazonaws.com/uploads/sites/30/2024/02/Conflicts-full-document-FINAL-pdf-1.pdf

3.51 The outcome of the Law Commission's review in this area will be important in the context of the metaverse given the extent of digital assets being traded in the metaverse. Whilst the issues relating to digital assets and the metaverse may be similar, the metaverse will involve not only the trade of digital assets but other interactions in a virtual reality landscape. It is hoped that given the significant focus of the Law Commission in recent years on innovative technologies and the issues these present to the law and regulations in the UK now and in the future that eventually the metaverse as a novel and distinct category will be considered by the Law Commission.

3.52 The Law Commission identifies the issues with private international law insofar as it applies to digital assets. Many of the same issues will also apply to the metaverse. This is because in most cases the jurisdiction concerning property rights is determined by reference to the location of the asset (*lex situs)*. An asset which only exists in virtual reality, within the metaverse, will not be attached to any physical jurisdiction. Equally where there is an act or event which has occurred, one will look at where this damage was caused (*lex loci damni)* or where the act was committed (*lex loci delicti commissi)*. If the event has happened within a virtual reality world it will be difficult to determine both the place where the act has taken place or where the harm has been suffered. It may in some cases be able to be said that this should be where the real-life user is based but this may not always be the case. Where there is a contractual dispute consideration will be had as to where the contract was concluded (*lex loci contractus)* and where it is performed (*lex loci solutionis)*. Again, in the metaverse it may be hard to determine where the contract is being concluded or performed in the traditional sense. In addition, considering the domicile of a contracting party is likely to be difficult, especially if they are operating via a DAO.

3.53 The Law Commission[66] identifies two central underpinning considerations in respect of jurisdiction:

1 where it would be just and fair to bring the case; and

2 when sovereignty can be exerted over a defendant based on the principles of public international law.

3.54 The issues with fairness encompass issues such as how easy it would be for witnesses to give evidence. In the metaverse some of these issues could be mitigated by using the technology itself.

3.55 Despite something happening virtually in the metaverse there will in most cases be human actors involved controlling the avatars, who will themselves be based in physical territories. The common law should have sufficient flexibility to be able to determine the impact of this in respect of jurisdiction.[67] The Law

66 https://cloud-platform-e218f50a4812967ba1215eaecede923f.s3.amazonaws.com/uploads/sites/30/2024/02/Conflicts-full-document-FINAL-pdf-1.pdf

67 Difficulties will arise where the avatar is being controlled by AI or by a company or a DAO

Commission considers that the location of a digital file can be traced to help with determining jurisdiction, be that to the physical location of the computer or where the file is localised. The issues in respect of the metaverse are likely to be slightly more complex given that there may not be the transfer of any digital file in the traditional sense. There may be nothing to download or store outside the metaverse environment. In such a case reference is likely to have to be had to where the server for the specific platform is located.[68] This may be complicated where something is run through various server systems[69] especially when recorded on the blockchain and decentralised given the way this is processed and the use of intermediaries such as exchanges.

3.56 Harrak considered the issue of private international law in respect of smart contracts and blockchain. He considered that conflict of law rules of a smart contract should be considered on the same basis as a contract in real life.[70] Harrak states that:

> 'in our view, the difficulty encountered to regulate DLT transactions in general is rather a matter of lack of legal imagination than a matter of thinking that distributed ledgers should comply with classical national rules. Distributed ledgers should be accepted as they are, a reality, a powerful one, a necessary one, which allow new and various transactions…Questioning the validity of distributed ledgers or trying to set some legal conditions to their use will only result in failure.'[71]

3.57 In Harrak's opinion smart contracts, regardless of whether or not they fit into traditional legal criteria, will still succeed. It is the law that will need to change to accommodate. This seems to some extent to be the stance taken by the Law Commission in its report on DAOs in which it identifies the benefits of the structure as we embark on the digital revolution and that it will be for the common law and eventually, if necessary, legislators to accommodate.

OMNITERRITORIALITY

3.58 The metaverse is borderless, therefore to determine the choice of law is it correct still to use traditional territorial boundaries? In a shift to an immersive use of the internet, as envisaged with the metaverse and Web3, should we still be using the same criteria as in real life? Thought is required as to whether the underlying principles of jurisdiction should still apply in respect of a virtual reality metaverse where there is scope for real-time cross border interactions in most cases without a need or want to know where the other person is based.

68 Ashton Investments v OJSC Russian Aluminium [2006] EWHC 2545 (Comm)

69 An issue cited in United States v Microsoft Corp 584 US (2018)

70 Bonomi, Lehmann, Lalani 'Blockchain and Private International Law' International and Comparative Business Law and public Policy, v4 BRILL – https://library.oapen.org/bitstream/handle/20.500.12657/87971/1/9789004514850.pdf Chapter 17' Do Smart Contracts Need New Conflict-of-Laws Rules? Mehdi El Harrak

71 Bonomi, Lehmann, Lalani 'Blockchain and Private International Law' International and Comparative Business Law and public Policy, v4 BRILL – https://library.oapen.org/bitstream/handle/20.500.12657/87971/1/9789004514850.pdf

3.59 The main issue relating to jurisdiction in respect of digital assets is that there is still a territorial requirement needed in most cases. The same issue will apply in the metaverse. The Law Commission does recognise that the courts have largely been sympathetic as to the issue of jurisdiction in the context of cryptocurrency; however, this may be more a reflection of the significant harm that has been experienced as a result of some of the unscrupulous issues arising in the context of cryptocurrency. It remains to be seen how this will be viewed in the context of a dispute arising in the metaverse between parties of equal bargaining power.

3.60 'Omniterritoriality' is a concept where there are 'phenomena that cannot be linked to a specific country because they have simultaneous and equally valid connections to jurisdictions all over the world.'[72] Given the advancements in the technology, and the issues with disparate laws and regulations it may be appropriate for the metaverse to have its own jurisdiction.[73] This is an interesting concept and one which will need further exploration.

UNIDROIT principles on digital assets and private law

3.61 UNIDROIT is an independent organisation tasked with 'modernising, harmonising and co-ordinating private and in particular commercial law as between States and groups of States and to formulate uniform law instruments, principles and rules to achieve those objectives'[74] There are currently 65 Member States including the UK and the USA.

3.62 In Rome between 10 and 12 May 2023 UNIDROIT considered draft principles on Digital Assets and Private Law which were prepared by its working group. The principles are not intended to apply to any specific technology nor to any specific jurisdiction. They are aimed at both common law and civil law. These principles would apply therefore to digital assets within the metaverse. The principles are aimed at proprietary rights in respect of digital assets only. These are non-binding 'soft laws' or guiding principles that reflect a flexible way for different member states with different legal systems and traditions to bring into effect key principles.

3.63 The draft principles are designed to try and establish some form of certainty when dealing with digital assets.[75] Under the principles it is considered

72 M Lehmann, 'Extraterritoriality in Financial Law' in A Parrish and C Ryngaert (eds), *Research Handbook on Extraterritoriality in International Law* (2023) p 427

73 Jesse Valente, Governing the Metaverse, 9 U. Cin. Intell. Prop. & Comput. L.J (2024) available at http://scholarship.law.uc.edu/ipclj/vol9/iss2/3

74 https://www.unidroit.org/about-unidroit/

75 The Principles are designed to '*reduce legal uncertainty which practitioners, judges, arbitrators, legislators, and market participants would otherwise face in the coming years in dealing with digital assets' and are designed to be implemented by countries* https://www.unidroit.org/wp-content/uploads/2023/04/C.D.-102-6-Principles-on-Digital-Assets-and-Private-Law.pdf

that digital assets should be categorised as property and that autonomy of choice of law should be respected. This, they consider may provide an incentive for choice of law to be included within contracts and dealings with digital assets. The principles consider that the defining feature of a digital asset is that they can be subject to control. In addition, it recognises that traditional rules for establishing a choice of law may not be appropriate for a digital asset. The rules set out a suggested model for determining choice of laws.

PUBLIC INTERNATIONAL LAW, CONFLICT OF LAWS AND THE METAVERSE

International criminal law

3.64 There are two distinct considerations in respect of jurisdiction in public international law. These are the jurisdiction to set laws and controls and the jurisdiction to enforce. The issue of when a state has jurisdiction to set public international laws was considered by the International Court of Justice in *Arrest Warrant of 11 April 2000 (Democratic Republic of Congo v Belgium)* ICJ 14 February 2002. It is widely accepted that criminal jurisdiction of a state applies when an offence is committed on its territory, or by its citizens. It is generally accepted that jurisdiction can apply where the victim is a citizen of the state. In addition, it is widely accepted that where the offence is so serious that it has an impact on a state's national interests, such state may be able to assert jurisdiction. In most cases a state only has jurisdiction to enforce criminal jurisdiction as against another state in its own territory if it has the permission of that other state. The only exceptions arise in the context of war.

3.65 There is however, one set of offences for which there is universal jurisdiction, where any state can assert jurisdiction in respect of a crime regardless of the nexus of the offence, victim or offender to that state – piracy. Cited as the true universal crime, any state can arrest and try a pirate captured by them. Over time the concept of which crimes may attract universal jurisdiction has however slightly expanded but is still considered as reserved for the most heinous of truly international crimes. More complex is whether it is possible to have universal law in absentia.

3.66 In the metaverse there will be criminal offences committed. In most cases, the prosecuting state should be able to identify the basis upon which they have jurisdiction; be that because the infringing user lives in their state in real life or the victim does. It is also likely that other prosecutions will be justified on the basis of national interest reasons. It is, however, possible that there will be cases where it is not be possible to easily identify a traditional basis for jurisdiction due to the fluid nature of the metaverse. Traditional international criminal law considerations tend to have focused on atrocities and crimes that go to the root of humanity: war crimes; crimes against humanity; and genocide. Under the UN World Summit Outcome Document there is a commitment from states to protect their citizens against war crimes, crimes against humanity and genocide. We do not know how far this may apply in the metaverse. As identified by the European Parliament[76] however there is already a military metaverse and a risk that metaverse technologies may be weaponised.[77] There is also the risk of terrorism, war and genocide in the metaverse predominantly arising from misinformation[78] which will also pose a challenge.

A NEW FORM OF JURISDICTION

3.67 There is a strong argument for adjusting conflict of law principles in respect of the metaverse. International law may have to be changed to add suitable flexibility on jurisdiction or even introduce a new concept of jurisdiction. There should be a new jurisdiction framework established for the metaverse with treaties and multinational entities established to oversee this framework.[79] Resolving the issue of jurisdiction is vital when dealing with the metaverse but it requires the support of the metaverse platform owners and the different states.

CAN THE METAVERSE SELF-REGULATE?

3.68 The Metaverse Standards Forum is a not-for-profit organisation established with the mission to create an 'open and inclusive metaverse'.[80] Whilst the Forum does not create its own standards its task is to develop resources with a view to aiding stakeholders to create a safe metaverse. The existence of the Forum itself, with key stakeholders being involved, lends legitimacy to the idea of creating a set of standards in the metaverse.[81]

3.69 Nick Clegg, former Deputy Prime Minister and later President, Global Affairs of Meta emphasises the need for technologists to build a safe metaverse.[82] This could be termed 'safety by design' just as we have the ICOs 'privacy by design'. He stresses that this is not the sole responsibility of one company but requires a collaborative approach. There is certainly a need for legislators, lawyers and technologists to work together.

76 https://www.europarl.europa.eu/RegData/etudes/STUD/2023/751222/IPOL_STU(2023)751222_EN.pdf

77 https://warontherocks.com/2022/02/the-full-potential-of-a-military-metaverse/

78 Garon 'When AI Goes to War: Corporate Accountability for Virtual Mass Disinformation, Algorithmic Atrocities, and Synthetic Propaganda' (2022) Northern Kentucky Law Review v.49 number 2 – 'disinformation can be exploited by belligerent nations, terrorist networks, and non-state actors to foster territorial conflict and genocide'

79 https://dergipark.org.tr/en/download/article-file/3660505

80 https://metaverse-standards.org

81 Thomas A. Hemphill (2023) The 'Metaverse' and the challenge of responsible standards development, Journal of Responsible Innovation, 10:1, 2243121, DOI: 10.1080/23299460.2023.2243121

82 https://nickclegg.medium.com/making-the-metaverse-what-it-is-how-it-will-be-built-and-why-it-matters-3710f7570b04

3.70 The Tech Giants – Google, Meta and Microsoft are all part of the metaverse trade body, the XR Association[83] which amongst other functions has created a number of policy and insight documents for the XR community. In April 2022 the XR Association together with the US think tank, the Bipartisan Policy Center prepared a comprehensive report on the key issues relating to the metaverse and potential solutions.[84] It identified policy concerns relating to XR in respect of:

1 Privacy – this is the main concern of users;

2 Safety and Security;

3 Use and adoption;

4 Equality

3.71 The XR Association highlights the importance of guidelines within this space, to ensure that there are rules but believe that these should have sufficient flexibility to react to emerging technology and risks.[85] It has created a number of guides for XR developers to try and promote the building of a safe metaverse. They reference amongst others the following guidance and framework initiatives:

1 Cyber-XR Coalition – call for immersive technology standards for accessibility, inclusion, ethics and safety.[86] This is aimed as a blueprint for developers building safe XR environments. It is designed at uniting the industry with one voice with a clear set of guidelines and principles putting 'trust, inclusion and accessibility' front and central as the guiding mantra of building out XR products;

2 The XRSI Privacy Framework[87] – this was devised in 2020 and creates a general 'privacy framework' for XR and spatial computing;

3 IEEE Global Initiative on Ethics and Extended Reality (XR) report.[88] This addresses harms such as cyber stalking.

TERRITORIAL BOUNDARIES IN THE METAVERSE

3.72 In many cases traditional territorial boundaries are unlikely to have a direct application in the metaverse. The 'microstate' of the Free Republic Liberland however evolved in 2015 from a region created in the metaverse into

83 https://xra.org

84 https://bipartisanpolicy.org/download/?file=%2Fwp-content%2Fuploads%2F2022%2F04%2FXR-Report_Final-Copy.pdf

85 https://bipartisanpolicy.org/download/?file=%2Fwp-content%2Fuploads%2F2022%2F04%2FXR-Report_Final-Copy.pdf

86 https://cyberxr.org/wp-content/uploads/2021/05/Immersive_Technology_Standards.pdf

87 https://xrsi.org/wp-content/uploads/2020/09/XRSI-Privacy-Framework-v1_002.pdf

88 https://standards.ieee.org/wp-content/uploads/import/governance/iccom/social-multi-user-spaces-vr.pdf

its own real life 'state' on the border of Croatia and Serbia[89] covering 7.2 square kilometres in a disputed territorial region. Whilst it is not currently recognised by either Croatia or the United Nations as a state it has published its own constitution, some laws[90] and considers itself a state based on the Montevideo Convention on the Rights and Duties of States adopted in 1933.[91] The state has been built on the Liberland Merit (LLM) blockchain, and you need a cryptocurrency wallet to be able to access any service in the country. The President of Liberland in his 2024 New Year speech confirmed that the justice and security system was being built using blockchain technology.[92] Laws are passed by posting a draft on the software repository GitHub and enabling feedback from citizens.[93] Its website terms and conditions make it clear that there is no central oversight over the Liberland Smart Chain and that this is being built by the users themselves on a public blockchain.[94]

3.73 Where real-life territories seem to have found some relevance in the metaverse is through the use of their embassies in the metaverse. Barbados opened the first embassy in the metaverse.[95] Israel has subsequently also opened an embassy in the Korean metaverse, with a symbolic olive tree, the national tree of Israel, inside it.[96]

3.74 Not everyone however, is satisfied that using a virtual embassy fulfils the requirements of being a diplomatic mission under the Vienna Convention on Diplomatic Relations 1961.[97] They argue that under the Convention an 'embassy' is defined as the 'buildings and land'.[98] With a virtual embassy there would be a real-life ambassador but they would not reside in the receiving state. Barbados's metaverse embassy is available to all those it has diplomatic relationships with in real life. For critics one of the negative aspects in respect of the Barbados's metaverse model is a lack of reciprocity, which they feel is fundamentally against the idea of diplomacy and the purpose of an embassy. Further issues such as immunity relating to the virtual embassy remain unclear but reference is made to Estonia's data embassy in Luxembourg which was previously afforded protection against searches.

89 http://www.cointrust.com/market-news/liberland-from-virtual-metaverse-to-a-real-nation-on-the-map
90 http://liberland.org/en/laws
91 http://liberland.org/en/news/500-why-liberland-is-more-than-just-a-micronation-a-closer-look-at-the-emerging-country
92 http://liberland.org/en/news/538-liberland-president-vit-jedlicka-gives-a-new-year-speech-for-2024
93 http://liberland.org/en/news/483-legislation-in-liberland
94 http://liberland.org/en/terms-and-conditions
95 To be hosted on decentraland – https://diplomatmagazine.eu/2022/08/30/barbados-to-establish-the-world-first-embassy-in-the-metavesre/. Both Sweden and the Maldives have already had virtual embassies in Second Life.
96 https://www.koreatimes.co.kr/www/nation/2024/06/113_336705.html
97 Zhahira, T., & Christianti, D. W. (2023). The establishment of a virtual embassy according to the 1961 Vienna Convention on diplomatic relations: the case of Barbados' metaverse embassy. Jurnal Bina Mulia Hukum, 8(1), 106-127. https://doi.org/10.23920/jbmh.v8i1.1336
98 Article 1(i)

3.75 Despite the criticism, there is recognition that the nature of diplomatic rules is such that they must evolve based on common consensus and accordingly there is the opportunity for virtual embassies in the metaverse to be recognised but in so doing, further considerations and framework are necessary.

CONCLUSION

3.76 This chapter considers the underlying principles for establishing a legal framework for the metaverse. The key-takeaway points are:

- Existing legislation designed for existing technologies will be suitable to cover many of the legal issues which may arise in the metaverse and in many circumstances the common law should be able to react. There are however, challenges that this technology creates both in itself and its symbiotic relationship with blockchain technology, cryptocurrency and digital assets.
- Great strides are being made by the Law Commission in considering many of the challenges the existing laws face with the metaverse and Web3.
- The UK has established the Digital Regulation Cooperation Forum (DRCF). A multi regulatory task force of key UK regulators addressing the challenge that emerging technologies impact a whole range of regulated areas.
- Legislators, in particular international legislators (notably the EU and its focus on 'virtual worlds', and the UAE) are closely monitoring the metaverse and whether changes need to be made to their legislation. The EU Parliament has adopted regulation on 'Virtual Worlds' affirming its commitment to ensuring the principles of the EU are safeguarded.
- Whilst the option of self-regulation of the metaverse sounds attractive, its flaws lie in the ability to properly regulate the public law issues, especially as the metaverse expands. Unelected Tech Giants being given the responsibility to make determinations about public law issues presents a considerable risk. The law, legal and political system in democratic societies have evolved to implement longstanding checks and balances on holding the ruling powers to account where they are dealing with issues which impact its citizens beyond a merely private law basis. Today we still do not hold Tech Giants to the same standards[99] and until now their role has been firmly rooted in private law principles; the relationship between the 'citizens' of the metaverse and the Tech Giants who own and control the metaverse has always been purely contractual. That contract is often incapable of being negotiated and inevitably prepared by the Tech Giant itself and overwhelmingly weighted in their favour. For this reason, suitable public law protections and governance are needed. It is positive that Interpol

99 Some steps are being taken under the EU Digital Services Act Package

has a presence in the metaverse, but until it can properly deal with public law issues outside real life legislative framework will still be needed.

- Given the cross-border nature of the metaverse, where borders are (often unknowingly) being crossed multiple times, in real-time, there are serious challenges with dealing with jurisdictional issues and conflicts of law in the metaverse. For now, real-life laws and precedent may work as a band-aid, but a combination of specific international treaty dealing with the metaverse, and technological solutions may be a better way of addressing such challenges.
- The idea of territorial jurisdiction may be a concept that is too antiquated and not relevant to the metaverse, and needs a rethink. This in itself is clearly not a quick or easy process.

Chapter 4

Are there human rights in the metaverse?

> *'We should declare metaverse to only be a success if it augments the human in a decentralized human-centric model of data ownership.'*
>
> Davi Ottenheimer, Vice President of Trust & Digital Ethics, Inrupt

4.01 The Council of Europe explored the idea of human rights in the metaverse in their 2023 paper and felt that the metaverse should be designed with human rights as a key priority.[1] The Human Rights Act, the Universal Declaration of Human rights, the European Convention on Human Rights and the decisions of the European Court of Human Rights will all still apply to the metaverse insofar as they relate in real life to citizens of states who have ratified those convention.

4.02 It is more complex however, to consider whether the avatars themselves should attract human rights (a form of 'humanised' avatar) or whether it is simply the underlying human user who has such protection. Digital subjects in the metaverse are not necessarily equivalent to humans in real life, as they do not have their own emotions and morality.[2] Any emotions and morality of the avatars must be created by humans and it is they who project real-life ethics and morality onto avatars, given their resemblance to real-life people. There are however, avatars who are deep-fakes or a chatbot being autonomously controlled and therefore they either have no underlying human persona or that persona is deliberately being manipulated to represent another. From an ethical perspective further thought is required on the extent to which avatars themselves should attract any form of protection akin to human rights.

WHAT ARE HUMAN RIGHTS IN THE METAVERSE?

4.03 Many organisations are starting to consider the issue of human rights in the metaverse. In 2022 the Norwegian Board of Technology and Norwegian Human Rights Institution put together a report on the Metaverse and Human Rights.[3] Under the report they consider that there are potential benefits of using the metaverse to protect human rights but there are also risks with the impact of the metaverse on human rights. They accept that there will be blurred lines

1 https://rm.coe.int/the-metaverse-impact-on-and-its-impact-on-human-rights-the-rule-of-law/1680ae6bce.

2 https://doi.org/10.1007/s11569-022-00426-x Grinbaum and Adomaitis 'Moral Equivalence in the Metaverse' (2022), Springer Nature B.V. 2022.

3 https://www.nhri.no/wp-content/uploads/2023/04/The-metaverse-and-human-rights-1.pdf.

between 'real life' and virtual reality, which will itself have an impact on human rights. In real life it is typically the state that is empowered to uphold human rights[4] but in the metaverse, at least for now, this will be private entities – the platform owners who are tasked with this role.[5] There are therefore serious concerns with being able to hold these private entities to account in the same way as individual states.

4.04 The EU have identified what it considers to be the eight human rights values for its citizens in respect of the metaverse,[6] these are:

1 Freedom of choice;

2 Environmental sustainability;

3 Human-centric;

4 A focus on health – both physical and mental;

5 Education;

6 Safety;

7 Transparency;

8 Inclusivity.

ETHICS IN THE METAVERSE

4.05 The Council of Europe has explored the idea of ethics in the metaverse.[7] It has highlighted that there are ethical issues as relating to:

1 Issues relating to 'digital humans';

2 The idea of 'virtual abundance'; and

3 The impact of the metaverse on 'autonomy and privacy'.

4.06 There is a need for regulators to carefully consider the ethics of emerging technologies. These ethical risks form the basis from which rules and regulations can be developed. Whilst some of the ethical risks in the metaverse will be the same as in real life there must be proper ethical considerations in respect of the blurring of real life and virtual reality.

4 And is the one accountable to supranational courts in respect of such rights where they have ratified the relevant Treaty.

5 https://www.nhri.no/wp-content/uploads/2023/04/The-metaverse-and-human-rights-1.pdf.

6 https://citizens.ec.europa.eu/document/download/5d55a9e4-a0f2-4974-b01b-a8382eb6cb4d_en?filename=ECP%20on%20Virtual%20Worlds_Final%20Report.pdf.

7 https://rm.coe.int/the-metaverse-impact-on-and-its-impact-on-human-rights-the-rule-of-law/1680ae6bce.

ARE EXISTING HUMAN RIGHTS RELEVANT IN THE METAVERSE?

4.07 There have been significant changes in both technology and society since the Universal Declaration of Human Rights in 1948. At that point the internet did not exist, let alone any concept of the metaverse. It is therefore questionable whether those declarations made almost 70 years ago remain relevant for the metaverse.[8]

4.08 Today, the digital divide is one of the most significant challenges for the metaverse. This is the division between those who have access to reliable internet and those that do not. The World Economic Forum consider that internet access is a universal human right[9] and that there are socio-economic divisions between those who are using the metaverse (or capable of using the metaverse as a result of their access to the internet) and those who are not using it.

WHAT ARE NEURORIGHTS?

4.09 The Council of Europe[10] identified that one of the key ethical risks in the metaverse is the ability for users' thoughts to be manipulated. Neurorights are 'ethical, legal, social or natural principles of freedom or entitlement related to a person's cerebral and mental domain'.[11] Put simply, a person should have the right not to have their thoughts manipulated. There are specific calls for new technologies to be regulated to prevent impeding these rights, with some even going as far as saying their infringements should be criminal offences[12] and others considering that mental integrity is a moral right and should be fundamentally protected given the harm that can be caused to someone's autonomy by another being able to pervade their innermost thoughts.[13]

4.10 The Australian Human Rights Commission released its paper in March 2024 on the impact of neurotechnology on Human Rights.[14] The Human Rights Commissioner expressed her concern with the general lack of safeguards and

8 Emerging Areas of Human Rights in the 21st Century, the role of the Universal Declaration of Human Rights, edited by Marco Odello and Sofia Cavandoli, Routledge Research in Human Rights Law, Routledge – Taylor & Francis, London and New York, 2011 chapter 1 'virtual world, real rights?: Human rights and the internet, Diane Rowland.

9 https://www.weforum.org/agenda/2023/01/davos23-immersive-experiences-close-digital-divide/.

10 https://rm.coe.int/the-metaverse-impact-on-and-its-impact-on-human-rights-the-rule-of-law/1680ae6bce.

11 https://www.europarl.europa.eu/thinktank/de/events/details/neurotechnology-and-neurorights-privacy-/20231019WKS05721.

12 https://sciencemediahub.eu/2023/11/08/neurorights-do-our-brains-need-to-be-protected-by-legislation/.

13 Lavazza and Giorgi 'Philosophical foundation of the right to mental integrity in the age of neurotechnologies' Neuroethics 16, 10 (2023). https://doi.org/10.1007/s12152-023-09517-2.

14 https://humanrights.gov.au/sites/default/files/document/publication/protecting_cognition_-_background_paper_on_neurotechnology_and_human_rights_1.pdf.

legislation globally in respect of neurotechnology and called for international consideration on the issue. She considered that the use of neurotechnology, such as BCI,[15] does have a considerable effect on an individual's human rights. There is the widespread concern that the use of neurotechnology, especially in advertising, could be used to manipulate a user.

4.11 Supporting the view of the Australian Human Rights Commissioner, the NeuroRights Foundation in its 2024 report[16] found that a majority of companies using neurotechnology did not have proper safeguards in place. In its analysis of 30 companies – all using some form of neurotechnology – it found many did not restrict their unfettered access to neural data, some did not have any privacy information available at all, most did not refer to the neural data as being personal data in their privacy policy and a majority could transfer the data to third parties.[17] At this stage it concluded that processes were woefully lacking.

4.12 Whilst many states have not expressly recognised a form of neurorights, in December 2020 the Chilean Senate amended its constitution to protect against infringement of neurorights. Further in 2023 its Supreme Court held that there was a fundamental right to mental privacy in the case of *Guido Girardi Lavin v Emotiv Inc* – case 105065-2023.[18] In the UK, the Human Rights Act 1998, s 9 already provides that everyone has the right to freedom of thought. It is expected that such a right may need further exploration in the context of the metaverse especially as the technology continues to become more and more immersive and as a result detaching the virtual experience further from real life.

RIGHT TO LIFE IN THE METAVERSE AND PROHIBITION OF TORTURE

4.13 At least in the current gamified form of the metaverse avatars will die and respawn. This is unlikely to be considered a breach of human rights by anyone. The intention of the Human Rights Act 1998 was clearly to protect against death in real life as opposed to in virtual life. Therefore, should your avatar be killed by another user of the metaverse this would not fall foul of this protection.

4.14 Should the metaverse however evolve into the concept of one all-encompassing virtual space where an avatar is a virtual representation of an individual to be used across the multiple platforms then there may be justification for the right to your virtual or digital representation not being killed or destroyed. More so if this results in your use of the metaverse with that avatar being terminated or even your profile being deleted. It may be at that stage there should be a more general right to a virtual representation of yourself in such way as

15 Which has direct relevance to the metaverse and its future expansion.

16 Safeguarding Brain Data: assessing the privacy practices of consumer neurotechnology companies by Jared Genser, Stephen Damianos and Rafael Yuste, April 2024.

17 https://www.perseus-strategies.com/wp-content/uploads/2024/04/FINAL_Consumer_Neurotechnology_Report_Neurorights_Foundation_April-1.pdf.

18 The case was brought against Emotiv Inc on behalf of data relating to Guido Girardi.

chosen by you to use in the metaverse, as opposed to the right to the virtual life of your avatar.[19]

4.15 Article 3 is perhaps more complex in the context of the metaverse. This right does not stipulate that the treatment has to be actually carried out real life. Instead, this protection looks more at the harm that is being protected against. If the real-life human has been subjected to inhumane or degrading treatment or punishment as a result of action taken in the metaverse then suitable protection should be afforded. A general comment on the Optional Protocol to the Convention against Torture and Other Cruel, Inhuman or Degrading Treatment or Punishment (OPCAT) was submitted by the Interdisciplinary United Nations Working Group on Human Rights and Digital Technology to the United Nations Subcommittee on Prevention of Torture and Other Cruel, Inhuman or Degrading Treatment or Punishment to say that the right against the deprivation of liberty should be specifically extended to expressly include digital spaces.[20] The Working Group recommended that digital spaces should be specifically considered to be a place where there can be a deprivation of liberty under the OPCAT. They specifically reference the risks present in respect of the metaverse and the harm that can be caused by depriving someone of their rights in this space, as well as being able to access and utilise this space. They suggested that clarification should be added to the OPCAT to say 'Places of deprivation of liberty shall also include any digital or non-physical spaces in which an individual's freedom of movement, expression, or access to essential services is limited or controlled'.[21] This opens the door to recourse where there are human right violations carried out in the metaverse.

4.16 There have been some discussions over how to punish someone in the metaverse. One suggestion is the idea of avatars being put into some form of prison.[22] The idea of punishment in the metaverse is directly aligned with Article 3 protection. Those building the infrastructure of the metaverse must consider how to balance protection of individual users against punishing those that infringe its rules. This is not a new balance in society, but it is one which is now being tasked to technology developers rather than law-makers.

FREEDOM OF EXPRESSION, ASSEMBLY AND ASSOCIATION IN THE METAVERSE

4.17 Freedom of expression should not be impeded in the metaverse.

19 Especially since the avatar is never actually alive.

20 https://www.ohchr.org/sites/default/files/documents/hrbodies/spt-opcat/cfis/gc1-art4/submission-spt-gc-article4-UNWG-HRDT.pdf.

21 https://www.ohchr.org/sites/default/files/documents/hrbodies/spt-opcat/cfis/gc1-art4/submission-spt-gc-article4-UNWG-HRDT.pdf.

22 https://www.thenationalnews.com/weekend/2022/10/14/avatar-jail-does-the-metaverse-need-its-own-police-force/

4.18 As discussed in previous chapters the current iteration of the metaverse is however, premised on controls imposed by the platform owners – who tend to be Tech Giants. The right to freedom of expression is designed to protect the right to a free press, ability to protest and providing a voice to citizens.[23] The metaverse platforms of today, or at least the proto-metaverse platforms, often seek to stifle this right through moderation, user terms and fair use policies.

4.19 Given the cross-border element of the metaverse it is complex to balance freedom of expression against the need for moderation due to geopolitical considerations.[24] There are interesting considerations since what may be censored in one country may be considered morally abhorrent to censor in another. One such example of this is in respect of LGBTQ+ material, which in some countries has legal restrictions on its promotions on social media.[25] This censorship itself however would be considered as a breach of Article 7 of the Universal Deceleration on Human Rights.[26] Should material be unobtainable if you enter the metaverse from one country, but not another? This feels at odds with the entire concept of a free-roaming metaverse. Should the metaverse evolve as desired to enable full interoperability with one all-encompassing metaverse it will be difficult to rationalise the differing censorship between states.

4.20 The Council of Europe considered the impact of the metaverse on freedom of expression and its moderation.[27] They noted the considerable challenges that will be faced in balancing the potential harm from the real-time explosion of content in the metaverse, which will include discriminatory and hate language, against freedom of expression. Further with the rise of deliberate use of misinformation and 'fake news' they considered the potential harms that could arise in the metaverse from this information being presented in an immersive environment where its impact would be more intense on the users and could even be used to manipulate their thoughts. Accordingly, in the metaverse the rights under Article 10 have a direct impact on the Article 9 rights of freedom of thought, conscience and religion.

CIVIL AND POLITICAL RIGHTS IN THE METAVERSE

4.21 The International Covenant on Civil and Political Rights was adopted by the General Assembly of the UN in 1966 and ratified by the UK in 1976.

23 Article 10 of the Human Rights Act 1998.

24 Emmie Hine, 'Content Moderation in the Metaverse Could Be a New Frontier to Attack Freedom of Expression' Philosophy & Technology (2023) 36:43.

25 Such as in Russia which introduced the Amendments to Article 5 of the Federal Law 'On the Protection of Children from Information Liable to Be Injurious to Their Health and Development' amongst other reforms. There are also restrictions as well in Hungary and Uganda.

26 Emmie Hine, 'Content Moderation in the Metaverse Could Be a New Frontier to Attack Freedom of Expression' Philosophy & Technology (2023) 36:43.

27 https://rm.coe.int/the-metaverse-impact-on-and-its-impact-on-human-rights-the-rule-of-law/1680ae6bce.

This Treaty is important in the context of the metaverse as it provides the right of individuals to determine their own political views,[28] to not be subject to unlawful interference or unlawful attack on honour or reputation in respect of such views[29] and in most cases to hold such views without interference.[30] Further the Treaty prohibits propaganda for war and national, racial or religious hatred that constitutes incitement to discrimination, hostility or violence.[31]

4.22 The Council of Europe considered the impact of the metaverse on political rights and felt that there was some opportunity that it could be used for greater engagement of citizens with politics.[32] They noted, however, that there is also the adverse risk of censorship of political views in the metaverse. As discussed above this would not be in line with the International Covenant on Civil and Political Rights. The Council of Europe cautioned against the risk of deep fakes and social augmentation being used to convey political viewpoints. This has already been seen in the run up to the UK 2024 General Election. There is also the risk that where certain political groups have a higher representation in the metaverse, other viewpoints may not be easily heard or available. Some consider that the metaverse could actually undermine democracy, given it does not require truthfulness and, similar to social media platforms, political views may be distorted.[33]

4.23 Censorship of political views and activism could go further in the metaverse than in real life. This is because, at least at this time, the metaverse is being built on platforms owned by private companies, which will have an interest in what happens within their space. There is a risk that activism could be shut down if this had a negative impact on a business and political discussions could even lead to immersive advertising trying to influence voting or political persuasion.[34] It is not a stretch to consider the harm that could be caused if the metaverse was used to try and influence a user's political beliefs or to manipulate an outcome of a real-life election. Sufficient protection is needed to safeguard the metaverse from political interference given these risks.

RIGHT TO EDUCATION AND THE METAVERSE

4.24 Article 26 of the Universal Declaration of Human Rights provides that everyone has the right to education. It goes further to stipulate that this shall

28 Article 1.
29 Article 17.
30 Article 19.
31 Article 20.
32 https://rm.coe.int/the-metaverse-impact-on-and-its-impact-on-human-rights-the-rule-of-law/1680ae6bce.
33 Aziz Z. Huq, Militant Democracy Comes to the Metaverse? 72 Emory L.J. 1105 (2023).
34 as discussed by Professor Turner from Stanford University at https://www.db.com/what-next/digital-disruption/Metaverse/democracy-Demokratie/index?language_id=1&kid=wn.stageGHP.democracy.en.

'promote understanding, tolerance and friendship among all nations, racial or religious groups, and shall further the activities of the United Nations for the maintenance of peace'. The metaverse is a fantastic educational tool and its use, with sufficient safeguards in place, could foster relationships across borders and religions. The metaverse could enable poorer areas to have access to teachers and students to not be limited by their geographic location.[35] The key aspect to note, however, is that States will need to ensure that there are no discriminatory barriers in place which may impact on this right to education carried out via the metaverse.

4.25 The Brookings Institution emphasise that those developing the educational part of the metaverse must ensure that they are thinking about how children learn and that this is meaningful and relevant.[36] The metaverse could give educators the opportunity to dispense with traditional forms of education through its new and immersive delivery. Education through the traditional school system is heavily regulated in the UK by the Department for Education with comprehensive safeguarding provisions which may not be readily adhered to in the metaverse. Schools and teachers should therefore, before engaging with the metaverse as part of the education of those in their care, be cautious and ensure proper safeguarding checks have been undertaken as well as suitable provisions concerning data protection, equality and human rights. In practice this is likely to be difficult to do given the expansive nature of the metaverse, so until there are technological safeguards in place we expect to see limits put around the use of the metaverse within the education system. It is likely this will be limited to pre-vetted spaces and activities. Ofcom's regulation under the Online Safety Act 2023 and its Protection of Children code of practice specifically aimed at protecting children goes some way to start to regulate the protection of children in the metaverse but it will become necessary for those using the metaverse in an education setting to update safeguarding policies and procedures to take into account any use of the metaverse as well as providing updated staff training especially on the risks of harm and safeguarding in the metaverse.

RIGHTS OF THE CHILD IN THE METAVERSE

4.26 The UN Convention on the Rights of the Child came into force in the UK in 1992. The Convention applies in many countries of the World but was never ratified by the United States of America.

4.27 The Preamble recognises amongst other rights that:

> 'The child should be … brought up in the spirit of the ideals proclaimed in the Charter of the United Nations, and in particular in the spirit of peace, dignity, tolerance, freedom, equality and solidarity'[37]

35 https://about.fb.com/news/2023/04/how-the-metaverse-can-transform-education/.

36 https://www.brookings.edu/wp-content/uploads/2022/02/A-whole-new-world_Education-meets-the-metaverse-FINAL-021422.pdf.

37 https://www.unicef.org.uk/wp-content/uploads/2016/08/unicef-convention-rights-child-uncrc.pdf.

4.28 The Committee on the Rights of the Child General Comment No.25 (2021) considered the implementation of the Convention in a digital context and stipulate that:

> 'The rights of every child must be respected, protected and fulfilled in the digital environment'[38]

4.29 The Committee highlighted that the four principles to protect a child in the digital space are:[39]

1 Non-discrimination;

2 Acting in the best interest of the child;

3 The right to life;

4 Having respect for the views of the child.

4.30 When discussing the right to life they highlight that measures should be taken to protect children from, amongst other issues: gambling; sexual abuse; cyberbullying; and extremist, sexual and violent content, all of which are considerable risks in the metaverse. All states must work with technology companies to ensure that the metaverse can meet these objectives and suitable protection is embedded into the infrastructure. The Committee remind parties to the Convention that steps may be necessary to meet their objectives and calls for independent monitoring. As discussed in **Chapter 3** the Online Safety Act 2023 may at this stage fail to properly cover avatar to avatar interactions should they fall under s 55, which may present risks in respect of meeting these objectives. Ofcom have however focused initially on the protection of children in respect of its obligations as regulator under the Online Safety Act 2023 and have prepared a Code of Practice with the aim of protecting children whilst balancing their human rights. It is expected that Ofcom will cover the metaverse platforms insofar as the Online Safety Act 2023 applies.

4.31 The Committee on the Rights of the Child General Comment No 25 (2021) further considers the impact of advertising and marketing on children in the digital environment. They consider that the best interests of the child should be the central consideration and that immersive advertising, advertising in virtual reality and augmented reality and neuromarketing should be banned for children. This is a clear message to those seeking to utilise advertising in the metaverse that this is unlikely to be compatible with the rights under the above Convention. States, which include the UK, who are parties to the Convention will need to be able to reconcile this position with the expansion of the metaverse. The Committee go so far as to stipulate that states should prohibit this form of

38 https://tbinternet.ohchr.org/_layouts/15/treatybodyexternal/Download.aspx?symbolno=CRC/C/GC/25&Lang=en.

39 https://tbinternet.ohchr.org/_layouts/15/treatybodyexternal/Download.aspx?symbolno=CRC/C/GC/25&Lang=en.

advertising so effective controls will need to be found to protect children in the metaverse from this type of advertising.

4.32 Children in particular are likely to be most affected by harms to which they are exposed in the metaverse. There are considerable risks of children being exposed to discrimination, misinformation and even criminal harms in the metaverse. Reports have shown that due to the immersive nature of the metaverse harms committed, such as abuse, can appear real and have a greater impact on a child.[40] The Council of Europe considered that there is a need for additional safeguarding and monitoring of children and young people's activity in the metaverse as well as putting in place comprehensive guidelines in order to comply with the Lanzarote Convention[41] and its own Strategy for the Rights of the Child 2022–2027.[42]

4.33 One of the objectives of the Council of Europe's Strategy for the Rights of the Child 2022 – 2027 is the 'access to and safe use of technologies for all children'.[43] In preparing the strategy 28 children were consulted in Belgium and Italy for their view on technology. The report on the consultations show that children are acutely aware of the risks presented with technology both from other users, such as cyber bullying, but also in respect of addiction and advertising.[44] The EU is currently trying to reach an agreement in respect of the implementation of framework for the prevention of online child abuse. Given the balance of the use of technology to monitor this, against data protection legislation, there is a current derogation in respect of the e-Privacy regulations in force until at least April 2026.[45]

4.34 In 2023 UNICEF prepared a report on the impact of the metaverse and extended reality on children.[46] It acknowledges that there are both risks and opportunities with the metaverse for children. Risks focus on the safety of the metaverse and exposure to harm, such as harassment and abuse, whilst amongst the many opportunities include education and even socialisation. The report highlights that steps need to be taken to properly exclude children from parts of the metaverse which are not suitable for them. There need to be effective controls given the significant impact of harm the child may suffer from being immersed into an unsuitable environment.

40 https://www.carnegiecouncil.org/media/article/protect-children-metaverse.
41 Protection of Children against Sexual Exploitation and Sexual Abuse.
42 https://rm.coe.int/the-metaverse-impact-on-and-its-impact-on-human-rights-the-rule-of-law/1680ae6bce.
43 https://www.coe.int/en/web/children/strategy-for-the-rights-of-the-child.
44 https://rm.coe.int/council-of-europe-child-consultations-to-inform-the-elaboration-of-the/1680a697d5.
45 https://www.europarl.europa.eu/news/en/press-room/20240212IPR17636/child-sexual-abuse-online-agreement-on-extending-current-rules-until-april-2026.
46 https://www.unicef.org/innocenti/media/756/file/UNICEF-Innocenti-Rapid-Analysis-Metaverse-XR-and-children-2023.pdf.pdf.

4.35 The report[47] highlighted that amongst other health concerns XR technology does impact the development of children. UNICEF voiced its concerns that studies have shown that children exposed to this type of technology find it difficult to distinguish between real life and virtual reality. The technology itself could therefore have a significant impact on a child's perception of reality making harms more serious to them but also impacting on their day-to-day life in the real world. Since the technologies are so new it is very hard to see the longer-term impact on children exposed to the metaverse.

4.36 The use of blockchain technology within the metaverse adds further complications. This is because any decisions and actions a person makes as a child will be permanently contained on their public digital record. The House of Commons Justice Committee's First Report of Session 2017–19[48] considered whether disclosing offences committed by a child under the age of 18 was appropriate given the impact of this on access to employment, education, insurance housing, travel and that it disproportionately affected certain demographic groups. The Committee questioned whether disclosing such records would be in contravention of the UNCRC. The permanent record of any potential infractions or misdemeanours committed in the metaverse on a publicly accessible blockchain is equally not in the spirit of the Convention nor Article 8 of the European Convention on human Rights.

WOMEN AND GIRLS

4.37 The Alliance for Universal Digital Rights (AUDRI) has created a framework aimed at safeguarding women and girls in the digital environment given the historic treatment and risk faced by women in real life. These prioritise the right to safety, right to freedom and the right to dignity.[49] Their nine principles are:[50]

1 Universal and equal rights

2 Personal safety and data privacy

3 Digital self-determination

4 Digital access for all

5 Freedom of expression and association

6 Secure, stable, and resilient networks

7 Linguistic and cultural diversity

8 Universal standard and regulation

9 Good digital governance

47 https://www.unicef.org/innocenti/media/756/file/UNICEF-Innocenti-Rapid-Analysis-Metaverse-XR-and-children-2023.pdf.pdf.

48 https://publications.parliament.uk/pa/cm201719/cmselect/cmjust/416/416.pdf.

49 https://audri.org/digital-principles/.

50 https://audri.org/wp-content/uploads/2023/02/Digital-Principles-AUDRi-2023.pdf.

4.38 These illustrate the need for safeguards to be put in place to protect women in the metaverse. Conscious effort should be made to ensure that some of the harms which exist in real life cannot manifest without control and sanction in the metaverse.

PROTECTION AGAINST DISCRIMINATION IN THE METAVERSE

4.39 Whilst the Human Rights Act 1998 does not prohibit discrimination generally[51] a user's human rights in the metaverse should not be denied because of discrimination – either direct or indirect

4.40 The metaverse should therefore be designed and built in an inclusive way to enable everyone to use it. Unless the metaverse is built in this way then the purist's version of one metaverse is unlikely to be achievable. As above there are concerns over the impact of the digital divide on inclusivity in the metaverse. The World Economic Forum have identified that 33% of the world's population still do not have access to broadband internet.[52] Many parts of the world do not have reliable internet connections, nor the access to the VR technology required to access the metaverse. Where the internet is unreliable the cost tends to be higher as well. There are calls for universal access to digital services, a mission being taken up by the EDISON Alliance in its '1 Billion Lives Challenge'.[53] Initiatives have already been taken up in numerous African and Southern Asia including Rwanda and Bangladesh.

COMMUNICATIONS SURVEILLANCE

4.41 As discussed earlier the metaverse has the opportunity to be used as a form of communication surveillance tool. Accordingly, it should be subject to the International Principles on the Application of Human Rights to Communications Surveillance which was developed in 2013 and is sometimes referred to as the 'necessary and proportionate principles'.[54]

4.42 The principles evolved out of the Snowden investigation into international intelligence systems and operations[55]. The principles are not binding but have been identified as guiding standards to uphold human right principles with digital advancements in surveillance and have been used as a framework by legislators.

4.43 The 13 principles are:

51 Discrimination generally however is likely to fall under the Equality Act 2010.
52 https://www.weforum.org/impact/digital-inclusion/.
53 https://www.weforum.org/impact/digital-inclusion/.
54 https://necessaryandproportionate.org/principles/.
55 https://www.ohchr.org/sites/default/files/Documents/Issues/Privacy/ElectronicFrontierFoundation.pdf.

1 Legality
2 Legitimate aim
3 Necessity
4 Adequacy
5 Proportionality
6 Competent judicial authority
7 Due process
8 User notification and right to an effective remedy
9 Transparency
10 Public oversight
11 Integrity of system and communications
12 Safeguards for cooperation
13 Safeguards against illegitimate user

CHARITY IN THE METAVERSE

4.44 Existing charities warn users not to forget about real-life issues when they are in the metaverse,[56] the metaverse however, presents new opportunities for charity.[57] Some charities are already accepting cryptocurrencies for donations.[58] Charity law, and regulation by the Charity Commission, will still apply in the metaverse.

TECH GIANTS, HUMAN RIGHTS AND THE METAVERSE

4.45 Some commentators consider that Tech Giants are expected by their investors to build their products to respect human rights.[59] The United Nations Office of the High Commissioner for Human Rights has established B-Tech Project aimed at helping technology businesses implement the UN Guiding Principles on Business and Human Rights given the risks identified in this sector in respect of human rights generally.[60]

56 https://www.wfpusa.org/articles/escape-to-metaverse-we-must-not-abandon-world-crises/.
57 https://forwork.meta.com/gb/nonprofit-solutions/.
58 Examples include Red Cross https://www.redcross.org.uk/get-involved/donate/ways-you-can-give/donate-in-crypto and Save the Children https://www.savethechildren.org/us/ways-to-help/ways-to-give/ways-to-help/cryptocurrency-donation.
59 https://www.humanrights.dk/files/media/document/Tech%20giants%20and%20human%20rights_2021.pdf.
60 https://www.ohchr.org/sites/default/files/documents/issues/business/b-tech/BTech-Institutional-Investor-Business-Models-Tool.pdf

4.46 Human rights groups such as Amnesty International have called for Tech Giants to be subject to specific human rights regulations to protect against the potential harms that can be caused as a result of their immense power and market dominance. The Deputy Director of Amnesty Tech has said that 'unregulated algorithms are optimised to maximise profit and engagement, which fans the flames of ethnic violence, disinformation and gross human rights violations'.[61]

CONCLUSION

4.47 This chapter considers the principles of human rights in the metaverse. The key-takeaway points are:

- Human rights of the individual users of the metaverse will, in so far as they apply, be protected by the Human Rights Act 1998, the Universal Declaration of Human rights and the European Convention on Human Rights. The first consideration should therefore be where the human user is based;
- Consideration will be required as to whether an avatar itself has stand-alone human rights. Complications arise where the avatar is not controlled by a human but by artificial intelligence or a corporation;
- Given the changes brought about as a result of the technological advances in metaversal technology, especially concerning immersive advertising, the use of haptic technology,[62] and brain computing interface technology, thought is needed as to whether additional rights need to be afforded fundamental protection. One such consideration is the explicit protection of 'neurorights'.
- Given the metaverse allows the user to defy reality, context is key when determining whether human rights are being infringed. There are different fundamental expectations when the metaverse is being used in the professional context to participate as part of a digital twin project as opposed to game play. A user may expect their avatar to be killed as part of a game but not so when participating in a research project in the metaverse.

61 https://www.amnesty.org/en/latest/news/2023/05/us-big-tech-must-be-regulated-to-protect-human-rights-despite-us-supreme-court-decision/.

62 Such as haptic suits and gloves.

Chapter 5

Intellectual property in the metaverse

'Think of the metaverse as a portal to any world you want to explore.'

Dave Waters, Nvidia Omniverse

5.01 Perhaps one of the key legal areas for considerations in respect of the metaverse, if not *the* key legal issue, is intellectual property rights. The rise of the metaverse sees the online domain, where intellectual property rights have come to the fore, collide with real-life where rights are usually more focused on tangible rights. It is perhaps symbolic that the virtual digital landscape places significant importance on these intangible rights.

5.02 At the core of the metaverse would be intellectual property rights and how these are owned, used, sold and exploited. The European Union Intellectual Property Office (EUIPO) confirms that it is already dealing with several legal issues in respect of the metaverse that it has started to address and encompass within its guidelines prepared in 2023,[1] the International Trademark Association prepared a white paper in 2023 considering the issue of trademarking in the metaverse[2] and in March 2024 the UK Intellectual Property Office released its own research into IP and the metaverse given its perceived lack of guidance on intellectual property in the metaverse.[3]

IS THE CURRENT INTELLECTUAL PROPERTY LAW SUITABLE FOR THE METAVERSE?

5.03 Again, one of the key risks with intellectual property in the metaverse is the global nature of the metaverse, whilst most registered intellectual property rights are, by their nature, territorial. The very nature of registered intellectual property rights is a legitimate form of monopoly. Blockchain technology however has significant benefits for use in recording intellectual property ownership rights.

1 https://ec.europa.eu/info/law/better-regulation/have-your-say/initiatives/13757-Virtual-worlds-metaverses-a-vision-for-openness-safety-and-respect/F3411618_en..

2 https://www.inta.org/wp-content/uploads/public-files/perspectives/industry-research/METAVERSE_REPORT-070323.pdf

3 https://www.gov.uk/government/publications/ip-and-metaverses-an-externally-commissioned-research-report/ip-and-metaverses-an-externally-commissioned-research-report.

5.04 As the metaverse expands, and use of the blockchain increases, there is certainly the need to consider whether the traditional ways in which intellectual property rights have been dealt with remains appropriate or whether these can in part be replaced by the use of the blockchain. Distinction between registered and unregistered rights may become obsolete with the rights being recorded on the blockchain as part of the product itself, with royalties being divided automatically via smart contract. In fact the EUIPO has already started to incorporate the use of the blockchain for its IP registers via its Digital Evolution Programme[4] and is creating an authentication platform on the blockchain to avoid counterfeiting.[5]

METAVERSE PLATFORMS AND INTELLECTUAL PROPERTY

5.05 As discussed further in **Chapter 8**, at this stage much of the metaverse in its current iterations is governed by the terms of use dictated by the various platform owners. These platforms regulate how intellectual property rights created in the metaverse can be owned, used and transferred. The terms also clearly demarcate which rights are retained by the platform owners themselves. Whilst some platforms permit users to create digital products or games within their ecosystems, or enable users to incorporate some of their existing real-life intellectual property into their system,[6] the virtual land and infrastructure itself is very carefully carved out as belonging to the tech platform.

5.06 This may change in the future, especially where there is a decentralised metaverse[7] or an all-encompassing virtual world. As we move towards a complete virtual world, it would be difficult to rationalise democratic values and free-trade should the Tech Giants seek to effectively own the very basis of this virtual world.

TRADE MARKS IN THE METAVERSE

5.07 The International Trademark Association highlights the opportunity of businesses to utilise their existing brands in the metaverse but also to create new brands for their digital goods and services in the metaverse.[8]

4 https://www.tmdn.org/network/-/euipo-connects-to-tmview-and-designview-through-blockchain.

5 https://euipo.europa.eu/ohimportal/en/-/news/a-new-era-in-anti-counterfeiting-technology? TSPD_101_R0=089375ec4aab200050e16c09ec1ae82b8dee4f156373c51976256c443232eeeb65282fcee9e728a8086ec7fbd1143000458daf62d6cd2defb37e1ea7def6f6e5472a2b03c30eb61ce472d46f144177398748ad8cf1e386caf544473bfe382427.

6 And licence the rights of use to the platform.

7 https://www.gov.uk/government/publications/ip-and-metaverses-an-externally-commissioned-research-report/ip-and-metaverses-an-externally-commissioned-research-report.

8 https://www.inta.org/wp-content/uploads/public-files/perspectives/industry-research/METAVERSE_REPORT-070323.pdf.

Expansion

5.08 As discussed in **Chapter 8** in more detail, to be able to properly determine the different goods and services being exploited in the metaverse, their different elements need to be deconstructed. Descriptions labelling a good or service as the 'virtual' equivalent in the metaverse does not necessarily relate to the same real-life goods or services. A virtual car is not the same as a real-life car, a virtual drink is not the same as a real-life drink and a virtual watch is not the same as a real-life watch. The same is true of services. Services being performed virtually will be different from those being performed in real life. There will be different scope and different methods deployed. All the elements that go into determining into what classes a trade mark should be registered will be different to some extent as between real life and the virtual world.

5.09 Brand owners will need to evaluate their trade mark portfolios to ensure that their real-life goods and services and their corresponding pre-existing trademarks are properly protected in the virtual world.

5.10 The International Trademark Association raises concerns that replicating a real-life product in the metaverse may not necessarily mean that there is an infringement of the trade mark.[9]

5.11 This issue was considered in one of the leading metaverse cases, *Hermes International v Rothschild* 1:22 cv-00384-JSR determined in June 2023 by the New York District Court. In this case Mason Rothschild (aka Sonny Estival) was selling NFTs of 'MetaBirkins'. Hermes, the owner of the trademark for Birkin, the luxury handbag brand successfully brought a case against Rothschild for, amongst other breaches, trademark infringement and trademark dilution. The NFT was not a digital handbag, but utilised the Birkin trademark. The judgment confirms that Hermes has sold over $1 billion worth of Birkins in the USA and that its trademark was capable of protection from being infringed by its use in the NFTs. This case goes some way to protect existing trademarks from digital exploitation and is likely to be cited globally as why courts should afford protection to real-life trademarks being exploited in the metaverse. As this is a US decision, it is still far from certain as to whether it would be sufficient to bar use of a trademark in the UK and any case will ultimately turn on the facts. Where the virtual product is the same as the real-life product, and the trademark the same (or slightly amended to reflect it being virtual) we would expect the courts to take a dim view of the use of another party's trademark.

5.12 In 2022 Nike brought action against StockX in New York relating to the use by StockX of the Nike trademark within their NFTs.[10] A judgment is still pending, but the respondents appear to be trying to distinguish the circumstances from the Hermes case since the NFT in question were not digital trainers per

9 https://www.inta.org/wp-content/uploads/public-files/perspectives/industry-research/METAVERSE_REPORT-070323.pdf.

10 *Nike, Inc. v. Stock X* LLC, No. 1:22-cv-00983-VEC.

se but a blockchain product to certify the provenience of different shoes. The respondents are seeking to validate their use of the Nike trademark on the basis of the first sale doctrine, discussed in more detail below, the use was fair use[11] and there is no confusion. This has to date been a drawn-out battle, with Nike alleging that they have discovered a high number of fake shoes authenticated as being genuine Nike trainers.

Classes

5.13 Trademarks are classified and registered based on the NICE classifications which have 45 different classes. In 2023 the NICE classifications were updated in class 9, class 35, class 36, class 38, class 41 and class 42 to incorporate virtual goods and services.[12] The guidelines introduced 'downloadable digital files authenticated by non-fungible tokens [nft]' in class 9 and minting (creating) of NFTs under class 42.[13] Some consider that there should instead be a new class, a class 46 for digital goods and services.[14]

5.14 Of note, the term NFT itself is not capable of stand-alone registration. The guidelines consider that the NFT is simply the record or the digital certification of the substantive digital asset.[15] The EUIPO highlights that practitioners should use the real-life impact of the virtual goods and services rather than its virtual representation. Again, as set out in **Chapter 8** it is important to look at what the goods and services actually are, and that these should be deconstructed.

Distinctiveness

5.15 In its decision in respect of METAVERSE DRINK[16] and METAVERSE FOOD[17] the Board of Appeal of the EUIPO upheld the decision that the term 'metaverse' where products would be capable of being sold online lacked distinctiveness since:

> 'The Metaverse does not refer exclusively to an alternative reality with avatars and virtual products. The virtual space is constantly evolving and developing new forms and opportunities offered by advances in information technology. More and more frequent examples indicate that the Metaverse could be another form of online commerce.'[18]

11 Permitted under US law.
12 In the 12th edition of the NICE classifications.
13 https://guidelines.euipo.europa.eu/2058843/2065747/trade-mark-guidelines/6-25-downloadable-goods-and-virtual-goods.
14 https://www.inta.org/wp-content/uploads/public-files/perspectives/industry-research/METAVERSE_REPORT-070323.pdf.
15 https://guidelines.euipo.europa.eu/2058843/2065747/trade-mark-guidelines/6-25-downloadable-goods-and-virtual-goods.
16 R2356/2022-2.
17 R2357/2022-2.
18 https://euipo.europa.eu/tunnel-web/secure/webdav/guest/document_library/contentPdfs/law_and_practice/appeal/2023_decisions_overview_Q3_en.pdf.

5.16 The EUIPO's position is that given the metaverse has not yet been properly defined, and it can effectively cover a whole array of online concepts then simply adding 'metaverse' before a descriptive trade mark will not make it distinctive and in the above case this was effectively just describing drink or food available online.

Territory

5.17 Given the idea of the metaverse is to enable seamless real-time interactions between users based anywhere in the world it is difficult to reconcile this with the territorial nature of trade marks. It may be, however, that new lines will have to be drawn such as territorial scope per different platform, or region of the metaverse or different 'lands'.

5.18 Jurisdiction is currently key for trademarking in real life. The International Trademark Association consider that one way of dealing with the issue of jurisdiction is to pin this to the law and jurisdiction set out in the platform owners terms of service.[19] This is difficult for a number of reasons, not least that this will only work until there is proper interoperability between platforms, in which case you may end up with different levels of protection depending on the law and jurisdiction dictated by the Tech Giant platform.

Well-known trade marks and passing off in the metaverse

5.19 In 2022 Juventus Football Club brought a case against Blockeras s.r.l in respect of the infringement of its trade mark caused by the minting and sale of trading card NFTs featuring the Juventus trade mark. The Rome Court granted an injunction against Blockeras and amongst other seminal points:

1) Affirmed the position of the EUIPO that NFTs are simply a record or certificate and is not itself descriptive of the goods.
2) Juventus Football Club had already attempted to enter the same market previously.
3) Certain brands are sufficiently well-known to cover the virtual world. This would be akin to a passing off claim under the law of England and Wales where the goodwill of Juventus was effectively being traded on by Blockeras s.r.l.

5.20 Furthermore, the case of *Yuga Lab v Ripps*,[20] under which the owner of the Bored Ape Yacht Club[21] was successful against Ripps in respect of their

19 https://www.inta.org/wp-content/uploads/public-files/perspectives/industry-research/METAVERSE_REPORT-070323.pdf.

20 *Yuga Labs Inc v Ryder Ripps, Jeremy Cahen* case number 2:22-cv-04355-JFW-JEMX.

21 which came to prominence as one of the first collectable NFTs and at its height one sold for $3.4 million https://coinpaper.com/4902/most-expensive-bored-ape-record-breaking-nft-sales.

sale of Ryder Ripps Bored Ape Yacht Club which the Californian courts found amounted to trade mark infringement. Although the claim by Yuga lab was brought in the United States in respect of its unregistered trademarks, should such a case have been brought under the law of England and Wales, it would instead likely have fallen under the law of passing off. This tort effectively seeks to protect against a person trading on the goodwill of another, so as to mislead others.

COPYRIGHT IN THE METAVERSE

5.21 The Intellectual Property Office raises concerns over the extent to which copyright will be afforded to some new forms of items created in the metaverse unless they fit within one of the statutory list under the Copyright, Design and Patents Act 1988 and whether the law on derivative works will be suitable for application in the metaverse.[22] It is an interesting concept to consider the extent to which copyright would apply to a virtual play or a virtual book read by an avatar.

5.22 Software coding itself does generally fall within the scope of copyright protection,[23] however, as the metaverse evolves it is likely that those seeking protection will not be the actual developers but those using coding from within the metaverse platforms. The European Innovation Council and SMEs Executive Agency have considered this point and believe that creations in the virtual world will be considered as graphical user interfaces and capable of protection as artistic works as highlighted by the ECJ in C-393/09 *Bezpečnostnǐ softwarová asociace – Svaz softwarové ochrany v Ministerstvo kultury*.[24]

5.23 As discussed in **Chapter 10** issues have been raised already in respect of the extent to which copyright in real-life products is protected from being exploited virtually when the products are brought into the metaverse. There is still uncertainty over how the courts will interpret the issue of copyright where certain rights have been exploited in attempts to try and circumvent other rights retained or owned by (often third party) copyright holders.

5.24 In some cases, this will be specifically dealt with via licensing provisions[25] but these are often unclear at this stage. It would be best practice where possible to ensure that suitable licensing provisions are put in place to ensure that copyright in real-life artistic works can be exploited in the metaverse

22 https://www.gov.uk/government/publications/ip-and-metaverses-an-externally-commissioned-research-report/ip-and-metaverses-an-externally-commissioned-research-report.

23 Under the WIPO Copyright Treaty 1996 and Directive 2009/24/EC.

24 https://intellectual-property-helpdesk.ec.europa.eu/news-events/news/intellectual-property-metaverse-episode-iv-copyright-2022-06-30_en.

25 Issues have been raised in respect of the Bored Ape Yacht Club and the pulp fiction scripts – https://intellectual-property-helpdesk.ec.europa.eu/news-events/news/intellectual-property-metaverse-episode-iv-copyright-2022-06-30_en.

and the extent to which this can and cannot be done. It is those cases where the real-life copyright holder is not the same as the virtual exploiter of such rights that we expect to see cases brought to establish common law on this area.

DESIGN RIGHTS IN THE METAVERSE

5.25 The Intellectual Property Office (IPO) considers that design rights are key in the metaverse and are likely to cover a magnitude of the intellectual property rights in the metaverse.[26] Design rights can be either registered or unregistered rights. There are concerns over the over use of unregistered design rights in the metaverse and the IPO advises instead that steps should be taken to protect such rights via registered design rights, given the cross-border nature of the metaverse.[27] Whilst it highlights that academics have questioned whether digital products are capable of design right protection the IPO has confirmed that both it and the EUIPO do believe they are capable of such protection.[28]

5.26 Design right protection in the metaverse is slightly behind that of trademark protection and as we have seen the NICE classifications have already been developed to encompass virtual goods and services so we expect the LOCARNO classifications to do the same.

PATENTS IN THE METAVERSE

5.27 As a new frontier there are many innovations still to be had in the metaverse. These are both in the form of hardware and software. The real-life elements required for a patent will still apply in the metaverse and interesting patent applications have already been seen from the likes of Apple, Meta and Nike.[29]

5.28 Like trademarks, patents typically have territorial scope. Some of the restrictions seen in the UK and EU, especially concerning software patenting, are not necessarily the same in other jurisdictions and are likely to continue into the metaverse. There are also likely to be policy decisions which will impact on whether something is patentable in different territories.[30]

26 https://www.gov.uk/government/publications/ip-and-metaverses-an-externally-commissioned-research-report/ip-and-metaverses-an-externally-commissioned-research-report.

27 https://www.gov.uk/government/publications/ip-and-metaverses-an-externally-commissioned-research-report/ip-and-metaverses-an-externally-commissioned-research-report.

28 https://www.gov.uk/government/publications/ip-and-metaverses-an-externally-commissioned-research-report/ip-and-metaverses-an-externally-commissioned-research-report.

29 Examples include Apple's technology to exclude certain avatar, Meta patent for personalisation of avatars and Nikes 'Cryptokicks' https://intellectual-property-helpdesk.ec.europa.eu/news-events/news/intellectual-property-metaverse-episode-iii-patents-2022-05-30_en.

30 Iony Randrianirina 'Patent Law and Metaverse'. Metaverse and the Law, Ap 2023, Lyon, France hal-04314534 – https://hal.science/hal-04314534/file/16%20-%20Iony%20Randrianirina%20-%20Patent%20Law%20and%20Metaverse% 20-%202024.pdf.

5.29 One concern that has been raised in respect of patents in the metaverse is about whether novelty can be claimed where the defining feature is that the process is happening virtually but is based on the real-life prior art process.[31] Whilst in principle computer simulations will be capable of patent protection it will not necessarily be straight-forward.[32] We can expect to see lines drawn around the distinction between software programmes and processes in the metaverse.[33]

5.30 Where something is actually being invented in the metaverse itself, via the avatars, there are concerns that it would not be capable of patent protection since it would be a virtual product and should be properly categorised as computer software and incapable of protection.[34]

TRADE SECRETS IN THE METAVERSE

5.31 Trade secrets will be paramount in the industrial metaverse. Significant steps are already being taken to try and ensure sufficient protection of industrial trade secrets, especially given the degree of collaboration needed for digital twins to function properly.

5.32 EU Directive 2016/943 protects trade secrets. This remains in effect in the UK under the Trade Secret Regulations. Further the National Security Act 2023 protects against the theft of trade secrets by foreign powers.

5.33 To qualify as a trade secret reasonable steps have to be taken to keep the information secret. It is likely that this element will be called into question in the metaverse, especially where there are collaborations and exchange of sensitive information. As discussed below, suitable steps will have to be taken to ensure that the contractual collaboration agreements make specific provisions over the identification and protection of trade secrets.

OTHER INTELLECTUAL PROPERTY CONSIDERATIONS

Avatars

5.34 An interesting aspect of intellectual property rights in the metaverse is the rights that are comprised within the avatars themselves. At this stage many of the platforms retain the underlying intellectual property rights in the avatars,

31 Nega 'What will patents look like in the metaverse?' Chicago-Kent Journal of Intellectual Property – https://studentorgs.kentlaw.iit.edu/ckjip/what-will-patents-look-like-in-the-metaverse/.

32 European Patent Office's decision G1/19.

33 Software programmes are not capable of patent protection.

34 Iony Randrianirina 'Patent Law and Metaverse'. Metaverse and the Law, Ap 2023, Lyon, France hal-04314534 – https://hal.science/hal-04314534/file/16%20-%20Iony%20Randrianirina%20-%20Patent%20Law%20and%20Metaverse %20-%202024.pdf.

however, with a movement towards the interoperability of metaverse platforms there is a challenge to this. The Metaverse Standards Forum has created a working group to develop the 'Avatar and Character Translation Framework'.[35] They acknowledge that many avatars are now customised and call for technological solutions to enable the portability of avatars between platforms. Further we expect to see a rise in avatars being used to promote brands and act as metaverse influencers. We have already seen celebrities represented in the metaverse via avatars. With the greater ability for interoperability there will be a need to ascertain who owns the avatars and the rights comprised therein.

5.35 The idea of the use of real-life traits and likeness in the metaverse was considered in the Pennsylvanian case of *Pellegrino v Epic Games Inc*.[36] In this case Pellegrino brought a case against the owners of the Fortnight game for misappropriating his likeness and trademark signature moves[37] within their 'emotes'. The Phone It In emote is sold by Fortnight and Pellegrino is not credited. The court dismissed the claim and found in favour of Epic Games on the basis that the avatars did not look like Pellegrino and was therefore the use of his likeness was transformative and permitted under the First Amendment protection[38] since the move had effectively become transformed into an identifying feature of Fortnight rather than Pellegrino. This is an interesting case to consider as we move towards a fully digitalised future, and the extent to which lines may be drawn where the courts will be likely to consider that an avatar likeness has sufficient goodwill to be protected under the laws of passing off under the law of England and Wales. As discussed in **Chapter 10**, the law of England and Wales does not recognise the right of publicity or image rights but there is protection such as in the *Rihanna*[39] case of passing off where the individual has generated sufficient goodwill in their image that effectively the use of their image amounts to the misrepresentation of their endorsement of the product.

5.36 Some consideration is needed as to whether an avatar would be capable of attracting other intellectual property rights. Characters can be protected as design rights. It is possible for signature moves to be protected as motion trade marks in the EU.[40] Depending on the process used to create the character there may be copyright in the character.

5.37 Where the avatar is used in the course of trade it is possible that such avatar could be capable of trademark protection but caution should be exercised prior to any registration to ascertain whether the platform retains the rights in the avatar.

35 https://metaverse-standards.org/news/blog/metaverse-standards-forum-announces-the-formation-of-interoperable-characters-avatars-working-group/.

36 *Pellegrino v Epic Games Inc* 2020 Case 2:19-cv-01806-JP.

37 Signature dancing moves whilst playing the saxophone known as the 'Phone It In' emote.

38 As an expressive work protected under the First Amendment has to be balanced in the US against the plaintiff's right of publicity and privacy.

39 [2015] EWCA Civ 3.

40 https://www.euipo.europa.eu/en/news/from-videogame-characters-to-ai-avatars-an-ip-story.

Collaborations

5.38 The metaverse will see multiple different collaborations which will have an impact on intellectual property rights in the metaverse.[41] Some of these will be formal and others informal. Some will see collaborators across multiple different jurisdictions and territories and some will see software and digital items being created in real-time within the metaverse itself. It will be important that there are clear contractual agreements in place setting out the expectations of all parties in respect of any collaboration. Such agreements will need to ensure that they properly deal with the ownership and exploitation of all intellectual property rights in the metaverse; this is not only in respect of the current iteration of the metaverse but its future evolution as a decentralised part of Web3.

Exhaustion of rights

5.39 Questions have been raised over whether the principle of 'first sale doctrine' applies in the metaverse.[42] The principle prevents the owner of the trademark and copyright from being able to enforce certain rights[43] where the goods have been legitimately purchased and sold on. The Intellectual Property (Exhaustion of Rights) (EU Exit) Regulations 2019 apply in the UK and seek to retain the EEA position on exhaustion of rights. It is likely that in the metaverse we will see few instances of digital goods actually being sold but instead licenced with restrictions. This would mean that we would be unlikely to see any determination on the exhaustion of rights in the metaverse save in exceptional circumstances. There is certainly an interesting legal argument whether there should be rights akin to real-life assets for digital assets, especially since they are now being recognised as a form of property – should users be permitted to sell on their old avatar skins or digital handbags?

LICENSING IN THE METAVERSE

5.40 It is unclear whether existing licences would cover expansion into the metaverse and it would be best practice where possible that these are revised to expressly stipulate what can and cannot be exploited in the metaverse and at what times.

5.41 Typically, intellectual property licences are limited to specific territories and specific media. Given the technological advances of the metaverse, which transcend traditional boundaries it would be wise to ensure that licences are properly prepared to reflect this. The New Emerging Issues Subcommittee of the Emerging Issues Committee of the International Trademark Association stresses the importance of being specific with what restrictions exist in respect of

41 https://www.gov.uk/government/publications/ip-and-metaverses-an-externally-commissioned-research-report/ip-and-metaverses-an-externally-commissioned-research-report.
42 https://www.wipo.int/wipo_magazine/en/2022/01/article_0006.html.
43 such as the right to sell – and create a 2nd hand market for digital assets.

the metaverse, which may be delineated at this stage by the different metaverse platforms, and whether any technological solutions, such as smart contracts, can be implemented.[44]

5.42 The IPO raises concerns that existing licences fail to properly deal with transposing real-life products into virtual assets and the use of virtual goods and services in the virtual world.[45] Further more research is needed to consider the extent to which intellectual property rights can be owned and licensed to DAOs. Given the emerging landscape, with new corporate entities and new concepts, there is the need for greater consideration to ensure that the exploitation of intellectual property in the metaverse is properly dealt with.

ENFORCEMENT OF INTELLECTUAL PROPERTY RIGHTS IN THE METAVERSE

5.43 The IPO highlights that interoperability and decentralisation cause significant challenges for holder of intellectual property rights.[46] It considers it would be beneficial to put the emphasis on the enforcement of copyright infringement on the platforms themselves in the same way that is done in the EU under Directive 2019/790.[47]

5.44 Enforcement in the metaverse will be complex given the overall lack of monitoring and difficulties in identifying and tracing the other users. We have already seen a number of large brands[48] taking enforcement action to protect their real-life brands from being used in an array of different ways in the metaverse. We expect this trend to continue as we move into the new digital world. Some of the issues will be novel and relate only to the metaverse, but for others we can learn from existing case law relating to the use of real-life intellectual property within computer games.[49]

Coexistence in the metaverse

5.45 We expect to see effective use of co-existence agreements to try and set parameters around the use of trademarks in the metaverse. For the metaverse

44 https://www.inta.org/wp-content/uploads/public-files/advocacy/committee-reports/20231218_TRADEMARK-LICENSING-IN-THE-METAVERSE.pdf.

45 https://www.gov.uk/government/publications/ip-and-metaverses-an-externally-commissioned-research-report/ip-and-metaverses-an-externally-commissioned-research-report.

46 https://www.gov.uk/government/publications/ip-and-metaverses-an-externally-commissioned-research-report/ip-and-metaverses-an-externally-commissioned-research-report.

47 https://www.gov.uk/government/publications/ip-and-metaverses-an-externally-commissioned-research-report/ip-and-metaverses-an-externally-commissioned-research-report.

48 Nike, Hermes, Miramax, Roc-A-Fella, Bored Ape Yacht Club.

49 Such as claims brought by Solid Oak Sketches relating to copyrighted tattoos in the NBA 2K game and AM General LLC claim against Call of Duty relating to the use of the Humvee where the Courts have relied on the the *Rogers v. Grimaldi* case (1989) 875 F.2d 994 (2d Cir. 1989) https://globalipconvention.com/blog/metaverse-and-intellectual-property-safeguarding-innovation-in-a-virtual-realm.

to reach its potential as a fully functioning virtual world, just as in real life, we expect to see brands wanting to use the same name for different goods and services, and with different audiences in the metaverse. Whilst the foundations are being developed, we expect to see a 'land grab' by larger organisations. The same real-life principles should apply, that trademarking should be proportionate and apply only to that being used in the course of trade.

THE FASHION BUSINESS IN THE METAVERSE

5.46 A 2023 survey of Gen Z (ages 22–26) reported by Roblox found that '64% say that, given a choice, dressing up their avatar would be more important than dressing up in the physical world'.[50] Many fashion brands have already moved into the metaverse. Anna Wintour, Director of Vogue said: 'Fashion has always been about creative freedom and about challenging norms. Whether or not you're already getting dressed in a metaverse, the new thinking in digital fashion and virtual fashion is fascinating to see'.[51]

5.47 It is important that those in the fashion industry fully appreciate the bundle of intellectual property rights being created as they enter into the metaverse and move from real-life fashion to navigating the complexities of software coding. As highlighted by Simon Windsor, who brought Balenciaga into the metaverse with Dimension Studio, the metaverse is changing both fashion itself and the fashion industry.[52]

5.48 Mckinsey, in its 2022 report into the fashion industry, stated that most brands who have moved into the metaverse have done so by way of a collaboration with the different platforms themselves.[53] It is important therefore that any commercial agreement between the brands and the platform is carefully drafted to ensure that should the platform or brand attract negative publicity then there are adequate safeguards in place. For both the brand and the metaverse platform, protection of their own reputation will go above and beyond any individual deal. At this stage many of the collaborations have been between specific platforms and specific brands, but if the metaverse evolves into connected multiverses or even one metaverse then further consideration will need to be had in respect of what limits brand owners could put on the use of their branded products in the metaverse. For example, could it be agreed or even written into code that an avatar wearing a brand's clothing would be prevented from entering a specific land or universe or engaging in a specific act? This could all be possible by

50 https://blog.roblox.com/2023/11/insights-latest-digital-expression-fashion-beauty-trends-report/.

51 https://www.voguebusiness.com/technology/global-vogue-titles-unveil-oceanic-metaverse-world-to-showcase-digital-talent.

52 https://www.mckinsey.com/industries/retail/our-insights/how-the-fashion-industry-can-get-into-a-metaverse-mindset.

53 https://www.mckinsey.com/~/media/mckinsey/industries/retail/our%20insights/state%20of%20fashion/2022/the-state-of-fashion-2022.pdf.

way of smart contract. A brand owner for example could physically prevent the avatar from wearing accessories by another designer or from entering another designer's land or even from entering a casino or partaking in gambling wearing their designs.

5.49 Careful consideration will be necessary in respect of the brand's intellectual property rights and those created as a result of the collaboration. We would also expect some form of exclusivity arrangement between the brand and the platform, at least for a defined period of time. Robert Triefus, Vice President and Chief Marketing Officer at Gucci confirmed that metaverse deals can be lucrative[54] and whilst he would not disclose the commercial structure of the specific deals one would expect these to differ from real-life collaboration deals in terms of the metrics and how a successful collaboration is measured. These will be based on impressions,[55] interactions and engagement via the metaverse. The collaboration between Brat Summer and Roblox brought via the Dress to Impress game reported seeing over 640,000 CCU and 10.5 million people using Roblox during the event.

5.50 Some brands, such as Nike, are taking a different approach[56] and instead have acquired software companies specialising in virtual reality. This demonstrates the use of targeted acquisition to expand into the metaverse, however, comprehensive due diligence should be undertaken given the inherent risks of any emerging technology.

CONCLUSION

5.51 This chapter considers the principles of intellectual property rights in the metaverse. The key takeaway points are:

- Intellectual property law will form the backbone of the metaverse for the conceivable future.
- Thought needs to be had as to whether the metaverse should be treated as an extension of the internet and intellectual property law dealt with in a similar vein, or whether due to the new challenges it presents with an immersive real-time virtual world there is the need to reconsider some of the underlying principles.
- Contractually the owners of the metaverse platforms are seeking to dictate the terms upon which intellectual property rights are owned and used within their space. This may be challenged in the future but for now it is the starting point for any issue concerning intellectual property in the metaverse.

54 https://www.mckinsey.com/~/media/mckinsey/industries/retail/our%20insights/state%20of%20fashion/2022/the-state-of-fashion-2022.pdf.

55 Likely measured in the same vein as with massive multiplayer online games (MMOG or MMO) like Roblox being CCU or the number of concurrent users at the same time.

56 Acquired RTFKT in 2021 – https://about.nike.com/en/newsroom/releases/nike-acquires-rtfkt.

- Real-life brand owners need to take steps to ensure they have sufficient protection of their brands insofar as they may be exploited in the metaverse.
- Licensing terms need to be carefully reviewed to ensure that they properly cover the exploitation of the goods and services in the virtual world. Traditional territorial boundaries and mediums are likely to be redundant in the metaverse.
- We have already seen swift action being taken by large brands against the digital exploitation of their trademarks and this trend is likely to continue as we move more and more into the metaverse.

Chapter 6

Digital identity, data protection, privacy and the metaverse

'Privacy and safety need to be built into the metaverse from day one.'

Mark Zuckerberg, Meta

6.01 For the metaverse to properly operate a vast amount of personal data, some of which are new types of data and highly sensitive, will be travelling digitally across borders in real-time. In the UK data protection in the metaverse will at this stage remain governed by the Data Protection Act 2018 and the UK GDPR. Once passed those in the UK will also be subject to the Data (Use and Access) Bill which was introduced into Parliament in October 2024 and is intended to update the Data Protection Act. In the EU it will remain subject to GDPR. There are serious concerns however, over the suitability and adaptability of these current laws for the metaverse. The European Parliament considers that the GDPR is probably not suitable for the metaverse in the long-term due to the unique issues, such as biometric data and the international flow of data.[1] The ICO further recognises the need to update data protection regulation[2]. There are also potentially different roles and responsibilities in the metaverse, which may not translate directly into the distinction between a 'Controller', 'Joint Controller' and 'Processor' which we see in the current regulation of data protection in the UK and EU.[3] Finally, there are also cross-border considerations in the metaverse, with the ability for sensitive personal data to move between safe and unsafe territories almost instantaneously.

6.02 Web2 and the current iteration of the internet has caused a fragmentation of digital ownership. The different platforms own and retain the data, rather than the data moving around with the users. With Web3 and the metaverse there are calls for the creation of a digital identity as discussed later in this chapter. This data is effectively the online persona of the individual and it is felt that all such data generated online about a user should be owned and controlled by the user. The EU has already implemented a framework for the creation and protection of its citizen's digital identity. The identity belongs to the individual and is available to move freely with the user without restriction. This identity must be protected. This is a massive step towards the creation of a metaverse in the purer sense of the term; the ability of users to seamlessly move between different platforms and perhaps one day to have just one metaverse. The Data (Use and Access)

1 https://www.europarl.europa.eu/doceo/document/TA-9-2024-0032_EN.html
2 https://ico.org.uk/about-the-ico/the-data-use-and-access-dua-bill/information-commissioner-s-response-to-the-data-use-and-access-bill/.
3 https://www3.weforum.org/docs/WEF_Metaverse_Privacy_and_Safety_2023.pdf

Bill looks like it will also start to take some steps to move the concept of data protection into the realms of Web3 with provisions relating to the expansion of smart data beyond open banking and the creation of a framework for digital verification and an emphasis on digital identity.[4]

DATA IN THE METAVERSE

6.03 Certain types of data being collected in the metaverse are novel. What really sets the metaverse apart from Web2 is the significant amount of data being produced as a result of the XR real-time interactions, together with the advancements in the different technologies being developed to optimise the XR experience such as haptic gloves. The World Economic Forum list some of the new types of data in the metaverse as being:[5]

1 'Body based data;

2 Biometric data;

3 Inferred data;

4 (Geo) Spatial data;

5 Immersive experience data;

6 Psychographic data;

7 Digital asset (individual generated content) data;

8 Transaction data'.

6.04 To be able to create an effective and personalised metaverse that users want to use, the types of data that become key are those which provide learning in respect of the users' interaction with the metaverse, such as changes in heart-rates, breathing, eye-movement, body placement and movement. With advancements in technology such as BCI (brain computing interface) data being extracted and utilised in the metaverse will quite literally be someone's thoughts and desires as well as neural signals. When combined with artificial intelligence analysis and learnings, this personal data is exceptionally sensitive data. It is effectively the blueprint of the users.

6.05 As the technology improves, we expect to see an avatar become a digital twin of oneself (also referred to as a virtual doppelganger) – reacting in real-time in the same way as a human user. With the use of virtual GPs and healthcare it is entirely possible for avatar's to eventually mirror health conditions of the users so that treatment can be trialled and monitored via the metaverse. Data

4 https://researchbriefings.files.parliament.uk/documents/LLN-2024-0063/LLN-2024-0063.pdf.
5 https://www3.weforum.org/docs/WEF_Metaverse_Privacy_and_Safety_2023.pdf

collected via the metaverse can already be used to try and detect autism, ADHD and dementia.[6]

DATA AND COMPETITION LAW

6.06 Just as with the online world generally, data is an extremely valuable commodity in the metaverse. There is also a considerable risk of users being exploited in respect of such data given the inequality between the users and the metaverse platforms. There are, therefore, not only privacy and data protection law considerations as discussed below but also competition law issues.

6.07 Tech Giants have already been subject to a number of investigations from competition authorities based on their practices and the extent of data being collected online generally.[7] This will only seek to grow in the metaverse where the data will be more extensive, and with the abundance of biometric data having a potentially revolutionary impact on immersive marketing techniques. Consumers must be made clearly aware of what data is being obtained from their use of the metaverse, how and why this is being processed. This requires proper consideration of how this information is brought to users' attention as discussed further below and the consequences of whether a user can decline to permit the processing of certain data.

6.08 Where the terms go beyond what is necessary, there is one dominant party (such as a metaverse platform) and a user is prevented from being able to properly exercise freedom of choice, then there is likely to be exploitative abuse which may be contrary to anti-competition laws.

DATA PROTECTION IN THE METAVERSE

6.09 Data protection in the metaverse will still face all the challenges experienced in real life with the processing of personal data. However, it will also face other challenges because of the nature of the data being collected. This is effectively the data which is necessary to bridge the gap between real life and virtual reality so that users can experience and participate properly within an immersive environment.

6 https://www.edps.europa.eu/data-protection/technology-monitoring/techsonar/extended-reality_en

7 As discussed by Adrian Kuenzler 'Direct Consumer Influence – the Missing strategy to integrate data privacy preferences into the market' Yearbook of European Law, Vol 39, No 1 (2022) pp 423 – 458 the German Federal Cartel Office investigated the impact of Facebook/Meta's dominance in social media and the impact this had on users genuinely being able to opt-out of data processing and accordingly the exploitation of personal data. Further competition investigations focus on the privacy implications such as the Google/DoubleClick and Facebook/WhatsApp mergers.

6.10 Data will be processed in the metaverse to enable services to work, as well as to process transactions.[8] Some data may only be needed to optimise services or experiences, but some data will be fundamental for the metaverse to function. This data will be wide ranging, especially as the metaverse evolves – it will range from highly sensitive medical data in the industrial metaverse being deployed in healthcare to educational data, including data on special educational needs, collected in the virtual classrooms. The World Economic Forum highlights that the fundamental principle underpinning privacy laws and regulation should be the freedom of choice.[9]

An emerging risk

6.11 Since 2021 the Information Commissioners Office has had an emerging technology team which keeps an eye on emerging technologies. The team has now identified the metaverse as one of eight new technologies to focus on in respect of privacy and data protection in their 2024 Tech Horizon Report.[10] This illustrates the rapid adoption of the metaverse technology and the significant risk presented by it in respect of data protection.

6.12 In July 2024 TechUK wrote an open letter to the incoming Government expressing concern about existing data protection laws in the context of emerging technologies generally.[11] They consider amongst others that there is a need to properly address automation, to address international transfers and establish Smart Data schemes. TechUK call for legislative reform to introduce an agile cross-border regime. This would be welcomed in the metaverse given the significant data protection and privacy challenges caused by the immersive nature of virtual lands.

6.13 Prior to the 2024 General Election the Data Protection and Digital Information Bill was making its way through Parliament. This Bill was lost when Parliament was dissolved. As part of the 2024 King's Speech, however, there was a commitment made to pass a new Digital Information and Smart Data Bill and a Cyber Security and Resilience Bill. In October 2023 the Data (Use and Access) Bill started to make its way through Parliament. It is hoped that this shows the intention to put data protection front and centre especially in the context of technology and innovation.

8 https://www3.weforum.org/docs/WEF_Metaverse_Privacy_and_Safety_2023.pdf

9 https://www.weforum.org/agenda/2023/08/why-the-metaverse-is-pushing-the-notions-of-what-we-call-privacy/

10 https://ico.org.uk/media/about-the-ico/research-reports-impact-and-evaluation/research-and-reports/technology-and-innovation/tech-horizons-report-1-0.pdf

11 https://www.techuk.org/resource/techuk-co-signs-a-letter-urging-the-next-government-to-modernise-the-uk-s-data-protection-framework.html

6.14 In the US there are calls for reform to federal privacy laws to reflect the challenges found in the metaverse[12] and to implement a similar type of framework as the GDPR in the EU.[13] The Information Technology and Innovation Foundation considers that there should be a uniform federal framework on data protection which should comprehensively cover the concerns raised in respect of the metaverse and protect against the harms it exposes.[14]

Regulatory concerns over privacy in the metaverse

6.15 The Information Commissioner's Office has concerns over data privacy in the metaverse which include data collected via VR hardware and the personal data of children.[15] It also raises potential issues with the way that data could be transferred between different platforms to create the seamless user experience and the risk to data protection of poorly-executed data transfer. If, however, this is done well then it may actually serve to enable users to retain control over their data. It is too early to tell, however, but all systems should be designed with privacy in mind.

6.16 One reason for the concern of the ICO is the large amount of data that will be collected by users of the metaverse (especially via VR headsets). This is not only data generated in respect of the user, but also from those who are in the vicinity of those using the metaverse whose data may inadvertently also be captured as a result of their proximity.[16] There are also serious other concerns over the use of personal data for automated decision-making in the metaverse and for profiling.

6.17 One of the unique features of the metaverse is that the technology removes the distinction traditionally found in Web2.0.[17] Users can seamlessly move between the real and the virtual world. As a result, there are calls for clear parameters for data protection and privacy just as would be appropriate in real life; for example medical data should not be treated any differently just because it is being collected via the metaverse. Clear boundaries are needed to distinguish between what is considered appropriate in real life and how that is reflected in the metaverse.

12 https://itif.org/publications/2021/03/04/balancing-user-privacy-and-innovation-augmented-and-virtual-reality/

13 Anushkay Raza 'Our Changing Reality: The Metaverse and the importance of Privacy Regulations in the United States, 12 Global Bus. L. Rev 30 (2023)

14 https://itif.org/publications/2021/03/04/balancing-user-privacy-and-innovation-augmented-and-virtual-reality/

15 https://ico.org.uk/about-the-ico/research-reports-impact-and-evaluation/research-and-reports/technology-and-innovation/tech-horizons-report/immersive-virtual-worlds/

16 https://ico.org.uk/about-the-ico/research-reports-impact-and-evaluation/research-and-reports/technology-and-innovation/tech-horizons-report/immersive-virtual-worlds/

17 https://www.weforum.org/agenda/2023/08/why-the-metaverse-is-pushing-the-notions-of-what-we-call-privacy/

6.18 The Digital Regulation Cooperation Forum (DRCF) considered the issue of privacy in the metaverse in their December 2023 immersive Technologies Foresight Paper and felt that it was something that did need to be addressed by regulators, specifically the use of biometric data and cybersecurity.[18] The DRCF felt that certain data protection issues associated with immersive technologies needed to be considered irrespective of whether there was mass adoption of XR. There is concern that biometric data may be used to learn what a user likes or how they may react to certain XR experiences, and therefore enable their exploitation for marketing or advertising purposes.

6.19 The DRCF calls for transparency as to how this data is being used and collected. This right is already enshrined within the DPA; however, the emphasis on this reflects the importance of empowering users to properly understand what data is actually being collected, how it is being used and what redress they have. Consideration has to be had as to how this can be done effectively in the metaverse so that this is clear to the users. The DRCF has expressed concern that users are not forced, or feel like they are being forced, to have to share data to be able to use the platform. It is necessary not only to work with regulators but also with developers to ensure that a proper balance can be achieved.

6.20 Legal academics consider that the focus should be on addressing the data protection and privacy issues which are caused by XR rather than on the technology itself.[19]The DRCF confirms that the Information Commissioners Office and Competition and Markets Authority are working together in respect of addressing the potential risk of exploitation of behaviour data.[20]

Solutions

6.21 The World Economic Forum considers that the idea of 'digital trust' will be fundamental if there is to be an all-encompassing metaverse.[21] It stresses the importance both of privacy by design and security by design in respect of the metaverse – with an emphasis on the idea of 'human first' as a safeguard for privacy in the metaverse. They consider that those building the metaverse should design it fundamentally with privacy at its heart to combat some of the failings that we see with Web2.0.

6.22 One of the key issues with privacy in the metaverse is the cross-border nature of the metaverse. Not all jurisdictions adequately protect personal data. This presents a significant risk. With this in mind contractual provisions between

18 https://www.drcf.org.uk/__data/assets/pdf_file/0027/273195/DRCF-Immersive-Technologies-Foresight-Paper.pdf

19 Hine et al 'Safety and Privacy in Immersive Extended Reality: An analysis and policy recommendation' Digital Society (2024) 3:33

20 https://www.drcf.org.uk/__data/assets/pdf_file/0027/273195/DRCF-Immersive-Technologies-Foresight-Paper.pdf

21 https://www3.weforum.org/docs/WEF_Metaverse_Privacy_and_Safety_2023.pdf

different parties are imperative. Any contractual relationship in the metaverse should include carefully drafted provisions in respect of the flow of data, especially the flow of personal data, and ensure that those with whom you are contracting will not fetter your ability to comply with regulatory standards and legislation.

6.23 It is important that the metaverse is built around the idea of privacy and data protection given the unique risks it presents, and there should be transparency so that users are fully aware of what is being collected.[22] Going further, developers of the metaverse should not only be transparent over what data is being collected but should let users know why it is being collected, how it is being collected and what it will be used for and could be used for in the future. To properly respect privacy, those building the metaverse should ensure that users are active participants with sufficient knowledge to be able to make informed decisions over what they do and do not do in the metaverse and how this impacts their privacy.

6.24 The European Data Protection Supervisor considered that there are positive uses of the metaverse in respect of privacy and, whilst it is still too soon to know, they believe that technological features could be developed to actually enhance data protection generally using the metaverse.[23]

Privacy policies in the metaverse and legal basis for data processing

6.25 Under the GDPR and DPA there must be a lawful basis for processing personal data. For certain data, such as biometric data and special category data it is necessary to obtain specific consent for such processing.

6.26 Meta Horizon uses a supplemental privacy policy in respect of its metaverse. The privacy policy set out what additional data is acquired using the VR products and includes information relating to the data collected in respect of the avatar.[24] The policy goes on to explain in detail what data is collected and why this is being collected. It states that this includes:

1 Information collected from the headset such as head position and movement;

2 Audio;

3 Data from tracking eyes, facial expressions, hands and body;

4 Metadata from playing the games

22 https://www.tcs.com/what-we-do/research/white-paper/user-privacy-protection-metaverse-experience

23 https://www.edps.europa.eu/press-publications/publications/techsonar/metaverse_en

24 https://www.meta.com/gb/legal/privacy-policy/?utm_source=horizon.meta.com&utm_medium=organicsearch

6.27 There are separate privacy notices for each of the specific body tracking data being collected where more detail is provided. It also makes it clear where the right for Meta to collect the data has been granted by the user themselves or where it is necessary for the metaverse to function. For example, Meta consider that it has a legitimate interest in processing body tracking data to be able to provide an 'engaging virtual, mixed and augmented reality experiences that rely on these features'.[25]

6.28 Those building the metaverse will need to consider how the privacy policies can be properly brought to the attention of the users. The traditional method of displaying the privacy policy on a website will not be appropriate in the metaverse. Lawyers and tech experts will need to work together to try and weave an authentic method into the metaverse to draw attention to how data is being collected and used, but still retain the look and feel of an immersive 'real-life' experience. In real-life interactions however, data is not being extracted, processed and recorded on external servers or on the blockchain. Where that data is recorded in a more permanent basis steps are then typically taken to draw attention to privacy notices or contractual provisions. It may be that a hybrid approach is appropriate in the metaverse; users converge with privacy gatekeeping avatars who explain what and how personal data is being collected and processed and what can be done with it and then the information in a written format is automatically sent to the user.

6.29 Privacy policies also need to ensure that they properly reflect the risks for the user's personal data associated with using the metaverse. They need to be clear where data cannot be deleted especially if this is being recorded on the blockchain.

CYBER SECURITY IN THE METAVERSE

6.30 Cyber security in the metaverse is essential. The volume of highly sensitive and valuable data, both personal data and non-personal data, that is generated in the metaverse makes it a significant target. The metaverse must be built with exceptional and highly advanced cyber-security to protect users. It is important that there is a clear framework with suitable cyber-security standards established.[26]

6.31 There will however, be the need to find a solution to traditional forms of passwords and verifications in the metaverse, especially if there is to be the effective ability to move between different platforms seamlessly.[27]

25 https://www.meta.com/gb/legal/quest/legal-bases/

26 https://www.weforum.org/agenda/2023/06/how-to-protect-against-immersive-cyber-security-threats-in-the-metaverse/

27 https://bpb-eu-w2.wpmucdn.com/blogs.bristol.ac.uk/dist/1/670/files/2023/05/REPHRAIN-White-Paper-Metaverse-and-Web-3.pdf

CONSENT IN THE METAVERSE

6.32 The World Economic Forum[28] considers that consent may not always be the most suitable lawful basis upon which to process data in the metaverse. Consent for data processing in the metaverse is unlikely to present itself in the same way as in real life.

6.33 Under the GDPR valid consent must be given freely. There are hurdles in meeting the threshold for consent under Article 7 of the GDPR[29] and data subjects have the right at any time to withdraw their consent to any data processing.[30] This is likely to cause issues in the metaverse where consent is used given the volume of data to which this could relate. Whilst it does not impact on any data processed up to the time that consent is revoked, a significant amount of data will likely still be processed in the time between that consent being revoked and action being taken.

6.34 Under the Data Protection Act 2018 consent is unlikely to be the easiest or most appropriate lawful basis to process most personal data in the metaverse. The ICO is clear that consent requires a positive step. It is not passive and is a high threshold. Given the idea of the metaverse is to transcend the real life – having to obtain and document consent is likely to make the interaction where data is being processed much more artificial. Thought needs to be had as to how consent may be obtained in the metaverse for data processing given pre-selected boxes to obtain consent are not permitted.

6.35 Consent is underpinned by trust. In an immersive environment it is questionable whether valid consent can be properly given; whether there is actually freedom of choice if the consequence is limited functionality or a less immersive experience. In addition, thought must be had as to how consent can effectively be withdrawn in the metaverse. It is likely that functionality may be impacted if consent is not granted for certain data processing, which would have a more significant impact in an immersive environment than where this is done traditionally online. This is likely to call into question the balance of power between those processing data in the metaverse and the data subjects.

6.36 The fact, however that the metaverse platform will have a dominant position compared with the individual users is not itself a barrier for valid consent but it will be taken into consideration in respect of whether there is freedom to consent and the ability to withdraw consent (save for in circumstances where it is strictly necessary for the services being provided).[31]

28 https://www3.weforum.org/docs/WEF_Metaverse_Privacy_and_Safety_2023.pdf
29 (EU) 2016/679 (General Data Protection Regulation)
30 Article 7(3)
31 This was considered in the Opinion of Advocate General Rantos on 20 September 2022 in respect of Case C252/21 Meta Platforms Inc., formerly *Facebook Inc.Meta Platforms Ireland Limited, formerly Facebook Ireland Ltd.,Facebook Deutschland GmbH v Bundeskartellamt,*

BODY BASED DATA AND BIOMETRIC DATA IN THE METAVERSE

6.37 One key privacy concern in respect of the metaverse is the abundance of body-based data. This data includes data about head positioning, eye movement, hand movement and body movement. This data is valuable but can also be extremely sensitive. This data may actually also become health data depending on what can be learnt from that data.

6.38 The data will include special category data which should be afforded suitable levels of protection. The unique features of an iris, known as iris signatures for example, are considered to be more effective than fingerprints for biometric authentication and security. This data will be collected via the use of VR headsets and smart glasses, and therefore suitable protection needs to be put in place to protect this data. Given the unique nature of this data it will not be possible to anonymise the data and will almost certainly always be at least considered pseudo-anonymous data.

THIRD PARTY DATA

6.39 Data will inadvertently be collected from third parties who are just in the vicinity of users wearing smart glasses or VR headsets. This data will accordingly be processed via the metaverse.

6.40 In such circumstances the user themself is likely to be considered as the Data Controller based on the decision of the Court of Justice in the EU case of C-212/13 *František Ryneš*. Whilst this was a case based on CCTV, it will be applicable in the context of the metaverse. It is likely however, that a user will be able to rely on having a legitimate interest to justify the processing. That said, there should still be some restrictions put on what can be done to data relating to third parties who are incidentally brought into the metaverse without their consent; for example there should be restrictions to prevent their image being manipulated.[32]

SMART GLASSES

6.41 In 2019 the European Data Protection Supervisor specifically looked at the data protection implications of smart glasses.[33] The glasses typically record and integrate a varying range of XR. The recording of personal data in a range of different formats is uppermost among the concerns regarding their use. The

32 REPHRAIN, a collaborative of academics from Bristol, Bath, UCL, Kings College and Edinburgh tasked with exploring protecting people online considered this in their white paper https://bpb-eu-w2.wpmucdn.com/blogs.bristol.ac.uk/dist/1/670/files/2023/05/REPHRAIN-White-Paper-Metaverse-and-Web-3.pdf

33 https://www.edps.europa.eu/sites/default/files/publication/19-01-18_edps-tech-report-1-smart_glasses_en.pdf

data ranges from video and audio recordings of public and private interactions, as well as the potential use of scanning other types of personal data. Personal data, such as emails, are also often incorporated on the screen of the glasses, which again undermines the concept of data privacy. There is a significant risk of hacking.

6.42 At this stage the European Data Protection Supervisor considers that GDPR is sufficient to cover the risk in respect of smart glasses but reminds manufacturers and legislators of their obligation to keep data privacy in mind. As above, where smart glasses record other people, this is data processing and should be treated like private CCTV for which the user is considered the controller.[34]

6.43 The European Data Protection Supervisor suggests that a Data Processing Impact Assessment should be done for all smart glasses regardless of whether one is actually required.

PRIVACY AND THE BLOCKCHAIN

6.44 The whole of idea of the blockchain is to establish a permanent record of all data on the ledger. This is often considered to be at odds with the idea of privacy and current data protection laws. As we move into the Web3 era the idea of privacy and data protection will need to be reconsidered. One of the tenets of data protection in the post-GDPR landscape is that incorrect data should be capable of rectification.

6.45 The European Parliament commissioned a study in 2019 to consider whether blockchain was compatible with the GDPR.[35] The study highlights that in certain circumstances the blockchain may be able to assist with certain requirements of GDPR but in other cases there are still significant challenges which are unlikely to be reconciled at this stage. With a blockchain-based metaverse the amount of personal data contained on that blockchain, as a permanent record, and the significant amounts of different types of data make this extremely challenging. The study called for some guidance from the regulators on the impact of privacy and the blockchain. It further suggests that there may be opportunities to add a form of certification for blockchain to deal with some of these challenges and look for how they can be solved. The study considers at this stage that each different blockchain should be considered separately rather than looking at the technology as one distinct stand-alone technology.

6.46 Whilst data protection is an important right, enshrined in the EU in the GDPR, Recital 4 of GDPR makes it clear that there are times when this may

34 CCTV even in a private home is data processing as determined in the CJEU case of C-212/13 – František Ryneš

35 https://www.europarl.europa.eu/RegData/etudes/STUD/2019/634445/EPRS_STU(2019)634445_EN.pdf

be at odds with other rights. The technological advancements and benefits of blockchain, and use of blockchain in the metaverse will have to be balanced against data protection issues.

6.47 Recital 4 states:

> The processing of personal data should be designed to serve mankind. The right to the protection of personal data is not an absolute right; it must be considered in relation to its function in society and be balanced against other fundamental rights, in accordance with the principle of proportionality. This Regulation respects all fundamental rights and observes the freedoms and principles recognised in the Charter as enshrined in the Treaties, in particular the respect for private and family life, home and communications, the protection of personal data, freedom of thought, conscience and religion, freedom of expression and information, freedom to conduct a business, the right to an effective remedy and to a fair trial, and cultural, religious and linguistic diversity.

6.48 It may be possible that with technologically advanced encryption such as homomorphic encryption the data may be treated as being anonymised, but at this stage this is not recognised by the court. It is also technologically possible to edit or prune parts of the blockchain, but this is not yet commonplace and goes against many positive uses of the blockchain. This would be very difficult to achieve in the metaverse with the volume of data.

Technological protections with blockchain

6.49 There are potential technological solutions to try and improve privacy issues with blockchain, especially the public blockchain, and therefore by extension the metaverse when this is based on the blockchain. Whilst this does not replace the need to comply with data protection legislation and process personal data correctly, it does help to demonstrate responsible design.

6.50 One such technological solution is the idea of knowledge proof or ZKP. In its simplest form the idea of the ZKP is that data is not made available, but instead is verified and then this verification is used instead of the data on the blockchain. This means that personal data is not added onto the blockchain, only the verification. The verification is tested technologically to such an extent that it would be considered technologically impossible for the verifying entity to be able to fulfil the tests if it did not have the underlying data. The verifying entity therefore effectively shields the personal data. The ICO consider ZKPs to be a privacy-enhancing technology or a PET which helps to aid privacy by design.[36] In creating its European Digital Identity Wallet the EU recommends that technology such as zero-knowledge proofs should be deployed.[37]

36 https://ico.org.uk/media/about-the-ico/consultations/4021464/chapter-5-anonymisation-pets.pdf
37 REGULATION (EU) 2024/1183 Recital (14)

6.51 Other forms of PETs recognised by the ICO include homomorphic encryption, which is an advanced level of encryption to protect the data. Depending on the level of homomorphic encryption[38] the data are afforded additional cyber security protection.

6.52 Given the metaverse, especially variations based on blockchain technology, is still very much in its infancy, steps should be taken now to explore what technological safeguards can be implemented to protect privacy and data protection principles.

CHILDREN'S PRIVACY IN THE METAVERSE

6.53 There is a considerable risk to the personal data of children in the metaverse.[39] The ICO Children's Code should be followed when providing goods and services in the metaverse to those under 18 years old, as well as being followed by the metaverse platforms themselves where they are used by children under 18 years old.[40] The code is not binding law but is considered good practice. As part of the code, it is recommended that geolocation is restricted for children, however this will have an impact on the ability of children to seamlessly enter and use the metaverse.

WHAT IS DIGITAL IDENTITY IN THE METAVERSE?

6.54 The World Economic Forum considers that digital identity in the metaverse is more than just an avatar, but all digital data that exists about someone.[41] This data creates a digital representation of a user, representing not only information input by the user (self-identifying characteristics) but also those garnered as a result of interactions within the metaverse (regardless of whether this reflects the user's real-life identity, known as 'inferred data'). The World Economic Forum explored the different layers of the metaverse identity and types of identity in its 2024 report 'Metaverse Identity: defining the self in a blended reality'.[42] It considers that focusing on the idea of digital identity can help to frame an inclusive metaverse and take into consideration failings from Web2.

6.55 The idea of identity in the metaverse is complex, not least because of it merges real life and a virtual world but the metaverse will also be a melting pot of different cultures, religions, sexualities and genders. The World Economic Forum

38 FHE – full encryption; and partial FHE and SHE

39 https://epthinktank.eu/2024/04/26/protecting-children-in-virtual-worlds-the-metaverse/

40 https://ico.org.uk/for-organisations/uk-gdpr-guidance-and-resources/childrens-information/childrens-code-guidance-and-resources/introduction-to-the-childrens-code/

41 https://www.weforum.org/agenda/2024/01/what-is-a-metaverse-identity/#:~:text=We%20all%20leave%20a%20collection, humans%20to%20include%20digital%20entities.

42 https://www3.weforum.org/docs/WEF_Metaverse_Identity_Defining_the_Self_in_a_Blended_Reality_2024.pdf

are calling for putting the idea of digital identity front and centre when building the metaverse.

6.56 The concern with digital identity generally in Web2 is that users do not tend to own this information, typically it is held and retained by the different platforms and therefore does not move across different platforms with the users.[43] This is not conducive for seamless interactions across the metaverse. The idea of having a portable digital identity that is owned by the user and moves with that user across the metaverse is one that is being advanced by the EU and its protection of its citizens' digital identities as set out below.

6.57 The idea of identity in the metaverse goes to the root of creating the metaverse and how data created within the metaverse should be dealt with. As a result, its governance is important and it is imperative that a suitable framework is established. The World Economic Forum called for the creation of a distinct digital identity and that specific regulations should be implemented to protect these.[44] As below the EU has now implemented the European Digital Identity Wallet which seeks to address these concerns.

Multiple identities in the metaverse

6.58 The World Economic Forum highlights that, just like in real life, a user is likely to have multiple different identities within the metaverse depending on the social context.[45] The identity that a user might want to portray in the industrial metaverse may not be the same identity that the same user wants to use in social interactions or even in virtual workspaces. The metaverse needs to be able to adapt to such different identities.

Framework for a digital identity

6.59 The EU passed Regulation 2024/1183 in April 2024 establishing the European Digital Identity Framework. The framework is designed to enable people to control their online data themselves.[46] It creates the idea of user-controlled digital identity which must be recognised across the EU by 2030.[47] The Regulation also creates the European Digital Identity Wallet which will enable users to authenticate and share their digital identity data.[48] The European Digital

43 https://www.weforum.org/agenda/2022/12/digital-identity-metaverse-why-we-need-to-regulate-it-and-how/
44 https://www.weforum.org/agenda/2022/12/digital-identity-metaverse-why-we-need-to-regulate-it-and-how/
45 https://www3.weforum.org/docs/WEF_Metaverse_Identity_Defining_the_Self_in_a_Blended_Reality_2024.pdf
46 REGULATION (EU) 2024/1183 Recital (2)
47 REGULATION (EU) 2024/1183 Recital (3)
48 REGULATION (EU) 2024/1183 Recital (7)

Identity Wallet must eventually be accepted by very large online platforms to authenticate access if the user wants to do this.[49]

6.60 The purpose is to create harmonised rules which enables EU citizens to have full benefit of digitalisation.[50] The Regulation recognises the need to protect users against cyber breaches and cyber crimes.[51]

6.61 The DRCF has also identified digital identity as a key topic that it intends to investigate in due course.[52] We expect that it has kept a firm eye on the EU development of a framework on digital identity. Whilst the EU framework will not apply in the UK, it does set in motion the recognition by legislators of the concept of needing to regulate a digital identity. It is likely to pave the way to future regulation in many other jurisdictions. The Data (Use and Access) Bil starts to adopt the idea of a framework for voluntary digital identity verification goods and services.[53]

Decentralised digital identity

6.62 The blockchain has sought to try and protect digital identity using technological solutions. One such solution is DIDs or Decentralised Identifiers. These enable users to establish a verification process on the blockchain for their own digital identity data. This enables users to retain control over their digital identity but use it for verification purposes in a similar manner as two stage authentication.

KNOW YOUR CLIENT IN THE METAVERSE

6.63 There is a concern that artificial barriers may come about if the metaverse has an over dependence on traditional forms of identification given not everyone in the world has a recognised forms of identity such as a passport.[54] Someone should not be prevented from using the metaverse simply because they do not have such documents. Concern is however raised over the risk of money-laundering in the metaverse and the need to do suitable Know Your Client (KYC) and AML checks on users.

6.64 Many issues have been raised about protecting identity documents in the metaverse from cyber criminals. The World Economic Forum considers that

49 REGULATION (EU) 2024/1183 Recital (57)
50 REGULATION (EU) 2024/1183 Recital (6)
51 REGULATION (EU) 2024/1183 Recital (4)
52 https://www.drcf.org.uk/__data/assets/pdf_file/0027/273195/DRCF-Immersive-Technologies-Foresight-Paper.pdf
53 https://researchbriefings.files.parliament.uk/documents/LLN-2024-0063/LLN-2024-0063.pdf.
54 https://www3.weforum.org/docs/WEF_Metaverse_Identity_Defining_the_Self_in_a_Blended_Reality_2024.pdf

new forms of verification of identity could be used in the metaverse given its immersive and real-time nature, such as the biometric data discussed earlier in the chapter.[55] Notwithstanding the benefits which come from the use of Zero Knowledge Proofs or Decentralised Identifiers some concern is still needed as to KYC in the metaverse.

CONCLUSION

6.65 This chapter considers the principles of privacy and data protection in the metaverse. The key-takeaway points are:

- Data is extremely valuable in Web3 and following the digital revolution. The metaverse will generate an abundance of novel personal data, such as eye movement and biometric data, all of which presents data protection challenges.
- Data protection regulators are taking a keen interest in the metaverse, and identify that it as a technology that they need to monitor.
- Blockchain technology is difficult to reconcile with certain GDPR principles. Should the metaverse utilise this form of technology additional steps will be needed to address whether the existing data protection framework remains suitable. There are technological solutions to try and protect personal data on the blockchain including Zero Knowledge Proofs. This technology should be incorporated into the metaverse by design. Significant steps should be taken to safeguard all personal data.
- The metaverse should be designed with privacy and protcction of data at its heart.
- Steps are being taken to protect an individual's digital identity. The DRCF identifies digital identity as a key topic that it intends to explore. The EU passed Regulation 2024/1183 in April 2024 establishing the European Digital Identity Framework.
- The idea of a digital identity, which can be safeguarded, highlights that not only is data a key commodity in a digital world, but that it should be owned and controlled by the individual themselves and not the Tech Giants just by virtue of their ownership of underlying technology.
- Upholding the integrity of someone's digital identity goes directly to the spirit of data protection principles; it is imperative that a user is fully informed of all decisions relating to their digital identity, that they can freely move this data where they choose and they are in charge of how their digital identity is used and exploited.

55 https://www3.weforum.org/docs/WEF_Metaverse_Identity_Defining_the_Self_in_a_Blended_Reality_2024.pdf

Chapter 7

Money and the metaverse

'I don't even really talk about money anymore because it's more about exchanging value. As long as we are all on a common value exchange platform, then it makes it easy. But as we build out the metaverse, the concept of value is different in each of these islands of the metaverse. In one virtual reality, we might use stable coins, in another one, we might be using Bitcoin, and in another one, we might be using NFTs. They are all different ways to create an exchange value. And the challenge is interoperability.'

Kirsty Duncan, Founder and CEO Women in Payments

7.01 The metaverse is already changing the way in which people interact with each other, entertain themselves, and even trade. Therefore, it is only reasonable to expect money to work in a certain way within these virtual world. Money in the metaverse is, as you might expect, non-fungible. That means many applications will eventually revolve around crypto currency and NFTs – transactions are private, anonymous, and instantaneous.

7.02 Virtual worlds' economies are, to many people, relatively scary. It is the next big unknown following the social media revolution of the past two decades. The concept of sharing one's entire life online was unheard of at the turn of the millennium. And yet, here we are now – and, by the turn of the next decade, metaverse user penetration is expected to reach around 39.7% – over two billion users.[1] This indicates that, by 2030, metaverse economies will already be booming with people making a sustainable living from virtual and augmented trading.

7.03 Metaverse economies will grow as a result of virtual assets becoming more sophisticated and more desirable over time. What is more, the metaverse will become more accessible to creators – and both scenarios are partly supported by the rise of generative AI, which is already creating stunning environments, models, and animations for virtual worlds.[2]

7.04 Ultimately, we are approaching an exciting time not only for metaverse applications, but also for economic growth. Meta observes that, by 2035, metaverse purchases will offer growth of up to $3.6 trillion each year to America's GDP.[3] Building new economies such as these will require legal frameworks, especially

1 https://www.statista.com/outlook/amo/metaverse/worldwide.
2 https://landvault.io/blog/ai-improving-access-to-metaverse.
3 https://about.fb.com/news/2023/05/economic-potential-of-the-metaverse/.

given the complexities of real-time interactions across multiple borders such as will be in the metaverse.

7.05 However, before we dive any deeper into the metaverse's financial frameworks, let's consider how far digital money – and therefore cryptocurrency – has come.

A BRIEF HISTORY OF DIGITAL MONEY

7.06 Digital money is a term used to describe many different types of transactions. In the mainstream, it's typically used to refer to funds held in e-wallets and digital transit – such as via PayPal or Wise. *Virtual* currencies however offer a different kind of digital money.

7.07 Cryptocurrencies, as we have come to define them, first emerged around the turn of the 2010s, shortly after a developer known as Satoshi Nakamoto – about whom we actually know very little[4] – first established Bitcoin, the first-ever decentralised currency. Shortly after, he established the blockchain, the foundation for virtual currencies for decades to come.

7.08 Bitcoin (BTC) emerged as a defiant response to 2008's financial crisis. Nakamoto reportedly developed BTC as a 'trustless' form of currency, whereby there would be no third party or trust to hold and manage transactions. This was a peer-to-peer or 'P2P' concept of currency that would simply travel from buyer to vendor. There would be no administrative red tape, no processing time, and no prying eyes.

7.09 Nakamoto intended to establish BTC as a more trustworthy currency by effectively removing trust. As strange as that may sound, a 'proof of work' system was established, through which anyone making and handling money on the blockchain could see where the currency began, what work was completed, and who took part in transactions.

7.10 This concept slowly gained popularity over the decade to pass. Nakamoto designed his currency as a finite resource which would effectively counter its limitations through 'halving' events where supply and demand would be kept under close watch.

A MAINSTREAM DREAM

7.11 Bitcoin is inarguably the forerunner of decentralised finance and Web3 concepts the world over. Ideologically, it takes the dream of removing money

4 Despite cases being brought in which the Defendant asserted he was Satoshi Nakamoto – *Crypto Open Patent Alliance v Craig Steve Wright* [2024] EWHC 1198 (Ch).

from centralised banks and institutions and instead places it – and the data surrounding it – in the hands of people who are actually using it.

7.12 That, however, has proved to be a controversial dream, at least when it comes to bringing cryptocurrencies into the mainstream. With long-established financial institutions on the whole reacting coldly to BTC and other digital currencies, and real-world global finance being reluctant to accept cryptocurrencies, those seeking financial freedom look keenly toward bolder ways to start using virtual money.

7.13 The metaverse has emerged as the perfect platform for crypto transactions. In decentralised digital worlds buried deep away from fiat transactions,[5] there is currently little red tape and middle management. This carries significant risks and as discussed below will almost certainly be subject to increasing regulation as the popularity of the metaverse increases. It is not to say cryptocurrencies *won't* have a place in the real world– but they do certainly have a place in the virtual world, they will aim to make metaverse applications more accessible and appealing to wider audiences.

7.14 Whilst virtual currencies remain popular in everyday life, despite concerns over BTC's volatility, the metaverse, however, offers the opportunity for people to embrace non-fiat transactions, and it is certainly shaping up to be the future of Decentralised Finance (DeFi).[6] It is pretty fitting that virtual money would help pave the way for virtual worlds!

7.15 When we speak of 'tokenisation' we are actually speaking about the creation of a node on the blockchain which creates a token. When real-life assets are put onto the blockchain the very act of creating the digital replica on the blockchain creates the token. These tokens may be purely utility tokens[7] or may be traded and become a financial instrument.[8]

7.16 In this chapter, we will explore further how money works in the metaverse – from its foundations and fundamentals, to financial instruments, challenges, payment systems, and future innovations.

REGULATION

7.17 What is clear is that regulation in the financial industry in the UK is not looking to become more relaxed with the new virtual landscape.[9] The

5 The term used to refer to 'real-life' currency.
6 Decentralised Finance.
7 This is a token which just enables the use of the services on the blockchain / DLT.
8 A security token is a financial instrument.
9 The FCA has confirmed that both it and HM Treasury are looking at further regulations – https://www.drcf.org.uk/__data/assets/pdf_file/0028/285337/Consumers-and-digital-assets-ICO-and-FCA-joint-insights-paper.pdf.

Financial Services and Markets Act 2023 (FSMA 2023) classifies the promotion of cryptoassets as a regulated financial activity for the purpose of the Financial Services and Markets Act 2000.[10] This means that to promote cryptoassets in the UK firms will effectively need to be registered with the Financial Conduct Authority (FCA). The FCA publishes rules and guidance in respect of such promotion.[11] The FCA is responsible for supervising crypto businesses in respect of their anti-money laundering and counter-terrorist financing requirements under the Money Laundering, Terrorist Financing and Transfer of Funds (Information on the Payer) Regulations 2017.

7.18 In the UK tokens and sale of all NFTs do not automatically fall to be regulated. It currently depends on whether these fall under the jurisdiction of the FCA or not.[12] The UK typically takes a purpose-based approach, looking at what the cryptoasset is actually intended to do. Where this replicates traditional finance then it will almost certainly fall to be regulated. The Law Commission identifies that the law needs to consider the idea of tokenisation in different concepts since such tokens have different values and different uses.[13]

7.19 The FCA together with the ICO considered the issue of digital assets in their May 2024 insight paper given the regulatory issues relating to digital assets from both a financial and data protection perspective.[14] The FCA highlighted that one of the fundamental issues is to uphold the trust for consumers in the digital assets. The issues with digital assets are the risk of harm should the consumers not be able to access their assets or obtain suitable information from the issuers. The FCA has confirmed that even with regulation there is still an inherent risk with digital assets, but the goal is to try and create a safe environment which mitigates harm to consumers and the risk of exploitation for money laundering and financing of terrorism.[15]

7.20 The Competition and Markets Authority (CMA) has established the Digital Market Unit under the Digital Markets, Competition and Consumer Act 2024 (DMCC 2024) to monitor competition in respect of digital assets.

7.21 The Prudential Regulation Authority has also been clear that it expects the risks around 'tokenisation' to be addressed by the banks. The Bank of England considers that financial institutions need to be prepared for innovations including

10 FSMA 200, s 69.

11 https://www.fca.org.uk/publication/finalised-guidance/fg23-3.pdf.

12 Being if they fall under the Money Laundering, Terrorist Financing and Transfer of Funds (Information on the Payer) Regulations 2017 and/or the Financial Services and Markets Act 2000 (as amended).

13 https://cloud-platform-e218f50a4812967ba1215eaecede923f.s3.amazonaws.com/uploads/sites/30/2024/07/DAOs-scoping-paper-110724.pdf.

14 https://www.drcf.org.uk/__data/assets/pdf_file/0028/285337/Consumers-and-digital-assets-ICO-and-FCA-joint-insights-paper.pdf.

15 https://www.drcf.org.uk/__data/assets/pdf_file/0028/285337/Consumers-and-digital-assets-ICO-and-FCA-joint-insights-paper.pdf.

tokenisation and blockchain technologies.[16] It confirms that it has already implemented technology to enable tokenisation, created the Digital Securities Sandbox (with the FCA) and is considering the adoption of digital currency. The Government has confirmed that it will retain the National Payment Vision, which the Independent Future of Payment Review called for in 2023, to set out the Government's intention for UK payments in the future.[17]

7.22 The Financial Action Task Force (FATF), the global money laundering and terrorist financing watchdog, prepared guidance in 2021 on virtual assets.[18] The guidelines are designed as best practice to regulate activities relating to virtual assets given the risks that are present.

7.23 It is likely we will have to wait a little time to see exactly how the metaverse virtual financial asset landscape will be regulated. In the meantime, a keen eye is being kept on this space by the FCA and CMA via their work in respect of the DRCF. As part of its 2023 report into the Future Financial Services Regulatory Regime for Cryptoassets the Government considers that cryptoassets should still meet the underpinning standards required of similar financial services.[19]

FOUNDATIONS OF METAVERSE ECONOMICS

7.24 In the metaverse, real money takes a back seat.

7.25 Creating value systems within the metaverse is an exciting proposal – given that building the metaverse revolves around the creation of virtual worlds, it stands to reason that the only currency usable within these worlds is virtual, too.

7.26 Economics within the metaverse revolve around a concept of limitless trade – users exchange virtual currency for virtual goods, with the desire for limited administrative slowdowns which we expect from fiat transactions and traditional goods exchanges.

7.27 When creating virtual worlds, storefronts, and experiences, we are also creating virtual economies. By rooting trade in cryptocurrencies transactions are instantaneous, and growth is fast. There is clear ownership over digital goods and

16 https://www.bankofengland.co.uk/-/media/boe/files/paper/2024/the-boes-approach-to-innovation-in-money-and-payments.pdf.

17 https://www.gov.uk/government/publications/future-of-payments-review-2023/update-on-the-national-payments-vision.

18 https://www.fatf-gafi.org/content/dam/fatf-gafi/guidance/Updated-Guidance-VA-VASP.pdf.coredownload.inline.pdf.

19 https://assets.publishing.service.gov.uk/government/uploads/system/uploads/attachment_data/file/1133404/TR_Privacy_edits_Future_financial_services_regulatory_regime_for_cryptoassets_vP.pdf.

assets, and a huge potential scope for creating Web3 assets that hold incredible value within the metaverse itself.

7.28 For example, digital assets such as NFT art, avatar clothing, accessories, and even virtual real estate are all valuable and achievable through a clearly defined, decentralised metaverse economy. Essentially, through the metaverse, we are breaking down the rules of real-world trade and transactions and reinventing a fairer, more accessible economy for all.

7.29 These economies hold vast potential. Buyers might pay directly with crypto coins or trade other digital assets to obtain items, for example. What's most exciting about metaverse economies is that they can exist seamlessly alongside real-world trading.

7.30 People taking part in metaverse economies can use the assets they buy to build digital lives or play immersive games – without ever having to tie up cards or bank accounts along the way. You can simply pull up your chosen crypto wallet, head to a virtual store, and start making purchases. Digital assets form part of an 'engine' that drives economic development.[20] Metaverse economies revolve around the idea that what we create for, and give to, society should generate purchasing power. With blockchain technology there is immutable logging – and that, unlike with real-world economies, people can literally create tradeable assets and, effectively, currency from nothing at all.[21]

7.31 Ideologically, this creates a fairer, more level economic playing field – which embodies the very principles that underpin cryptocurrencies. Metaverse trading will remove any administrative slowdown and exclusive elements that prevent people from making money and investing in the assets they desire.

7.32 We also need to consider metaverse economies' place alongside real-world economies through the lens of enhancement. It's easy to assume that metaverse trading will grow purely inside its own virtual reality playgrounds – but there are ample, exciting opportunities for metaverse economies to grow through enhancing real-world experiences, too. Consider the application, for example, of AR (augmented reality) assets in everyday life. There are multiple ways metaverse economies could expand through adoption of AR enhancements such as:

- Surgery assistance in healthcare

20 https://www.researchgate.net/publication/366211214_Economic_Systems_in_Metaverse_Basics_State_of_the_Art_and_Challenges/link/652154323ab6cb4ec6c3dd42/download?_tp=eyJjb250ZXh0Ijp7ImZpcnN0UGFnZSI6InB1YmxpY2F0aW9uIiwicGFnZSI6InB1YmxpY2F0aW9uIn19.

21 https://www.researchgate.net/publication/366211214_Economic_Systems_in_Metaverse_Basics_State_of_the_Art_and_Challenges/link/652154323ab6cb4ec6c3dd42/download?_tp=eyJjb250ZXh0Ijp7ImZpcnN0UGFnZSI6InB1YmxpY2F0aW9uIiwicGFnZSI6InB1YmxpY2F0aW9uIn19.

- Travel guides for people on vacation
- Live comments on real-world events
- Augmented trainers and teachers during physical education
- Customisation of furnishings and fittings
- Live translation of real-world conversations[22]

7.33 Therefore, we can expect for now that both types of economy can coexist peacefully – with neither at this stage under threat from the other. VR experiences in the metaverse are more immersive and therefore more likely to grow its economies, but AR applications keep a door open for millions of people unlikely to dive deep into virtual worlds. As the metaverse becomes more pervasive and all-encompassing there will inevitably be a convergence of the virtual and real-life economies and it is for this reason it is important that the legal backbone of money and economics in the metaverse is carefully designed to ensure that in the future there is this seamless integration. This is why the Government itself has identified the need to ensure that there is a clear regulatory framework with the objective of ensuring that the UK financial market remains stable and retains its integrity.[23]

7.34 We simply need to look at some of the most successful metaverse projects that are already solidifying their own economies. Decentraland, for example, is arguably one of the most successful metaverse projects currently live. Using its own currency based on the Ethereum blockchain, it has become a thriving playground where people can purchase and develop digital assets, get paid, and even build their own virtual real estate. For other examples of successful economies already hitting the mainstream, we need to look at the world of gaming. Roblox, for example, is immensely popular with young people in particular. Millions of people engage with the platform, using Robux to develop games, worlds, and even work alongside brands. Roblox could help lay down a template for successful metaversal economies for the years to come.

A LEGAL FRAMEWORK

7.35 With the building of new economies, clear legal and regulatory frameworks need to be set up to protect the interests of everyone involved in trading. With the metaverse, as a result of traditional systems being relatively slow to embrace cryptocurrency, there are still some uncertainties over how

22 https://www.brookings.edu/articles/metaverse-economics-part-1-creating-value-in-the-metaverse/.

23 https://assets.publishing.service.gov.uk/government/uploads/system/uploads/attachment_data/file/1133404/TR_Privacy_edits_Future_financial_services_regulatory_regime_for_cryptoassets_vP.pdf

payments and asset transfers will be regulated within the metaverse itself, at least with regards to the years and decades to come. This is more so where we speak about the use of virtual assets (including use of NFTs) to trade, as opposed to those held for investment only.

7.36 Like the legal framework generally in the metaverse it is likely that for some time there will be a patchwork of laws and regulations dealing with financial regulation. At least at the outset it is likely that this will be jurisdiction-specific, designed to protect the citizens of the various jurisdictions from harm.

7.37 In the UK, unlike other jurisdictions,[24] there remains a piecemeal approach to the regulation and legislation of cryptoassets generally, with an absence of a standalone law. The FSMA 2023 goes some way to start to regulate cryptoassets in the UK. The FSMA 2023 brought about reform to the Payment Systems Regulator (PSR) and make clear that it regulates the Digital Settlement Assets.[25] It further amends the Banking Act 2009 and Financial Services (Banking Reform) Act 2013. It also, as above, brings the promotion of qualifying cryptoassets into the remit of the FCA and FSMA. We can expect to see, a more and more sophisticated regulation of virtual assets (perhaps even as distinct from digital assets) as the use of the metaverse increases. It is, already, as set out above on the horizon of UK regulators, as can be seen by the involvement of both the FCA and the CMA in the DRCF and its interest in digital assets.[26] Legislators need to consider the underlying risks and harms when setting their policy on cryptoassets, those of money laundering, and harm to consumers. These risks will remain the same in the metaverse.

7.38 There are a few international cases that set promising templates for regulation of metaverse activities. Japan, for example, has established a 'Web 3.0 Policy Office',[27] which aims to establish policies and regulation in line with growing interest in the metaverse and other Web3 applications. Specifically, Japan's office, set up in 2022, opens up government officials to thoughtful discussions about legal frameworks within the metaverse and particular about the economics of the metaverse against the backdrop of the same.

7.39 The EU has established the MiCAR (the Markets in Crypto-Asset Regulation – EU 2023/1114) which governs crytoassets in the EU and is being phased in after June 2024. This framework will eventually cover asset-referenced tokens, e-money tokens and cryptoasset service providers. The Regulation highlights the need for proper regulation of financial services in the digital age,

24 As discussed below MiCAR sets to harmonise EU states with a comprehensive framework for cryptoassets

25 Which are cryptoassets used to make payments.

26 As can be seen with their May 2024 report on consumer attitudes on the risks and benefits of engaging with digital assets – https://www.drcf.org.uk/__data/assets/pdf_file/0028/285337/Consumers-and-digital-assets-ICO-and-FCA-joint-insights-paper.pdf.

27 https://www.meti.go.jp/english/press/2022/0715_002.html.

and in particular those which use DLT.[28] It highlights that certain cryptoassets will already be categorised as financial instruments, whilst others are not. The EU, therefore, believes that there is a need to create a framework to cover all cryptoassets given this gap but this should not impede on the competitiveness of EU cryptoassets. The Regulation will require specific information to be provided by retail purchasers of cryptoassets and contained within the white paper. This again shows the EU leading the way in the advancement of a legislative framework for digital assets and we expect it will be used as a basis for many other jurisdictions. MiCAR is, however, not without its staunch critics who consider that it costs a significant amount of money to comply with the Regulation which will results in people moving away from the EU market.[29]

7.40 On 1 September 2024 the Qatar Financial Centre established its digital asset framework which provides for the exploitation of digital assets and tokenisation. In the US, meanwhile, the IRS has stood fairly clear on how it interprets cryptocurrencies, NFTs, and other tradable assets within the metaverse (and outside of it). Specifically, the IRS refers to these commodities as 'digital assets'.[30] Right now, that means US tax officials are not classing these assets as a currency. Despite that, the IRS's laws clearly state that assets can be used to pay for certain goods and services, or 'digitally traded'. One could perhaps interpret the latter to refer to sales within the metaverse. We are yet to know what Donald Trump's presidency may bring about in terms of digital assets and cryptoassets regulation in the US but he has seemed to be a supporter of such assets and their opportunities during his campaign and the desire to bring some certainty to this landscape.[31]

7.41 Ultimately, we are at a point where legal financial regulations are yet to be fully agreed upon when it comes to the metaverse – and some might argue that establishments are taking too long to adapt to its increasing popularity. Others will argue that the lack of update in respect of the technology means that it is not necessary at this time and given their focus is instead on cryptocurrencies generally the monitoring by the FCA and CMA is sufficient for now when balanced against the potential harm.

TECHNOLOGICAL SOLUTIONS?

7.42 What is fundamental with the concept of money, as highlighted by the Bank of England, is the idea of 'trust'.[32] There is a potential technological

28 Distributed ledger technology – such as blockchain.

29 Matthias Lehmann, 'MICAR – Gold standard or regulatory poison for the crypto industry?', (2024), 61, Common Market Law Review, Issue 3, pp. 699-726, https://kluwerlawonline.com/journalarticle/Common+Market+Law+Review/61.2/COLA2024047

30 https://www.irs.gov/businesses/small-businesses-self-employed/digital-assets.

31 https://www.reuters.com/sustainability/boards-policy-regulation/crypto-industry-pushes-policy-sea-change-after-trump-victory-2024-11-14/

32 https://www.bankofengland.co.uk/-/media/boe/files/paper/2024/the-boes-approach-to-innovation-in-money-and-payments.pdf.

solution for the regulation of the use of 'virtual money' within the metaverse whilst the underpinning legal framework is developed. As established, asset creation, sharing, and recording all take place via blockchain. This is, again, an immutable technology—meaning that each individual transaction is effectively regulated by a record that cannot be edited. Therefore, any legal concerns over the legitimacy of trade within the metaverse are effectively moot. There are clear records that cannot be challenged – this is more than just paper and wet ink that could be falsified.

7.43 Individual transactions are already protected, to an extent, through the use of blockchain contracts. At the very least, this technology helps to some extent to prevent financial fraud and theft – beyond individual users losing access to their crypto wallet keys. Definitions regarding theft and the metaverse – and Web3 in general – are still in flux. Ultimately, protecting financial rights and pursuing alleged theft in virtual worlds present a new range of complex challenges that our existing legal frameworks (and the experts within them) are still trying to figure out.

The digital pound

7.44 The Bank of England is currently working with HM Treasury to design and develop a digital pound.[33] This will not be a cryptocurrency but a Central Bank Digital Currency (CBDC)[34] that can be used in both wholesale and retail transactions. It is likely we will see real-life fiat money, with the centralised governance, moving into the metaverse as well in some guise likely via forms of CBDC.

Stable coins

7.45 There is continued interest in the use of stablecoins as part of metaversal economy development. Stablecoins, such as Tether, take the best of both worlds from centralised and decentralised systems. Crucially, stablecoins *are* tethered to central assets to some extent, but not in the way you would expect from fiat.

7.46 Therefore, these coins offer a more stable and less volatile trading experience, hence the name. This lack of volatility could help to encourage businesses and traders who are still unsure of metaverse economics into the digital landscape.

33 https://www.bankofengland.co.uk/the-digital-pound/digital-pound-working-groups?sf186429079=1.

34 In December 2023 130 countries where looking at establishing CBDC – https://publications.parliament.uk/pa/cm5804/cmselect/cmtreasy/215/report.html.

In-game currency

At this stage it would be remiss to fail to discuss the current use of in-game currency by many of the proto-metaverse platforms. In many games the in-game currency is just digital content which has little or no value outside of the game itself.

In August 2024 the House of Commons considered the idea of loot boxes in video games.[35] This shone a spotlight on the idea of currency and its economics in the proto-metaverses. There are concerns that loot boxes constitute gambling but they are not currently regulated by the Gambling Commission despite calls for them to be regulated.

The Office of Fair Trading has had the idea of in-game purchasing in its cross-hairs since 2013 where it felt that the practice exploited children and payments were being taken without knowledge and proper transparency.[36] The Office of Fair Trading highlights that in-game purchases sit within the consumer protection regulations and the regulation of payment services.[37]

MONEY CREATION IN THE METAVERSE

7.47 With all this talk of economics and legal frameworks, we need to take a step back and look at the basics – how do people make money in the metaverse, and how do we even assign value to certain assets and what is traded between users?

7.48 We have to consider the main reasons why people use the metaverse at all – right now, it is all about gaming, investing in collectibles, hosting events, socialising with others, and investing in real estate. There is a value system already in place in the metaverse, and it is tied to cryptocurrencies, cryptoassets and digital assets. Depending on where you buy and sell, different stores and platforms will accept a variety of crypto coins[38] and value their wares based on work put into creativity and marketing.

7.49 That said, yet again, we are in a position where there is no formal system for measuring the precise value of digital assets in the metaverse. Therefore, people trading within virtual worlds need to consider a few different factors to determine value – just as we might with physical commodities in the 'real world'.

35 https://researchbriefings.files.parliament.uk/documents/CBP-8498/CBP-8498.pdf.
36 https://assets.publishing.service.gov.uk/media/5a7c6a29e5274a5590059b52/oft1519.pdf.
37 Under the Payment Services Regulations 2017.
38 Or in game currency.

7.50 For example, it is reasonable to apply more value to, or expect more money for, digital assets that can be used between different games and virtual worlds and digital scarcity is a big valuation factor.[39] Through blockchain, creators can establish scarcity with unique contracts for each work published. That means, for example with a piece of NFT artwork, there is only one legitimate copy.

7.51 Even further, we have to consider viral trends – community factors such as value perception amongst peers can increase asset pricing. Consider this to be much like supply and demand in the real world.

7.52 If a certain product in real-world economics becomes scarce or particularly sought after due to endorsements or trend factors, you can expect pricing to increase. We have seen this with the 'meme coin' phenomena where the value of such coins came about through community engagement. This is much the same as you can expect in the metaverse – if certain assets and items start becoming popular in virtual communities, there's every chance they will increase in price. In turn, we would expect some form of legal protection to guarantee the representations of scarcity being made. As discussed in **Chapter 5** issues relating to passing off and trading on the goodwill of another are also relevant points of discussion when it comes to trends and endorsement. Court cases have already been brought as a result of alignment with both real life and virtual trends.[40]

7.53 There are several ways for people to make money in the metaverse that are fairly similar to trading options in the real world. For example, as mentioned briefly earlier, real estate is booming in the metaverse – a great example is the 'land' marketplace available through Decentraland, where people can buy and sell metaverse plots for various applications. This is discussed in more detail in **Chapter 11**.

7.54 The metaverse is also a fantastic opportunity for artists and creators to auction digital work to collectors outside of the physical realm. Users can buy unique pieces they can install in virtual worlds and showcase as collector's items. Other artists might create clothing, hairstyles, and accessories that users can apply to their avatars for use across different worlds and applications.

7.55 Interestingly, the metaverse already has some real-world banking connections, too. JP Morgan offers a platform called Onyx, running on blockchain,[41] which allows people to set up their own enterprises and start making crypto money exclusive to virtual worlds.

39 https://www.linkedin.com/pulse/valuation-digital-assets-metaverse-michel-maus-evzbe/.
40 Examples include the Bored Ape Yacht Club, the MetaBirkin and CryptoNike.
41 https://www.jpmorgan.com/onyx/index.

7.56 Yet again, we're looking at the infancy of money creation and value attribution in the metaverse. And yet, we have to keep pointing to statistics that claim virtual worlds are becoming increasingly mainstream. While cryptocurrencies remain volatile, there is enough big-name interest flowing into the metaverse right now for confidence in virtual world trading to remain high.

7.57 What will set metaversal money-making apart from real-world trading and finance accrual is how markets are affected. Although famously volatile, coins like BTC are relatively unaffected by political and socioeconomic events. That means even if sterling or the euro takes a hit in the real world, value will typically remain strong in the metaverse. Therefore, over the years to come, traders will need to build robust expectations of how crypto markets will affect their business.

7.58 How trading will continue to evolve in the metaverse will depend on how mainstream finance and business embrace cryptocurrencies in the years leading up to 2030. Despite the benefits of Web3 being clear to millions, we are still some way away from banks and institutions embracing virtual currencies with open arms.

7.59 In the meantime, however, if you even glance at worlds within the metaverse, you'll see that trading and business are thriving – a great sign for the strength of the virtual economy to come.

FINANCIAL SERVICES

7.60 Now we are a little clearer on how people make money in the metaverse, and how financial regulation could look for the years ahead, we also need to consider how financial institutions intend to operate in virtual worlds.

7.61 As mentioned, JP Morgan already has a foothold with its own cryptocurrency division – but will creators and inhabitants within virtual worlds be able to access loans, banking instruments, and investment portfolios? The answer is *yes*, eventually – but as with other topics we've discussed so far, there is a *but* involved – simply because Web3 is still emerging, and the metaverse is still in flux.

7.62 Currently several banks and institutions have footprints in the metaverse. Among them is Deutsche Bank, who, some time ago, advised it would be launching an immersive, 3D banking experience for people exploring metaversal worlds.

7.63 Specifically, Deutsche Bank talks about live events and apparel – yes, even banks are embracing the idea that people can exchange crypto coins for branded avatar items – with a view to eventually offering product advice within the metaverse itself. Right now, for many banks, it's a platform where people can attend talks and learn more about *potential*. The infrastructure is not yet ready for much more.

7.64 Several experts interested in financial services adapting to the metaverse suggest that users will be able to deposit and withdraw money within digital worlds, and speak with financial advisors without having to attend a physical office. Deutsche Bank, in fact, suggests the latter might be the case soon enough. Certainly, from a conceptual standpoint, there are no reasons why people shouldn't be able to interact with virtual advisors regarding taking out loans or making investment decisions. It is perhaps just one step beyond speaking with an advisor over video conference – it's really not that great a leap!

7.65 The knock-on effect of this is for banks to start offering crypto wallets within the metaverse itself. Again, we have to look at JP Morgan as the trailblazer. Its platform, Onyx,[42] is already live within Decentraland, and with a generic user base ever-growing, now is the perfect time for the bank to embrace crypto.

7.66 Ultimately, banks need to start taking metaverse applications seriously. The virtual revolution, and Web3, are no longer pipe-dream possibilities – we are looking at a very real revolution taking place beyond our physical plane.

7.67 Banks could start becoming metaverse-ready by thinking carefully about the types of products and instruments they are developing.[43] For example, do they already provide secure crypto wallet services? Are they developing digital twin technology to help people secure and access their physical assets or deeds outside of the real world? Perhaps a bank could use digital twinning to help people access and extend credit or loans within the metaverse itself. Recorded on blockchain contracts, users could take out digital mortgages or access lines of crypto credit by putting up digital twins for cars, businesses, or properties as collateral.

7.68 That's not a world away from how we are managing things in the real world. In the metaverse, arguably, security is greater for all parties involved where the blockchain is being utilised but there are still concerns about cybersecurity. Banks and lenders have a clear, immutable contract of what's put up towards a loan, and users can rest assured knowing their paperwork is digitally twinned – it won't readily be lost or subject to fraud.

7.69 Investments in the metaverse, as discussed, take on an entirely different shape. Here, people will trade in digital artwork and properties as opposed to physical assets – meaning banks could present special investment portfolio options purely to carry these types of assets.

42 https://www.jpmorgan.com/onyx/index.

43 https://www.avanade.com/-/media/asset/solutions/avanade-banks-creating-value-in-metaverse-pov.pdf.

7.70 Where a bank's traditional retirement or growth portfolio strategies might not account for cryptocurrencies, digital assets, or NFTs, new, metaverse-friendly products could pick up the slack. In the years to come, financial experts will gain more insight into what drives value in the metaverse, and how advisors could potentially help their customers and clients to build wealth.

7.71 There is also fantastic scope for financial education – specifically, with regard to financial instruments and investment growth in a digital universe. Therefore, banks that *don't* take advantage and start developing new platforms and technologies risk falling behind the pack. Financial education offered in the metaverse could operate via VR or AR – and banks could also train their personnel using mixed media and AI conversations to build knowledge and service capabilities.

7.72 The general idea is that, within the metaverse, there should be the same opportunities people have in the real world in order to grow wealth and save money. However, these opportunities should be tailored specifically to the exciting range of digital instruments that are already unfolding. A bank that offers a crash course in metaversal financial basics will appeal hugely to people who are completely new to digital banking and Web3 assets and finance. Established institutions could lend millions of people a helpful bridge towards a world of incredible new opportunities. It is interesting to see banks like JP Morgan go all in on embracing metaversal finance. After all, many institutions are still hands-off when it comes to committing to crypto – mainly because of the lack of financial tethering at play.

7.73 And yet, there are infinite possibilities for the individual user, businessperson and bank account owner in the metaverse – with traditional fiat checks and measures fast appearing outdated and unnecessary, more banks need to take bolder steps in approaching Web3.

PAYMENTS IN THE METAVERSE

7.74 In the UK payment providers are regulated by the Payment Systems Regulator (PSR) which also regulates payments involving cryptoassets. The PSR stresses that it is important that there are strong safeguards in place to protect consumers from harm.[44]

7.75 Whilst cryptocurrencies provide a firm backbone for financial transactions in the future metaverse. At least for now, there are fiat transactions and trades taking place right this second. Traditional financial transactions are much like what you expect from paying for game assets and perks in the real world. Although payments between e-wallets and banks are faster than ever

44 https://committees.parliament.uk/writtenevidence/111710/html/#:~:text=As%20part%20of%20the%20recent,can%20be%20used%20for%20payments.

nowadays, there are still central delays and checks that can slow processes down. Metaversal financial transfers are even faster than regular e-wallet users can imagine – there's no waiting for emails, or for banks to let payments through. In the real world, we are reliant on systems where checks and measures dictate the speed at which products and services are delivered. The decentralisation of blockchain based payments is more compatible with the real-time nature of the metaverse where payments are being made cross-border on a 24/7 basis in real time.[45]

7.76 Using crypto wallets in the metaverse enables payments to be made instantaneously, and immutable contracting allows for greater security on individual purchases. It also means additional privacy for buyers, too, meaning transactions in the metaverse won't appear itemised on bank statements or via e-wallets. Businesses in the metaverse can streamline transactions with other corporate clients and with customers through the use of high-speed gateways, either through creating regular contract agreements or by using digital invoices. Individuals, too, can trade easily via the metaverse using individual payment links. People can share wallet and payment links with each other to instantly transfer funds – taking place either within a digital world, or outside of it.

7.77 Currently, in most metaverse platforms the payment methods will still be dictated by the platform owners. Currently payment methods include both traditional payments, such as credit and debit card and PayPal as well as cryptocurrencies and tokens.[46] Metaverses which are built on the blockchain typically require purchases to be brought in cryptocurrencies.[47] Most blockchain metaverses require connection to a cryptographic wallet.

7.78 With such a financial revolution taking place within the metaverse, it makes sense that there should be a scalable and reliable security solution in place. Again, immutable contracts will protect individuals to an extent, but businesses and traders need to take steps to secure their transactions in case of criminal activity. Blockchain technology has intensive security measures set up to ensure financial data is encrypted and that money travels to where it is expected. However, that is not to say the metaverse is completely protected against security challenges and threats that are likely to arise for the years to come. For example, while we have said fraud-proofing is possible through relying on blockchain transactions, criminal activity evolves alongside technology.

7.79 Right now transaction verification on the blockchain takes place in an instant – meaning buyers feel secure in that they are buying from a legitimate source with a blockchain contract, and sellers know that they won't have to chase for payment or wait for funds to clear.

45 Carlos Cantú, Cecilia Franco and Jon Frost, BIS Papers No 144, The economic implications of services in the metaverse (2024) – https://www.bis.org/publ/bppdf/bispap144.pdf.

46 Such as Robux in Roblox and Linden dollar in Second Life.

47 MANA is used in Decentraland, SAND in Sandbox.

7.80 Of course, there are a few outlier issues – the *Frosties* case blew open discussions regarding cryptocurrency and fraud. Blockchain's recorded contracts however, helped to ensure perpetrators were caught – meaning that anyone purchasing assets via the metaverse can rest easy knowing the paper trail isn't difficult to follow.

7.81 To many people, the idea of buying and selling within the metaverse might sound complex or difficult to visualise, at least at first. However, with the support of banks already immersed in digital worlds (as discussed in the last section) who offer education and guidance, it is likely that people of all ages and backgrounds will get to grips with the economics.

7.82 And, again, that is part of what many blockchain technology companies stand for – making Web3 finance as accessible and as beneficial for as broad an audience as possible, and thankfully, the metaverse's financial playground allows for an incredible amount of innovation in this regard.

CHALLENGES AND RISKS

7.83 One of the main reasons why adoption of cryptocurrencies in the metaverse and in general has been so hands-off is because of cyber security concerns. As discussed, there are already some regulatory practices in place, and there is also evidence to suggest that fraudulent activity *does* exist.

7.84 That aside, faking contracts or claiming ownership falsely when it comes to metaversal activity and digital goods is still challenging. The very nature of blockchain contracts makes sure of that. However, we need to be realistic about the potential for challenges in metaverse money as the technology evolves over time. Many of the high profile cryptocurrency frauds have come about as a result of the individual bad players as opposed to the technology itself.[48]

7.85 There is the argument that, with a lack of any kind of formal regulation, everyday people are at risk from fraudulent activity. A lack of knowledge in market fluctuations and crypto volatility could lead some vulnerable people into schemes where they simply do not recognise the risk.[49]

7.86 Individual financial loss is one thing, but there are also widespread challenges to expect. A lack of any kind of formal compliance in the metaverse means that, to an extent, 'anything goes.' What is scaring a lot of people about the metaverse and money used within is this idea of the great unknown.

48 For example Centra Tech/Sohrab Sharma, FTX/ Sam Bankman-Fried, OneCoin/'Cryptoqueen', Bitclub Network, Thodex.

49 As identified by the FCA and ICO in their consumer research https://www.drcf.org.uk/__data/assets/pdf_file/0028/285337/Consumers-and-digital-assets-ICO-and-FCA-joint-insights-paper.pdf.

7.87 A general lack of financial regulation and therefore assured security are among the biggest challenges facing widespread metaversal adoption and trading.[50] The metaverse is however still in flux in respect of money. It does not really seem to know which way to turn. It is still unclear on how to measure, regulate, and even tax virtual money.

7.88 As mentioned, several companies and banking institutions are already taking bold steps forward to try and embrace Web3 before it's too late. After all, late adoption doesn't just put businesses behind the interest curve, but also puts customers at risk. The sooner they start to develop security protections and plans, the faster they can reassure metaverse users. Companies are already taking steps relatively early in the metaverse revolution by developing gateways and crypto solutions to help businesses and individuals gain confidence in using virtual money, so that future companies are prepared and protected against any challenges that lie ahead.

7.89 For now, ultimately, individuals are themselves responsible for the activities that take place. Every transaction they make carries risk – admittedly, as it does in the real world – but, right now, these risks are higher simply because there are no official, overall agreements in place as to how transactions should be policed. One way around this would be for more territories, like Japan, to set up policy departments to discuss crypto matters with the view to changing existing legislation. However, getting international buy-in also presents a challenge.

7.90 The clock is ticking for international bodies to find ways to cooperate with each other and agree upon ways to measure and manage metaversal finance and other legal challenges. There is a need for international regulation of money in the metaverse, setting key protections and standards.

Inflation

7.91 There is also the matter of natural challenges arising in the metaverse with regard to money and digital asset value. As discussed, cryptocurrencies are inherently volatile despite not being tethered to political or social change. It is decentralisation, admittedly, that helps to create this volatility – there are no ingrained systems tethered to underpin cryptocurrency values.

7.92 Inflation is one such threat that could realistically affect metaverse trading and asset value. That said, BTC is already a few steps ahead of the threat thanks to its limited supply of around 21 million coins. Once these coins are fully minted, the production of BTC will cease. That, at least, provides a safety net against inflation.

50 https://www.mckinsey.com/featured-insights/in-the-balance/the-role-of-legal-and-compliance-in-the-metaverse.

7.93 Real-world inflation, however, might not have as much of an impact on crypto trading within the metaverse as many might assume. It has, after all, weathered highs and lows experienced by fiat money in the past, and for some territories, cryptocurrencies have helped to support economies where fiat has reduced massively in value.

7.94 Ultimately, the challenges that could face the metaverse and money traded within it are potentially solvable, provided people and economies come together and collaborate. By breaking down unnecessary barriers caused by centralisation we can instead focus on working together to create a sustainable series of economies.

AML IN THE METAVERSE

7.95 Although blockchain contracts irrefutably establish what deals have taken place within the metaverse at any given time, there are still concerns that money laundering is difficult to police because of the lack of centralisation. The metaverse has compliance challenges based on its current setup. However, that doesn't mean there are not technological solutions around the corner.

7.96 Much like traditional money laundering, money laundering in the metaverse goes through the same process,[51] however, there are new challenges created as a result of the immersive technology and the lack of effective regulation. One of the risks is that criminals can use the metaverse to effectively shield the user – not only their identity but also their location. This makes it harder to identify whether the user is in a high-risk jurisdiction and to run effective anti-money laundering checks.

7.97 One of the best ways to prevent money laundering in the metaverse is simply to boost education and to set up suitable gatekeeping services. Ensuring that everyone understands financial risks in the metaverse and that there is technology in place to prevent financial loss will take considerable time and effort.

FUTURE INNOVATIONS

7.98 Of course, to start reaching a sustainable consensus regarding how to safeguard and grow metaverse economies, we need to start developing strategies and innovations that will support users, traders, and businesses. There needs to be interoperability between fintech providers and solutions for true financial ease of use.

51 Annelieke Mooij 'Regulating the Metaverse Economy – how to prevent money laundering and the financing of terrorism' (2024) SpringerBriefs in Law.

7.99 We also need to consider innovations in AI and how they might affect the metaversal landscape in years to come. Already, we are seeing major leaps and bounds in generative AI, meaning it has never been easier to create avatars, digital real estate, and other visual assets in a matter of minutes. Quite how this will affect digital asset value in time to come remains to be seen. Using AI to build storefronts, avatars, accessories, artworks, and even whole worlds means that there will be less time spent waiting for experiences to arise. It's also going to encourage more people to get involved, with businesses setting up quickly and easily – whereas previously, 'development time' and expensive set up costs may have turned businesses away from growing their brands in the metaverse. Metaverse business owners can simply get straight into creating assets without having to invest incredible amounts of time and money. AI is, for all intents and purposes, helping the metaverse to grow at such a blistering pace.

7.100 With AI, metaverse economies can expand faster than we've ever seen traditional economies grow. Therefore, we are yet again reinventing the wheel – and potentially seeing something completely new and exciting in terms of economics as we know it.

7.101 The Internet of Things or 'IoT', also holds exciting potential for metaversal economics and the way people trade. Ultimately, without physical devices, which form the IoT, people have no way of accessing the metaverse – which is why its innovations are pivotal to how we can expect money in metaversal worlds to evolve in the years to come. IoT innovations in Virtual Reality (VR) are helping people to experience more and more real-world things in the metaverse. In the years to come, we may well be holding and physically manipulating items in the metaverse using IoT objects and wearable tech beyond our current remit.

7.102 That would mean digital assets within the metaverse could become more than just representations, or purely visually impressive. We could start to interact with these assets in new ways – meaning that, hypothetically, these extra dimensions add more value to the metaverse.

7.103 It's a process of digital twinning – where we are effectively building a new economic state around a mirrored world – one that's going to run parallel to the physical world, but without any of the centralised and unnecessary control systems.

7.104 It is perhaps bold to assume that, through AI, the IoT, and digital twinning, we could potentially create universes parallel to our own – to many it sounds like pure science fiction. And yet, economies and businesses are already thriving in the metaverse because people are already seeing value from Web3. The metaverse is here to stay, and for as long as innovations promise new experiences, its value will continue to build and its economies thrive.

CONCLUSION

7.105 This chapter considers the principles of money and finances in the metaverse. The key-takeaway points are:

- In the new virtual world there is a need for new types of finance and money.
- Existing digital asset, digital currency, cryptocurrencies and NFT will be tradable commodities in the metaverse.
- The Financial Services and Markets Act 2023 classify the promotion of cryptoassets as a regulated activity.
- Regulatory oversight will still be required to avoid a 'wild west' payment landscape. In the UK the DRCF is closely monitoring the metaverse and with both the FCA and CMA key players it is understood that financial regulation and 'money' in the metaverse will be keen topics of interest
- Safeguards can be put in place from a technological perspective. The use of blockchain (and other forms of distributed ledger technology) can be used to mitigate some of the challenges perceived by the regulators with cryptoassets and payments in the virtual world.
- The key tenet with money in the metaverse is trust. In real life the economy is underpinned by trust and it is essential that regulators and legislators take all necessary steps to safeguard this trust in the virtual world. There is a need for consistency and suitable legal frameworks which reflect the need for a new virtual economy which exists both in the metaverse and in the real world.

Chapter 8

Contracting and doing business in the metaverse

'The metaverse is barely being born. The opportunities to capitalize in this area are immense. Get involved and learn it quickly.'

Dave Waters, Nvidia Omniverse

8.01 The metaverse is a new frontier for businesses. The Brookings Think Tank has said that 'beyond its application in traditional businesses, the metaverse will create a whole new economy, just like the internet did. New companies, new jobs, and new job descriptions will come into being to build and manage the metaverse'.[1] Whilst many traditional businesses will therefore expand into the metaverse, there will also be new types of businesses that will be specifically created for the metaverse.

8.02 There are many business uses for the metaverse. Nokia[2] identified the top six as being engineering, training, healthcare, staff onboarding, remote assistance, networking and socialising. Whilst there are clear opportunities and benefits for businesses from using the metaverse, this also creates unique legal implications and risks which must be properly considered when advising those looking to venture into the metaverse space; be that to trade or to bring other parts of their operations into the virtual space.

8.03 Real-life considerations and commercial law principles will still apply when carrying on business in the metaverse. Business users will need to ensure that they have in place comprehensive insurance coverage in the event of action being taken against them. Some of the new risks in the metaverse that need to be insured against include those arising as a result of issues caused by technological faults and criminal behaviour.[3] Importantly, tax considerations need to be factored into any decision of a trader to carry out business in the metaverse. Tax in the metaverse is complex given the lack of traditional territorial boundaries. In the absence of any new rules and regulations existing principles will apply.[4] Traders will need to identify which tax regime will apply as well as whether there are import and export duties payable.

1 https://www.brookings.edu/articles/ai-makes-rules-for-the-metaverse-even-more-important/.
2 https://www.nokia.com/metaverse/six-metaverse-use-cases-for-businesses/?did=D00000004855&gad_source=1&gclid=EAIaIQobChMIyomU_veNhQMV34hQBh3viQnOEAMYASAAEgJ4lfD_BwE.
3 https://www.pwc.com/us/en/tech-effect/emerging-tech/the-metaverse-and-insurance.html.
4 https://www.pwc.co.uk/services/tax/insights/tax-in-digital-economy-metaverse.html.

8.04 This chapter explores some of the key commercial law considerations in respect of the metaverse and supporting businesses looking to expand into this area.

METAVERSE GOODS AND SERVICES

8.05 Goods and services in the metaverse are not the same as those with the same name in real life. By deconstructing the actual goods and services being offered in the metaverse you can then identify the different expectations for those goods and services, decide what should be documented in any contractual agreement and see where a breach of those rights is likely to cause material damage or be a fundamental breach of contract. It is always necessary therefore to carefully disassemble the different elements of the goods and services being offered to understand what is actually being traded in the metaverse.

8.06 An avatar buying a can of coca cola from a shop in the metaverse for example, is not the same as someone going into a shop in real life and buying a can of coca cola; a virtual stadium tour in the metaverse is not the same as a stadium tour in real life and travel in the metaverse is not the same as travelling in real life. In real life, assets such as cars depreciate in value due to their physical use, but this is not the case in the metaverse; similarly, in the metaverse issues concerning the type of fuel that a car runs on are irrelevant and play no factor in the purchasing decision. In the metaverse an avatar's property does not provide them shelter, in real life this is one of its primary purposes.

8.07 In the coca cola example, in real life the store is selling a can of coca cola, typically having purchased this from a supplier. The can of coca cola in real life comprises both the drink and the branded can. In most cases the branding is secondary to the underlying product and therefore the cost associated with the branding and packaging is typically wrapped up in the cost of the product. You may pay more for 'branded' goods but the branding alone is not the sole purpose of the product. The purpose of the can of coca cola in real life is the drink; in the metaverse the avatar cannot drink the coca cola, so the can of coca cola in the metaverse is purely the visual representation of the brand and little different from any digital goods brought for an avatar, be that a pair of glasses or even branded skin.

NFTs

8.08 Many businesses in the metaverse use or sell NFTs. An NFT is a non-fungible token. It is digitally recorded, normally on the Ethereum blockchain, which means that there is a permanent record of the unique transaction. There are many use cases for NFTs[5] including digital art, ticketing, gaming, education

5 PWC Australia identified these at https://ww.pwc.com.au/digitalpulse/101-non-fungible-token-nfts.html.

and recording part of the supply chain all of which will be important in the metaverse.[6]

SELLING IN THE METAVERSE

8.09 Selling is one of the key opportunities for business users of the metaverse. Businesses can sell both digital goods and services in the metaverse. Whilst most goods in the metaverse will be digital products, there is the opportunity for a cross-over between digital goods and real-life goods being sold, such as an avatar buying a digital representation of a product in the metaverse and then the user being sent physical goods matching the digital products. The now defunct Starbucks Odyssey enabled users to obtain real-life rewards from their online interactions.[7] Hilton Hotels has created Slivingland on Roblox which enables users to earn Hilton rewards in the metaverse which can then be used in real life Hilton hotels.[8] This is one of the first cross-overs between the metaverse and real life.

8.10 In April 2024 Walmart enabled users of Roblox to be able to buy real-life goods via its platform. As part of the experience users can trial digital twins of real-life products and once purchased via the Roblox platform the users get both the digital product for immediate use in the metaverse and the real-life product simultaneously be shipped to them.[9] Whilst this is initially being trialled on Roblox with Walmart it is expected that this will become a new revenue stream for both the retailers and the metaverse platforms.

8.11 In the future the metaverse platforms could deploy smart contract technology to automatically trigger the real-life product being shipped where the corresponding virtual asset is purchased. Care would need to be had to deal with cooling off periods under consumer protection laws, especially where there may be different periods for the real-life product as opposed to the digital products. If a consumer uses the digital product this may preclude a cancellation of the contract but despite being linked, the contract for the real-life product should still be capable of being cancelled. Given the reforms under the Electronic Trade Documents Act 2023 electronic trade documents such as electronic bills of lading could also now in theory be transmitted digitally via the metaverse and there are significant opportunities for utilising blockchain technology for these types of

6 https://www.ft.com/partnercontent/crypto-com/nfts-identity-in-the-metaverse.html.

7 https://techcrunch.com/2022/12/08/starbucks-opens-up-its-blockchain-based-loyalty-program-and-nft-community-to-first-beta-testers/?guccounter=1&guce_referrer=aHR0cHM6Ly93d3cuZ29vZ2xlLmNvbS8&guce_referrer_sig=AQAAAGyDPFT5n_M0j-JvbcSMj_QDO1ab0Z3HaTD-aLhPComQ_R9_GVzZzQWIIhpO0QuXe_O2wh8WjLENqYLGoZ24ANGrJcKuWpyX_3vTLtFZAB5VeybMxdJ76y0Me9Ddgd6-nHMv1DGKRcr2q65vGeMEUiKU2wn5HavruU1hM4HjfQ6W.

8 https://stories.hilton.com/hilton-for-the-stay/step-into-paris-hiltons-slivingland-on-roblox-to-unlock-real-hilton-honors-rewards.

9 https://digiday.com/marketing/walmart-and-roblox-are-teaming-up-to-make-virtual-e-commerce-a-reality/.

documents. The advancements permitted now as a result of this legislative update would benefit the logistic aspect of the real life/metaverse goods cross-overs.

8.12 Caution, however, should still be exercised since Roblox in their terms of business make it clear that virtual assets purchased on their platform do not entitle the users to those assets in real life.[10] It is likely that, should this Walmart trial be successful, and if other businesses expand to offer the simultaneous cross-over between the metaverse and real life, these terms would be updated to make it clear when each apply. Care should be taken to review the position carefully. Consideration should also be had as to what happens where there is a conflict between the platform terms and other terms.

Online Safety Act 2023

8.13 Any user that is providing services to other users within the metaverse will have to comply with the Online Safety Act 2023. There are some requirements that only apply to large service providers and there are still some points of clarity required in respect of the metaverse[11] but generally speaking all those that operate an online service within the metaverse environment need to comply with the Act.

8.14 There will be a transition period, which is likely to be until around the end of 2024, as new rules are developed by Ofcom and take effect, but all online providers should start to implement steps now to comply with the Act. Ofcom's current guidance[12] encourages online service providers to:

1 undertake a risk assessment of the nature and types of harms present in respect of their services both generally and how they may impact children;

2 address how they can control and minimise these risks;

3 look to update terms and conditions to make it clear how they are protecting users;

4 ensure there are systems to enable users to report concerns and complain

8.15 There are extensive fines for non-compliance with the Act. These are fines of up to £18,000,000 or 10% of worldwide revenue, whichever is higher, as well as other sanctions and enforcement powers.

Platform terms – general

8.16 Any interaction in the metaverse will currently principally be governed contractually by the relevant platform terms. Prior to any business commencing on the relevant platform its terms should be carefully considered to determine whether

10 https://www.roblox.com/info/terms?locale=en_us.

11 Around aural communications.

12 https://www.ofcom.org.uk/online-safety/illegal-and-harmful-content/guide-for-services/.

or not there are any restrictions in respect of the commercial use of that platform. Each platform has its own rules for how users can trade in their metaverse, for example the Voxel platform's code of conduct includes the expectation that 'you.. [are]... to behave as you would want others to behave toward you'.[13]

8.17 On almost all platforms the platform owners have contractually excluded any liability for the actions of users and have, as far as they legally can, limited liability. Assemblr Metaverse[14] for example, permits commercial use of its metaverse but excludes any liability of the platform for disputes between users[15] and Vertikal[16] makes it clear that they are not responsible for third party services.[17] On most metaverse platforms the owners have the right to remove or suspend any user who infringes their terms of use. This has been the case in respect of virtual worlds for a considerable length of time and was the catalyst for one of the first cases involving virtual worlds *Bragg v Linden Research Inc.*[18]

Key metaverse platform terms – specific terms

8.18 What is interesting at this stage is the comparison between the different ways in which the metaverse platforms are seeking to protect themselves, and limit their liability, for user-to-user interactions.

8.19 In Decentraland[19] users can buy and sell in the different lands. The rules for each land are governed by the terms and conditions set by the owner of that land but everyone still remain subject to the Decentraland Content Policy. Any NFT is owned by the creator of the NFT and any sale is governed by the terms and conditions of that creator. Any content created on Decentraland is owned by the creator and again the creator may impose their own terms and conditions in respect of its sale or use.[20] Decentraland under its Terms of Use disclaims any liability for any user-to-user content or interactions.[21]

8.20 In Sandbox[22] the users have control over any game that has been created by them including how it is charged. Sandbox terms set out guidelines for users in

13 https://www.voxels.com/conduct.

14 'an easy, beginner-friendly metaverse' – https://www.assemblrworld.com/metaverse.

15 https://www.assemblrworld.com/pages/assemblr-metaverse-terms-and-conditions#:~:text=Assemblr%20Metaverse%20does%20not%20have,or%20transmit%20using%20the%20Service.

16 Which is a 'hub of art and culture in the Metaverse' https://www.vertikal.art/vertikal-metaverse-for-nft-art-nft-photo-nft-collectors-art-gallery-and-nft-communities-v2.

17 ttps://www.vertikal.art/vertikal-metaverse-terms-and-conditions-v2.

18 *Bragg v. Linden Research, Inc.*, 487 F. Supp. 2d 593 (E.D. Pa. 2007) (No. 06CV4925).

19 described as 'a virtual social world, the first decentralized metaverse' https://decentraland.org.

20 https://decentraland.org/terms/.

21 https://decentraland.org/terms/.

22 which enables 'users ... to create, buy, transfer, and trade unique digital game assets in voxel art ... which can then be used on The Sandbox for game-making purposes' https://www.sandbox.game/en/terms-of-use/.

respect of any game created. The payment transactions happen on the Ethereum blockchain outside of the control of the platform. The terms make it clear that the users are responsible for their content and a number of representations and warranties have to be made under the terms. The users also indemnify the platform owners of Sandbox under the terms in respect of the use of their content and any fault of their staff.[23]

8.21 Roblox[24] permits both premium users and creators to sell virtual content. Under their terms of use any dispute is between the users in the first instance but this can be escalated to Roblox to try and help to resolve.[25] This puts Roblox more on a judicial or dispute resolution footing. Roblox terms also clearly disclaim any liability for any user or creator content, there is a limit of liability and an indemnity. Roblox has separate creator terms, as well as incorporating advertising terms and other terms and conditions.

REGULATION (EU) 2019/1150

8.22 Whilst most of the different metaverse platforms have sought to contractually disclaim any liability towards its business users, the European Union Regulation (EU) 2019/1150 will apply to business users of the metaverse. These Regulations apply where a platform enables a business user to sell directly to consumers via its platform, such as a store in the metaverse. The Regulations are intended to promote fairness and transparency for the business users of 'online intermediation services'. Most metaverse platforms will be considered to be online intermediation services and therefore where a party is based within the EU the relationship will be subject to these Regulations.[26]

8.23 The Regulations largely reflect the fact that businesses have today generally come to rely on platforms to be able to carry out their businesses, and unfortunately such platforms typically are set up with standard form terms of business with limited or no scope to negotiate these. The Regulations provide for fair practices for business users when using online intermediary services to conduct their business. Under the Regulations any change to terms and conditions must be notified to business users on a durable medium with no less than 15 days' notice before the change takes effect. The terms need to contain full details of where a decision can be taken to suspend or terminate a business user. Further the business user cannot be prevented from using their trading identity by the platform.

23 https://www.sandbox.game/en/terms-of-use/.
24 a platform described as 'reimagining the way people come together' https://www.roblox.com/info/about-us?locale=en_us
25 https://www.roblox.com/info/terms?locale=en_us.
26 Article 2(2) – the other requirements are that the platform must qualify as a 'information society services' (Article 2(1) and there must be a contract between the platform and the business user).

8.24 The Regulations also deal with how a platform ranks business users in their listings. The way that a platform ranks businesses must be disclosed to the business user in advance. It would be interesting to see how such provisions will apply in respect of the metaverse, especially as the nature and way businesses are ranked will change as a result of this technology; it is not the same as SEO ranking in Web2.

8.25 In the event of a dispute between the platform and the business user, mediation is encouraged under the Regulations and the higher share of costs for trying to resolve matters in this way should be paid by the platform owner.

8.26 Whilst the Regulation will not apply under the law of England and Wales, it may still offer part of the protection (albeit not guaranteed) to business users who use metaverse platforms which cater to EU business users where general contractual updates have been put in place to cater to the Regulations. Care should, however, be taken to ensure that the terms still apply and there has been no specific carve out just for EU business users. It would be useful for the UK to consider the need for a similar type of legislation to protect its traders who use the metaverse to trade. Legal commentators have highlighted that it was never really intended that intellectual property laws would be the main laws governing virtual worlds in the real-world[27] and instead principles of contract law should be used to provide the necessary safeguards which real-life products are afforded. This shift has moved digital products and virtual reality goods and services from contractual principles based on reciprocated bargaining powers into an intellectual property landscape where the owners retain control and dictate the terms of use of their asset. Laws designed to govern intangible assets being used online in a two-dimensional way are not appropriate for the metaverse and should not be used to govern real-life interactions, albeit using XR technology. Instead, real-life analogies are more appropriate.

User-to-user contracting in the metaverse

8.27 When contracting in the metaverse it is still important to ensure that all the basic real-life legal principles of a contract have been fulfilled. Has there been offer and acceptance? Is there valid consideration and an intention to create legal relations? Careful analysis is required when any contract between users in the metaverse is concluded. Such contracts may not necessarily look the same as contracts being concluded in real life but any agreements should still properly reflect what is actually being agreed. It is important that care is taken to understand what may be happening technologically as well as visually playing out via the XR every step of the way. Attention must be paid as to whether limits have been placed around the law and jurisdiction applicable to the contract and whether there are limits on how the contract must be enforced, such as mandatory

27 Joshua A.T. Fairfield, Mixed Reality: How the Laws of Virtual Worlds Govern Everyday Life, 27 Berkeley Tech. L. J. 55 (2012).

ADR as opposed to litigation. These are key areas of concern for contracts being concluded in the metaverse.

8.28 Historically we have drawn legal distinctions between contracts concluded in-premises and off-premises.[28] This will be blurred in the metaverse. The store may look like it is real life, it may enable test driving or trial use of the products, but the user will most likely still be physically in their own home and therefore susceptible to greater influence and control.

8.29 Unlike purchasing items in Web2 through online shops, shopping in Web3 or the metaverse will, however, be more like shopping in real life. Avatars will browse the store and interact with the products and each other. They will be able to try on the products and potentially test drive others. Virtual stores may advertise products in their 'store', and may even require a user to take multiple steps to obtain such items, but this is still likely to be considered as an invitation to treat in the same way as in real life and a Web2 website. The buying avatar will therefore make the offer for the sale, which may or may not be accepted by the selling avatar or underlying seller.

8.30 Care must be had over whether sufficient notice has been provided of any terms governing a contract between users. Any express terms of a contract will need to be identified since they may not be presented in the way traditionally expected. They should, however, be presented ahead of the contract being formed and developers will need to ensure that this is the case. Issues regarding the incorporation of contractual terms between users are a key issue in the metaverse. Consideration must be had as to how the terms are communicated to another user. It is important that any terms of a contract are clearly communicated to the other users so that they can be relied upon. Such terms are unlikely to be 'written' in the conventional sense. It may be instead that terms are projected in written form into the virtual space or read out by an avatar in a virtual marketplace. Where this is the case there are likely to be evidential issues as well as questions around incorporation. Warning must still be had as to Lord Justice Denning's obiter that:

> 'The more unreasonable a clause is, the greater the notice which must be given of it. Some clauses I have seen would need to be printed in red ink on the face of the document with a red hand pointing to it before the notice could be held to be sufficient'[29]

8.31 Technologists should therefore ensure that the most onerous and key terms are properly brought to the user's attention. One way may be that such terms appear as giant pop ups that must be clearly acknowledged.

8.32 The use of augmented reality may actually assist with making informed decisions about a product or a retailer. With XR, users may be able to access

28 Distinction is drawn under The Consumer Contracts (Information, Cancellation and Additional Charges) Regulations 2013.

29 *J. Spurling Limited v Bradshaw* [1956] WLR 461.

extensive reviews and details about a product prior to purchasing it. There is, therefore an argument that contracts supported by XR should actually be held to be more enforceable than traditional contracts.[30]

8.33 It is not fatal for a contract that users do not know each other in real life nor whether a party can be identified.[31] This is principally an evidential issue should there be a need for a claim. The cases of *D'Aloia v Persons Unknown & Others*[32] and *Osbourne v Persons unknown and others*[33] and *Jones v Persons Unknown*[34] have all permitted service of proceedings via NFT (non-fungible token). It is also possible that in the future service of proceedings may be expanded in other ways in respect of metaverse technologies. The Civil Procedure Rules 1998 have the necessary flexibility to enable service of a claim form by alternative means[35] and the court can even dispense with service of the claim form altogether.[36] A claim for breaching a contract in the metaverse could in theory even be served in virtual reality through the metaverse itself with the permission of the court.

8.34 As set out above, time must also be taken to deal with the relationship between user-to-user terms and platform terms. Where there are conflicts between such terms it is not clear how these would be determined in real life.

Implied terms

8.35 There will always be relevant implied terms to consider in respect of any contracts concluded in the metaverse. Any contract in the metaverse will incorporate statutory implied terms such as the Consumer Rights Act 2015. As discussed below – any digital content supplied to a consumer must be of satisfactory quality,[37] fit for purpose,[38] free from defect,[39] safe[40] and durable.[41] If the contractual relationship is business to business there is likely to be some argument since, although the Sale of Goods Act 1979 would typically provide an implied term that the goods are fit for purpose digital assets are not the same

30 Scott R. Peppet, Freedom of Contract in an Augmented Reality: The Case of Consumer Contracts, 59 UCLA L. REV. 676 (2012), available at https://scholar.law.colorado.edu/articles/119.

31 As referenced on H Beale (ed), Chitty on Contracts (34th ed 2021) para 5-037 shown at https://s3-eu-west-2.amazonaws.com/cloud-platform-e218f50a4812967ba1215eaecede923f/uploads/sites/30/2021/11/Smart-legal-contracts-accessible.pdf.

32 [2022] EWHC 1723 (Ch).

33 [2023] EWHC 39 (KB).

34 [2022] EWHC 2543 (Comm).

35 CPR 1998, r 6.3 and 6.15.

36 CPR 1998, r 6.16.

37 CRA 2015, s 34(1).

38 CRA 2015, s 34(3)(a).

39 CRA 2015, s 34(3)(b).

40 CRA 2015, s 34(3)(c).

41 CRA 2015, s 34(3)(d).

as goods under the Sale of Goods 1979.[42] This is the established position in respect of software generally as reflected in *St Albans City and District Council v International Computers Ltd.*[43]

8.36 Terms may be implied into a contract in the metaverse to give business efficacy to the contract. It is for this reason it is important to deconstruct the different elements of what is being offered and purchased in the metaverse to identify the user's expectations as set out above. For example if you are sold an object in the metaverse which is promoted as being unique then this should not be available for sale to anyone else and if a product is promoted as being suitable for the metaverse it should be possible to use it in all metaverses. There are also numerous issues in respect of the terms of sale in respect of 'land' in the metaverse which are discussed further in **Chapter 9.**

Smart contracts

8.37 Where the metaverse is on the blockchain smart contracts will be utilised. Smart contracts are effectively computer software or protocols which automatically trigger something else to happen. The transaction is all recorded on the blockchain. With a smart contract, the specific action therefore will trigger certain pre-programmed consequences. They are sometimes attached to a written agreement but they do not have to be.[44]

8.38 The Law Commission presented its advice to the Government on smart contracts in 2021.[45] In their report they considered that the law of England and Wales could accommodate smart contracts but further consideration was still needed to clarify whether computer coding on its own could satisfy the test of being a contract. They did not feel it necessary to have a separate class of contract introduced for smart contracts nor special rules or laws implemented to cover these.

8.39 The Law Commission confirmed that any specific issues concerning the agreement should be expressly stated in the smart contract. They identified ten key issues to consider in the preparation of any smart contract:

(1) contemplate the scope and purpose of the contract – what consequences are required and why;

42 https://www.lawsociety.org.uk/en/campaigns/consultation-responses/law-commission-consultation-on-digital-assets#:~:text=Digital%20assets%20are%20not%20analogous,for%20purchasers%20of%20digital%20assets and the Law Commission consultation on digital assets – Law Society response 4th November 2022.

43 [1996] 4 All ER 481.

44 Levi and Lipton distinguishes these as 'code only smart contracts' and 'ancillary smart contracts' – https://corpgov.law.harvard.edu/2018/05/26/an-introduction-to-smart-contracts-and-their-potential-and-inherent-limitations/.

45 https://s3-eu-west-2.amazonaws.com/cloud-platform-e218f50a4812967ba1215eaecede923f/uploads/sites/30/2021/11/Smart-legal-contracts-accessible.pdf.

(2) determine the format of the smart contract – will there be an accompanying written contract or will the terms only be contained in the code itself – how will it be recorded?

(3) identify whether the code itself is intended to form part of the contract or just be used to perform the contract and ensure that this decision is properly recorded as part of the smart contract itself;

(4) establish the language of the contract – is this the code or not, and what takes priority if these are inconsistent. Again, ensure that this is recorded on the blockchain;

(5) include provisions within the smart contract about key technological issues which could arise, such as what happens if there are fundamental issues with the code, this is especially important if the code is considered to form part of the contract itself;

(6) ensure that it is clear in the smart contract itself what part of the smart contract is contractual and what is not contractual. Some parts of the code for example may be non-contractual whilst it may be useful to have some parts of the code that is contractual. The coding will often include natural language as well as the code, so should this be considered as part of the contract or not?

(7) agree whether to include written descriptions or clarification in respect of any coding as part of the contract and consider whether this should form part of the contract. Should the accompanying written clarifications be binding and, if so, what should take priority in the event of inconsistencies?

(8) review whether other systems or platforms and their terms should be incorporated into the smart contract. This is likely to be required within any smart contract in the metaverse which utilises the public blockchain of the metaverse;

(9) ensure that there are proper termination provisions within the smart contract coding and the ability to suspend the contract if necessary; and

(10) include provisions on jurisdiction and choice of law.

8.40 We would also suggest that, as relevant, the smart contract includes other boiler plate provisions to avoid unnecessary points of dispute. Important provisions include severability of specific clauses, or even parts of the code and how notices can be served.

8.41 Smart contracts are enforceable provided that the contract meets the legal test of being a contract.[46] The classic early example of a smart contract is a vending machine, which would clearly constitute a binding contract. It is important therefore that the basic principles of offer, acceptance, consideration

46 https://corpgov.law.harvard.edu/2018/05/26/an-introduction-to-smart-contracts-and-their-potential-and-inherent-limitations/.

and an intention to create legal relationships are met. This may not be as straight forward as in real life since at least part of the process will be processed automatically by the technology.

8.42 There are serious issues with the concept of consideration in smart contracts.[47] This is because, prima facie, a smart contract does not necessarily distinguish between a gift and a contract; a gift could be coded into a smart contract. It would prima facie look and act largely in the same way as a contractual smart contract. The distinguishing feature of the smart contract is the software coding and automated response, not necessarily whether the elements of a contract have been properly fulfilled. It will therefore be important to carefully consider any smart contract to ensure all elements of a contract have been properly fulfilled. The timing of the smart contract will be important, since under the law of England and Wales, any contract would fail should it be considered that there was in fact past consideration.

8.43 One of the main complexities with smart contracts will be having the technological prowess needed to understand and negotiate these agreements.[48] Legal practitioners should work with technologists to ensure that they understand exactly what is being done at what point of the process. One of the difficulties with smart contracts is with their amendment and termination.[49] This is important when contracting in the metaverse if this is being done by smart contract, which will be the case at least for those using blockchain based technologies. In this situation, consideration will have to be had as to the extent to which these agreements can actually be negotiated and, even where negotiation is technically possible, the technological barriers and costs of doing this.

8.44 It is unlikely that, for now at least, extensive legal terms will be incorporated into any agreement which is executed in the metaverse only via smart contract and instead, even when a smart contract is being used, there is likely to be some form of accompanying written terms, be that in the traditional sense or otherwise. If a user is contracting with someone in the metaverse via smart contract it will be difficult for lawyers to get full transparency and be able to properly advise on the contract without understanding the code. When advising users contracting in the metaverse any legal advisor will have to ensure that they are fully abreast of all the intricacies which may not be readily presented in the same format as a traditional written contract.

8.45 On 15 July 2024 the UNCITRAL Model Law on Automated Contracting was adopted by the United Nations Commission on International Trade Law.

47 K. Werbach & N. Cornell, 67. Duke Law Journal 2017, pp 313, 340. https://scholarship.law.duke.edu/cgi/viewcontent.cgi?article=3913&context=dlj.

48 https://corpgov.law.harvard.edu/2018/05/26/an-introduction-to-smart-contracts-and-their-potential-and-inherent-limitations/

49 https://corpgov.law.harvard.edu/2018/05/26/an-introduction-to-smart-contracts-and-their-potential-and-inherent-limitations/

This seeks to establish a framework for smart contracts and is reflective of the international focus on the digital economy and move towards Web3.[50]

FIDUCIARY DUTIES WHEN DEALING WITH VIRTUAL ASSETS

8.46 In *Tulip Trading v Van Der Laan*[51] the Court of Appeal was asked to consider whether in certain circumstances software developers could owe fiduciary duty to owners of cryptocurrency and therefore be subject to tortious liability. The position as to whether there is a fiduciary duty was never actually decided[52] since this case was discontinued prior to a full determination of the merits of such an argument. The Court of Appeal however did not dismiss the potential idea of developers having a fiduciary duty out of hand.

8.47 The Law Commission[53] does not consider that software developers should owe a fiduciary duty in a majority of circumstances and, whilst it closes the door on making any recommendation for legislative change, it does consider that in the future it may need to be determined through the common law depending on the facts presented. The Law Commission believes however, that such circumstances should be rare.

8.48 The *Tulip Trading* case potentially starts, at least embryonically, the idea that virtual property should be capable of suitable protection and those tasked with custody of such property, whether as holding the metaphoric key (or the actual private keys) have a trusted position which should by extension include fiduciary duties. Whilst on the whole the Law Commission does not support the extension of fiduciary duties to software developers' it does feel that this should be considered further by the UKJT. This is important for the context of the metaverse, where the idea of virtual currency and virtual goods and assets are common-place.

CONSUMER PROTECTION IN THE METAVERSE

8.49 The protection of consumer rights in the metaverse will be vital. Law and regulation in the real world have evolved to create special protection for consumers, given the disadvantaged position of power that they have generally in any contractual bargaining. Existing consumer protection legislation will continue to apply.

8.50 The EU Commission considers that it already has a robust framework of consumer protection regulation to protect consumers in virtual worlds and the

50 https://unis.unvienna.org/unis/pressrels/2024/unisl362.html

51 [2023] EWCA Civ 83, [2023] 4 WLR 16.

52 The case was simply about whether there was potential legal merit in the argument.

53 https://cloud-platform-e218f50a4812967ba1215eaecede923f.s3.amazonaws.com/uploads/sites/30/2024/07/DAOs-scoping-paper-110724.pdf.

metaverse including Regulation (EU) 2023/988 on General Product Safety and Directive 2005/29/EC on Unfair Commercial Practices.[54] In the UK, consumers will seek to rely on the Consumer Rights Act 2015. This legislation seeks to distinguish between real-life goods, services and 'digital content'. For now, therefore, under UK consumer protection laws goods in the metaverse would be considered as digital content and digital services will just fall under the generic protection afforded to services. This is unlike the Digital Content Directive[55] which is applicable in the EU where digital services are treated differently to real-life services.

8.51 Chapter 3 of the Consumer Rights Act 2015 deals with the rights afforded to consumers in respect of digital contents. Under the Consumer Rights Act 2015 digital content has to be of satisfactory quality, fit for purpose and supplied as described. Digital services will still be treated as services and must be performed with reasonable care and skill.

8.52 In the metaverse there is the considerable risk that consumers will be subject to exploitation. The users will be confronted with the option to buy something through an immersive experience,[56] but in many cases the real-life user will be buying this from the perceived safety of their own home. This is why there has been for many years enhanced protection for sales concluded with a consumer within their home.[57]

8.53 In the UK the Consumer Contracts (Information, Cancellation and Additional Charges) Regulations 2013 will apply and developers will need to identify the most appropriate way to convey the relevant mandatory information to the consumers in the metaverse, including the right to cancel. It is a criminal offence under the Regulations not to supply a consumer with specific information. It is likely however, that the Regulations will need to be updated to reflect the change caused by the metaverse and its technology.

8.54 Under the Consumer Contracts (Information, Cancellation and Additional Charges) Regulations 2013 digital content being supplied during the cancellation period results in the right to cancel under regulation 29(1) being lost provided certain information is provided to the user.[58] This reflects the historical idea that, once supplied, the benefit of digital content is immediately depleted.

54 https://digital-strategy.ec.europa.eu/en/library/eu-initiative-virtual-worlds-head-start-next-technological-transition.

55 Directive (EU) 2019/770.

56 Which Rathore describes as 'virtual consumerism' in 'Virtual Consumerism: An Exploration of E-Commerce in the Metaverse (2017) International Journal of New Media Studies Vol 4 Issue 2 where he describes the types of experience that users will experience such as virtual showrooms with virtual mirrors for both real-life products and digital products.

57 Previously this was dealt with by the Mail Order Transactions (Information) Order 1976 then the Consumer Protection (Distance Selling) Regulations 2000 which was replaced by the Consumer Contracts (Information, Cancellation and Additional Charges) Regulations 2013 and the Consumer Contract Regulations in 2014.

58 Regulation 37(1).

This is not necessarily the case in the metaverse, where there is perhaps little distinction between purchasing a digital handbag and a real-life handbag. If a user changes their mind once they have purchased the virtual goods should they not be able to return the product? This right will be lost in the metaverse, even if the virtual product is not used, since in most cases virtual goods will be immediately supplied to the user on purchase. In real life there is no restriction on someone handling a product prior to returning it provided that their handling of the goods has not diminished their value by.[59] Where the handling of goods in real life goes beyond what you would expect in a shop, such additional diminishment in value can be deducted from the purchase price when it is returned. This is because in real life it is recognised in most cases that the goods themselves would have some underlying value and depending on the condition it would be expected that a refund would be afforded in some form. Consideration should be had as to how this should also apply to virtual goods purchased. Consumers should have the right to change their mind about virtual goods in the same way as they do with real-life goods. We have come a long way with digital products and no longer are they akin to shrink-wrapped computer programmes on a CD-Rom. The virtual product has its own intrinsic value that can be recouped by the vendor if it is resold.

THE REGULATORY PERSPECTIVE

8.55 The DRCF highlights the importance of protecting consumers in the metaverse but does consider that there are also many opportunities for consumers in the metaverse and that it is likely that in reality the technology and will probably react to the demands of consumers.[60] People will effect change in practice within the metaverse (and even in real life) by voting with their wallets. Again, however, this is likely to require input not only from lawyers but technologists to form the way in which consumer protection should be afforded in the metaverse.

8.56 The Competition and Markets Authority (CMA) considered that digital design itself can actually harm consumers.[61] The CMA identifies that the way in which goods and services are presented to a consumer digitally does have an impact on the consumer's behaviour. This can be manipulated and harm caused. This will become key in the metaverse, especially since those goods and services will be presented in real time to the consumer and in an immersive manner. Proper oversight and regulation are key as goods and services move into the metaverse. The CMA has established the Digital Markets Unit which monitors digital businesses, given the considerable risks to consumers in this area and it is envisaged that much more work will be done on the impact of how goods and services are presented in the metaverse and how this impacts on the consumer.

59 Regulation 34(9).

60 https://www.drcf.org.uk/__data/assets/pdf_file/0027/273195/DRCF-Immersive-Technologies-Foresight-Paper.pdf.

61 https://assets.publishing.service.gov.uk/media/624c27c68fa8f527710aaf58/Online_choice_architecture_discussion_paper.pdf.

ENVIRONMENTAL, SOCIAL AND GOVERNANCE (ESG) CONSIDERATIONS IN THE METAVERSE

8.57 ESG is firmly on the agenda for all businesses. From June 2023 the European Commission's new sustainable finance package requires finance businesses in the EU to prioritise ESG in their investments.[62] All businesses are now finding themselves accountable to different stakeholders on their ESG rating – be they shareholders, suppliers, customers or funders. KPMG has undertaken an extensive study into sustainability and the metaverse[63] in which it concludes that whilst the metaverse will consume a lot of energy its use may actually result in a reduction in travel generally including international travel which would in turn have a significant impact on the environment.

8.58 KPMG[64] further highlights that there are considerable opportunities for the metaverse to have a positive impact on social issues because the metaverse is borderless and could enable opportunities which ordinarily would not be available for many people. The examples given includes being able to study or work anywhere in the world. The metaverse is potentially very positive for those with some disabilities and mental health problems, although for some – for example, the blind or partially sighted – they may be restricted from being able to properly access the metaverse and face more barriers than in real life. Nokia[65] believes that the metaverse generally brings considerable sustainability benefits to businesses.[66]

ADVERTISING IN THE METAVERSE

8.59 Advertising in the metaverse, and the protection of users, are important considerations.[67] Any advertising is going to be truly immersive; users will be consumed by any marketing saturating the metaverse. It is for this reason that any advertising will have to be done responsibly.

62 https://ec.europa.eu/commission/presscorner/detail/en/ip_23_3192.

63 https://assets.kpmg.com/content/dam/kpmg/dk/pdf/dk-2022/Shaping%20the%20Metaverse%20towards%20sustainability_final.pdf.

64 https://assets.kpmg.com/content/dam/kpmg/dk/pdf/dk-2022/Shaping%20the%20Metaverse%20towards%20sustainability_final.pdf.

65 https://www.nokia.com/metaverse/industrial-metaverse/sustainability-is-the-top-benefit-of-the-metaverse-at-work/.

66 Nokia's research with EY put sustainability as the highest ranking benefit this was 41% for those looking to move into the metaverse and 51% who were already in the metaverse – https://www.nokia.com/metaverse/industrial-metaverse/sustainability-is-the-top-benefit-of-the-metaverse-at-work/.

67 McKinsey highlight that 'leading brands are already rewriting the rules of marketing' in the metaverse https://www.mckinsey.com/capabilities/growth-marketing-and-sales/our-insights/marketing-in-the-metaverse-an-opportunity-for-innovation-and-experimentation.

The Consumer Protection from Unfair Trading Regulations 2008 apply to advertising to consumers in the metaverse and prohibits unfair commercial practices.[68]The Business Protection from Misleading Marketing Regulations 2008 Directive 2006/114/EC of the European Parliament and of the Council of 12 December 2006 concerning misleading and comparative advertising (codified version) was implemented into UK law under the Business Protection from Misleading Marketing Regulations 2008 and applies in respect of advertising to businesses in the metaverse. These regulations provide that advertising cannot be misleading which means it either deceives or is likely to deceive a trader.

8.60 The Advertising Standards Authority (ASA) has reminded advertisers that its codes and regulations continue to apply to advertising in the metaverse as they do in real life.[69] The purpose of the ASA is to make sure that all advertising is responsible.[70] When speaking about the evolution of the ASA to deal with the metaverse they have said 'we expect one thing to remain the same: the ASA will be here doing all we can to make sure UK advertising is legal, decent, honest and truthful'.[71] Whilst it may be more complicated to do this where the platform is decentralised,[72] the ASA now uses an artificial intelligence based Active Ad Monitoring system to monitor online advertising and state that they will develop their framework to bring 'greater transparency and broader accountability'.[73] As advertisers are using more and more sophisticated forms of advertising technology, so the regulators are developing more and more sophisticated ways of monitoring this.

8.61 We expect to see a combination both of new forms of advertising in the metaverse and established methods of online advertising, including sponsorship, endorsements and virtual billboards. Any advertising in the metaverse must be obvious as such.[74] It is important therefore that any advertising in the metaverse is correctly identified as advertising. This may be far from easy in the metaverse given images or products being promoted are unlikely to be static adverts, and will be immersive. Advertising warnings are likely to impact on the aesthetic in the metaverse so we expect to see creative variations in respect of the same. Any advertising warnings however must be sufficiently clear to ensure that it is

68 Section 3 – the Consumer Protection from Unfair Trading Regulations 2008.

69 https://www.asa.org.uk/news/things-can-only-get-meta-a-brief-guide-to-ad-regulation-in-the-metaverse.html.

70 https://www.asa.org.uk/about-asa-and-cap/about-regulation/our-purpose-and-strategy.html.

71 https://www.asa.org.uk/news/at-60-the-asa-and-advertising-continues-to-change.html.

72 https://www.shs-conferences.org/articles/shsconf/pdf/2023/26/shsconf_copeji2023_02003.pdf.

73 https://www.asa.org.uk/about-asa-and-cap/about-regulation/our-purpose-and-strategy.html.

74 https://www.asa.org.uk/static/uploaded/3af39c72-76e1-4a59-b2b47e81a034cd1d.pdf.

obvious that it is advertising[75] before the user engages with it.[76] Whilst at this stage advertising in the metaverse would not be considered as advertising on broadcast media, should the metaverse increase in popularity and its use increase as expected, it is likely new rules will apply or even the Broadcasting Code[77] could be extended to cover these platforms.

8.62 Where users of the metaverse are able to click through from something in the metaverse to purchase something – affiliate marketing – this will be governed by the ASA and the Cap Code will apply. As it evolves the metaverse is likely to include a significant amount of affiliate marketing.

Marketing agreements

8.63 Any agreement for marketing in the metaverse should be carefully governed by detailed commercial agreements given action can also be taken against the brand owners by the ASA where the CAP Code is infringed. Brands looking to create specialist metaverse platforms or 'microverse'[78] like Nikeworld and McDonald's My Happy Place will need to specifically negotiate commercial terms which should include specific considerations around ownership of intellectual property rights created for the projects, what can be used for other projects by the developers, and revenue shares.

Virtual influencers

8.64 We expect to see a rise in the use of influencer avatars in the metaverse, since we are already seeing AI-created influencers on social media.[79] Both real-life and virtual influencers in the metaverse will have to make it clear where they have been paid to promote a specific product in the metaverse. This may be their avatar using a specific product or even branded skin – or even potentially the look of an avatar should this itself be considered a trade mark or representation of a brand. Any influencers in the metaverse will have to comply with both the

75 The ASA Rulings in respect of influencers on social media are illustrative. In ASA Ruling on Emma Louise Connolly 18 August 2021 the ASA ruled that Instagram posts had to ' ensure that they made clear the commercial intent of their posts in future, and to ensure that their future ads were obviously identifiable as marketing communications, and that identifiers such as '#ad' were clearly and prominently displayed' – https://www.asa.org.uk/rulings/emma-louise-connolly-g21-1114838-emma-louise-connolly.html.

76 ASA Ruling on Prettylittlething.com Ltd on 7 April 2021 highlights that there should have been '#ad placed upfront' https://www.asa.org.uk/rulings/prettylittlething-com-ltd-a20-1082593-prettylittlething-com-ltd.html and in ASA Ruling on Britvic Soft Drinks Ltd a video in which Millie Mackintosh endorsed J20 'we considered consumers would not be aware before engagement that the post was an ad' https://www.asa.org.uk/rulings/britvic-soft-drinks-ltd-a15-305687.html.

77 https://www.ofcom.org.uk/tv-radio-and-on-demand/broadcast-codes/broadcast-code.

78 https://in.mashable.com/tech/27591/microverse-is-the-next-big-thing-in-metaverse-all-you-need-to-know.

79 https://www.euronews.com/next/2024/03/22/meet-the-first-spanish-ai-model-earning-up-to-10000-per-month.

UK Code of Non-broadcast Advertising and Direct & Promotional Marketing (CAP Code) and the Consumer Protection from Unfair Trading Regulations 2008.

8.65 It is important that users ensure that any terms of use for the metaverse platforms are compatible with how they are intending to use the metaverse for their marketing and advertising.[80] Particular attention is required in respect of the ownership of any intellectual property rights generated. For example, in Roblox an IP licence is always granted in favour of Roblox for any avatar created by a user whereas any intellectual property in a virtual item that is created remains with the creator.[81] There is a risk therefore under such terms where the avatar itself is the advertising commodity, such as a metaverse influencer for example, and the advertiser wants to monetise the avatar itself either on other platforms or offline in real life. As discussed in **Chapter 5** there is a question over whether image rights can be afforded to an avatar, as well as the use of image rights in avatars relating to public figures.

In-game advertising

8.66 The Committee of Advertising Practice has issued guidance in respect of advertising for in-game purchases. This will cover the gaming use of the metaverse. Any in-game advertising cannot be 'materially misleading'.[82] The CAP Code will apply to in-game advertising where virtual currency is used to purchase an item. This is currency which is directly purchased with real money. It does not cover advertising where the in-game currency is earned by playing the game, even if this is a hybrid and users can also purchase the in-game currency to top it up.[83] This is likely to be complex to determine in the metaverse, especially as the metaverse continues to evolve. However, developers should not seek to try and avoid the Code by introducing gamification rewards since, as with all regulation and regulators, the implementation of the Code is likely to evolve as more harms are identified. Extensive regulation will be required in due course to protect users in the metaverse given the risks with advertising in this forum. Where real-life currency is used to purchase items in the metaverse then this will be covered by the Code.

Advertising of cryptoassets

8.67 Until October 2023 the ASA dealt with technical claims in respect of the advertising of cryptoassets, however, this has now been taken over by the Financial

80 https://www.shs-conferences.org/articles/shsconf/pdf/2023/26/shsconf_copeji2023_02003.pdf.

81 https://www.shs-conferences.org/articles/shsconf/pdf/2023/26/shsconf_copeji2023_02003.pdf.

82 Code 3.1.

83 https://www.asa.org.uk/static/4028c436-5861-4035-8d98c148d3c66b7e/Guidance-on-advertising-in-game-purchases.pdf.

Conduct Authority (FCA) for qualifying cryptoassets.[84] The FCA now governs the promotion of cryptoassets.[85] Many cryptoassets are considered financial promotions[86] and subject to the Financial Promotion Rules for Cryptoassets.[87] The aim of the FCA rules is to protect consumers. The rules only apply where the asset is transferrable and fungible. Should these rules be breached there are criminal sanctions, compensation and any contract would be rendered unenforceable. If a cryptobusiness is registered with the FCA it would be able to promote its own cryptoasset. Financial promotions of cryptoassets must be fair, clear and not misleading.[88] Proper risk warnings will be required for financial promotions. Many NFTs however, will remain outside of the scope of the FCA and instead require compliance with the ASA. The ASA ruled that advertisers were required to make it clear that any such NFT is an unregulated cryptoasset.[89]

Product placement

8.68 Product placement will be a significant concern within the metaverse but this will be different from the issues we have seen with product placement in real life. This is because the product placement in the metaverse will be both immersive and interactive. There is the scope for such marketing to be specifically directed and tailored to the specific user. In **Chapter 4** we explored whether there should be protection for neuro-rights.

8.69 Product placement for broadcast media is dealt with under Rule 9 of the Broadcast Code and whilst at this stage advertising in the metaverse will not fall under the Broadcast Code given the risks inherent in respect of advertising in the metaverse it is likely that there will be additional restraints imposed on advertising in the metaverse which may be akin to those currently imposed in respect of broadcast media.

BUSINESS STRUCTURES

8.70 Whilst traditional business entities[90] still exist in the metaverse, there has been a rise of Decentralised Autonomous Organisations (DAOs) within the

84 https://www.asa.org.uk/news/financial-conduct-authority-rules-on-advertising-cryptoassets.html.

85 https://www.fca.org.uk/news/news-stories/guidance-crypto-firms-help-them-comply-marketing-rules.

86 Financial promotions are subject to section 21 of the Financial Services and Markets Act 2000 ('FSMA').

87 https://www.fca.org.uk/publication/policy/ps23-6.pdf.

88 COB 4.2 and as applicable Principle 7 or Principle 12 and PRIN 2A.5.3R – https://www.fca.org.uk/publication/finalised-guidance/fg23-3.pdf.

89 The ASA ruled in respect of social media advertising in Turtle United NFT on 21 December 2022 – https://www.asa.org.uk/rulings/turtle-united-nft-a22-1162126-turtle-united-nft.html.

90 such as limited companies, limited liability partnerships, public companies, charities, partnerships and sole traders

blockchain community. The metaverse platform Decentraland is itself owned via a DAO.[91] A DAO is effectively a virtual organisation whereby decisions about governance are made collaboratively by the individual members who are connected via the software coding and their decisions trigger an automated output actioned via a smart contract. The individual owners can participate in a vote, as they would in a traditional company, and once a pre-agreed threshold is reached it would automatically trigger the agreed output executed via the smart contract. Everything is recorded on the blockchain, enabling transparency. This means there is no traditional hierarchy within the organisation. A DAO is currently not recognised as its own distinct legal structure in the UK. They are however recognised in Liechtenstein, Panama, the Marshall Islands, the US state of Wyoming, the Cayman Islands and Switzerland.

8.71 The Law Commission put out a call for evidence in 2022 on DAOs[92] and one point it wanted to address was why so few DAOs are based in the UK. Interestingly the Law Commission is also exploring whether there should ever be circumstances where a smart contract should have its own legal personality.[93] The Financial Markets Law Committee has also established a working group exploring DAOs and their impact on wholesale financial markets.[94]

8.72 In July 2024 the Law Commission released its 'Decentralised autonomous organisations (DAOs) a scoping paper' in response to its 2022 call for evidence.[95] At this stage it does not recommend that it is necessary to have specific legislative framework to address DAOs, principally because, as discussed below, there is not yet an established view on DAOs and therefore these are currently taking many different guises from the purely philanthropic to DeFi investment vehicles.

8.73 The Law Commission has confirmed that there are many different varieties of DAO and that its definition is still not yet settled. In fact, it confirms that being labelled a DAO itself may not be sufficient to indicate any specific type of structure and it is necessary to dissect how each specific DAO has been structured, the underlying protocols in the smart contracts, how it is effected and its purpose, to be able to make any decision as to its legal treatment and the way it is taxed. It may be premature to determine whether there is one collective way in which such systems can be governed or how they can behave or act. Just like smart contracts themselves it may be that traditional legal structures[96] can largely remain the same, perhaps with some evolution to reflect a change in

91 https://decentraland.org/dao/.

92 https://s3-eu-west-2.amazonaws.com/cloud-platform-e218f50a4812967ba1215eaecede923f/uploads/sites/30/2022/11/DAOs-Call-for-Evidence-LC.pdf.

93 https://s3-eu-west-2.amazonaws.com/cloud-platform-e218f50a4812967ba1215eaecede923f/uploads/sites/30/2022/11/DAOs-Call-for-Evidence-LC.pdf.

94 https://fmlc.org/projects/decentralised-autonomous-organisations/.

95 https://cloud-platform-e218f50a4812967ba1215eaecede923f.s3.amazonaws.com/uploads/sites/30/2024/07/DAOs-scoping-paper-110724.pdf.

96 Such as sole trader, partnerships, unincorporated associations, limited liability, public limited.

societal expectations, but the governance and running of the organisation is what is moved onto the blockchain instead to reflect a desire for transparency.

8.74 The Law Commission[97] considers that at one extreme is the idea of the 'pure DAO': these are set up by developers to be truly decentralised, typically via governance and control being entirely delegated to token-holders. In fact in some cases the DAO is so decentralised as a result of its structure that some consider there is no one actually making any decisions. The Law Commission considers in such cases it may be difficult to ascertain who is legally culpable but it would expect there to be some form of liability and instead it would likely fall to the courts to determine the exact nature of the relationships, most likely retrospectively.

8.75 This is perhaps more complex, at least for now, when contracting with businesses in the metaverse. Since we do not yet have full clarity on this new type of business, and for many ordinary users they will either be incapable of having access to the underlying specifics of the smart contract protocols or they would not understand them even if they did. In fact, in most cases we expect that most would not even properly consider the specific details of their contracting party[98] and therefore we expect to see a number of disputes where someone has contracted with a DAO without knowing that they have done so.

8.76 At this stage a standalone DAO[99] would not automatically attract limited liability status akin to a company or limited liability partnership and depending on how it has been structured it may be treated more like an unincorporated association[100] or even a traditional partnership.[101] There is clearly a risk with the lack of limited liability and distinct legal personality. Under the Partnership Act 1890 each partner is jointly and severally liable for all acts of its partner. Therefore, unless the DAO is correctly governed with suitable indemnities setting out the liability and responsibilities of the partners then, if it is determined to be a partnership,[102] each partner stands liable for all decisions taken by the other partners, regardless of whether they have supported them or not.

97 In its July 2024 paper at https://cloud-platform-e218f50a4812967ba1215eaecede923f.s3.amazonaws.com/uploads/sites/30/2024/07/DAOs-scoping-paper-110724.pdf.

98 This is the case with contracting parties generally even with traditional business structures, it is common-place to see contracts concluded without full consideration of whom are the contracting parties with numerous assumptions being made across the board. This typically only comes to light in a dispute where a contract may have been found to have been made with a foreign subsidiary or even non-trading or previously struck off entities.

99 Without a legal wrapper.

100 The Law Commission considers that it is likely to turn on the purpose of the DAO: https://cloud-platform-e218f50a4812967ba1215eaecede923f.s3.amazonaws.com/uploads/sites/30/2024/07/DAOs-scoping-paper-110724.pdf.

101 https://s3-eu-west-2.amazonaws.com/cloud-platform-e218f50a4812967ba1215eaecede923f/uploads/sites/30/2022/11/DAOs-Call-for-Evidence-LC.pdf.

102 The Law Commission question whether most pure DAO's would be categorised as partnerships and ultimately it will turn on the facts as to whether the legal test for a general partnership is satisfied or not placing significant reliance on the commentary in R I Banks, Lindley & Banks on Partnership (20th ed 2017).

8.77 There are clear risks for those looking to contract with a DAO in particular where this type of entity is not recognised in the jurisdiction. Given on the whole the DAO structure itself does not attract its own distinct legal personality under English Law you will need to delve deeply into any contractual relationship to understand the contracting parties and who will be liable in the event of a dispute and really understand how the DAO is structured and whether it meets the criteria as an unincorporated association, partnership or even a trust. Under the law of England and Wales a DAO per se would not be able to contract in its own name nor would it be able to hold property.

8.78 Given the DAO does not itself have a distinct legal personality in the UK there are likely to be insurance issues for DAOs seeking insurance and they are likely to be insured as either an unincorporated associated or a partnership. In the event that the insurance terms are not complied with by the insured then cover would not be available. Given the novelty of the DAO care must be taken to ensure that insurance is properly in place prior to contracting with a DAO. There are also risks from a regulatory perspective for its members if the DAO is participating in a regulated activity.

8.79 It is unclear at this time how a claim through the courts in England and Wales would deal with a DAO even where it has been properly incorporated in a different jurisdiction and holding legal status in that jurisdiction as a DAO. Types of structures used by DAOs in other jurisdictions include existing entities such as ownerless foundations[103] and special purpose trusts[104] as well as other new forms of entities created for DAOs[105] such as a Blockchain-based Limited Liability Company as used in Vermont, DAO LLC in Wyoming and decentralised organisations in Tennessee. Places such as the Marshall Islands have changed their laws to enable DAOs to qualify as limited liability entities.

8.80 Caution must be taken when considering the nature of any business entity in the metaverse. It is possible for a DAO to include some form of incorporated entity such as a limited company within its structure (or may be a digital legal entity as identified by the Law Commission) but then separate out different parts of the operation and governance. Any investigation will need to explore first principles to identify the entity. Where the DAO is treated either as an unincorporated association or partnership then all its members or partners could be at risk of being jointly and severally liable for any decisions made, damages or contractual liabilities. This means that one member could be sued in their own name for the entire breach.

8.81 The EU Commission is currently undertaking its own study into DAOs which is expected to be published in 2025.

103 Such as used in Cayman Islands, Panama and Switzerland.

104 Used in Cayman Islands and Guernsey.

105 https://s3-eu-west-2.amazonaws.com/cloud-platform-e218f50a4812967ba1215eaecede923f/uploads/sites/30/2022/11/DAOs-Call-for-Evidence-LC.pdf.

8.82 For now, if there is knowledge that a user is contracting with a DAO it is important first to properly unravel the true nature of that entity and take suitable steps to mitigate some of the risks of enforcement, as discussed more in **Chapter 16**. This may, for example include some form of security being held in escrow should there be a default.

COMPETITION LAW AND MONOPOLIES IN THE METAVERSE

8.83 Competition and anti-trust law will apply in the metaverse and there is a need for proper regulation and scrutiny.[106] The buying sprees undertaken by the Tech Giants in new and emerging technologies is likely to continue to be the practice in the metaverse as it has been with AI.[107]

8.84 The different competition regulators are already closely following developments in the metaverse. The Competition Commission for the European Commission has confirmed that it is keeping a close eye on the metaverse.[108]

8.85 Some legal commentators believe that current anti-trust laws are not suitable for governing and controlling the risk of monopolies of the Tech Giants and call for new forms of regulation.[109] They compare the level of control that Tech Giants have over online platforms to that of the railway companies in the late 1800 which resulted in the United States in The Sherman Anti-trust Act 1890.

A VIRTUAL WORKPLACE

8.86 In the metaverse the workplace is virtual. This is not the same as remote working, but an immersive experience where users can seamlessly interact with each other. The communication methods are integrated eradicating the disjointed nature of remote working.

8.87 The World Economic Forum highlights the six potential benefits of the metaverse for staff.[110] These are staff onboarding, helping to create the company's culture, training, recruitment, removing barriers and remote working. Meta has even created a specific work metaverse called 'workplace'.[111]

106 https://www.weforum.org/agenda/2023/03/metaverse-competition-regulation-and-other-stories-you-need-to-read-this-week/.

107 Bar Atrakchi-Israel & Yifat Nahmias, Metaverse, Competition, and the Online Digital Ecosystem, 24 MINN. J.L. SCI. & TECH. 235 (2023).

108 https://www.pymnts.com/cpi-posts/eu-eyes-competition-and-antitrust-in-metaverse/.

109 Bar Atrakchi-Israel & Yifat Nahmias, Metaverse, Competition, and the Online Digital Ecosystem, 24 MINN. J.L. SCI. & TECH. 235 (2023).

110 https://www.weforum.org/agenda/2023/01/6-world-of-work-challenges-the-metaverse-will-address-davos2023/.

111 https://en-gb.workplace.com.

8.88 Employers looking to move staff into the metaverse will need to ensure that they can sufficiently monitor their staff in this environment. Working in the metaverse is likely to be much more than just remote working or existing video conferencing. In the metaverse users will be working, interacting and conversing in the same physical space. There will be challenges for Human Resource departments to adapt to this new landscape. It is important that staff policies and processes are updated to reflect this new way of working. Employers need to remember that they remain vicariously liable for the actions of their employees whilst they are working in the metaverse. Given the nature of the landscape in the metaverse, and the risk of complacency as a result, employers should ensure that all staff are clear on their expectations when working and engaging with other members of staff in the metaverse. This would include work events in the metaverse, such as attending a virtual concert together or virtual bar.

HEALTH AND SAFETY AND OCCUPATIONAL HEALTH IN THE METAVERSE

8.89 In England every employer is responsible for ensuring the health, safety and welfare of their employees at work under the Health and Safety at Work etc Act 1974. There are potential serious health and safety risks for those working in the metaverse with the extensive use of virtual reality technology.[112] Employers will be required to undertake proper risk assessments in respect of the risks to their staff of using VR equipment as well as them spending prolonged periods of time in the metaverse.

8.90 Working in the metaverse will be intense and will require a considerable amount of concentration. Given the enhanced visibility in the metaverse workplace, and therefore scrutiny, it is likely that workers will feel unable to take sufficient breaks from their work. There is the heightened risk of computer vision syndrome (CVS) and studies show that the maximum length of time someone should spend using VR headsets is 70 minutes.[113] People have complained about stiff joints from prolonged periods of time in the metaverse and it is recommended that breaks involving some form of physical activity should be regularly scheduled.[114] VR headsets have been linked with heterophoria, cyberkinetosis and physiological changes.[115]

8.91 Whilst wearing VR equipment the user's awareness and ability to engage in real life will be reduced. Employers need to ensure that employees are operating the VR equipment and working from the metaverse in a safe space where the risk of them colliding with other objects is minimised. Employers should ensure that there are suitable insurances in place to cover the location

112 Potential challenges of working in a virtual space, Peter Sipka, Italian Labour Law e-Journal Issue 1, Vol. 16 (2023) ISSN 1561-8048.

113 https://www.etui.org/publications/working-metaverse-what-are-risks.

114 https://dl.acm.org/doi/pdf/10.1145/3544548.3581306.

115 https://www.etui.org/publications/working-metaverse-what-are-risks.

where the employee is physically located. There have been studies that have found that there may be short term effects on a user's reaction time and hand/eye coordination following the sustained user of virtual reality and therefore this should be factored into working patterns to ensure that the user can safely travel home if necessary.

8.92 There are positives however for staff working in the metaverse. Studies have found there to be an increased sense of wellbeing and that workers leaving the metaverse at the end of a shift felt like they had left work unlike complaints with remote working and work impeding onto family life.[116]

TRAINING IN THE METAVERSE

8.93 Under the Health and Safety at Work etc Act 1974, s 2(2)(c) there is a requirement that all employers provide all training necessary to ensure the health and safety of its employees at work. There are many opportunities for the metaverse to be used for training within organisations. PWC found that of the businesses it questioned 34% considered that training was one of the main benefits of the metaverse.[117]

8.94 Employers have to ensure that where training is deployed in the metaverse, especially if this replaces other forms of training, that this is suitable and sufficient training to meet their statutory obligations.

CONCLUSION

8.95 This chapter considers business in the metaverse. The key-takeaway points are:

- It is vital to understand exactly what is being traded in the metaverse. This will involve the deconstruction of the underlying goods and services into its raw components. This is important to understand what would be a condition of any contract, where there may be misrepresentation and what terms may be suitable to be implied into any contract.
- Currently the different platforms are governed by contractual terms of use. These set parameters over what can and cannot be done on each platform. In most of these liability of the platform has been excluded as much as legally possible.
- Regulation (EU) 2019/1150 is relevant to business users of the metaverse and seeks to offer some protection for EU traders when dealing with the non-negotiable terms of the tech platforms.

116 https://dl.acm.org/doi/pdf/10.1145/3544548.3581306.

117 https://www.pwc.com/us/en/tech-effect/emerging-tech/virtual-reality-study.html.

- Basic principles of contracting should not be forgotten in the metaverse. It is essential that careful consideration is given to ensure that all requirements are properly fulfilled, even if this is effected by the underlying technology or takes place in a new and immersive environment.
- Existing consumer protection laws are considered, at least by the EU to be sufficiently robust to deal with the metaverse. In the UK some attention is needed as to whether it is necessary to distinguish digital services and real-life services in the same way that is done by the EU in the Digital Content Directive.
- Technologists will need to work with lawyers to work out the best way in which mandatory terms are brought to the attention of users and how best to properly incorporate contractual terms.
- Advertising in the metaverse requires careful consideration. Existing laws and regulations will apply but we also expect to see extensions to this to deal with the metaverse especially with constraints around the use of biometric data for advertising decisions and the use of immersive advertising for children.
- Novel business structures are emerging in Web3 and blockchain. These will rise to prominence in the metaverse. It is important that there is careful consideration as to the exact legal entity as this will have a significant impact on all interactions in the metaverse, from its ability to own assets, to contract and to be sued for breach.
- Employment law in the metaverse is, at least for now, likely to remain under the laws as to where the real-life employee is physically based but this is likely to change. There are serious considerations as to vicarious liability, as well as health and safety.

Chapter 9

The industrial metaverse

'The real future of the metaverse is not for consumers'

Pekka Lundmark, CEO of Nokia

9.01 The industrial metaverse is the term used to describe the application of the metaverse to the industrial sector. It forms what is being termed as Industry 4.0. The World Economic Forum estimated in March 2024 that the industrial metaverse was estimated to grow to a value of $100 billion by 2030, with 75% of companies in advance industries already using digital twin and fuelling the next industrial revolution.[1]

9.02 The industrial metaverse typically uses digital twins to digitally recreate specific parts of the industrial process. This enables users to design, train and test different processes throughout the industrial supply chain process in real-time. There are numerous opportunities for the use of the metaverse in the industrial space and different initiatives trying to connect digital twins together to recreate real life. In many cases the use of digital twins is being combined with artificial intelligence; data is extracted from the digital twin simulations and is used to train the artificial intelligence systems and gain insights and learnings.

9.03 Historically it was often a dangerous and expensive task to test new iterations in industrial processes, but all this has been revolutionised with the industrial metaverse whereby users can converge together and stress test different options and scenarios in an immersive virtual environment where, subject to connectivity issues, different users can be based anywhere in the world. For example, Siemens created a digital twin to mirror a 73,000 sqm factory and boasted an increase in productivity of 20% and Unilever created a digital twin of its production line which has reduced capital expenditure by 70%.[2]

9.04 Whilst there are many opportunities for the industrial metaverse, when surveyed over 36% of people considered that there were unique legal and regulatory challenges of the industrial metaverse.[3] One of the key challenges with the industrial metaverse is the lack of consistent regulations.[4]

1 https://www3.weforum.org/docs/WEF_Navigating_the_Industrial_Metaverse_A_Blueprint_2024.pdf.

2 https://assets.new.siemens.com/siemens/assets/api/uuid:e36f2de7-f3c4-481f-bb20-9791dc12bbec/the-emergent-industrial-metaverse-update-2024.pdf.

3 https://onestore.nokia.com/asset/i/213304.

4 Tantawi, K., Fidan, I., Huseynov, O. et al. Advances in industry 4.0: from intelligentization to the industrial metaverse. Int J Interact Des Manuf (2024). https://doi.org/10.1007/s12008-024-01750-0.

9.05 Despite the difficulties with regulations, the industrial metaverse itself has the potential to revolutionise how regulators themselves can assess and monitor their industry. The metaverse enables regulators to assess the impact of its new rules and consider potential real-life implication, which is being explored by innovators such as Simulnova Software Ltd.[5] The EU established the Virtual and Augmented Reality Industrial Coalition in 2020 to bring together industry and policy-makers.[6] Amongst others it puts its objectives as encouraging:

1 the growth of sustainable XR across Europe;

2 standard operating systems and protocols such as the Open Metaverse Interoperability Protocol (OMI);

3 discussions between different industries concerning XR;

9.06 This chapter covers the idea of the industrial metaverse, which is looking to solve real-life industrial issues using the metaverse.

DIGITAL TWINS

9.07 A digital twin is a virtual simulation of a real-life object. This may be part of a machine, a full virtual working model of a machine or even property, buildings and whole cities. A digital twin typically uses both AI and data sensors as well as XR. Data is typically collected via an internet of things (IoT) device or sensor and artificial intelligence is used for modelling and prediction.

9.08 One of the leading industrial metaverse platforms is the NVIDIA Omniverse which enables users to create digital twins. A number of high-profile enterprise clients use the NVIDIA Omniverse including BMW, Mercedes-Benz, Siemens Energy and the UK Atomic Energy Authority.[7]

Legal issues with digital twins

9.09 There are currently many gaps in most of the regulation of Industry 4.0.[8] This stems from the fact that there are new legal issues arising from the emerging changes in morals and ethics in the digital revolution; states are wanting to balance this risk against fostering innovation, international competition and digital sovereignty.

5 https://www.techuk.org/resource/guest-blog-digital-twins-and-virtual-testing-of-regulatory-remedies.html.

6 https://digital-strategy.ec.europa.eu/en/policies/virtual-and-augmented-reality-coalition#:~:text=The%20Virtual%20and%20Augmented%20Reality%20Industrial%20Coalition%20is%20a%20platform,Media%20and%20Audiovisual%20Action%20Plan.

7 https://www.nvidia.com/en-gb/omniverse/platform/enterprise-systems/.

8 Elizaveta A. Gromova, Natalia S. Koneva and Elena V. Titova, Legal barriers to the implementation of digital industry (Industry 4.0) components and ways to overcome them Journal of World Intellect Property (2022) 1–20.

9.10 One of the main issues with digital twins is also their most important feature, the acute need for accuracy as between the real-life object and the virtual object. If the digital twin fails to accurately replicate the real-life object then much of its value is depleted. There is a considerable legal risk for developers designing digital twins, should the digital twin not exactly mirror the real-life object. In order to create the digital twin a significant amount of data has to be extracted from the real-life object and this data has to be fed into the digital twin and enable real-time updates to ensure that the digital twin remains up-to-date and relevant. This data has to be accurate or it will result in inaccurate models and in turn the digital twin will not be accurate and therefore not useful. Complexities however arise when different parties create different parts of the digital twin. Careful consideration must be had as to where liability sits where there is an inaccuracy and whether this is as a result of the sensors or as a result of the coding. Liability is therefore a key consideration in any contract dealing with digital twin technology.

9.11 The Centre for Digital Built Britain, a University of Cambridge initiative which ran for five years until 2022 created a framework for its national digital twin initiative known as the Gemini Principles.[9] Since this time, however, there has been an explosion in the use and abilities of AI. The national digital twin project was designed to try and build federated digital twin ecosystem infrastructure to enable collaboration between different stakeholders. There are nine guiding principles broken down under the headings of 'purpose', and 'trust' and 'function'. At its heart is the guiding principle that the digital twin must be for the public good. Further, digital twins should prioritise governance, security, openness and the integrity of data.

9.12 Digital twins are suspectable to cyber-attack. It is important that suitable security measures are put in place to minimise risk associated with ransom attacks and even terrorist attacks focused on key infrastructure. Nokia confirms that from its surveys the main concern for the use of the industrial metaverse is cyber and information risks given the significant amount of data.[10]

9.13 Digital twins require a significant amount of power and are intrinsically linked to the 5G movement. There are risks to the digital twin and its integrity in the event that there is a power outage or internet failure.

9.14 The Alan Turing Institute has created the TRIC-DT Innovation and Impact Hub for digital twins.[11] The aim of the Hub is to create an open access platform for digital twin technology. The Alan Turing Institute is running a number of different projects including the Trustworthy and Ethical Assurance for Digital Twins (TEA-DT) project. As part of the project the platform assists

9 https://www.cdbb.cam.ac.uk/DFTG/GeminiPrinciples.
10 https://onestore.nokia.com/asset/i/213304.
11 https://www.turing.ac.uk/research/research-projects/tric-dt.

participants with identifying the ethical objectives of their product and legal considerations to understand best practices.

9.15 Many businesses venturing into the industrial metaverse space are already highly regulated and as a result they will need to be able to persuade their regulators of the safety and security of the use of digital twins and its benefit to their business.[12]

Contracting in relation to digital twins

9.16 It is of fundamental importance that there is a bespoke and comprehensive agreement for the development of any digital twin by a third party. Oliver Röpke, President of the European Economic and Social Committee (EESC) considers that there is a need for new types of licensing and collaboration agreements to deal with this emerging technology.[13]

9.17 Key issues to include within such an agreement include the risk of inaccurate replications and data. Clear provisions should be put in place for liability where there is a discrepancy between the real-life object and its digital twin.

9.18 There is a strong movement, as discussed below, for the need for active collaboration between different parties within the industrial metaverse in order to maximise its value. It makes no sense to have your digital twin sitting in isolation when in real life the object is part of a wider process or ecosystem. As a result, there is a call for the industrial metaverse being coded in a common software language to enable a 'plug and play' type of system.[14]

9.19 Any contract will have to be clear who owns the data generated via the digital twin. Consideration will have to be had as to what that data can be used for and for what duration.

9.20 There is a need for true collaboration between organisations and enterprises to be able to create a true industrial metaverse.[15] The Alan Turing Institute refers to the need for an 'ecosystem of digital twins' or EDTs.[16] It is important that any relationship is clear over what data is confidential, what data can be shared and for what this can be used. The Climate Resilience Demonstrator has created a template data exploration licence which deals with the sharing of

12 https://onestore.nokia.com/asset/i/213304.

13 https://www.eesc.europa.eu/en/our-work/opinions-information-reports/opinions/initiative-virtual-worlds-such-metaverse.

14 https://assets.new.siemens.com/siemens/assets/api/uuid:e36f2de7-f3c4-481f-bb20-9791dc12bbec/the-emergent-industrial-metaverse-update-2024.pdf.

15 https://www.siemens.com/global/en/company/digital-transformation/industrial-metaverse/the-emergent-industrial-metaverse.html.

16 https://www.turing.ac.uk/research/research-projects/ecosystems-digital-twins.

data for the purpose of the project.[17] Under the licence the data can be stored on the servers of those hosting or creating the digital twin and the data can be shared with authorised third parties. The licence prevents the commercial exploitation of the data being shared without the consent of the owner of that data.

The National Digital Twin Programme (NDTP)

9.21 The UK Government has established the National Digital Twin Programme (NDPT) which is overseen by the Department for Business and Trade. The NDPT is designed as a national programme to grow digital twin technologies in the UK.

9.22 Whilst at this stage there is no specific regulation or law specifically covering digital twins in the UK, the principles of the NDTP go some way to establishing the key framework considerations in respect of building a digital twin and in turn the priorities identified as fundamental by the relevant government departments. One of the seven principles of the NDTP is to 'establish the rules of the road'[18] and therefore the learnings taken from this programme are expected to go some way to developing future standards, codes, rules, governance and legislation concerning digital twins.

9.23 With this in mind the rules established by the NDPT for someone to contribute to the programme are important. They set the tone on the minimum requirements that are expected when building a digital twin and go some way to setting out the underpinning fundamental requirements of the UK Government on the idea of digital twins. The Government has stipulated that to contribute to the NDPT it is necessary that the digital twin is safe, secure, trustworthy, ethical, sustainable, adaptable and interoperable.[19] We expect these principles to form the backbone of any future regulation or legislation concerning digital twins.

9.24 Current NDPT projects include the modelling of digital twins to test the use of different energy sources in the Isle of Wight with the aim of the Isle of Wight being autonomous and self-sufficient in respect of energy.[20]

9.25 In January 2024 the Virtual Energy Programme and the National Digital Twin Programme signed a memorandum of understanding to collaborate on data sharing in the energy sector.

17 https://digitaltwinhub.co.uk/download/credo-data-exploration-license-template/.
18 https://www.gov.uk/government/publications/what-a-digital-twin-is-and-how-you-can-contribute/national-digital-twin-programme-ndtp-principles.
19 https://www.gov.uk/government/publications/what-a-digital-twin-is-and-how-you-can-contribute/national-digital-twin-programme-ndtp-principles.
20 https://www.gov.uk/government/case-studies/energy-system-national-digital-twin-programme-ndtp.

SUPPLY CHAIN

9.26 One key use case for the industrial metaverse is within the supply chain. Some of the issues that global supply chains faced during the Covid-19 pandemic and resulting global lockdowns may have accelerated the adoption of this technology for those involved with global supply chains. The industrial metaverse is already being implemented by industry leaders; for example Kraft Heinz has joined with Microsoft to create a digital twin of its supply chain to explore amongst other issues why there were issues with their ketchup packets getting stuck in machinery during production.[21]

9.27 Deloitte joined with the Manufacturing Leadership Council to investigate the industrial metaverse and its use in the supply chain.[22] Its key areas of concern included having access to necessary talent in order to develop the infrastructure required as well as intellectual property and cyber security.

9.28 Nokia highlights the use of the industrial metaverse to be able to track the supply chain virtually and identify where there may be weaknesses along the way.[23] This includes energy consumption and logistics, meaning accurate forecasts can be created. Nokia highlights that the food and beverage industries are embracing the use of the industrial metaverse in particular to improve its supply chain from inception all the way to the end customer.[24]

9.29 The World Economic Forum highlights the use of digital twins by Amazon Robotics to analyse its warehousing functionality.[25] These are being built by Nvidia Omniverse and are used to run simulations of the robotics being deployed in the Amazon warehouses.[26]

9.30 The World Economic Forum has developed the Advanced Manufacturing and Supply Chain Hub as part of its Global Collaboration Village[27] which includes hubs on 'advanced manufacturing and supply chain' and a hub for energy. The platform uses XR to enable users to collaborate within the ecosystem.

21 https://digitaltwininsider.com/2022/06/07/metaverse-ketchup-how-kraft-heinz-is-using-digital-twin-technology-to-boost-optimization/.

22 https://www2.deloitte.com/uk/en/insights/industry/manufacturing/industrial-metaverse-applications-smart-factory.html.

23 https://onestore.nokia.com/asset/i/213304.

24 https://onestore.nokia.com/asset/i/213322.

25 https://www3.weforum.org/docs/WEF_Navigating_the_Industrial_Metaverse_A_Blueprint_2024.pdf.

26 https://www.youtube.com/watch?v=-VQLqs6s9y0.

27 https://www.weforum.org/agenda/2024/01/global-collaboration-village-xr-technology-manufacturing-supply-chains/.

SMART FACTORIES

9.31 One application of the industrial metaverse to manufacturing is the use of smart factories, examples being Mercedes-Benz which has joined forces with Microsoft to map out its manufacturing facilities[28] and Mars which collaborated with Accenture to create a digital twin of its factory in Illinois.[29] These are typical digital twins of real-life manufacturing facilities which use real-time data collected from real-life facilities to power an XR version of the facility. They are used to simulate the production lines and test new functionalities and productions. Smart factories combine a variety of different technologies including artificial intelligence, internet of things and virtual reality. 83% of manufacturers believe that that smart factories will revolutionise manufacturing.[30]

9.32 The World Economic Forum published its White Paper in January 2023 on The Future of Industrial Strategies: Five Grand Challenges for Resilient Manufacturing.[31] It identified the five challenges for industrial businesses as:

1 sustainability;

2 resilience;

3 developing new techniques;

4 suitable workforces;

5 socio-environmental concerns.

9.33 In real life there are numerous legal considerations impacting manufacturers. The Supply of Machinery (Safety) Regulations 2008 deal with the supply of machines into the UK market. It is an offence for a manufacturer to supply machinery unless it complies with this regulation. As part of the regulations there is the requirement to carry out a risk assessment on the products and supply certain evidence that the machinery is safe. The industrial metaverse and digital twins will enable manufacturers to stress test the machinery in a virtual environment to ensure it can comply with these regulations. The testing necessary to pass the UKCA and CE marking could be simulated in the metaverse. The identification of hazards can take place in the metaverse and reduce exposure to the same.

28 https://news.microsoft.com/2022/10/12/mercedes-benz-and-microsoft-collaborate-to-boost-efficiency-resilience-and-sustainability-in-car-production/.

29 https://newsroom.accenture.com/news/2022/accenture-collaborates-with-mars-to-develop-factory-of-the-future-using-ai-cloud-edge-and-digital-twins.

30 https://www.deloitte.com/content/dam/assets-shared/docs/industries/energy-resources-industrials/2024/gx-smart-factory-brochure-new.pdf.

31 https://www3.weforum.org/docs/WEF_The_Future_of_Industrial_Strategies_2023.pdf.

PRODUCT LIABILITY

9.34

The General Product Safety Regulations 2005 govern product safety in the UK and is overseen by Office of Product Safety and Standards and enforced by Trading Standards. Any business which manufactures, imports, distributes or sells goods to consumers must ensure that the goods are safe.[32] Producers have the further obligation under the General Product Safety Regulations 2005, reg 7(3) to take measures to be informed of risks of harm that the product may cause.

The metaverse has the opportunity to assist businesses with testing products to ensure that they are safe. There is the risk, however, that faults in testing using simulated environments may actually cause harm and expose the product to failings under The General Product Safety Regulations 2005 and other safety standards. There is the risk that any software failure could result in product liability issues or production failures.[33] Digital twins are vulnerable to cyber attack.[34] If a digital twin is attacked then this exposes a product to risk of malfunction, which may have a significant impact on the integrity of the product and its compliance with safety laws.

ENVIRONMENTAL LAW

9.35 Sustainability is being touted as one of the key benefits of the industrial metaverse.[35] EESC, however, stress that the metaverse uses a large amount of electricity and believes that there is a need for regulation to control this.[36]

9.36 Environmental considerations in the UK are governed by the Environment Act 2021. The legislation brings in the framework for new environmental targets for the UK including on the priority areas of air quality, water, biodiversity and waste reduction.[37] The legislation further enables the different national authorities of the UK to regulate producers' environmental obligations in respect of prevention of waste and increasing a minimum level of reuse/recycling/redistribution.[38] Depending on the specifics of this it is likely that use of the

32 Section 5 The General Product Safety Regulations 2005.

33 https://www.swissre.com/institute/research/sonar/sonar2023/digital-twins-virtual-testing-maintenance.html.

34 https://www.ibanet.org/Digital-twinning-technology-lawyers-urged-to-remain-vigilant-of-legal-risks.

35 https://onestore.nokia.com/asset/i/213304.

36 https://www.eesc.europa.eu/en/our-work/opinions-information-reports/opinions/initiative-virtual-worlds-such-metaverse.

37 Environment Act 2021, s 1(3).

38 Environment Act 2021, s 50(1) and conditions set out in Sch 4.

industrial metaverse will aid producers in meeting these objectives by reducing the environmental impacts of research, design and development phases, all of which are suited to being carried out in the industrial metaverse. In addition, it will enable the real-time monitoring of emissions to enable changes to be tested and then implemented with the desire to reduce the same. Siemens stresses the fundamental importance of the industrial metaverse in reducing emissions and the consumption of natural resources.[39] The World Economic Forum's Global Collaboration Village[40] has a focus on conservation and climate change.

9.37 The Climate Change Act 2008[41] commits the UK to reduce its greenhouse gas emissions to net zero by 2050. Scotland has set a target to be net zero by 2045 and Wales by 2030. The use of digital twins is an effective way of helping to achieve these objectives. Through the use of digital twins Tata Consulting Services boasts that it has enabled one production plant to cut its energy use by 15% and reduce CO_2 emissions by the same amount.[42]

9.38 The Climate Resilience Demonstrator (CReDo) has been established to create an infrastructure of digital twins of key infrastructure impacted by climate change.[43] The project is using data from Anglian Water, BT and UK Power Networks to create connected digital twins. CReDo has confirmed that it is working with some regulators already but is looking to try and engage with all regulators dealing with key infrastructure such as housing, transport and aviation.[44] The first phase of the project is looking at creating a digital twin of energy – both primary and secondary substations, and water – including sewage, pumping, water treatment and recycling, and telecommunications.

9.39 The European Digital Twin Ocean (European DTO) project [45] is an ambitious EU initiative which seeks to recreate the oceans, including not only mapping out the ocean floor but including biodiversity data and chemical data. It is aimed at trying to combat the impact of climate change on our oceans.

SPECIFIC AREAS

9.40 We turn now to specific areas which have adopted the industrial metaverse and consider some of the legal implications in respect of the same.

39 https://assets.new.siemens.com/siemens/assets/api/uuid:e36f2de7-f3c4-481f-bb20-9791dc12bbec/the-emergent-industrial-metaverse-update-2024.pdf.
40 https://www.globalcollaborationvillage.org/explore-the-village.
41 As amended by Climate Change Act 2008 (2050 Target Amendment) Order 2019.
42 https://azure.microsoft.com/en-us/blog/the-net-zero-journey-why-digital-twins-are-a-powerful-ally/.
43 https://digitaltwinhub.co.uk/climate-resilience-demonstrator-credo/.
44 https://digitaltwinhub.co.uk/climate-resilience-demonstrator-credo/taking-action/.
45 https://research-and-innovation.ec.europa.eu/funding/funding-opportunities/funding-programmes-and-open-calls/horizon-europe/eu-missions-horizon-europe/restore-our-ocean-and-waters/european-digital-twin-ocean-european-dto_en#:~:text=Aims%20to%20model%20the%20ocean%27s,predictions%20of%20its%20future%20behaviour.

Automotives

9.41 The automobile industry is heavily regulated both in the UK and globally. In an industry in which safety is paramount and there is considerable pressure to reduce carbon emissions it is not surprising that industry leaders are embracing the industrial metaverse. It is predicted that by 2030 the metaverse in respect of automotive sector will be worth $626.5 billion.[46] Renault has created an industrial metaverse of its manufacturing process[47] and it is estimated that by 2025 it will save about €580 million and will reduce warranty costs by about 60%.[48]

9.42 The automotive industry is embracing the metaverse in a number of ways including Skodaverse[49] which offers metaverse gaming experience in Fortnite and the use of NFTs in its vault and MINIverse[50] a gamification of the Mini buying experience and customisation of vehicles in MXE (Maserati Experience Engine).[51] It is expected that the industry will eventually embrace the metaverse from the initial design stages all the way to the final vehicle being test driven.

9.43 On or after 1 February 2024 all new models of vehicles will need to comply with the GB Type Approval. The UK Government is in the process of considering what international approvals will be accepted.[52] The UK is a party to the United Nations Economic Commission for Europe (UNECE) which seeks to harmonise specific standards in the production of vehicles.[53] UNECE is participating in the UN Virtual Worlds Day 2024 designed to 'harness the metaverse to advance the sustainable development goals'.[54]

9.44 In the EU, Regulation (EU) 2019/2144 deals with the safety requirements necessary for the approval of vehicles. Chapter 2 of the Regulations deals with obligations on manufacturers to be able to show that all new vehicles are compliant[55] and 'ensure that vehicles are designed, constructed and assembled so as to minimise the risk of injury to vehicle occupants and vulnerable road users'.[56]

46 https://www.motorfinanceonline.com/comment/driving-into-the-future-the-metaverses-impact-on-in-car-experiences/.
47 https://tw3partners.fr/industrial-metaverse-renault-revolution/.
48 https://media.renaultgroup.com/renault-group-launches-the-first-industrial-metaverse/.
49 https://www.skodaverseworld.com/?menu=metaverse.
50 https://www.mini.com/en_MS/home/progress/welcome-to-the-miniverse.html.
51 https://www.accenture.com/mu-en/case-studies/automotive/maserati-experience-engine.
52 https://www.gov.uk/government/consultations/updating-gb-type-approval-for-road-vehicles/updating-gb-type-approval-for-road-vehicles.
53 the UNECE 1958 Agreement concerning the adoption of harmonized technical united nations regulations for wheeled vehicles, equipment and parts which can be fitted and/or be used on wheeled vehicles and the conditions for reciprocal recognition of approvals granted on the basis of these united nations regulations (revision 3)- https://unece.org/trans/main/wp29/wp29regs.
54 https://www.itu.int/metaverse/un-virtual-worlds-day/about/.
55 Regulation (EU) 2019/2144 section 4(1).
56 Regulation (EU) 2019/2144 section 4(4).

The metaverse will be able to help manufacturers more readily demonstrate their compliance with this.

9.45 In the UK most car manufacturers have signed up to the Motor Ombudsman and the New Car Code which is governed by Trading Standards.[57] The Code states:

> 'Once you have ordered your new car, it is our responsibility to ensure that the car supplied to the retailer is manufactured to a high quality standard which will meet with your expectations.'

9.46 The industrial metaverse will be able to help car manufacturers ensure that their vehicles meet these standards before production even starts. The more of the design, development and testing that can be carried out virtually the lower the costs.

Energy

9.47 The Virtual Energy System or VirtualES was established by the National Grid ESO in 2021 with the aim of trying to help the UK to achieve its net zero and carbon free commitments.[58] The VirtualES aims to create connected digital twins in the energy sector which enable shared data and learning across the sector. The ambition of the VirtualES is to create a complete virtual mirror of the whole GB energy system which will operate and update in real time to mirror the real-life system.

9.48 In August 2023 the Virtual Energy System released its common framework.[59] The VirtualES equates the work it is trying to do to the Open Banking movement which sought to revolutionise FinTech. Its framework establishes technological requirements and the need for a governance framework in the virtual energy sector. The aim is to create an environment which fosters collaboration but retains integrity with the regulators. The digital twins are built on an open framework with shared protocols and requirements in respect of data requirements. New digital twins can be plugged into the system and together use and share the real-time data collected within the system. The VirtualES highlights that there is a significant need for a common governance structure within the digital energy sector to ensure that there is proper coordination and collaboration. The VirtualES has said that it would like to adopt a co-led form of governance. This would require a new organisation be established to oversee the initiative. The organisation would be backed by the Government but would have its own independent remit. This is yet to be formed but it shows what the industry and key stakeholders are seeking in this area.

57 https://www.tradingstandards.uk/media/mcl-new-car-code-2015.pdf.
58 https://www.nationalgrideso.com/future-energy/virtual-energy-system.
59 https://www.nationalgrideso.com/document/285406/download.

9.49 The VirtualES governance framework says that it has seven design principles.[60] These are:

1 Transparency;

2 Legitimacy;

3 Accountability;

4 Stakeholder engagement;

5 Responsiveness;

6 Participation;

7 Empowerment.

9.50 The VirtualES promotes six values.[61] These are:

1 transparency between users sharing data;

2 participants taking responsibility for their involvement, actions and data;

3 collaboration between users;

4 agility and responsiveness;

5 inclusion and treating participants fairly;

6 innovation.

9.51 The VirtualES stresses the importance of fitting within existing regulation of the energy sector.

9.52 ARUP which has been tasked to consider aspects of the VirtualES considered that there would be the need to consider the use of data within the governance framework.[62] One option is a data licence to enable users to access data for the purpose of the project and the other is the idea of a data trust.

Healthcare

9.53 The industrial metaverse is having a significant impact on the healthcare industry but currently it is under-regulated.[63] The metaverse is being used to train surgeons on simulated bodies and organs (as digital twins themselves). Dubai

60 https://www.nationalgrideso.com/document/285406/download.

61 https://www.nationalgrideso.com/document/285406/download.

62 https://www.nationalgrideso.com/document/268931/download.

63 It is estimated that the medical metaverse will be worth $71bn in the US by 2030 but there remains gaps in licensing and legal regulation according to Solaiman in the 'Metaverse: Legal & Ethical Challenges for Cross-Border care in Virtual Worlds' International Collaborations: The Future of Health Care – The Journal of Law, Medicine and Ethics, 51 (2023) 287 -300.

has created a virtual hospital as a digital twin of a real-life hospital.[64] In addition, the metaverse is being promoted as having the ability for patients to have virtual GP, healthcare appointments and assist patients suffering with mental health conditions.

9.54 Where the metaverse is being used to diagnose a medical condition, or being used as part of the treatment of a condition it would be considered as a medical device under definitions in both UK and EU regulation.[65] In the UK medical devices are regulated by the Medicines and Healthcare products Regulatory Agency (MHRA). Medical devices have to be registered with the MHRA and governed by the Medical Devices Regulations 2002, the General Product Safety Regulations 2005 and the Medicines and Medical Devices Act 2001. Software is capable of falling within the remit of being a medical device and is subject to regulation by the MHRA.[66] To register with the MHRA you need to be based in the UK or appoint a UK Responsible Person, this means international providers which are looking to provide medical services to UK users via the metaverse will have to take steps to register in the UK. In the EU a medical device is regulated under Regulation (EU) 2017/745 of the European Parliament and of the Council of 5 April 2017 on medical devices.[67]

9.55 Given the cross-border nature of the metaverse there are serious considerations in respect of the licensing and liability of medical professionals operating in the metaverse. Rules relating to such professionals are not universal, nor are rules on medication. From a pragmatic perspective there are different brand names for different medications throughout the world and some practices which may be lawful in one territory are unlawful in another. Should the medical metaverse reach its potential it will be important that there is a clear framework put in place to protect patients. There will need to be clear parameters drawn over territorial scope, who is liable for what, how and where sensitive personal data is stored and protected.

64 https://www.pwc.com/m1/en/industries/healthcare/the-future-of-healthcare-in-the-metaverse.html.

65 A 'Medical device' is defined under section 2 of the Medical Devices Regulations 2002 and Article 2(1) under Regulation (EU) 2017/745 of the European Parliament and of the Council of 5 April 2017.

66 https://assets.publishing.service.gov.uk/media/64a7d22d7a4c230013bba33c/Medical_device_stand-alone_software_including_apps__including_IVDMDs_.pdf.

67 Article 2(1) a medical device 'means any instrument, apparatus, appliance, **software**, implant, reagent, material or other article intended by the manufacturer to be used, alone or in combination, for human beings for one or more of the following specific medical purposes:

- diagnosis, prevention, monitoring, prediction, prognosis, treatment or alleviation of disease
- diagnosis, monitoring, treatment, alleviation of, or compensation for, an injury or disability,
- investigation, replacement or modification of the anatomy or of a physiological or pathological process or state,
- providing information by means of in vitro examination of specimens derived from the human body, including organ, blood and tissue donations,
- and which does not achieve its principal intended action by pharmacological, immunological or metabolic means, in or on the human body, but which may be assisted in its function by such means.

CONCLUSION

9.56 This chapter considers the industrial metaverse. The key-takeaway points are:

- The industrial metaverse is fuelling the next industrial revolution. As such it is likely we will see changes in the way industry is regulated as they adapt to this new landscape.
- The industrial metaverse sees the coming together of the leading emerging technologies, XR, IoT and AI. It has resulted in pioneering digital twins which are revolutionising.
- One of the key challenges in this area is the lack of specific regulation for the industrial metaverse in an area which is already heavily regulated. It is likely, however, that due to the revolutionary nature of this space that regulators themselves will change to incorporate this technology. Many stakeholders in the industrial metaverse will already be regulated themselves and therefore there will be existing safeguards. Once the products move into real life, existing regulations and laws will apply.
- Digital twins require precision. This presents a risk across the supply chain for those creating, operating and using digital twins. Comprehensive agreements are required to ensure that liability is properly attributed to the correct person or stakeholder at the correct point of the process.
- Issues relating to cyber-security and trade secrets are key in the industrial metaverse. This requires a combination of technological solutions and legislative framework.
- Guidance can be taken from existing large-scale digital twin programmes to try and establish a framework and standard for establishing and operating digital twins.
- Leading technology platforms are seeking to create the underlying infrastructure upon which to build digital twins and virtual factories. At its heart there is a need for collaboration, which should be properly documented.
- Consideration is needed as to product liability and environmental considerations within the metaverse. Both of which should be properly reflected in any commercial contracts to reflect understanding in respect of the same.
- Key areas where the industrial metaverse is thriving is in respect of 'smart factories', in the motorsport industry, healthcare and in the energy sector.

Chapter 10

Sport, entertainment, culture and the arts in the metaverse

'I think both the metaverse and web3 will certainly represent the future of fan engagement because it's giving fans brand new ways to engage with the sport.'

Max Proctor, Doppelgänger

10.01 The metaverse creates significant opportunities in sport, entertainment, culture and the arts. In sport, Manchester City has collaborated with Sony to recreate the Etihad Stadium in the metaverse,[1] SSC Napoli have expanded into the Sandbox platform,[2] the NFL has created NFL Zone in Fortnite,[3] the Paris 2024 Olympic Games had a replica digital twin of their different arenas[4] and the International Olympic Committee has formed a virtual world to bring to life the winter youth Olympic games for Gangwon 2024 which is in six languages and has customisable avatars.[5] The Premier league is embracing VR technologies through its collaboration with the VR software company Rezzil.[6]

10.02 Real-life entertainment is already crossing over into the metaverse. Major artists like Travis Scott, Eminem, Ariana Grande and David Guetta have performed concerts in the metaverse and in February 2024 Disney's $1.4 billion investment into Fortnight and Epic Games was announced paving the way for a new form of cross over between the metaverse and amusement parks.[7]

1 https://www.sportspromedia.com/news/manchester-city-sony-metaverse-digital-fan-experiences/.
2 https://sscnapoli.it/en/ssc-napoli-enter-the-metaverse-partnering-with-the-sandbox/.
3 https://www.nfl.com/news/nfl-continues-metaverse-exploration-with-persistent-fortnite-experience-nfl-zone.
4 https://www.hostcity.com/news/sporting-venues/paris-2024-digital-twins-being-used-plan-next-olympic-and-paralympic-games.
5 https://olympics.com/ioc/news/gangwon-2024-has-launched-the-first-ever-metaverse-experience-for-youth-olympic-fans.
6 https://www.auganix.org/vr-news-premier-league-signs-multi-year-deal-with-vr-developer-rezzil/?utm_campaign=Weekly%20Spatial&utm_medium=email&_hsmi=300335517&utm_content=300336447&utm_source=hs_email.
7 https://venturebeat.com/games/disney-invests-1-5b-in-fortnite-maker-epic-games-to-build-a-persistent-game-universe/.

10.03 The metaverse is already being used to experience key cultural heritage sites in various countries including in Wales[8] and Saudi Arabia.[9] The metaverse enables users not only to interact with heritage sites but even to transport them back in time to experience the site at the time of its significance.[10]

SPORTS LAW CONSIDERATIONS IN THE METAVERSE

10.04 There are many sports law considerations in the metaverse. The principal issues are around intellectual property rights, as well as the protection and preservation of brand and image rights for leagues, players and teams. It is important, however, to distinguish between the expansion of real-life sporting events and sports teams into the metaverse, principally for fan engagement and brand enhancement, as opposed to the creation of new forms of virtual e-sport in the metaverse.

10.05 The metaverse may help to improve accessibility issues for athletes and eventually reduce disability discrimination.[11] That said, currently many of the real-life issues which impact on diversity, equality and inclusion are however also known to be present in the sporting metaverse at this time, including social class barriers and sex discrimination.[12]

INTELLECTUAL PROPERTY CONSIDERATIONS IN THE METAVERSE

10.06 Many sportspeople are using NFTs to generate income. There are a variety of different items that are suitable for converting into NFTs including signed trading cards and digitally coded tickets. Action is required now by sports personalities to protect intellectual property rights in the metaverse since these NFTs can be extremely valuable with the most expensive being the 'Statute of Lebron' valued at $21.6million.[13]

10.07 It is important for any sports lawyer to keep a keen eye on the expansion of the metaverse and the protection of its client's digital image rights in this

8 https://www.gov.wales/croeso-i-gymru-wales-becomes-first-uk-nation-launch-metaverse-experience.

9 https://www.blockleaders.io/metaverse/saudi-arabia-announce-cultural-heritage-metaverse-platform and https://www.rcu.gov.sa/en/media-gallery/news/the-royal-commission-for-alula-enter-the-metaverse-with-first-fully-explorable-3d-model-of-hegra-s-tomb-of-lihyan-a-unesco-world-heritage-site/.

10 https://landvault.io/blog/cultural-preservation-in-the-metaverse.

11 https://www.emerald.com/insight/content/doi/10.1108/IJSMS-04-2023-0080/full/pdf?title=diversity-equity-and-inclusion-in-the-sport-metaverse.

12 https://www.emerald.com/insight/content/doi/10.1108/IJSMS-04-2023-0080/full/pdf?title=diversity-equity-and-inclusion-in-the-sport-metaverse.

13 Maeve Hyer, Physical Sports Needing Virtual Boundaries? An Analysis of Intellectual Property Issues Arising from Sport NFTs, 30 Jeffrey S. Moorad Sports L.J. 91 (2023) – http://digitalcommons.law.villanova.edu/mslj/vol30/iss1/4.

space. There is considerable growth potential in the metaverse and therefore any licensing agreement should specifically provide for use of image rights and trade marks in this virtual landscape. Consideration must be had as to whether a sportsperson registering an avatar in their name and likeness would infringe any rights already licensed to their club or sponsor. The same care and attention should be had to any sponsorship opportunities to ensure that the licensing agreement is sufficient well drafted to compensate for any use in this context. On the other hand the athletes need to be aware of where their clubs and sponsors are expanding into the metaverse and whether their contracts have already licensed the right for their intellectual property to be exploited.

10.08 There are some novel issues which arise in licensing considerations for sports personalities, especially when they are looking to move into the metaverse, which require not only intellectual property law considerations but also those of sports lawyers.[14] There may, for example be places where you want to restrict an avatar from venturing, such as a rival's sports stadium or places which may potentially damage the sportsperson's reputation such as a virtual casino.[15] You may also want to restrict them from being able to engage with competing brands of their sponsors to avoid any scenario where their avatar is seen promoting a rival team or product. In addition, depending on the sport, it is likely to require the involvement of not only the sports personality but also their club, and potentially their sponsors as well.

SPORTS DATA

10.09 The metaverse will be used as a training tool by athletes to simulate real-life scenarios. By its very nature the metaverse will generate a significant amount of data for analysis. One existing concern of athletes in real life is in respect of the collection and use of their sporting data. This is likely to only be intensified in the metaverse and so steps should be taken by practitioners to understand who has the rights to such data generated in the metaverse by the athletes – themselves, their clubs or even sponsors.

10.10 In 2020 a campaign dubbed 'Project Red Card' was formed and has reportedly gained the support of hundreds of football players, cricketer and rugby players. The campaign concerns the frustrations of professional athletes that, having typically given over broad rights to their image and other types of data to their clubs and teams, this data has been used for multiple different purposes none of which were in the contemplation, and it seems knowledge of the athletes. Rights to this data have been licensed to a number of third parties including gambling companies to use for statistical analysis.

14 Baker, Bradley J (2022) 'Impact Analysis of a virtual stadium: Measuring Sport in the Metaverse', Journal of Applied Sport Management: Vol 14: iss 4. http://doi.org/10.7290/jasm/vol14/iss4/7.

15 For example you could see the sports clubs preventing sport stars avatars from betting on specific sports.

10.11 The basis for the purported potential claims is data protection legislation and the extent to which the sports data should be considered personal data and whether consent has been granted in respect of this data. This is an interesting area and its determination will shape the law on sports data. How this is decided will have a significant impact on the metaverse, however, steps can be taken now by sports law practitioners to remedy these concerns going forward and ensure that data generated in the metaverse is owned and held where their clients intend.

10.12 Interestingly the recognition of publicity rights in the US as a distinct right largely stems from litigation flowing from baseball players rights in baseball cards.[16] In which the court stated:

> 'We think that, in addition to and independent of that right of privacy … a man has a right in the publicity value of his photograph, i. e., the right to grant the exclusive privilege of publishing his picture, and that such a grant may validly be made 'in gross,' i.e., without an accompanying transfer of a business or of anything else.'[17]

10.13 Whilst the right to publicity is not recognised by the courts of England and Wales – it is interesting to see whether the change in tide caused by Project Red Card may go some way to influence a concept of a right of publicity in the metaverse, especially where an avatar is a digital twin of the sportsperson.

PLAYER CONTRACTS

10.14 The same considerations as with e-sports generally are relevant in the metaverse relating to contracts between the player and the e-sport teams. With e-sport there is often felt to be a disparity between different player's contracts, which has already led to legal issues.[18] In some e-sports there are more formal requirements on player contracts, but in most there are not. Learning should be taken from traditional real-life sport contracts. In real life there are often governing bodies which have created player associations and collective bargaining arrangements but this is currently not the case in the metaverse or esports. In e-sport player contracts it is imperative that they cover issues such as player transfers and buy-out to move to a new team, as well as sponsorship and expectations.[19] In addition, it is important to cover share of revenue, which will largely depend on how and where revenue is generate as a result of the virtual sporting events.

10.15 High profile disputes relating to player contracts include the public dispute between Tfue and FaZe Clan which centred around FaZe Clan's rights to Tfue's third party sponsorship revenue. The complaint purports that the player

16 *Haelan Labs, Inc. v. Topps Chewing Gum, Inc.*, 202 F.2d 866 (2d Cir. 1953).
17 *Haelan Labs, Inc. v. Topps Chewing Gum, Inc.*, 202 F.2d 866 (2d Cir. 1953).
18 Ergashev Sanat, 'The Legal Frontier of E-Sports: analyzing regulatory challenges and solutions in the Cyber-arena' Uzbek Journal of Law and Digital Policy volume 1: issue 2 (2023).
19 https://esportsinsider.com/2023/06/why-esports-player-contracts-are-so-important.

contract entitled FaZe Clan to 80% of all of Tfue's revenue from any third party.[20] The dispute settled prior to a final decision [21] but highlights the tension between the e-sports teams and players regarding third party income. In the metaverse the opportunities of virtual sports players to generate money from their identity and data will only grow. Whilst this is a US case it reminds us that sports contracts in the metaverse still need to avoid being an unlawful restraint of trade.

10.16 It is expected that the key contracts in virtual sport in the metaverse will be between:

1. player;
2. teams;
3. sponsors;
4. metaverse platform;
5. the relevant metaverse sports league.

E-SPORTS

10.17 A significant amount of learning can be taken from the meteoric rise of e-sports, which has many parallels with virtual sports in the metaverse. Virtual sports are likely to be an extension of esports into a more immersive environment rather than a completely stand-alone new concept.

10.18 In its most simple form e-sports is competitive gaming. It is extremely popular. It is projected that in 2024 the e-sport market will reach revenues of $4.3 billion.[22] There are considerable opportunities for e-sports or electronic sports in the metaverse but as yet VR sport has not yet fully taken off.[23] It is however expected to become a growth area of the metaverse and in 2023 the Olympic Esports in Singapore saw competitions including virtual taekwondo, virtual baseball, virtual sailing and virtual shooting.[24]

10.19 Many interchangeable terms are currently in existence, such as virtual sports and cyber sports but ultimately these relate to the actual playing of the sport in the metaverse as opposed to real-life sporting events being mirrored in a virtual landscape. Given the way they are played, virtual sports are typically more active than most e-sports.

20 https://www.foley.com/wp-content/uploads/imported/ae331ba2932049e896a06c2e8bbc187a.pdf.

21 https://www.forbes.com/sites/christinasettimi/2020/08/26/fortnite-star-tfue-settles-dispute-with-faze-clan-ending-esports-first-major-employment-lawsuit/.

22 https://www.statista.com/outlook/amo/esports/worldwide#:~:text=The%20Esports%20market%20worldwide%20is,US%245.7bn%20by%202028.

23 https://www.techuk.org/resource/event-round-up-exploring-the-future-of-esports.html.

24 https://olympics.com/en/esports/olympic-esports-series/cycling.

REGULATION AND GOVERNANCE OF SPORT IN THE METAVERSE

10.20 There is the need for clear rules for all sports that are played in the metaverse. Virtual sports are similar to e-sport and many of the same issues in terms of governance and regulation will apply. There is the need to set a benchmark for the different virtual sports for the players, and a legal framework is necessary to protect all stakeholders. These are, however, challenging to clearly define at this stage given the fast pace nature of the industry and its rapid changes.[25]

10.21 There is currently not one single regulator of e-sports or virtual sports, and therefore the governance and rules for the different leagues and different sports at this stage depends on the governing body chosen for that virtual sport and league by the different organisers.

10.22 Virtual sports in the metaverse will need to decide whether they fall under the real-life sporting rules; e-sports generally or whether they should be distinct; it is likely that virtual sports will become a subset of e-sports and at least at the competitive level are likely to be dealt with in the same way as many other e-sports are currently, where the rules of the real-life sports will be capable of adaptation into the virtual sport, much like technological advancements, such as VAR, are being incorporated into real-life sports. This for example is the case for virtual sailing and virtual cycling, where, as below, there are not that many distinctions between the real-life rules and the virtual sport rules. As below, however, there are certain distinct areas where novel issues arise in the metaverse including where there is the inclusion of technological gamification included within the e-sport such as 'boosts' which are used on the Zwift platform.

Regulation of e-sports

10.23 The World Esport Association (WESA) is trying to create some standardised regulation for e-sports generally and has some of the leading industry experts involved.[26] WESA has created a code of conduct for teams and players,[27] Arbitration Rules[28] and social media and best practice guidelines.[29] The International Esport Federation has 144 different federations as members and has anti-doping regulations and statutes which are governed under the law of the Republic of Korea.[30] The Global Esports Federation, is looking to try and create

25 Ergashev Sanat, 'The Legal Frontier of E-Sports: analyzing regulatory challenges and solutions in the Cyber-arena' Uzbek Journal of Law and Digital Policy volume 1: issue 2 (2023).

26 WESA is seeking to 'become the global benchmark for industry-wide standards' – https://wesa.gg.

27 https://wesa.gg/wp-content/uploads/2019/05/WESA-Code-of-Conduct-Teams-and-Players-Final-03052019-1.pdf.

28 https://wesa.gg/wp-content/uploads/2016/12/WESA-Arbitration-Rules-2016.pdf.

29 https://wesa.gg/wp-content/uploads/2017/07/WESA-Social-Media-Policy-and-Best-Practices-Guidelines.pdf.

30 https://iesf.org/rules-regulations/.

a regulator for esports and established its GEF Metaverse Council in 2022.[31] The British Esport Federation is aimed at both grassroots e-sport up to competitive e-sport in the UK and seeks to try and educate people on e-sport and inspire people to get involved.[32]

10.24 The Esports Integrity Commission (ESIC)[33] is aimed at organisers, developers and leagues as opposed to players and has created six guiding principles. These are:

1 integrity and respect
2 fair process
3 standard codes
4 recognised sanctions
5 information sharing
6 confidentiality

DOPING

10.25 There are concerns around doping in e-sports generally especially the use of drugs to try and make a player more focused.[34] This will probably be the same in the metaverse, although XR will require more physical movement than normal e-sports. Any rules and regulations of virtual sports will need to cover rules on the prohibition of the use of performance enhancing drugs.

UNFAIR ADVANTAGE

10.26 In 2019 British Cycling disqualified Cameron Jeffers from the British eRacing Championships for using a bot to create an unfair advantage in the competition.[35] Sports regulations need to keep up to speed with advances in technology and the ways in which participants can exploit the technology to obtain an unfair advantage. This will be key in the metaverse as well as with e-sports generally.

CURRENT EXAMPLES OF VIRTUAL SPORTS AND THEIR RULES

10.27 The following examines examples of some of the current rules and regulations for virtual sports.

31 https://www.globalesports.org/about.
32 https://britishesports.org/about-us/.
33 https://esic.gg.
34 Such as ADHD medication https://www.britishsportslaw.org/esports-regulatory-concerns.html.
35 https://www.theguardian.com/sport/2019/oct/04/first-british-eracing-champion-banned-for-using-bot-to-gain-unfair-advantage.

F1 Sim Racing

10.28 F1 Sim Racing enables players to compete in virtual motorsport races. Some drivers compete professionally for an official Formula 1 Esports Team. The sport is governed by the Handbook[36] as well as the Championship Rulebook,[37] the Qualification Rulebook[38] and the World Champion Rulebook[39] depending on the different stages of the competition. The Handbook states that the drivers may also have to enter into an agreement with the promoter and operator of F1 Sim Racing.

Virtual Regatta

10.29 Virtual Regatta is a digital sailing platform. It joined the metaverse in 2023 with a pilot operation, which incorporated a conservation aspect drawing attention to the protection of oceans.[40] As part of this collaboration it partnered with Accenture.

10.30 E-sailing has attracted many participants and featured in the Olympic Esports and sponsors include Rolex. The rules for e-sailing in Virtual Regatta Inshore are adapted from the Racing Rules of Sailing and in comparison, see relatively small changes.[41]

SPORTING EVENTS AND STADIUMS IN THE METAVERSE

10.31 Many sporting venues have now moved into the metaverse. The leading examples include:[42]

1. Nikeland in Roblox which enables game play as well as shopping for digital Nike products for your avatar;
2. Netaverse, the home of the Brooklyn Nets – National Basketball Association;
3. Truist Park, the home of the Atlanta Braves – Major League Baseball;
4. Monte Carlo F1 in 2022;
5. Wimble World in 2022 in Roblox;

36 https://downloads.f1esports.com/Rules/2023/F1_SRWC_Participants_Handbook_v1.6.pdf.
37 https://downloads.f1esports.com/Rules/2023/F1_SRWC23-24_Rulebook_v1.0.pdf.
38 https://downloads.f1esports.com/Rules/2023/F1_Esports_2023_Qualification_Rulebook_v1.3.pdf.
39 https://downloads.f1esports.com/Rules/2023/F1_SRWC23_Rulebook_v0.7.pdf.
40 https://www.virtualregatta.com/en/news/metaverse-experience-tor/.
41 https://d7qh6ksdplczd.cloudfront.net/sailing/wp-content/uploads/2022/02/25122529/Virtual_Racing_Rules_220119.pdf.
42 Baker, Bradley J (2022) 'Impact Analysis of a virtual stadium: Measuring Sport in the Metaverse', Journal of Applied Sport Management: Vol 14: iss 4. http://doi.org/10.7290/jasm/vol14/iss4/7.

6. Etihad Stadium, the home of Manchester City;
7. Real Madrid Virtual World.

10.32 Whilst creating virtual stadiums in the metaverse are costly, these costs are significantly lower than building real-life stadiums.[43] Virtual stadiums do not have the same capacity restrictions as in real life, meaning more fan engagement.

10.33 There is however, likely to be a detrimental economic impact for the local community when events are hosted in the metaverse, which in real life is often cited in planning applications as justification for permission to build new infrastructure. Further there is likely to be an impact for the venue given the experience of attending an event is often more than just watching the sporting event but includes drink and food and merchandise. That said, digital merchandise can, however, still generate significant revenue.

10.34 Digital twins of sporting events and stadiums are already being created in the metaverse both to help with planning large sporting events and to offer opportunities for engagement for those unable to attend in real life.[44] Digital twins can be used to simulate different crowd control methods, seating and lighting to try and create the optimum experience for real-life visitors. In addition, with real-time data, organisers can monitor and react to evolving situations as well as sponsorship opportunities and post-match analysis. Whilst there is potential for using digital twins in large sporting events to reduce environmental issues, at this stage the technology is complex especially in the sporting environment and there remain privacy concerns.[45] It is also important to have comprehensive cyber security procedures and protocols in virtual stadiums to prevent cheating in the virtual sport.[46]

SPORTING BROADCASTING RESTRICTIONS AND THE METAVERSE

10.35 In 2022 the Government announced it intended to review broadcasting rules for sport to ensure that the main broadcasters have the ability to show the designated live sporting events on their digital media, coined the Digital Rights Review.[47] Accordingly, the Media Act 2024 extends the scope of coverage for listed events to include Public Service Broadcast streaming services but also other

43 Baker, Bradley J (2022) 'Impact Analysis of a virtual stadium: Measuring Sport in the Metaverse', Journal of Applied Sport Management: Vol 14: iss 4. http://doi.org/10.7290/jasm/vol14/iss4/7.

44 Glebova E, Book R, Su Y, Perić M and Heller J (2023) Sports venue digital twin technology from a spectator virtual visiting perspective. Front. Sports Act. Living 5:1289140. doi: 10.3389/fspor.2023.1289140.

45 Glebova E, Book R, Su Y, Perić M and Heller J (2023) Sports venue digital twin technology from a spectator virtual visiting perspective. Front. Sports Act. Living 5:1289140. doi: 10.3389/fspor.2023.1289140.

46 Baker, Bradley J (2022) 'Impact Analysis of a virtual stadium: Measuring Sport in the Metaverse', Journal of Applied Sport Management: Vol 14: iss 4. http://doi.org/10.7290/jasm/vol14/iss4/7.

47 https://www.gov.uk/government/news/review-of-broadcast-rules-around-major-sporting-events.

providers who will have the opportunity to show events.[48] Ofcom are intending to consult on its proposals in 2025.[49]

10.36 This is highly relevant to the metaverse, where sporting events will be made available on a virtual reality and interactive basis. The listed events include key sporting events such as the Olympics, the Grand National and the FIFA World Cup. Some of these as described earlier have already moved into the metaverse, albeit not to show live events but as a way of interacting as a virtual experience with the event. If the platform intends to show the event live[50] they will need to comply with the necessary regulations. They will either require authorisation or consent. Unless the metaverse platform meets the definition of a qualified provider, which at this stage they would likely not (but this may need to be reviewed in the future depending on the expansion of the metaverse and its adoption) then they would not be able to get exclusive rights to certain top tier events.

GAMBLING IN THE METAVERSE

10.37 In the UK the provision of gambling facilities is regulated under the Gambling Act 2005 and it is a criminal offence to provide gambling facilities without a licence.[51] In addition, there are restrictions on advertising of gambling under s 328 and this will still apply to remote gambling aimed at people in the UK.[52] The Government was looking to reform the Gambling Act 2005 but at the time of writing this has not happened but the Gambling Commission is however, looking to implement some of the changes proposed in the White Paper over the course of 2024 and early 2025 as a six-month pilot.[53] The 2023 White Paper is entitled 'High Stakes: gambling reform for the digital age'[54] and acknowledges change is needed to keep up with technological advances and to embed more online protection and to safeguard children.

48 It will be divided into 'qualifying' (PBS) and 'non-qualifying'.

49 https://www.ofcom.org.uk/tv-radio-and-on-demand/listed-sporting-events/what-will-future-rules-around-showing-major-sporting-events-look-like/.

50 The definition and scope of 'live coverage' is currently being defined by Ofcom and is subject to their determination following its 2024 call for evidence.

51 The Gambling Act 2005 applies to the provision of facilities for remote gambling provided at least one piece of remote gambling equipment is based in Great Britain or the facilities are used there (section 36(3)) and the person providing the facilities should have known that the facilities are being used in Great Britain (section 36(4)). In addition it is an offence to invite someone in Great Britain (or use equipment in Great Britain to do so) to gamble remotely in a prohibited territory (section 44).

52 The test under 333 (4) provides for information either coming to the attention of someone in Great Britain (a); intended to come to the attention of someone in Great Britain (b); data being made available with a view to it being accessed by someone in Great Britain (c) or data being made available where it is likely to be accessed by someone in Great Britain (d)

53 https://www.gamblingcommission.gov.uk/news/article/new-rules-boosting-safety-and-consumer-choice#:~:text=The%20changes%2C%20consistent%20with%20the,tightening%20processes%20to%20support%20age.

54 https://www.gov.uk/government/publications/high-stakes-gambling-reform-for-the-digital-age.

10.38 The Gambling Commission is keeping a firm eye on the metaverse via the multi-regulatory Digital Regulation Cooperation Forum.[55] Gambling in the metaverse will take many forms as it does in real life including virtual casinos and betting on virtual esports. There are numerous legal issues with gambling in the metaverse not least the issues in respect of jurisdiction given the cross-border nature of the metaverse. The Gambling Commission released its discussion paper in 2016[56] on esports and much remains relevant for application of gambling in the metaverse. The Gambling Commission considers that the same laws and regulations apply to betting on esports as they do to betting on physical sports and we expect the same position in respect of gambling on virtual sports carried out in the metaverse. Further the Gambling Commission highlighted that where sites enabled players to play against each other but also to bet on themselves to win they may fall under the definition of being a 'betting intermediary' and accordingly require licensing.

10.39 Some of the e-games on offer may themselves fall under the definition of gaming under the regulations and require a licence to be carried out. It is likely that this issue will continue in the metaverse. A close eye should be kept on any updates to the Gambling Commission's position on social gaming, which includes interaction with other players, which is currently that additional regulations are not required to cover this area but this may change should there be harms identified in this area, in particular if this takes off in the metaverse.

10.40 The Gambling Commission has confirmed that a licence is still required where digital currency is used, which may include in-game currency or commodities such as 'skins' for your avatar,[57] and highlight that digital technologies present an increased risk of money laundering.[58] This will be the case in the metaverse and it will be important for anyone looking to offer gambling in the metaverse have in place comprehensive anti-money laundering procedures.

10.41 The ESIC has created the gold standard in respect of betting in esports.[59] This includes compliance with suitable surveillance protocols as well as collaboration with the ESIC and Suspicious Betting Alert Network.

ENTERTAINMENT LAW CONSIDERATIONS IN THE METAVERSE

10.42 As with all new technologies many artists are seeking to expand into the metaverse. There are numerous entertainment law issues with the metaverse.

55 https://www.gamblingcommission.gov.uk/about-us/transparency/html/board-minutes-18-may-2022.

56 https://assets.ctfassets.net/j16ev64qyf6l/5KSPqqMxzZnmuK87nIjvP0/16b402e60ab5531829514e61e03c566e/Virtual-currencies-eSports-and-social-gaming-discussion-paper-August-2016.pdf.

57 https://www.gamblingcommission.gov.uk/licensees-and-businesses/guide/page/digital-and-virtual-currencies.

58 https://www.gamblingcommission.gov.uk/licensees-and-businesses/guide/digital-technologies-and-aml.

59 https://esic.gg/esports-betting-product-standard/.

Those involved in negotiating contracts for artists need to be clear over what rights can be used of the artist in the metaverse and whether there are any restrictions. It is important that tight controls are implemented over who has control over the avatar representing the artist to ensure that it does not engage in acts in the metaverse which may have an impact in real life and which may affect their brand or image or reputation.

10.43 Just as real-life celebrity and entertainment is likely to spill into the metaverse there is also opportunity for new types of entertainment in the metaverse which could merge real life and the metaverse.[60] Aespa is the first metaverse K-pop girl group which combines four real-life members and four metaverse members of the band.[61] In addition, Mika who is a virtual mega-star is peer-produced and permits fans 'reworking' the productions.[62]

10.44 There is significant potential for the metaverse in the entertainment industry both in respect of fan engagement, such as with virtual concerts but also with innovative NFTs such as behind the scene clips.[63] There is already a significant rise in the adoption of avatars by celebrities, such as John Legend.[64] The virtual avatar is controlled by a person in real life. Consideration must be had over who is authorised to control the avatar, since this is much more immersive and representative of the underlying persona of the celebrity than their social media account. Care should be had to specifically document what is and isn't permitted by anyone with control of a celebrities account given the potential risk of damaging their reputation by a wrong interaction or engagement in the metaverse.

VIRTUAL CONCERTS

10.45 There are various ways that musicians can perform in the metaverse[65] which include a mix of performances by avatars and real-life videos of the real-life artist.

60 https://www.techtarget.com/searchcio/feature/Examples-of-the-metaverse-for-business-and-IT-leaders.

61 Jeong, Minju; Kim, Seongcheol (2023): What makes 'aespa', the first metaverse girl group in the K-pop universe, succeed in the global entertainment industry?, 32nd European Conference of the International Telecommunications Society (ITS): 'Realising the digital decade in the European Union – Easier said than done?', Madrid, Spain, 19th – 20th June 2023, International Telecommunications Society (ITS), Calgary.

62 https://ieeexplore.ieee.org/stamp/stamp.jsp?arnumber=10058945.

63 Alanna Sadler, Legal Uncertainty in Virtual Worlds and Digital Goods: Do the Same Laws Apply? 32 U. MIA Bus. L. Rev 381 available at: https://repository.law.miami.edu/umblr/vol32/iss3/7.

64 https://ieeexplore.ieee.org/stamp/stamp.jsp?arnumber=10058945.

65 Chelsea Cohen, *Welcome to Web 3.0: A Reevaluation of Music Licensing and Consumption to Level the Payment Imbalance for Songwriters,* 45 Hastings Com. & Ent, L.J. 45 (2023).

10.46 Whilst there are a number of opportunities associated with virtual concerts there are novel legal considerations such as:

1) should dead artists be able to perform? This could happen with both holograms and in the metaverse but this may not reflect the actual wishes of the deceased artists;

2) should audience members have a right to privacy or not? In real life this is dealt with contractually on tickets but in the metaverse there could be the option to either increase or decrease privacy settings;

3) should you be able to share the concert with third parties in return for paying something to the artist?[66]

MUSIC

10.47 Any licensing agreement should specifically deal with the right to use the music within the metaverse. Typically, licensing agreements are limited to specific territories, however careful drafting will be required to provide for limitations on use of the music outside of the specific metaverse. At this juncture care should be taken to carefully limit on which platforms the music is licensed to be used and on what terms. This should all be documented in the licensing agreement.

10.48 There are legal issues with music licensing in the metaverse.[67] One issue is the need for clearance for any avatar performing a song. The licensing would deal with the fee for this performance. In addition, there is likely to be synchronisation for use within the metaverse and therefore the licence should deal with this. Further, different people may own the rights to the music in different territories and therefore it may be complex to negotiate the rights. An answer to this may be to impose technological restrictions on from where the music can be accessed in the metaverse, so for certain countries users will not be able to watch the concert or access the music – in the same way that streaming companies limit streaming in certain territories. Strictly speaking a licence would be required to synchronise any music via the relevant metaverse platform, which would require the consent of both the recording artist and composers but there are issues with this given the number of songs which could potentially be utilised within the metaverse.[68]

66 Breese, Jennifer L., Fox, Mark A., and Vaidyanathan, Ganesh, 'Live music performances and the internet of things' Issues in Information Systems, International Association for Computer Information Systems, Vol 23, no 3 pp 179 – 188, 2020, http://www.iacis.org/iis/2020/3_iis_2020_179-188.pdf.

67 Chelsea Cohen, *Welcome to Web 3.0: A Reevaluation of Music Licensing and Consumption to Level the Payment Imbalance for Songwriters,* 45 Hastings Com. & Ent, L.J. 45 (2023).

68 Kim, Kyungsuk, Music License in the Metaverse, International Journal of Internet, Broadcasting and Communication Vol 12, No 4 44- 54 (2023) – https://koreascience.kr/article/JAKO202302472082619.pdf.

10.49 Whilst there are many benefits for musicians in the metaverse it is necessary to ensure that musicians are properly protected for both the copyright in the sound recordings and the composition since in real life there is often discrepancy between the royalties received from the sound recordings (for the recording artists) and from the compositions (for the song writers).[69] In the United States the 2018 Music Modernization Act seeks to deal more coherently with streaming services and enable blanket licensing arrangements. NFT or the blockchain could be used to record ownership of digital copies of music in the metaverse which could be linked to a smart contract which automatically pays out to the artist on its use or transfer.[70]

10.50 There are numerous ways in which music will infiltrate the metaverse – pre-existing music will become commonplace, as will user-generated music created in the metaverse and even virtual collaboration in the metaverse. Going further, what is being termed the 'musical metaverse', will see the incorporation of the Internet of Musical Things (IoMusT).[71] This will see musical instruments using sensors, the blockchain and NFTs. This in turn will help with music licensing, division of royalties and even the sharing of digital assets and partaking in the governance of the same. Blockchain can be used to divide up and reflect the ownership of music rights and smart contracts could bring into effect any predetermined arrangement. Some believe that this innovation could even see the removal of the need for intermediaries in the music business.[72]

10.51 There are legal implications of music licensing in the metaverse. Action has already been threatened (and commenced) against Roblox in both 2021 by the National Music Publishers' Association and in 2022 by the Korea Music Content Association.[73]

10.52 Despite settling in around October 2021,[74] and Roblox denying the allegations,[75] The National Music Publishers' Association complaint[76] which was filed in the Central District of California on 6 September 2021 pleaded that:

> 'Roblox engages in copyright infringement on a massive scale by deliberately creating a centralized synchronization (or 'sync') library of unlicensed songs to be distributed, streamed, publicly performed and incorporated into game content. In

69 Chelsea Cohen, *Welcome to Web 3.0: A Reevaluation of Music Licensing and Consumption to Level the Payment Imbalance for Songwriters,* 45 Hastings Com. & Ent, L.J. 45 (2023).

70 Chelsea Cohen, *Welcome to Web 3.0: A Reevaluation of Music Licensing and Consumption to Level the Payment Imbalance for Songwriters,* 45 Hastings Com. & Ent, L.J. 45 (2023).

71 Turchet, Luca, Musical Metaverse: vision, opportunities and challenges, Personal and Ubiquitous Computing (2023) 27: 1811- 1827.

72 Turchet, Luca, Musical Metaverse: vision, opportunities and challenges, Personal and Ubiquitous Computing (2023) 27: 1811- 1827.

73 Kim, Kyungsuk, Music License in the Metaverse, International Journal of Internet, Broadcasting and Communication Vol 12, No 4 44- 54 (2023) – https://koreascience.kr/article/JAKO202302472082619.pdf.

74 https://www.nmpa.org/roblox-music-publishers-settle-copyright-licensing-dispute/.

75 https://www.courtlistener.com/docket/59972437/40/abkco-music-inc-v-roblox-corporation/.

76 *ABKCO Music Inc. v. Roblox Corp.*, U.S. District Court for the Central District of California, No. 2:21-cv-04705.

creating this library, Roblox reproduces each song included therein, charging users to upload music to be incorporated into their games. Roblox is fully aware that it is required to obtain licenses to exploit copyright music on its platform, including obtaining necessary reproduction, sync, and public performance licenses, but wilfully refuses to do so. Roblox is taking for itself Plaintiffs' creative and financial investments without permission and without compensation, on a platform that earns revenue only for Roblox and its users'[77]

10.53 One of the main issues with copyright of music and songs in the metaverse is that it is usually individual users who are the ones uploading the songs to the platform and when relevant breaching any copyright in the music.[78] It is difficult, however, for the copyright holders to try and trace and enforce against the individual users. This will prove even more complex with decentralised systems. A solution in the US, and the EU to some extent, would be to ensure that all metaverse platforms are classified as Online Service Providers. Should a platform be considered as an Online Service Provider it would be exempt from liability for breach of copyright by the users under the E-Commerce Directive (2000/31/EC) in the EU[79] and under the Digital Millennium Copyright Act of 1998 (DMCA), 17 U.S.C. in the US.[80] For such exemptions to apply, the platform must not have knowledge of the infringement and must take down the material if a request is received. There are however practical difficulties in making take down reports in the metaverse since it will require identification as to when and where the music was heard which may not be readily known or easy to identify.

10.54 In the UK the 'safe harbour' exemption will not apply. The metaverse platforms would also be subject to the Digital Copyright Directive (2019/790/EU) in the EU which under article 17 requires the platform to try and obtain permission from the copyright holders. This is more onerous that the E-Commerce Directive. The E-Commerce Directive no longer applies in the UK and the Digital Copyright Directive was never implemented in the UK. In the UK therefore the platforms should be seeking the right to the material from the copyright holders.

10.55 It may be beneficial for metaverse platforms to become a Collective Management Organisation (CMO) with simplified licensing requirements and liability.

IMAGE RIGHTS

10.56 In many countries around the world a person's likeness is protected – in the United States there are Personality Rights, there is a Right of Publicity in

77 https://fingfx.thomsonreuters.com/gfx/legaldocs/yxmvjaqnkpr/IP%20ROBLOX%20COPYRIGHT%20complaint.pdf.

78 Kim, Kyungsuk, Music License in the Metaverse, International Journal of Internet, Broadcasting and Communication Vol 12, No 4 44- 54 (2023) – https://koreascience.kr/article/JAKO202302472082619.pdf.

79 Article 14(1).

80 Section 512(c).

Canada and similar rights in France and Germany. This protects an individual from their personality being appropriated for commercial gain and is considered as a tort. This is a stand-alone right, different from a right against defamation or breach of privacy. In the metaverse there is the real risk of someone's personality being taken via an avatar and utilised for gain.

10.57 Under the law of England and Wales however, there are no Personality Rights, or Right of Publicity or Image Rights per se, and any protection in the metaverse will fall under a patchwork of different intellectual property rights and the law of passing off. In the *Rihanna v Top Shop* judgment[81] Kitchin LJ was clear

> 'There is in English law no 'image right' or 'character right' which allows a celebrity to control the use of his or her name of image… A celebrity seeking to control the use of his or her image must therefore rely on some other cause of action such as breach of contract, breach of confidence, infringement of copyright or, as in this case, passing off'[82]

10.58 This is likely to require further consideration in the metaverse where an avatar will be the digital representation of the celebrity. Legal commentators considering the evolution of image rights in the US identify that these rights evolved from baseball players having an interest in playing cards depicting their image[83] and separating out a distinct right of publicity[84] and suggest that this right would apply to avatars, but there are still questions over whether this would apply only to celebrities and those who have exploited their image.

10.59 For passing off to succeed however, it is necessary to demonstrate that the goodwill in the business has been damaged. This may not necessarily be the case in the unlawful replication of a celebrity's image or persona in the metaverse. We would expect anyone who finds themselves the victim of their persona being replicated in the metaverse to seek to try and bring a claim in a jurisdiction which does recognise Personality Rights and for this reason it is likely the courts in England and Wales will not see litigation on this given the unfavourable position.

DEEP FAKES

10.60 The metaverse will not be immune from the issues affecting celebrities generally in respect of deep fakes. In the metaverse, however, such deep fakes will be able to converse with other users and effectively take on a life of their own. Such deep fakes will have the potential to cause immense damage to a

81 Robyn Rihanna Fenty, Roraj Trade LLC, *Combermere Entertainment Properties, LLC v Arcadia Group Brands Limited, Topshop/Topman Limited* [2015] EWCA Civ 3.

82 Repeating the earlier decision in *Douglas & ors v Hello! Ltd & ors* (No 3) [2007] UKHL 21, [2008] 1 AC 1.

83 *Haelan Labs, Inc. v. Topps Chewing Gum, Inc.*, 202 F.2d 866 (2d Cir. 1953).

84 Jon M. Garon, Playing in the Virtual Arena: Avatars, Publicity, and Identity Reconceptualized Through Virtual Worlds and Computer Games, 11 Chap. L. Rev. 465 (2008).

celebrity's reputation as a result of their real-time interactions. As the graphics in the metaverse and with avatars progresses we expect to see more issues with deep fakes in the metaverse. In some cases, the behaviour may fall under the Online Safety Act 2023. In July 2024 Ofcom published its discussion paper on 'Mitigating the Harms of Deceptive Deepfakes' in which they discuss some of the technological ways in which technology companies are seeking to defend against 'deep fakes'[85] together with their regulation under the Online Safety Act 2023 and their upcoming codes of conduct.

LEGAL CONSIDERATIONS IN RESPECT OF CULTURE AND HERITAGE IN THE METAVERSE

10.61 In 1972 the Treaty on the Convention concerning the Protection of the World Cultural and Natural Heritage[86] was adopted in an effort to safeguard cultural heritage sites. The Treaty is overseen by the World Heritage Committee as part of UNESCO. At its heart the Treaty seeks to protect cultural and natural heritage from risks caused by natural disasters as well as damage and destruction caused by other means such as war. The Treaty recognises the global importance of certain sites and that their loss will be significant to future generations. The metaverse is already being adopted as a tool to virtually recreate heritage sites so that if needed they can be recreated in the future, to analyse the different impacts on the sites from natural and other types of risks and for people who may not be able to experience the site to visit virtually, especially in times of conflict. As a result, the creation of digital twins for the metaverse of these sites would be in line with the Treaty and the Article 4 obligation on states to do all they can to preserve, protect and ensure heritage sites are still available for future generations.

10.62 In 2003 UNESCO adopted the Convention for the Safeguarding of the Intangible Cultural Heritage. This provides for safeguarding cultural heritage for future generations. The metaverse is able to help preserve such heritage, however, as highlighted by Rouhani[87] cultural heritage is dynamic and continually changing. In addition, he highlights the risk that using technologies such as the metaverse to preserve controversial culture presents an ethical risk given access to these objects now goes beyond just interested academics but includes the general public. He explains that the metaverse is not only being used as a tool to record cultural heritage but has now expanded to managing heritage sites and even trading in respect of cultural heritage. He calls for guidelines such as the Getty Conservation Institute to be expanded and the ICOMOS Charter for the Interpretation and Presentation of Cultural Heritage Sites and International

85 Such as watermarking and labelling.

86 https://www.unesco.org/en/legal-affairs/convention-concerning-protection-world-cultural-and-natural-heritage.

87 Bijan Rouhani. 2023. Ethically Digital: Contested Cultural Heritage in Digital Context. SDH, Vol 7, No 1, 1-16.

Principles on Virtual Archaeology should be used despite it not specifically covering the metaverse.

10.63 The metaverse is being used for cultural heritage and to support conservation efforts.[88] The metaverse can be used to monitor heritage sites and to support archaeology. The use of digital twins can be used to identify areas of deterioration. The metaverse can be used to preserve culture, such as ancient characters and folk tales. There are issues however in respect of trying to create a cultural heritage metaverse including risks with certain sites being highly contentious politically and remote in their locations.

10.64 Ownership of the copyright in the digital copies of historic sites, artefacts and classical masterpieces raises moral and ethical complications given that in real life these do not have copyright protection. This is especially the case with disputed heritage sites where real-life political tensions could spill over into ownership issues in the metaverse.[89] This can be seen by the concerns raised by the Italian Government in respect of the Uffizi Gallery.

PROTESTS IN THE METAVERSE AND CONTROVERSIAL LANDMARKS

10.65 As part of a wave of international Black Lives Matter protests in 2020 a number of statues were pulled down, such as the Edward Colston statute in Bristol. In May 2021 the Secretary of State for Digital, Culture, Media and Sport established the Heritage Advisory Board which was tasked with creating new guidelines in line with the policy of 'retain and explain' a commitment to protecting and preserving historic statutes and monuments in the UK for the future.[90] The Government policy at the time of writing has been to push for historical statutes to remain in situ but in some cases as necessary to add an explanation and have set out comprehensive guidance on this policy.[91] The guidance considers that should it be felt necessary custodians can use alternative ways to explain the monument, which would include XR.

10.66 Those creating the metaverse will need to consider whether or not they want to include controversial landmarks or statues. Should such landmarks be included then there is a risk of protests in the metaverse – such protests have already started.[92] If a digital twin of a heritage site is destroyed in the metaverse

88 Zhang, X.; Yang, D.; Yow, C.H.; Huang, L.; Wu, X.; Huang, X.; Guo, J.; Zhou, S.; Cai, Y. Metaverse for Cultural Heritages. Electronics 2022, 11, 3730. https://doi.org/ 10.3390/ electronics11223730.

89 Bijan Rouhani. 2023. Ethically Digital: Contested Cultural Heritage in Digital Context. SDH, Vol 7, No 1, 1-16.

90 https://www.gov.uk/government/news/new-legal-protection-for-england-s-heritage.

91 https://www.gov.uk/government/publications/guidance-for-custodians-on-how-to-deal-with-commemorative-heritage-assets-that-have-become-contested/guidance-for-custodians-on-how-to-deal-with-commemorative-heritage-assets-that-have-become-contested.

92 https://nftevening.com/first-metaverse-protest-held-at-samsungs-decentraland-hq/ and https://www.arabnews.pk/node/2398501/media.

as a result of activism should this be treated in the same way as in real life given the importance of the site? One would assume not given the assumption that it can be easily fixed through backups of the data, however, it is certainly an aggravating feature of any virtual crime given the likely cultural significance. In real life the intentional destruction of cultural heritage sites are considered as a War Crime.[93]

10.67 The Parthenon Marbles and the Queen Nefertiti bust demonstrate the legal and ethical challenges with digitalisation of contested artefacts – both have been digitally scanned without the consent of the museums in which they are housed.[94] There are questions as to whether the artifact should reference the dispute and whether there should be restrictions on who can access this.

ART LAW CONSIDERATIONS IN THE METAVERSE

10.68 There are both opportunities and challenges for art in the metaverse. One issue with the displaying of art in the metaverse is that there are not consistent copyright laws globally plus there are issues now with art created using AI.[95]

Existing art and the metaverse

10.69 Existing artwork is being converted into software and brought into the metaverse. The art is copied into a digital XR format that can then be viewed in virtual reality. This is slightly different from art recorded onto NFT as a form of tokenisation (although the use of NFT for art is still an important topic in the metaverse). Whilst many consider that minting art into an NFT does not infringe the copyright in the underlying artwork[96] it is still unclear whether the conversion of artwork into an XR format would be considered an infringement of the rights of the copyright holder should consent not be provided. It is likely for now that artwork which is free of copyright can be converted, not least because these tend to be from the most historically famous artists where the work is already in the public domain.

10.70 Artists looking to move into the metaverse need to consider how their artwork will be displayed and their audience. The virtual gallery would not be owned by the artists and consideration needs to be had to ensure that the look is appropriate to the artwork. This should all be reflected in any agreement between the artist, the developer and the metaverse 'gallery' owner. There may also be the

93 Articles 27 and 56 Hague Convention – as annexed in 1910.

94 Bijan Rouhani. 2023. Ethically Digital: Contested Cultural Heritage in Digital Context. SDH, Vol 7, No 1, 1-16.

95 Hurst, W.; Spyrou, O.; Tekinerdogan, B.; Krampe, C. Digital Art and the Metaverse: Benefits and Challenges. Future Internet 2023, 15, 188. https://doi.org/10.3390/ fi15060188.

96 Alpini, 'NFT and NFTED Artwork between property and copyrightability' Peresona e Mercato 2023/1 – Saggi.

opportunity to protect parts of the work as a derivative work; consideration will have to be had as to where those rights lie and should be contractually recorded.

Art created in the metaverse

10.71 Much of the artwork created in the metaverse for sale is recorded on NFT but it does not necessarily need to be if it is just being displayed in a virtual format. The NFT is just the record of the artwork on the blockchain.

10.72 The metaverse is creating the opportunity for artists to collaborate. It is important that the parties enter into a collaboration agreement which clearly sets out the different expectations and ownership rights.

MORAL RIGHTS

10.73 One area of interest in respect of art in the metaverse is the moral rights afforded to artists when real-life art is converted into NFT or brought into the metaverse. This is the position which was considered in the *Mango* case.[97] In January 2024 the Commercial Court of Barcelona gave its judgment in favour of Mango (Punto Fa, S.L) in a case brought against it by Visual Entidad de Gestión de Artistas Plásticos (VEGAP) concerning the purported infringement by Mango of moral rights and economic rights in art which was converted into digital art NFTs.[98] The case concerned the art of three artists which Mango used as part of a virtual exhibition in Decentraland in 2022. Mango owned the physical artwork but VEGAP, the Visual Entity for Management of Plastic Artists alleged that they had not brought the rights to turn these items into NFT and accordingly the moral rights and economic rights of the artists were being infringed. The court found that Mango had not reproduced the works but by turning them into digital art they had in fact created new works and that they had a fair use argument given no economic benefit was obtained by Mango.

10.74 All human creators of artwork automatically have moral rights. This in addition to economic rights ascribed to the copyright in the artwork. Moral rights cannot be transferred but it is possible for these to be waived under the law of England and Wales. It is still unclear how a dispute similar to that in the *Mango* case would be viewed by the courts, however, it would be prudent for those wanting to use art in the metaverse to ensure that such rights are comprehensively waived. The moral rights under the law of England and Wales are contained in the Copyright, Design and Patents Act 1988, Ch VI as:

97 https://intellectual-property-helpdesk.ec.europa.eu/news-events/news/mango-prevails-court-supports-nft-art-exhibition-metaverse-general-court-upholds-yannick-noahs-tm-2024-02-15_en.

98 Juzgado de lo Mercantil, Barcelona, No 1900/2022.

1 the right to be identified as author;[99]

2 right to object to derogatory treatment of work;[100]

3 right not to have false attribution of work;[101]

4 right to privacy of certain photographs and film.[102]

10.75 Legal commentators believe that creating an immersive experience of an artwork is no different than the right to print copies of the art and therefore would not be infringing mortal rights.[103]

10.76 With regards to art which is created in the metaverse this is unlikely to attract its own moral rights under English Law given the right to be identified as author and to object to derogatory treatment do not arise for a computer programme or any computer-generated work under the Copyright, Designs and Patents Act 1988, ss 79(2) and 81(2).

CONCLUSION

10.77 This chapter considers sports, entertainment, culture and the arts in the metaverse. The key takeaway points are:

- Entertainment is moving into the metaverse. Consideration is needed in respect of the rights of personalities in this space and whether the existing law offers sufficient protection. In particular care is needed to ensure that new rights in the metaverse are properly licensed.
- Brand protection and the use of sports data will be important considerations in the metaverse.
- Virtual sports already exist. There is a need to determine how these are regulated, whether as an add-on to existing e-sports or as an add-on to the real-life sport or as an independent standalone sport itself. Players are being drafted for virtual sports and signing contracts to join sports teams. There is the need for input from governing bodies to safeguard rights usually afforded to sportspersons in real life within their contracts and restrictions to protect the integrity of the sport and participants.

99 Section 77(4) the author of an artistic work has the right to be identified whenever (a) the work is published commercially or exhibited in public, or a visual image of it is communicated to the public.

100 Section 80(1). Under section 80(4) an artist has the right where this is being published commercially or exhibited in public.

101 Section 84(1).

102 Section 85(1).

103 https://itsartlaw.org/2023/03/23/the-public-domain-and-immersive-art-how-copyright-law-impacts-interactive-art-experiences/#:~:text=For%20example%2C%20an%20immersive%20art,is%20protected%20by%20copyright%20law.

- Digital twin technology is being used to move real-life sport into the metaverse both to test capacity of venues but also for fan engagement. Strict security measures are required to stop any potential interference with the real-life game and to prevent cyber-attacks.
- Gambling regulations should still apply in the metaverse and suitable safeguards should be put in place. It may be necessary to have a licence in place for certain games in the metaverse.
- Licensing should deal with the right to use music within the metaverse. Care must be taken over other territorial rights which may arise given the cross-border nature of the metaverse. Where there is no licence in place there are considerable risks with the use of third parties' music in the metaverse without their permission.
- The metaverse has considerable potential for preserving cultural landmarks and practices. This is in line with UN Treaties but there are rights with intellectual property rights in such artefacts as shown with issues such as with the Parthenon Marbles and the Queen Nefertiti bust.
- Copyright will be created in respect of art created in the metaverse. There are potential issues of moral right infringements where art is brought into the metaverse, even where there are no copyright concerns.

Chapter 11

Purchasing property in the metaverse

> *'Metaverse real estate is one of the most exciting things that we've been dealing with for some time. It's real estate that is virtual, where parcels of land are sold. And, it's less new than you think. People have been working on it and building whole worlds for a very long time.'*
>
> Mark Rose, CEO Avison Young

11.01 Plots of land in the metaverse have sold for as much as USD$2.4m[1] and USD$4.3m;[2] large businesses such as Gucci and JP Morgan and celebrities such as Snoop Dogg all own land in the metaverse in one form or another and in 2022 it was reported that in the previous 12 months almost $2 billion had been spent on land in the metaverse.[3] Parcels of 'land' in the metaverse are being sold to users.[4] In real life there are specific laws and enhanced protection for land as real property. Real property is for many one of their most important possessions and their biggest asset.[5] For this reason, the law of property has evolved to safeguard real property rights given its economic, sociological, political, economic and cultural importance.[6] This chapter explores the principles underpinning traditional law of property in real life and its application in the metaverse.

11.02 The Royal Institution of Chartered Surveyors (RICS) has considered the idea of land in the metaverse.[7] It has confirmed that there are positive and negative aspects of real estate in the metaverse but regardless it is evident that the idea of the metaverse and buying and selling land in the metaverse is on the horizon. RICS considers that the value of land in the metaverse may not be based on the same factors as in real life. It highlights that while there is no single metaverse with finite land then the value of land in the metaverse will not be equivalent to that of land in real life. It considers that what makes land expensive in real life is that it is a finite resource. The World Economic Forum however

1 https://www2.deloitte.com/nl/nl/pages/real-estate/articles/real-estate-in-the-metaverse.html.
2 https://www.weforum.org/agenda/2022/03/metaverse-real-estate-prices-boom/.
3 https://www.bbc.co.uk/news/technology-63488059.
4 https://docs.decentraland.org/player/general/introduction/.
5 Bell highlights that some consider property to be 'the core of liberty' Abraham Bell and Gideon Parchomovsky, A Theory of Property, 90 Cornell L. Rev. 531 (2005) Available at: http://scholarship.law.cornell.edu/clr/vol90/iss3/1.
6 Bruce G. Carruthers and Laura Ariovich, The sociology of property rights, Annu. Rev. Sociol. 2004. 30:23–46.
7 https://ww3.rics.org/uk/en/modus/technology-and-data/smart-living/unreal-estate--buying-property-in-the-metaverse-.html.

views the different metaverse platforms as akin to different countries on Earth and accordingly believe there would be a finite amount of land in the metaverse.[8]

11.03 Whilst there are certainly fundamental property law issues to consider in respect of the metaverse, it is clear that the metaverse can also help with many factors of real property purchases in real life. These include the use of digital twins for planning and to virtually explore the neighbourhood.[9] This is already planned for the UAE and can be used for standard search enquiries to check highways and draining.

WHAT IS REAL PROPERTY?

11.04 Land is defined under the Law of Property Act 1925 (LPA 1925), s 205(1)(ix).[10] Whilst this is a complex definition, it covers the bundle of both tangible and intangible rights associated with real property and despite many of the rights being dealt with by way of contracts or deeds what makes real property unique is that the rights attach to the land itself and bind more than just those that are a party to the contract; it creates proprietary interests and rights in respect of the land itself.[11]

11.05 The difficulties in defining the concept of property is due to its historical, legal and economic importance. Historically the reason for the importance of land is its value and the extraction of that value.[12] Land is generally considered to be unlike other assets. It is permanent and capable of physical possession.[13] Land law in England and Wales remains firmly rooted in the feudal system. It is this structure that birthed the concept of a division of equitable and legal title. The concept of real property is derived from the remedies available, for real property – the remedies permitted the recovery of that item as opposed to damages only for its loss.[14]

8 https://www.weforum.org/agenda/2022/03/metaverse-real-estate-prices-boom/.

9 https://www.cbre.co.uk/insights/articles/how-can-the-commercial-real-estate-sector-use-the-metaverse.

10 Land is defined as "Land' includes land of any tenure, and mines and minerals, whether or not held apart from the surface, buildings or parts of buildings (whether the division is horizontal, vertical or made in any other way) and other corporeal hereditaments; also a manor, an advowson, and a rent and other incorporeal hereditaments, and an easement, right, privilege, or benefit in, over, or derived from land; … and 'mines and minerals' include any strata or seam of minerals or substances in or under any land, and powers of working and getting the same. .; and 'manor' includes a lordship, and reputed manor or lordship; and 'hereditament' means any real property which on an intestacy occurring before the commencement of this Act might have devolved upon an heir'.

11 Martin Dixon, Modern Land Law, 12th edition (2021) Routledge Taylor, Francis Group.

12 Abraham Bell and Gideon Parchomovsky, A Theory of Property, 90 Cornell L. Rev. 531 (2005).

13 Thompson, Modern Land Law, 2nd edition, Oxford University Press (2003).

14 Thompson, Modern Land Law, 2nd edition, Oxford University Press (2003).

WHAT IS 'LAND' IN THE METAVERSE?

11.06 Unlike in real life land in the metaverse is not real property. It is instead the right to be identified as the owner of a specific area of the metaverse and governed under the relevant terms of the platform. The user will not own the specific coding associated with that land. Where the metaverse is recorded on the blockchain it is expected that the land ownership would be recorded on the blockchain. Land in the metaverse is intangible property; the right to use a certain space and it be identified as your space. It is not the same as owning land in real life where you are said (rather inaccurately given the LPA 1925) to own '*cuius est solum, eius est usque ad coelum et ad inferos'*, which is roughly translated as 'everything from heaven to hell'.

11.07 In most instances ownership of land in the metaverse will be a licence in respect of the use of the land as a digital product. For the most parts it will be the same as all other digital assets that are sold in the metaverse. Decentraland identify Wearables and NAMES and LAND as digital assets which are linked to a user's digital wallet.[15]

11.08 Sir Geoffrey Vos, Master of the Rolls, identified the unique features of digital assets as being that they are intangible, have cryptographic authentication and use distributed ledger technology[16] The Law Commission was asked by the UK Government to consider whether the law was able to deal with digital assets given their unique characteristics and concluded that the common law of England and Wales can in the main already deal with digital assets due to its flexibility but it would recommend specific legislative reforms as necessary and introduced the idea of using technological specialists to assist judges.[17] One such specific proposed legislative change proposed by The Law Commission in February 2024[18] was to introduce a new distinct category of personal property to explicitly cover digital assets. The Law Commission identified following extensive research that certain digital assets did not fit into either 'things in possession' or 'things in action'. The Law Commission refers to the 2019 case of *AA v Persons Unknown*[19] in which the High Court recognised that there was an issue with classifying cryptocurrency as either 'things in possession' or 'things in action'.[20] As below Parliament have now introduced specific legislation to finally clarify that digital assets are property and the very next day after such legislation

15 https://decentraland.org/blog/about-decentraland/how-to-keep-your-digital-assets-safe-in-the-metaverse.

16 https://www.judiciary.uk/wp-content/uploads/2019/11/LegalStatementLaunch.GV_.2-1.pdf.

17 https://cloud-platform-e218f50a4812967ba1215eaecede923f.s3.amazonaws.com/uploads/sites/30/2024/02/Conflicts-full-document-FINAL-pdf-1.pdf.

18 https://cloud-platform-e218f50a4812967ba1215eaecede923f.s3.amazonaws.com/uploads/sites/30/2024/02/Feb-2024-digital-assets-and-personal-property-CP.pdf.

19 *AA v Persons Unknown* [2019] EWHC 3556 (Comm), [2020] 4 WLR 35.

20 The Court of Appeal confirmed that cryto-assets are property.

was introduced the High Court affirmed the position in the case of *D'Aloia v Persons Unknown*.[21]

11.09 Whilst The Law Commission's focus was on crytotokens the same will apply to many items in the metaverse. This would cover both cryptocurrency or tokens used in the metaverse but also other objects including 'land' or other assets purchased in the metaverse. The Law Commission however said that it does not consider that the proposed Bill would apply to all in-game assets.

11.10 The Property (Digital Assets etc) Bill was introduced into Parliament on 11 September 2024[22] and states:

> **Objects of personal property rights**
>
> A thing (including a thing that is digital or electronic in nature) is not prevented from being the object of personal property rights merely because it is neither—
>
> (a) a thing in possession, nor (b) a thing in action.

11.11 The Law Commission recognises that this statute would be interpreted based on common law principles but highlights that any digital assets falling under these provisions will have to meet the features of property as set out by Lord Wilberforce in *National Provincial Bank v Ainsworth*.[23] The Law Commission highlights the importance of 'rivalrousness' in the context of digital assets, being when one user is using an asset it is not possible for another user to also use the same asset. This has historically been a challenge with digital products but one which the blockchain has aimed to solve, especially with the use of NFTs.

A NEW APPROACH

11.12 There is certainly an argument for 'land' in the metaverse to be treated in the same manner as real property or land in real life. Whilst it may not necessarily fit within the traditional idea of real property, given the sums involved, and the risks associated with this 'land' the enhanced protection afforded in real life to real property however would be beneficial for virtual land in the metaverse.[24] It is worth keeping in mind that historically even leases were considered to fall under the law of personality and treated as a commercial arrangement rather than coming under land law.[25] This has changed over time given the importance of leasehold property and the need for certain rights and protection being attached to the land itself.

21 [2024] EWHC 2342 (Ch), [2024] WLR(D) 417.

22 This is slightly different from the suggested wording by the Law Commission – https://lawcom.gov.uk/property-digital-assets-etc-bill-introduced-into-parliament/.

23 *National Provincial Bank v Ainsworth* [1965] AC 1175.

24 Such as the requirements under LP(MP)A 1989, 2 which requires contracts of land to be made by signed writing

25 Thompson, *Modern Land Law* (2nd edn, Oxford University Press, 2003).

11.13 In the metaverse rights relating to the 'land' certainly are capable of attaching to the 'land' and being recorded on the blockchain. Accordingly, there is the capability of reflecting any proprietary rights for the land which are designated as belonging to that land in the metaverse to the 'land' and recording this all on the blockchain. The European Parliament's Policy Department for Citizens' Rights and Constitutional Affair in its 2023 report calls on legislators both in the US and EU to address the issue of land in the metaverse given the significant issues and risks.[26]

11.14 Property in the metaverse mirrors real life.[27] Virtual property has the same hallmarks of property as identified by Honoré in his Oxford Essays in Jurisprudence[28] but under western legal systems there has been a move from tangible rights to intangible rights and no longer are such rights directly attached to the land. Historically land transfers required the actual physical transfer of soil from the parcel of land and now instead we speak of the different interests in the land being transferred.

11.15 Where software mimics the real world it should be treated in the same way as the real-life equivalent.[29] Fairfield draws a distinction between something that is rivalrous and non-rivalrous. He considers that where items are non-rivalrous then it is appropriate for their use to be governed by intellectual property rights, however, where the item is rivalrous then this should be treated as 'virtual property' and afforded the rights more akin to those given to property. Land in the metaverse is rivalrous. Once it is sold it no longer available to any other user to purchase. The land is carved up and identified as parcels of land effectively in the same way that property in real life has been carved up. Ownership of land in the metaverse is being advertised as being permanent and capable of being used and sold by the owners.

11.16 The cases of *Bragg v Linden Research*[30] and *Eros, LLC v Simon*[31] show that the same issues exist with virtual property rights as in real life and whilst in the first instance terms of business will govern the relationship in respect of virtual property, there is a school of thought that the courts may actually reject

26 https://www.europarl.europa.eu/RegData/etudes/STUD/2023/751222/IPOL_STU(2023)751222_EN.pdf.

27 The Laws of the Virtual Worlds, F. Gregory Lastowka & Dan Hunter, California Law Review, vol. 92 no 1, January 2004

28 As set out in A. M. Honoré, Ownership, in Oxford Essays in Jurisprudence 107, 108-10 (A.G. Guest ed., 1961) Ownership, 107, 108-10 (A.G. Guest ed., 1961) in which ownership is considered to be 'the right to use, exclude, and transfer, and noting that some rights, such as rights to possess or manage, can be subsumed within these categories' (as quoted from The Laws of the Virtual Worlds, F. Gregory Lastowka & Dan Hunter, California Law Review, vol. 92 no 1, January 2004).

29 Fairfield, Joshua, 'Virtual Property' (2005), Articles by Maurer Faculty. 1787 – http://www.repository.law.indiana.edu/facpub/1787.

30 *Bragg v Linden Research, Inc.*, 487 F. Supp. 2d 593 (E.D. Pa. 2007) (No. 06CV4925).

31 *Eros, LLC v Simon*, No. 1:07CV4447 (E.D.N.Y. Oct. 24, 2007).

such terms in the future and insist on other forms of protection for users.[32] In some situations, the courts have actually already been able to reclassify purported interests from what they have been labelled by the parties.[33] Examples such as in property law where licenses and leases are often reclassified, and in contractual law when there is retention of title and rather than be considered as a licence, the interest is reclassified as a security interest in the item instead. The US case of *UMG Recordings, Inc v Augusto*[34] in particular is as an example of reclassification of rights from their original labelling. This case relates to CDs and not land. In this case the record label sought to try and argue that they had not sold the rights in the CD to the buyers but licensed the right to the music under the CD to the buyers. In this case the courts found that given the buyer of the CD never had to return the music on the CD then the CDs were being sold, not licensed, to the buyers. It further explores the cases of *Vernor v Autodesk, Inc*[35] and *Softman Products Co, LLC v Adobe Systems, Inc.*[36] These were both cases concerning the issue of reclassification of licensing in software but in both examples there is still some form of tangible product. This makes the analogies difficult in the context of the metaverse, since there is unlikely to ever be any form of tangible ownership rights passing. As with many other issues it may be that the historical distinction however, between tangible and intangible rights in respect of property are no longer of any real value or significance as society move more into the digital realm and the metaverse evolves. The Property (Digital Assets etc) Bill certainly seems to suggest that this is the case because an item can still be classed as property but fall into neither category. Therefore we would expect the courts to look at the underlying realities of what is being sold rather than labels.

CO-OWNERSHIP IN THE METAVERSE

11.17 The issue of co-ownership in the metaverse is complex depending on how the ownership rights are being recorded. Where the metaverse is based on the blockchain the property rights will be contained in the user's wallet. The idea of co-ownership then becomes problematic and issues of joint tenancy are largely redundant unless technological provisions can be put in place for assets to be held jointly in the metaverse and not held in specific shares. If the property or land is carved up to enable shared ownership then already the lines are being drawn to demark a tenancy in common. It is arguable that by reflecting ownership shares on the blockchain that any joint tenancy is severed. Centuries of protection afforded to those benefitting from resulting trusts are somewhat eradicated. That is not to say that there would be no argument that where joint property is held by one legal owner in the metaverse that there is no constructive trust. It is more than likely that a court would seek to afford beneficiaries with such protection in these circumstances.

32 Lastowka & Hunter, The Laws of the Virtual Worlds, 92 CAL. L. REV. 1 (2004).

33 Juliet M. Moringiello, What Virtual Worlds Can Do for Property Law, 62 Fla. L. Rev. 159 ().Available at: https://scholarship.law.ufl.edu/flr/vol62/iss1/4.

34 558 F. Supp. 2d 1055 (C.D. Cal. 2008).

35 555 F. Supp. 2d 1164 (W.D. Wash. 2008).

36 171 F. Supp. 2d 1075 (C.D. Cal. 2001).

CONVEYANCING IN THE METAVERSE

11.18 Whilst virtual estate agents sell virtual 'land' in the metaverse, as yet no standardised conveyancing process have been devised. In real life as part of the conveyancing process enquiries will be raised in respect of the property. The Conveyancing Protocol[37] includes both standardised enquiries and standard sale terms.

Searches

11.19 The first stage of the conveyancing process is to advise on searches. Standard searches include title searches, local authority searches, water and drainage searches and environmental searches. Other common searches include searches in respect of planning and highways. The searches are designed to identify common risks to properties and pull together search reports based on public information. Whilst not all of these searches would be relevant in the metaverse there will be factors which will affect all landowners in the metaverse and should form part of a standard search package. To be able to compile these searches however the necessary underpinning infrastructure will need to be put in place by the platform owners and those utilising the metaverse so that sufficient data would be available. Given this is all digital and the push for devising the metaverse with greater transparency this should be possible and would be desirable.

11.20 Searches that would be beneficial would include information on the ownership rights in the virtual land, the underlying platform and any restrictions, whether the land can be transferred or sold, the intended use of other properties in the vicinity, any restriction on use of the land (both from a technological perspective such as the underlying blockchain/ platform and the any restrictions in respect of the space, identification of public access routes (eg is the land on a main street, in a cul de sac or inaccessible) and proximity to public amenities. As the metaverse evolves so will the need for the searches to evolve. If for example there are portals to access other metaverses, where would these be in proximity to you and are you close to transport links.

11.21 In real life mortgage companies require searches to be carried out. This seeks to go some way to mitigate their risks in respect of their security over the property. The issue of mortgaging and securing a charge over land in the metaverse is discussed below, however, should there be any financing it would be anticipated that some form of searches would be required.

11.22 It depends upon which platform the land is on as to what searches can be carried out. On Decentraland for example you are able to search and see your land on a virtual map[38] whilst on Sandbox you can buy land via their raffle or specific land via a third party market-place.[39]

37 https://www.lawsociety.org.uk/topics/property/conveyancing-protocol.

38 https://decentraland.org/marketplace/lands.

39 https://docs.sandbox.game/en/owners/land/buy-land.

11.23 Searches as to title will be undertaken in real life. In the metaverse caution should be exercised to check that the person purporting to sell the 'land' has the right to sell that 'land'. 'Land' is typically available to be purchased either from the owners of the platform or from resellers. Terms upon which land can be sold may be contained within the terms of use on the specific platform or it may be recorded on the blockchain depending on how the transaction is taking place and how the platform itself is structured. On those metaverse platforms that are based on blockchain the land would typically be represented as an NFT. Checks can be made to confirm the ownership and provenience of the NFT prior to its transfer. This is however not straightforward and a cyber security expert should be involved to confirm the legitimacy and that the NFT is actually in the wallet of the seller prior to progressing the sale.

Enquiries

11.24 In respect of commercial property it is common to use Commercial Property Standard Enquiries (CPSE) to request due diligence in respect of the property. Whilst most of the CPSE deals with issues relating to bricks and mortar in real-life properties prior to the conclusion of any purchase of land in the metaverse suitable enquiries should be made. Care should be taken to develop standard enquiries which would be applicable to all commercial property owners in the metaverse.

11.25 In respect of residential property, it is typical for the seller to prepare standard documents in respect of the sale such as the Property Information Form and Fittings and Content Form. These forms are effectively standard enquiries to which the seller is responding. The risk remains with such forms that should these be incorrectly completed the seller is exposed to allegations of misrepresentation.

Contract of sale

11.26 Under the Law of Property (Miscellaneous Provisions) Act 1989 (LP(MP)A 1989), s 2 any contract for the sale of land must:

(1) be in writing;

(2) contain all the terms in one agreement;

(3) be signed by all parties.

11.27 If the requirements of the LP(MP)A 1989, s 2 are not complied with then the sale will be void.[40] Standard Conditions of Sale are typically used for residential property sales.[41] There is scope for developing similar standard sale

40 This was affirmed in the case of Bates v (1) Guy (2) Tebb [2017] UKFTT 882 (PC), 20 November 2017.

41 https://www.lawsociety.org.uk/topics/property/standard-conditions-of-sale.

terms for sale of land in the metaverse to standardise the process and protect the parties. Whilst the metaverse may revolutionise the way that affairs are conducted it would be beneficial to have safeguards akin to the LP(MP)A 1989, s 2, and whilst this does not have to be signed under-hand it should still ideally be in a written form.

MORTGAGES IN THE METAVERSE

11.28 The metaverse and blockchain has the potential to revolutionise mortgages.[42] Mortgages are being offered over virtual property in the metaverse.[43] The mortgages are secured against cryptoassets on the blockchain.[44] At this stage the mortgages are short term debt facilities.[45] The NFTs for the land are held by the metaverse mortgage company but the borrower is still permitted to develop the land.[46]

11.29 Chaplin in his 1890 Law Report[47] explains that the idea of the mortgage or a secured charge over property has been around for a very long time. He traces the idea of simple liens over property to Roman Law but confirmed that Roman Law did not distinguish between land and chattels. He states under Saxon Law the agreement was registered in either a court or monastery. At that time if possession was taken under the agreement then the lender did not take full ownership of the property but a '*pledgee's seisin*'. He confirmed that the word mortgage meant 'dead pledge'. It was not until the 1300s that the modern concept of the mortgage was used, with security over the land with an equitable interest in the land.

11.30 It is certainly not common today to have mortgages over chattels and therefore we expect to see extensive contractual provisions in play where finance is being secured against a virtual asset. It is unclear whether it would be sufficient for this to be registered purely on the blockchain or whether there would start to be a centralised register of mortgages held by the platform owners. How this is dealt with would be a true divergence between the centralised and decentralised systems.

TENURE

11.31 In the metaverse land is in theory capable of ownership on both a freehold and leasehold basis, in so far as certain users will 'purchase' land and

42 Dubey, Mokashi, Pradhan, Gupta, Walimbe, Technium, Metaverse and Banking Industry – 2023 The Year of Metaverse Adoption, Vol. 4, No.10 pp.62-73 (2022).

43 https://markets.businessinsider.com/news/currencies/metaverse-mortgage-terrazero-decentraland-virtual-land-real-estate-crypto-finance-2022-2.

44 https://metaworksholdings.com/2022/12/20/mortgages-in-the-metaverse/.

45 https://wishu.io/metaverse-mortgages-buying-property-in-decentraland/.

46 https://www.nationalmortgagenews.com/list/how-does-a-metaverse-mortgage-work.

47 H W Chaplin, The Story of Mortgage Law, Harvard Law Review, v4, no1 Boston, 15 April 1890.

then enable other users to rent their space and brand it as their space under a form of virtual lease.[48] Strictly speaking it is likely that this will be a license to use the space which will then be sub-licensed. It will be important to carefully check the platform terms to understand the basis upon which any 'land' is being sold.[49] It is important to confirm that under the platform terms that any land that is looking to be leased can actually be 'leased' or arguably more accurately sublicensed.

11.32 In real life there are many statutory protections afforded to leaseholders under the law of England and Wales. There has been much discussion under the law of England and Wales over whether what has been granted to a tenant is a licence or a leasehold interest in the property. This is interesting in the context of the metaverse, given in many cases the decisions looked not at labels afforded to the interest by the parties but the underlying features of the relationship. In *Street v Mountford*[50] the key feature of a lease was considered to the right to exclusive possession. This is at least technically possible in the metaverse.

11.33 Under the Law of Property Act 1925 most leases require the parties to enter into a deed to create a lease. There are a few exceptions but the formalities of entering into a deed in the metaverse are themselves likely to be fraught with complications especially with the uncertainty as to whether both parties being present together virtually in the metaverse would qualify.[51]

11.34 Importantly under any lease there are certain implied terms. These implied terms are likely to be relevant to those looking to obtain a 'leasehold interest' or at the least a 'sub-licence' to land in the metaverse. First, and importantly there is the right to quiet enjoyment. The application of this right in the metaverse may extend for example to the right not to have the landlord's avatar frequenting the land unless prior notice has been provided. It is also likely to extend to specific issues that are likely to only apply in the metaverse, such as rebranding or refashioning the land. If the tenant has acquired the use of the land with the appearance of a high-rise modern office then it would interfere with their enjoyment of the property if the owner of the land suddenly redesigned the look of the property to say be a Malibu beach house.

11.35 Another implied term in a lease with importance in the metaverse is that the landlord should not derogate from the grant. This means if the property is let for a particular purpose the landlord should not do anything to frustrate that use. In the metaverse there could be numerous infringements of this right; these may include for example the landlord seeking to technologically circumvent customers from being able to access a metaverse store.

48 https://www.wired.com/story/landlords-rentals-decentraland-metaverse/.

49 Radhakrishna, Legal Issues with Real Estate in the Metaverse, Proceedings of the International Conference on Law and Digitalization (ICLD 2022).

50 [1985] UKHL 4.

51 https://www.lawsociety.org.uk/topics/business-management/qa-on-how-to-use-electronic-signatures-and-complete-virtual-executions.

11.36 In real life depending on the nature of the lease there is some form of repairing covenant imposed on the landlord. This is interesting in the context of the metaverse. For example one would assume that should rights akin to a tenancy be implied into an agreement between a tenant and landlord in the metaverse this would require the landlord to ensure that the coding for the land is kept up to date and compatible with access via the metaverse. It would be prudent, however, to ensure that express provisions in respect of the repairing obligations and maintenance are detailed in any virtual lease.

FORFEITURE IN THE METAVERSE

11.37 It is common in real life for a lease to include a right of forfeiture. The right of forfeiture enables the landlord to bring the lease to an end as a result of a breach of covenants under the lease by the tenant and enables the landlord to take back possession of the land. The potential application of the right of forfeiture available to virtual landlords in the metaverse is important. Landlords want to avoid the argument that tenants should be able to breach provisions of the lease and instead be liable in damages only and not be mandated to return the property back to the landlord. Typically, forfeiture is used in practice in cases of non-payment of rents to enable the landlord to take back the property and either use it themselves or relet it. Regardless of whether the courts accept that there are property rights in any tenancy created between a landlord and tenant in the metaverse you can still protect a landlord in respect of a virtual lease with the contractual right to take back the land in certain situations. It may also be possible to use a smart contract to automatically take back the land in certain circumstances.

11.38 Where the landlord is looking to forfeit a lease in real life other than for non-payment of rent there are strict formalities required under LPA 1925, s 146. This includes the service of a formal notice on the tenant. It is likely to be complex to serve any form of notice on a tenant in the metaverse given its cross-border nature and potential lack of information on the underlying users. Whilst the use of NFT to serve proceedings has been accepted in respect of several litigation matters including *D'Aloia v Persons Unknown & Others*[52] and *Osbourne v Persons unknown and others*[53] and *Jones v Persons Unknown*[54] these all apply in respect of cryptocurrency frauds and it is unclear whether the courts would be as amenable to use of this method of service in other types of proceedings, in particular where forfeiture is being requested for a breach of a covenant other than non-payment of rent.

52 [2022] EWHC 1723 (Ch).
53 [2023] EWHC 39 (KB).
54 [2022] EWHC 2543 (Comm).

EASEMENTS IN THE METAVERSE

11.39 An easement is a third party right over someone else's land. This may be a positive easement, such as a right of way, or a negative easement such as a prohibition to build something on the land. To qualify as an easement, it is necessary for there to be two different pieces of land owned by different people, the right must be of benefit to the dominant land and a burden over the servient land. The easement must benefit the land, and not merely the owner of the land. A legal easement is now typically registered at the Land Registry and is usually created by way of a deed but can be created in other ways such as by way of an implied grant or prescription.

11.40 There is a need to ensure that there are adequate provisions in the metaverse to ensure suitable access to a user's land. Whilst land in the metaverse is different in so far as it is technologically possible to reprogramme the software should a parcel of land be 'landlocked', it is conceivable that as the metaverse evolves land owners will carve up the different parcels of land or grant tenancies over different pieces of land and it will be important that there are suitable easements put in place.

11.41 Justin B Slaughter calls for the introduction of the concept of the 'virtual easements' in respect of the metaverse.[55] He suggest these should be based on a combination of property law concepts and contractual law principles, since neither adequately solve the problem. Going further the use of the blockchain is well suited to be able to permanently record easements concerning the different parcels of virtual land in the metaverse.

RESTRICTIVE COVENANTS

11.42 In real life restrictive covenants can be created between landowners and provided it meets the criteria under the LPA 1925, s 79, the restrictions will run with the land. Restrictive covenants have come about in real life to protect certain key rights that the parties have agreed are important. In the metaverse it is likely that there will still be the need for restrictive covenants or at least the underpinning rationale in respect of restrictive covenants. Common restrictive covenants in real life include not causing a nuisance to neighbours, not using the property for certain trades, not building property on the land, not making certain alterations to the property and limits to use of the property. In some new builds there are stipulations on what colour frontage has to be used and upkeep of the gardens.

55 https://openyls.law.yale.edu/bitstream/handle/20.500.13051/5676/Virtual_Worlds_Between_Contract_and_Property.pdf?sequence=2.

METAVERSE CITIES

11.43 There are numerous digital twin projects which are seeking to use digital twin technology to recreate real-life urban infrastructures.[56] The World Economic Forum predict there will be at least 700 metaverse cities by 2030.[57] Some traditional town planning law considerations will be relevant in the metaverse. Whilst the land itself may be virtual, it still needs effective co-ordination and planning. In real life properties are subject to planning permission and substantial changes to the existing structures require permission which is determined in accordance with local and national planning policy.[58] In real life, however, ultimate recourse against the local authority decision-maker is judicial review. At this stage in the metaverse the decision is ultimately being made by the Tech Giants, and suitable provisions should be put in place to protect users of the metaverse from unreasonable decisions.

CONCLUSION

11.44 This chapter considers property in the metaverse. The key takeaway points are:

- The law has evolved to give special attention to real property given its importance and value. Whilst the metaverse will bring with it a new form of virtual property, it is hoped that the law will follow suit to afford more protection to virtual real property.
- In the metaverse land is a virtual asset. It will be dealt with as a digital asset. The Law Commission has highlighted the need to have a new sub-set of property for digital property to ensure that it is properly recognised under the law of England and Wales. New legislation is set to clarify the position.
- Co-ownership rights of land in the metaverse are complex. The blockchain has the ability to record this but there are complications whether this would sever any joint tenancy.
- Conveyancing will be needed in the metaverse. Steps should be taken now to devise suitable searches and enquiries akin to those of real property given similar risks are present in the metaverse as in real-life property purchases.
- Mortgages are already starting to be made available in the metaverse, but nowhere near to the same extent as in real life. Blockchain technology lends itself to mortgages.
- There is no reason why virtual property should not be capable of being held by virtue of a lease. Implied terms in a lease would be beneficial in

56 Examples include Seoul, Dubai and Santa Monica – https://www.weforum.org/agenda/2023/11/metaverse-digital-cities-urban/.

57 https://www.weforum.org/agenda/2023/11/metaverse-digital-cities-urban/.

58 Town and Country Planning Act 1990.

the metaverse to set expectations over the terms upon which the land can be used. It is likely that many of the real life implied terms will be helpful in the metaverse, but there are also likely to be further terms that should be incorporated into any virtual lease.

- Suitable protection should be afforded to virtual leaseholders to prevent arbitrary decisions to terminate. Protection rights akin to forfeiture should be afforded to virtual leases.
- Easements and restrictive covenants will be important for virtual land.

Chapter 12

Relationships and life in the metaverse

'We're here to celebrate the marriage of two Taco Bell lovers tying the knot in the Metaverse. You heard that right. This is a real wedding with a real couple, a real officiant, in an unreal Taco Bell Metaverse venue. At the Taco Bell Metaverse Wedding you'll get the chance to participate in an experience that includes a one-of-a-kind venue, unique wearables, a DJ, live dancefloor, and a few tasty Taco Bell surprises.'[1]

Taco Bell Metaverse Wedding

12.01 Family life will move into the metaverse as its technology evolves. Many laws have evolved to protect different aspects of home life, from traditional family law issues such as marriage, divorce and child arrangements, to issues surrounding education, travel and work. We expect the law to evolve to protect and safeguard users of the metaverse in their family and home-life albeit carried out in the metaverse.

VIRTUAL WEDDINGS

12.02 Whilst it may be possible to host a virtual wedding ceremony in the metaverse,[2] invite guests to attend a virtual reception, receive virtual gifts and even exchange virtual rings such marriages would not be considered legal under matrimonial law in England and Wales.

12.03 At this stage, those wanting to legally marry will need a legal marriage in real life, but would be free to have a non-legal wedding ceremony in the metaverse. The current law on marriage is based on the Marriage Act 1949 with subsequent supplemental updates.

12.04 In 2022 the Law Commission concluded its report into the law of marriage and considered that law reform was necessary to update the current legal position on marriage.[3] As yet however, these reforms have not been addressed by Parliament.

1 https://decentraland.org/events/event/?id=bacf6081-db0d-46d0-aed4-428970de3d88.

2 There have been several instances of metaverse weddings including the wedding of Sheel Mohnot and Amruta Godbol https://www.technologyreview.com/2023/03/15/1069848/taco-bell-metaverse-wedding/.

3 https://cloud-platform-e218f50a4812967ba1215eaecede923f.s3.amazonaws.com/uploads/sites/30/2022/07/A-new-weddings-law-LC-report.pdf.

12.05 The Law Commission highlights that much has changed since the laws on weddings originated in the 18th century. At that time it was inconceivable to entertain any discussion that weddings could in theory be held remotely. In fact at the time of such laws it was uncommon for marriages to take place outside of a community let alone between people living on different continents.

12.06 Whilst significant reform is recommended the Law Commission does not go so far as to endorse remote weddings save for considering these could be appropriate in limited and exceptional circumstances during times of national emergencies (as discussed below). What the Law Commission does recommend, however, is a move towards officiant-based rules, as opposed to venue-centric rules.[4] The Law Commission consider that whilst the law on marriage must be updated, there is still a need to safeguard legitimate marriages and protect people against sham marriages and forced marriages. The Law Commission considered that the law on marriage may need some form of carve out in times of national emergency where it is impossible to comply, but stop short of recommending that these should be commonplace.

12.07 The Law Commission did consider that some parts of the wedding formalities could however be done remotely[5] and accordingly these could be conducted via the metaverse. These include notices for civil weddings which could be permitted to be made online.

Remote weddings

12.08 In 2020, at the height of the Covid-19 pandemic, Governor Andrew Cuomo passed an Executive Order in New York enabling virtual wedding ceremonies.[6] Once all restrictions were lifted however the Order ended and virtual weddings were not permitted after 25 June 2022.

12.09 Virtual weddings are however, legal in Utah[7] and have been since 2020. Therefore, providing the officiant is located in Utah a wedding conducted virtually will be considered legal. In Utah the entire marriage registration process has moved online, providing for the eventual move into Web3.

12.10 The validity of remote weddings starts to paves the way for virtual weddings in the metaverse; albeit in the metaverse the individuals would at this stage be represented as avatars so as yet would not fall under current provisions. In the future as the technology evolves so too will the realistic nature of the digital representations of the users.

4 https://cloud-platform-e218f50a4812967ba1215eaecede923f.s3.amazonaws.com/uploads/sites/30/2022/07/A-new-weddings-law-LC-report.pdf.

5 https://cloud-platform-e218f50a4812967ba1215eaecede923f.s3.amazonaws.com/uploads/sites/30/2022/07/A-new-weddings-law-LC-report.pdf.

6 https://www.weforum.org/agenda/2020/04/coronavirus-covid-19-wedding-online/.

7 https://www.utahcounty.gov/dept/clerk/marriage/ceremony.html.

Legal recognition of virtual marriages

12.11 Virtual marriages may not be legally recognised in real life but as rules are largely yet to be written in respect of the metaverse there could be a divergence which enables virtual weddings to be recognised and the couple virtually married for the purpose of the metaverse as its own 'jurisdiction'. Studies have shown that virtual marriages help to free people from sociological issues and legal restrictions.[8] Given the ability of the metaverse to diverge from real life there is nothing preventing the decision to declare a marriage in the metaverse binding within the metaverse itself. The benefits afforded by real-life marriage in real life for example, such as joint ownership and intestacy rules could be applied in the metaverse for those with registered virtual metaverse marriages. Whilst there are studies relating to virtual marriages which have evolved out of online games,[9] it is yet to be seen how this may play out in the metaverse as it starts to move away from a purely gaming-centric model.

12.12 Consideration will have to be had as to whether it should be legally permitted to have both a real-life marriage and a virtual marriage. Given the lack of legal recognition of virtual marriages in gaming this question has never been properly addressed,[10] however, if virtual marriages in the metaverse were to gain legal recognition as a result of its immersive and real-time nature this is an area that the law will need to address and consider if legislation is needed to be updated. Studies have shown that those who have had virtual relationships describe it as feeling as being as real as in real life;[11] perhaps this is not surprising given the phenomena of internet dating generally and it is expected that dating will become more virtual as we move into the metaverse.

DIVORCE AND THE METAVERSE

12.13 Real-life divorce is likely to impact on a user in the metaverse. Digital assets will fall under section 24 Matrimonial Causes Act 1973, therefore should be recorded on the Form E and are capable of being transferred as part of Property Adjustment Order under the Matrimonial Causes Act 1973, s 24. One of the main complications is identifying the virtual assets that the other spouse may have and then trying to value these assets. As the metaverse moves onto the blockchain it will be easier to identify virtual assets.

8 J. Abraham and A.Falah, 'Is Virtual Marriage Acceptable? A Psychological Study Investigating The Role of Ambiguity Tolerance and Intimacy Illusion in Online Dating among Adolescents and Early Adults', 2017, Journal of Psychological and Educational Research, 24(2), 117 – 143.

9 Such as the study into the online game Audition carried out by Freeman et al in their paper 'simulating marriage: Gender Roles and Emerging Intimacy in an Online Game CSCW 2015, March 14-18, 2015, Vancouver, BC, Canada.

10 Despite the online virtual world 'Second Life' enabling people to engage in virtual relationships from the mid-2000s which includes engaging in virtual sex and buying virtual property together..

11 Kolotkin et al 'Does loving an avatar threaten real life marriage?' (2012) Journal of Virtual Worlds Research vol 5 number 3.

12.14 The types of virtual assets in the metaverse will be wide ranging. There will be digital assets directly purchased and used by avatars such as NFTs, but other assets will also have value. As data becomes one of the key commodities as we move into Web3, this virtual data will increase in value, especially as we move towards a digital identity. As in **Chapter 8** when discussing the specific assets comprised within the digital goods and services being purchased, it is imperative that divorce lawyers are able to deconstruct the digital asset accurately to understand exactly what bundle of rights exists and are owned by the matrimonial estate.

12.15 Legal experts call for establishing a framework for dealing with the tracing, identification, valuation (cash equivalent) and division of virtual assets in the metaverse on divorce.[12] In the UK this would be the preparation of the Financial Statement (Form E) but in the US it would be undertaken via discovery. It is important not only to identify the virtual asset but also where possible obtain the metadata to be able to justify any valuation. Suitable experts on digital assets and their valuation will be required if there are contested financial proceedings in the divorce. There are multiple different ways to value digital assets, which itself presents a challenge in financial proceedings. As the range of digital assets in the metaverse increases further we expect to see more challenges ahead for dealing with those on divorce. Lawyers need to keep in mind that it is not only the 'capital assets' owned in the metaverse but also any income that may be being generated from performing services in the metaverse or generated from digital assets that may be being used by third parties, such as stores owned by a party or income being generated from a digital asset being worn by another avatar.

12.16 As discussed in **Chapter 16** there are complications when tracing assets in the metaverse and on the blockchain.

12.17 There are very few cases dealing with digital assets on divorce. One case in the US that may be helpful to address the issue of the valuation of digital assets is the Nevada case *of LaFond v LaFond.*[13] In this case the court made the award over a percentage of the Bitcoin held by the husband as at a specific date rather than relying on the purported value of the Bitcoin. A similar decision has been reached by the UK courts in *DH v RH* [2024] EWFC 79, where the judge ordered a 50/50 split of the remaining cryptocurrency. Mr Justice MacDonald in this case stated:

> 'I accept that, as a class of assets, cryptocurrency renders the identification of ownership and control of assets harder'.

12.18 As discussed in **Chapter 17** there are serious considerations if legal advice is being provided in the metaverse, especially in family law matters and predominantly divorce and child law matters. This is because the spouse may

12 Tang, 'Cryptocurrency, NFTs, and the 'Metaverse': Addressing the Expanding World of Virtual Assets in Divorce Proceedings' (2022) Penn State Law Review Vol 127:1.

13 2022 WL 714430.

be able to access such advice via the VR headset and pose as their spouse. As a result there is a high risk of extremely sensitive information being accidently disclosed. This is because in the metaverse, via the VR headset the spouse would effectively become their spouse's avatar and would look the same, and through voice altering technology could easily pose as the other party. With an evolving metaverse they may not even need to converge with words but other forms of communication or be unwittingly even able to access to virtual files on a case.

Virtual infidelity

12.19 Since the Divorce, Dissolution and Separation Act 2020 provided for 'no fault' divorces (in effect from 2022) there has been no requirement to provide evidence for divorce based on one of the previous five grounds of adultery, unreasonable behaviour, desertion, consent after two years separation, or five years' separation. Instead, it just has to be pleaded that the marriage has irretrievably broken down. Therefore, irrespective of whether virtual infidelity would be considered as adultery or unreasonable behaviour, this is now irrelevant under the law of England and Wales.

12.20 Whilst it may not now be necessary under the law of England and Wales to now have to prove adultery, this is not the case in many other jurisdictions where fault-based divorces are still required.[14] In many jurisdictions virtual adultery would not be sufficient to prove adultery for with-fault divorces and calls have been made to modernise the law on adultery to encompass virtual adultery given the changes in interactions with the advancements in technology.[15] This should be considered in the metaverse given its immersive nature, which could result in intimate relationships despite the fact that there is no interaction in real life.

CHILD CUSTODY AND VIRTUAL PARENTING

12.21 Whilst some consider virtual parenting to be raising a virtual child,[16] it is perhaps more interesting from a legal perspective to consider the prospects of access and virtual visitation rights via the metaverse for a real-life child. There are many positives to be said for visitation rights taking place via the metaverse. This enables parents to have continued involvement with their children when they may not physically be located in the same country, and it also enables more cost-effective supervised visitation. Under the Children Act 1989, s 1 any decision concerning the upbringing of a child, the best interests of the child are paramount.

14 For example in the US many states have both fault and no-fault based divorces.

15 Kathryn Pfeiffer, Comment, Virtual Adultery: No Physical Harm, No Foul? 46 U. Rich. L. Rev. 667 (2012)..

16 https://www.theguardian.com/technology/2022/may/31/tamagotchi-kids-future-parenthood-virutal-children-metaverse.

12.22 All arrangements should be accurately contained in a Child Arrangements Order under the Children Act 1989, s 8. The Order needs to be clear whether any access in the metaverse is supervised or unsupervised. In addition, some thought may need to be had as to where the meeting will take place in the metaverse, since this must be suitable for the visit.

12.23 Consideration needs to be had, however, of the risk that the metaverse could be misused by parents subject to restrictions on visitation to interact with their children in this new realm. Some thought should be had to include specific restrictions concerning interactions in the metaverse. Depending on the circumstances this could be recorded on a Prohibited Steps Order.

PARENTAL RIGHTS IN THE METAVERSE

12.24 Under the Children Act 1989, s 3(1) parental responsibility is defined as 'all the rights, duties, powers, responsibilities and authority which by law a parent of a child has in relation to the child and his property'. With the advent of the metaverse there is the need to redefine the parameters of 'parental responsibility'. It is accepted that parental responsibility extends to decisions about education and schooling – consideration, needs to be had therefore what happens if one parent wants to educate via the metaverse, whilst the other separated parent (with parental responsibility) wants to educate in real life. Unless agreement is reached, it is likely such decision will require the intervention of the courts. Further consent to medical treatment undertaken via the metaverse is also likely to be included.

12.25 Consideration will need to be had as to how far parental responsibility extends to the responsibilities and rights in respect of a child's digital identity and generally in the metaverse. There is certainly an argument to be had, especially with the EU's new EU Digital Identity Wallet under the Digital Identity Regulations, that parental responsibility should extend to treating the digital footprint as the property of a child and decisions in respect of the same would amount to parental responsibility.

FAMILY DISPUTE RESOLUTION IN THE METAVERSE

12.26 The metaverse provides an effective platform for family law mediation. The technology could be used to help parties appreciate the other person's perspective by immersing them in the situation. Mediation in the metaverse would help to create a safe environment for participants and enable users to join from their own homes. That said, one of the criticisms of remote mediations during the Covid-19 pandemic was the fact that participants felt that joining sessions from home felt intrusive. This is likely to be intensified in the metaverse, especially if the parties come face to face. Further safeguards need to be in place to ensure that any children are not present, which is harder to control when the parties are not physically present. A comprehensive framework is needed to effectively create a suitable long-lasting framework for virtual mediation in the metaverse.

DOMESTIC VIOLENCE IN THE METAVERSE

12.27 Domestic violence is known to cross into the digital realm[17] and this is expected to be no different with the rise of the metaverse. The metaverse has the potential to be used for coercive control, psychological abuse, economic abuse and even sexual abuse. Whilst the abuse may not be physical per se, with haptic gloves and immersive technology, virtual physical abuse may not feel dissimilar to physical abuse in real life. It also certainly raises questions whether the misuse of haptic glove technology itself to cause discomfort could amount to physical abuse. Web2 technology has been used to cyberstalk as well as harass victims and technology-facilitated abuse is recognised as a form of domestic abuse.[18] In the metaverse the persistent unwanted presence of an abuser would be abusive, as would 'trolling' someone in the metaverse, preventing their access to their metaverse accounts or misusing someone's metaverse account.

12.28 The Domestic Abuse Act 2021 defines domestic abuse as abusive behaviour towards a personally connected person where both are aged 16 or over.[19] The types of abusive behaviour are listed at s 1(3). Where the definition is fulfilled, the police have the option to issue a domestic abuse protection notice under the Domestic Abuse Act 2021, s 22 prohibiting contact and restricting the person from coming within a specific distance of the victim's home. At this stage there is no restriction which applies to the perpetrator making contact with the victim via the metaverse, which due to its interactive and immersive nature means the victim may come face to face with the perpetrator in XR in their home. Some thought needs to be had around this aspect, especially when avatars are more realistic or if they evolve into more hologrammatic versions of individuals. Restriction may be appropriate not only to access rights in the real-world but also in the metaverse.

12.29 Under of the Domestic Abuse Act 2021, s 28 an application can be made for a domestic abuse order. This will either be with or without notice. This will be required within 48 hours of a domestic abuse protection notice being issued. The order can also be sought as part of family court proceedings, criminal proceedings and in civil proceedings. Section 35(1) provides that the court can 'impose any requirements that the court considers necessary to protect the person for whose protection the order is made from domestic abuse or the risk of domestic abuse'. This could include specific provisions which prevent access and contact via the metaverse. Careful consideration should be had as to any virtual interactions that the perpetrator may be able to utilise to contact and abuse the victim.

17 https://www.esafety.gov.au/women/reduce-technology-facilitated-abuse.

18 Technology-facilitated abuse is specifically detailed in the statutory guidance to the Domestic Abuse Act 2021 https://www.gov.uk/government/publications/domestic-abuse-act-2021/domestic-abuse-statutory-guidance-accessible-version.

19 Domestic Abuse Act 2021, s 1(2).

12.30 On 7 August 2023 the Culture, Media and Sport Committee published its report into the use of connected technologies in domestic abuse and called on legislative reform to protect victims of domestic violence using technology.[20] These technologies form the backbone of the metaverse via the use of smart devices and connected technologies. The Committee highlighted that such technology can be used to spy on victims, to locate them and to control them remotely. These are all potential risks of the metaverse, especially a truly immersive and purist view of one metaverse where all aspects of home life are digitalised and embraced via the immersive technology. Interestingly the Committee highlights that the solution should not be to move victims 'offline'. They recommend that more training is needed for the police on tech-enabled abuse and suitable steps should be taken by industry to protect victims against such abuse.

CHILD PROTECTION IN THE METAVERSE

12.31 Child protection support could be offered in the metaverse as a new avenue to monitor children at risk and subject to a supervision order. Use of virtual guardians already exists and this could be extended in the metaverse. Such guardians could alert the authorities to specific behaviour being carried out in the metaverse. In addition, the alerts could transcend the metaverse if the metaverse virtual guardian was able to monitor real-life interactions in real time using sensors and effectively recreate a digital twin of the home of the at-risk child. At this stage the costs are likely to be prohibitive but with the accessibility of the technology improving, this should ease with time.

12.32 The metaverse itself, however, can present child protection issues. Excessive use of the metaverse, especially to the detriment of other activities, especially education, is likely to raise concerns concerning a parent's ability to give their child sufficient care and lead to care order proceedings.

EDUCATION IN THE METAVERSE

12.33 The metaverse has a significant opportunity in the education space. There are already 'metaversities'.[21]

12.34 Parents have a duty under the Education Act 1996, s 7 to ensure all children of compulsory school age receive a suitable education. The suitability is based on age, ability and aptitude and subject to any special educational needs. The legislation states that this is via 'regular attendance at school or otherwise'. Remote learning via the metaverse would fall therefore within the Education Act 1996, s 7 provided this was suitable for the child. As set out above, all those with

20 https://committees.parliament.uk/publications/41099/documents/200210/default/

21 Such as EUI Department of Law – https://www.eui.eu/news-hub?id=eui-department-of-law-launches-first-course-in-the-metaverse.

parental responsibility have the right to be involved in respect of educational decisions about a child.

Safeguarding

12.35 In real life everyone who works in a school has a safeguarding responsibility. Schools have an important role in safeguarding children.[22] Governing bodies of schools have a requirement to ensure there are arrangements in place to safeguard its pupils under the Education Act 2002, s 175. Teachers have an obligation under the Teachers' Standards to safeguard children.[23] Senior leaders will need to ensure that safeguarding policies are updated to reflect any use of the metaverse by pupils.

Teaching in the metaverse

12.36 Teachers in England must comply with the Teachers' Standards[24] which came into force in September 2012. The Teachers' Standards are not prescriptive but instead outlines the required minimum expectations of teachers. Whether teaching in real life or in the metaverse these standards will need to be adhered to. The metaverse at this stage is a tool which could be incorporated within teaching but under standard one of the Teachers' Standards a teacher must ensure that there is a safe environment for pupils. Teachers will have to be confident that the metaverse environment being deployed is not putting the pupil in an unsafe environment. Just as teachers are required to ensure that their real-life classroom has clear rules on behaviour the same should be transferred into the virtual classroom. Teachers should ensure that pupils are not being exposed to cyber-bullying or other detriments caused by the new technologies.

12.37 Teachers also have to ensure that they take into consideration the capabilities of their pupils; therefore it is expected some students may need more assistance in a virtual environment than others.

WORK-LIFE BALANCE IN THE METAVERSE

12.38 One consideration in the metaverse will be the balance of work and homelife. Working in the metaverse will mean that users will not have to leave home to work, and can step into work via their VR headsets. Some countries have already put in place legislation to prevent employers making contact outside of

22 https://assets.publishing.service.gov.uk/media/6650a1967b792ffff71a83e8/Keeping_children_safe_in_education_2024.pdf.

23 https://assets.publishing.service.gov.uk/media/61b73d6c8fa8f50384489c9a/Teachers__Standards_Dec_2021.pdf.

24 https://assets.publishing.service.gov.uk/media/61b73d6c8fa8f50384489c9a/Teachers__Standards_Dec_2021.pdf.

work hours, known as the 'right to disconnect'.[25] The Labour Party pledged as part of its manifesto to incorporate the right to disconnect.[26]

Working in the metaverse

12.39 Some legal commentators question whether existing employment laws would be suitable for those working solely in the metaverse.[27] One issue being determining the place of work where this is exclusively a virtual workplace. This is important as there may be visa and tax implications depending on what is considered as the employee's place of work.

12.40 In June 2024 Ikea pioneered its 'Co-Worker Game' on Roblox, hiring staff to work in their metaverse shop.[28] The job advert had over 175,000 applications in a week, making it the highest number of applications ever for a job in the UK. The interviews were held virtually and staff are being paid the equivalent of the amount paid to its London staff. The role is fully remote but applicants must be based in the UK.[29] It will be interesting to see what Ikea uses as the 'place of work' given this has to be included as part of the principle statement under the written statement of employment particulars.

12.41 In August 2024 the Dubai Court of First Instance permitted part of an employee's salary to be paid in cryptocurrency for the first time provided the terms were sufficiently clear.[30] This paves the way towards working in the Web3 era. As discussed in **Chapter 7** the metaverse will create new economies and therefore it only seems correct that workers be paid via the same way.

12.42 Given the lack of traditional boundaries in the metaverse the issue of which law will govern any employment relationship will be key for those employed in the metaverse. Under the law of England and Wales it remains relatively uncertain whether the Employment Rights Act 1996 applies when the employee is based outside of the UK since territorial limits were repealed in 1999. The current position seems to require a connection to the UK. This is likely to be complex in the metaverse where the work is exclusively performed virtually. Rome I still applies.[31] A court would therefore look at the jurisdiction

25 There is the right to disconnect under Belgium law; the Employment (Amendment) Bill 2022 is currently making its way through the Kenyan parliament and the EU Parliament has been trying to implement laws on the right to disconnect since 2021: https://www.europarl.europa.eu/topics/en/article/20210121STO96103/parliament-wants-to-ensure-the-right-to-disconnect-from-work.

26 https://labour.org.uk/wp-content/uploads/2022/09/Employment-Rights-Green-Paper.pdf.

27 Potential challenges of working in a virtual space, Peter Sipka, Italian Labour Law e-Journal Issue 1, Vol. 16 (2023) ISSN 1561-8048.

28 https://www.ikea.com/gb/en/newsroom/corporate-news/ikea-is-opening-a-new-store-on-roblox-pub8a9272d0.

29 https://thecoworker.co.uk.

30 Case 1739 of 2024.

31 The Law Applicable to Contractual Obligations and Non-Contractual Obligations (Amendments etc) (EU Exit) Regulations 2019).

chosen by the parties under any employment contract and in the absence of this then it shall be where the employee carries out the work[32] or where there is no physical place (such as will be the case with work in the metaverse) where the business itself is located.[33] This is complex where the business is a DAO or where the business itself is just formed and carried out in the metaverse. Where the employee is not physically based in the UK care should also be had to check whether any local laws also apply.

12.43 Care should be exercised in the EU to ensure that Article 20 – 23 of Regulation (EU) No 1215/2012 is followed to determine where an employment contract can be enforced. This is where either the employee or employer is based in the EU[34] action can only be taken in the member state in which the employee lives.[35]

12.44 Where an employee is being employed in the metaverse by a DAO there are still some uncertainties in respect of the legal relationship given the uncertainties already in existence around DAOs generally under the law of England and Wales. Where these are considered as unincorporated associations any employment rights would have to be enforced against the individual members. Further all employees are entitled to a written statement of employment particulars when they start work, which must include the employer's name. If the DAO has no distinct legal personality, then the employer cannot be the DAO.

12.45 Platform workers carry out their work via a platform for the benefit of the users of the platform. They are often categorised by the platform as self-employed. The EU are looking to regulate this relationship and move the presumption to one of an employment relationship. Working in the metaverse would not necessarily fall within the proposed Platform Work Directive but there are still calls for legislative reform to cover those working in the metaverse.[36] Consideration has to be had as to whether the platform owners and operators should take on any liability for workers working in the metaverse – a form of occupier's liability given they are using their space to conduct the work. There are further questions as to how trade unions can operate and protect workers in the metaverse.

Discrimination in the metaverse workplace

12.46 Attention should still be had to the Equality Act 2010 when looking to move staff into the metaverse. Virtual reality headsets do not suit everyone, they

32 Article 8(2) Rome I.
33 Article 8(3) Rome I.
34 https://eur-lex.europa.eu/LexUriServ/LexUriServ.do?uri=OJ:L:2012:351:0001:0032:en:PDF.
35 Article 22.
36 Potential challenges of working in a virtual space, Peter Sipka, Italian Labour Law e-Journal Issue 1, Vol. 16 (2023) ISSN 1561-8048.

can make people feel sick and some people with disabilities will be unable to use them.[37] Virtual reality headsets also increase the risk of seizures for those with epilepsy, which is classed as a disability under the Equality Act 2010.[38] There is also the risk of indirect age discrimination with an employer looking to move staff into the metaverse.

12.47 There is the risk that the data being gathered from VR headsets may identify disabilities in the workforce. Employers should caution against this unless there are effective safeguards to handle and safeguard this data – but if such data are obtained then employers will need to ensure that reasonable adjustments are put in place. Employees have the right to privacy and if such information is gathered as a result of interactions in the metaverse then this should be kept confidential. This data would be considered special category personal data. Employers should ensure that suitable privacy notices are in place for their staff in respect of data processed via the metaverse.

12.48 Notwithstanding the above, there is also, however, the positive use of the metaverse to potentially help those with certain disabilities to become more employable.[39] With this in mind it is important to ensure that care is taken on a case-by-case basis to ensure that the role is suitable for the specific employee and whether any reasonable adjustments would be necessary.

12.49 The Institute for Ethics and Emerging Technologies considered whether employers will have the right to set policies on the use of metaverse avatars for their employees.[40] There is a considerable risk for employers if they start to set policies or protocol for avatars over aspects which would amount to protected characteristics in real life and therefore make decisions based on those amounting to discrimination if carried out in real life. It would seem prudent however to set some rules to ensure that the avatars working for your business are not offensive and depending on the role it may be necessary to ensure they comply with a particular style. There are still questions as to whether an employer can be held liable when an avatar is discriminated against, but the protected characteristic relates to the avatar only and not the underlying user.[41] It is likely that this would amount to discrimination by perception.

37 Felicia Rosioru, Workers' non-discrimination in the metaverse, SHS Web of Conferences 177, 01001 (2023) Legal Perspectives on the Internet, COPEJI 6.0.

38 https://www.etui.org/publications/working-metaverse-what-are-risks.

39 Seolhee Lee, Youngsun Lee, Eunhye Park, The Development of Metaverse-based Employability Promotion Program for the Young Adults with Disability, Journal of Digital Contents Society, Vol. 23, No. 8, pp. 1527-1537, Aug. 2022.

40 https://philarchive.org/archive/STUTDM-2.

41 Potential challenges of working in a virtual space, Peter Sipka, Italian Labour Law e-Journal Issue 1, Vol. 16 (2023) ISSN 1561-8048.

HOLIDAYS IN THE METAVERSE

12.50 There are many opportunities for tourism in the metaverse and it could eventually be worth $13 billion.[42] Recent examples of tourism in the metaverse include 'visits' to Notre-Dame following the 2019 fire, visits to the UNESCO World Heritage Site of Hegra and even virtual tours of Korea.[43] Qatar Airways has introduced QVerse which enables its travellers to experience virtual air travel in the metaverse complete with a virtual cabin crew member called Sama.[44]

12.51 Package holidays in real life are regulated under The Package Travel and Linked Travel Arrangements Regulations 2018. The Department for Business, Energy and Industrial Strategy guidance highlights that holiday providers have long been regulated in the UK given the risk to consumers in this area.[45] This is because consumers typically spend a large amount of their income on their holidays and with packaged holidays there can be multiple different businesses involved. At this stage virtual tourist trips organised and conducted exclusively in the metaverse would not be covered by the regulations, however, should the harms in respect of package holiday present in real life start to present itself in the metaverse we would expect some form of regulation to protect these consumers.

12.52 Where an existing package holiday provider introduces some form of metaverse engagement or XR experience as part of the package holiday then this would fall under the regulations. If the holiday does fall under the regulations, there are increased obligation on the organiser including being liable for all the different travel services in the package,[46] an obligation to provide appropriate assistance if the tourist is in difficulty[47] and having to provide compensation where there is a lack of conformity with what was agreed.[48] Therefore, package holiday organisers may find themselves having to take on the liability of the metaverse experience so they should ensure that they have in place detailed agreements with any metaverse experience provider.

12.53 To fall under the Package Travel and Linked Travel Arrangements Regulations 2018 there must be at least two 'Travel Services'.[49] What counts as 'Travel Services' is listed under the regulations as the provision of accommodation, car hire, travel and other tourist services. Incorporating a form of XR experience or metaverse engagement as part of a holiday would fall under

42 https://www.mckinsey.com/industries/travel-logistics-and-infrastructure/our-insights/tourism-in-the-metaverse-can-travel-go-virtual.

43 https://www.mckinsey.com/industries/travel-logistics-and-infrastructure/our-insights/tourism-in-the-metaverse-can-travel-go-virtual.

44 https://www.travelandtourworld.com/news/article/qatar-airways-leads-air-travel-innovation-with-qverse-and-ai/.

45 https://assets.publishing.service.gov.uk/media/62dea082e90e0766afece5ee/package-travel-regulations-2018-guidance.pdf.

46 Package Travel and Linked Travel Arrangements Regulations 2018, reg 15.

47 Package Travel and Linked Travel Arrangements Regulations 2018, reg 18.

48 Package Travel and Linked Travel Arrangements Regulations 2018, reg 16

49 2018 Package Travel and Linked Travel Arrangements Regulations 2018, reg 2(1).

the provision of 'any other tourist service'.[50] Where there is just one other 'Travel Service' plus something which falls 'any other tourist service' such as a metaverse experience, the metaverse experience would need to either be advertised as an essential feature of the holiday, account for a significant amount of the value of the holiday or be purchased after the other travel service has been performed.[51] Given the cross-overs we have already seen between real life and the metaverse then incorporating a metaverse element to a holiday is entirely conceivable.

CONCLUSION

12.54 This chapter considers life in the metaverse. The key takeaway points are:

- Virtual weddings would not be considered legal weddings under the law of England and Wales. Weddings however can be conducted remotely under the law of Utah which paves the way for legal weddings in the metaverse.
- Virtual weddings will not be legally recognised in real life but may be recognised in the metaverse. It remains to be seen how a virtual marriage should be treated in the metaverse but there is the opportunity for the platforms to recognise this and to afford similar rights afforded to married couples in real life.
- Real-life divorce will impact on a user in the metaverse. Digital assets may need to be traced, valued and distributed.
- The metaverse can be used as a tool for child access and visitation rights. Controls will be needed to prevent unauthorised contact in the metaverse and should be specifically included within any Prohibited Steps Order where this may be a concern.
- Parental responsibility rights will extend to the metaverse, in particular for healthcare, educational use and schooling.
- Domestic violence can take place in the metaverse. When dealing with protective orders specific restrictions should be included to limit access via the metaverse.
- It is essential that there are proper safeguards put in place in respect of education in the metaverse. Teaching in the metaverse will need to be in accordance with the Teachers' Standards.
- Existing employment law is likely to apply in the metaverse. This may be complicated in the metaverse since there may not be a real-life place of work, the employer may have an alternative business structure and wages may even be paid in tokens.
- Holidays in the metaverse may require regulation under The Package Travel and Linked Travel Arrangements Regulations 2018

50 2018 Package Travel and Linked Travel Arrangements Regulations 2018, reg 2(1).
51 Package Travel and Linked Travel Arrangements Regulations 2018, reg 2(6).

Chapter 13

Estate planning in the metaverse

'The digital afterlife offers more opportunity for continued bonds with our deceased loved ones and, I believe, also houses the greatest opportunity for advancement in how we memorialize and remember our loved ones.'

Cole Imperi, Founder of the School of American Thanatology

13.01 When considering the metaverse as a private client practitioner, advice could fall within one or more of the four pillars; estate planning, estate administration, trusts and/or Court of Protection matters. In the real world we consider actual assets, personal interests, personal benefits, and entitlements from trusts. The metaverse however encapsulates assets, interests, rights, and benefits in a virtual world. A world where regulation is still developing, and possibilities are potentially endless. A world where, without exposure to technology, the visualisation of the assets is not yet accessible to the average person.[1]

ESTATE PLANNING

13.02 Estate planning is arguably the foundation of all other private client matters, with a prominent focus on succession planning. Assets in the real world can nearly always be gifted, transferred or inherited. Therefore, a plan for passing on wealth on a multi-generational level, whether during an individual's lifetime or on death, can be achieved. The process for this in England and Wales is usually considered alongside tax regimes such as inheritance tax, capital gains tax, income tax and stamp duty land tax or (in Wales) land transaction tax. In addition, when gifting or passing on offshore assets, considerations are made to the *situs* of something and/or succession laws in different jurisdictions and double taxation treaties.

13.03 Assets and value in the metaverse typically will sit within a decentralised environment where jurisdiction is just in the early stages of being developed. Whilst one person on earth may have a collection of assets which can be documented through a paper trail, a credit search or record of ownership; their virtual double, alias, or avatar, does not have the same bread crumb trail that practitioners have traditionally become used to. As we move further and further

1 For example the asset is likely to be contained either on the metaverse platform itself behind passwords and authentication codes, or in digital wallets which again require passcodes and security measures to access.

into living double lives (in real life and in virtual life), the need for estate and succession planning will deepen as much as these two worlds will. It is going to be essential for private client practitioners to have an understanding of the ins and outs of the virtual world, in particular as Generation Z and Generation Alpha individuals become our clients.

13.04 In England and Wales, our laws of succession are flexible and are not forced in a particular direction like other jurisdictions. We have the ability to gift in accordance with our wishes during our lifetimes and similarly via a will on death. Where there is no will on death, we have the intestacy rules which provide for family to inherit as per the order of priority set out in the Non-Contentious Probate Rules 1987, r 22. We then also have further flexibility after death, where post-death variations can be made so far as they comply with the Inheritance Tax Act 1984, s 142. The metaverse is not as regulated as this, and to date, mainly relies upon the particular service provider and the terms agreed to when an individual engages with the metaverse.

13.05 So, the question arises, how do we offer succession planning advice to those who are engaging in the metaverse? One considers there to be three main obstacles sitting in the way of being able to provide accurate advice to clients on the succession of assets and interests in the metaverse – value, accessibility, and awareness.

Valuing assets

13.06 The first obstacle is value. We live in a real-life environment where most things are given a monetary value. For estate planning and succession planning purposes, it is this value which is often the focus of this process. Private client practitioners usually focus on the *'open market'* value as required by the Inheritance Tax Act 1964, s 160. Ownership in the metaverse, however, cannot be given this blanket approach because not only does the Great British Pound, the US Dollar or any other real-life currency not exist in the same way it does on earth, the value assets hold in the metaverse are not always monetary.

13.07 In addition to the issue of applying a monetary value to assets in the metaverse, when considering passing on assets on death through the means of a will, private client practitioners would usually want to have an idea of the value of an asset in the future. This allows us to consider which reliefs and exemptions can be used for inheritance tax purposes. Whilst we deal with the emerging market of the metaverse, and as it continues to develop and grow at substantial pace, placing a real-life value on to something and planning around the future of that value is impossible. It is now plausible and foreseeable for an asset worth £1 million on the current open market to be valued 500% more in the future. As a result of this uncertainty, providing advice on inheritance tax exposure becomes very risky.

13.08 It cannot be said, however, that all assets and interests in the metaverse do not carry a monetary value. In fact, the ability to apply a monetary value is developing as quickly as the concept of the metaverse itself. The ability to own and trade digital assets, such as NFTs, is enabling financial value to be applied to certain aspects of the metaverse and the assets held within it. NFTs provide a 'certificate of ownership', and therefore real-life evidence of possession of something digital. Having acknowledgement of legal ownership makes it far easier to be able to plan the succession of an asset in comparison to something which has no such 'certificate' or evidence of ownership, such as an avatar identity in a virtual reality gaming environment.

13.09 One can now purchase digital real estate within the metaverse using digital currencies and tokens. However, buying buildings and land in the metaverse is far from as regulated as purchasing land in England and Wales for instance. When property and land are purchased in England and Wales, records are obtained, and legal ownership is recorded at HM Land Registry. The regulation of land in the metaverse currently sits with the creators and service providers of that metaverse, each of which takes a different approach to rights and rewards given to purchasers. There are developments ongoing to establish legal ownership, so it is now common for NFTs to be a counterpart to owning land, buildings, and other assets, such as clothing, in the metaverse. This is not a blanket approach across all metaverses and digital environments. In addition, whilst NFTs may be issued as part of a metaverse or digital purchase, not all NFTs carry the same value. Some NFTs carry a capital trading value, one which could be sold for real life currency. Others carry rights, such as gaming rights or royalties, etc. Blockchains will enable a tracing record to be obtained of such transactions which is a step in the right direction for those looking to use trades in the metaverse as an investment product. As more people become familiar with the idea of using blockchains as a means of investment, accessibility will also become easier if users provide people with access to them for succession planning purposes.

Accessibility

13.10 This brings us on to our second obstacle for succession planning – accessibility. The security of assets in the metaverse is not on the same level as that in the real world. Whilst one would argue the security in the digital world, through the use of digital wallets and blockchains, is the most protected environment in existence, this could also be the biggest hindrance for people who are not accustomed to the environment. At present, whilst NFTs and other crypto assets can be traded and therefore have a financial value attached to them, when considering their succession, the ability for those assets to actually succeed or be inherited is essential. There will be some metaverse property which may not have a counterpart NFT attached to it and therefore there is no 'certificate of ownership' and subsequently nothing identifiable to pass on to others. There are most likely going to be some assets where monetary value cannot be attached to them, such as avatars or character identities, sentimental values attached to creations within the metaverse, and the reputation of someone in a metaverse environment.[2]

13.11 There are multiple layers of security attached to crypto assets. If this level of security was not present, the financial and investment value given to these assets today, which is forecast to continue to grow in the future, would most likely not be there. Digital wallets which are accessed through private keys and passwords are the literal key to financial value and wealth attached to assets in the metaverse. However, if the access is not available to the right people, the value attached to the assets will be nil. Therefore, whilst considering succession and estate planning of these assets may seem simple, this is only possible whilst those with access to that value are present and capable. Estate and succession planning can include gifting during a lifetime or leaving assets on death, these concepts will now be considered separately. It is important to encourage clients to ensure passcodes are safely and securely kept in a designated place to ensure executors can properly carry out their wishes in respect of their digital assets.

LIFETIME GIFTING

13.12 Lifetime gifting is easier if one person is gifting an asset to another, in a metaverse environment which allows you to trade assets.

13.13 The easiest example to think of is an asset with a counterpart NFT. The only requirements are for the NFT to have trading rights, and then the ability for the donor (the person gifting) to access the assets which can be valued and transferred within their digital wallet and then send them to the donee's (the person receiving the gift) public key. The donee then accesses the assets via their private key and receives any benefits attached to them (again, as long as they are transferable). The transaction will be recorded on the blockchain, and a record of the transaction will be available. This process is as simple as transferring funds from one bank account to another through an online format, in real life. The only key necessities are that both the donor and the donee need to be adept with the digital trading environment and that digital environment needs to allow the trade to take place.

13.14 What then happens to assets or identities in the metaverse which are not attached to a tradable counterpart such as an NFT? This could be an avatar in a gaming environment with an in-game value and reputation. This is where succession planning with assets in the metaverse is hindered and reaches a block. Unless the service provider allows for that avatar to be transferred from one living person's account to another, there is no way of planning around the succession of

2 Although this may not always be the case especially with avatars which may be able to transcend multiple metaverses. As discussed below there are issues with whether such assets are able to pass to another person whether as a lifetime gift or on death.

that asset in real life. This may seem irrelevant to the average person, however, as the digital world develops more, these experiences are obtaining financial value in the metaverse which people would rather pass on to those who can enjoy them during their lifetime, rather than leaving them to become a dormant asset. There is therefore the risk that as in-game investment becomes more popular there is going to be a generation of people who hold wealth within a locked environment who cannot pass it on due to the restrictions set by service and platform providers.

13.15 The question then arises; does someone with this type of value in the metaverse actually own that value? Or is it that they own the enjoyment of that value whilst is it accessible to them? It is hard not to argue the latter if you do not have the ability to do as you please with it, like any assets you legally own in the real world.

13.16 With non-transferable value in the metaverse, such as an in-game experience, the only way to currently pass on that value (whether monetary or not), is to divulge passwords and access to a living individual during your lifetime.[3] The concept of this proves to be rather uncomfortable as it is an all or nothing approach – you either give all of your value or none of it at all. Lifetime gifting of assets in the metaverse without fungible value is therefore restricted and until platform providers allow for partial transfers between people, it is not going to be possible to succession plan with these concepts.

LEAVING ASSETS ON DEATH

13.17 Leaving metaverse based assets to individuals or trusts on death presents even more restrictions and obstacles in comparison to what it does when gifting during one's lifetime.

13.18 There is no set precedent for what a will under the law of England and Wales should include so long as it is valid in accordance with the Wills Act 1837, s 9 which stipulates the following: (a) the will must be in writing, signed by the testator or by another in the testator's presence and with their direction; (b) the testator intended for the will to be effective; (c) the signature on the will is witnessed by two present witnesses; and (d) each witness attests or signs the will or acknowledges their signature in the presence of the testator.

13.19 When it comes to digital assets and interests, however, it is now best practice to have an express digital assets clause in a will even though this will not give personal representatives all of the access they need to deal with decentralised assets and interests on death. The definition of 'digital assets' will be key and notwithstanding the introduction of the Property (Digital Assets etc) Bill, it is currently suggested that the more in depth and explanatory the definition of

3 Which may actually be a breach of terms of use on certain platforms and could lead to suspension or being expelled under acceptable use policies etc.

'digital assets' is in a will, the more success personal representatives will have in accessing such assets. Private client practitioners should be encouraging clients to divulge the true extent of their digital personality and record this in the definition of 'digital assets' included in a will as far as possible.

13.20 The reason this detailed level of description is recommended is because there have already been test cases where personal representatives have failed to establish the right to access 'digital assets' particular to a service provider or licence manager. For example, Apple have now introduced the ability to add a 'Legacy Contact' to an Apple account.[4] Without this provision, personal representatives may not be granted automatic access to photos or digital information of a deceased person stored in the iCloud, without further evidence of the death and right to access such information, which could include a court order. This is just one example and with the emerging metaverse economy there could be an array of varying approaches by service providers which personal representatives are going to have to tackle. Best practice is therefore to try and give express powers in a will to at least give personal representatives a stepping stone to demonstrate there is intention for them to be able to access information, data and assets held in these digital environments.

13.21 In addition to the above inclusions in a will, private client practitioners should also be encouraging clients to review the terms and conditions of their various digital assets, identities, and interests. This will mean taking into consideration the terms of service when entering a metaverse environment to see whether or not they accept English and Welsh succession provisions. There are still not worldwide laws of succession, and each jurisdiction has its own rules and regulations. Where an individual has value in the metaverse, such as an in-game experience, whilst the law of England and Wales will say that if property rights can be established over an asset (in accordance with the Property (Digital Assets etc) Bill), one should be able to pass this interest on in a will or on death in general. It will come down to the terms of service of the metaverse or the jurisdiction it is attached to. There is therefore a huge risk that if the requisite permissions are not given, whether those be on an international legal level or a service agreement level, access to the assets and interests held in the metaverse could die with the testator.

13.22 Smart contracts are another key requirement to the running of trades and other types of exchanges in the metaverse. They require a set of actions to be completed before a result is provided and are, in some cases, foolproof. In the event someone enters into a smart contract and then dies before undertaking the required actions, the understanding would be that the objective of that smart contract would fail. However, if the deceased had completed their required actions and was waiting on other parties to complete theirs, the completion of said contract could be detrimental to the deceased's estate. As you can imagine,

4 How to request access to a deceased family member's Apple account – Apple Support (UK) – https://support.apple.com/en-gb/102431.

what the deceased would be getting out of a contractual agreement has a bearing on whether or not this automated process is beneficial. In the event these smart contracts fail at particular stages, there could also be a basis for a claim against the other parties to the smart contract. By their very nature, smart contracts enable parties from all over the world to engage with one another in a decentralised environment, therefore there will be situations which arise where litigation is required. The Law Commission acknowledges that where private international law disputes arise, in circumstances such as smart contracts, the decision as to which countries' laws should apply to a particular dispute is currently uncertain. Whilst in the real world, where someone enters into a contract, or is proposing to enter into a contract, provisions for the event of death can be included or attorneys can be appointed to see the completion through, the same cannot yet be said for smart contracts in the metaverse.

Awareness

13.23 Whilst a testator or living donor may be digitally savvy when it comes to investing, playing, or generally engaging in the metaverse, their plans for succession are only as useful as the knowledge of those being given access or management duties of the subject assets. For example, whilst Mr A may have engaged in smart contracts, incorporated lengthy descriptions in his will and complied with any service provider requirements for passing on metaverse interests on his death, if his executor isn't aware of the metaverse and the extent to which Mr A lived in it, the succession plan is worth nothing.

13.24 A testator needs to understand that whoever they are trusting to either administer their estate or to locate their assets, that person or persons needs to be made aware of their existence. As a species, humans generally find talking about their wealth and assets a taboo topic, however this should not be the case for assets stored and held in this emerging world. As more and more people begin to live a double life – a real life and a digital life – it is imperative, for estate planning purposes, that testators provide guidance to whoever may be responsible for those assets in the future and make them aware of their existence.

13.25 A quick internet search into the movement of cryptocurrency will show you that large percentages of cryptocurrencies have not moved hands or locations in years. The reasons for this lack of movement could be many; however, it is hard not to assume that some of this value has not moved because the owners are deceased or now lack the capacity to manage the asset and those left with the responsibility of managing and administering it, are not aware of it or cannot access it. The same is likely to happen to assets and value held within the metaverse. Unless executors, attorneys or deputies are made aware of the assets and how to access them, they do not stand a chance of being able to administer them and pass them on to beneficiaries or utilise them to benefit someone with no mental capacity.

ESTATE ADMINISTRATION

13.26 As previously mentioned, it is now accepted that digital assets, in particular cryptocurrencies, and electronic trade documents, are 'property' for the purposes of the Law of England and Wales and for UK taxes. Whilst they arguably did not fall within the usual definitions of 'property', the introduction of the Property (Digital Assets etc) Bill has expressly provided that digital assets are property.

13.27 In the event of a death, personal representatives of someone's estate are required to value the assets in the deceased's estate as of the moment before they died. The valuation given to an asset should be 'the price it might reasonably be expected to fetch if sold in the open market at that time' as per the Inheritance Tax Act 1984, s 60. Therefore, personal representatives will be expected to obtain a valuation for digital assets as of the day before the deceased died which, taking into account the issues of valuation and accessibility mentioned earlier in the chapter, will be difficult.

13.28 For the time being, HM Revenue and Customs (HMRC) has decided that where an individual dies in possession of digital assets, including crypto currency and tokens, those assets will be taxed in accordance with the individual's tax residency. Subsequently, if a UK resident and domiciled individual dies in possession of digital wealth, the wealth will be taxed in accordance with UK laws.

13.29 Where personal representatives are aware the deceased died with a digital personality, unless they can access that personality, they will be unable to value it and declare it accurately for inheritance tax purposes.

13.30 Guidance for personal representatives, at the moment, is varied. Some advisors say if personal representatives are aware of digital assets and have access to them, they should take steps to liquidate them and convert them into a real-life currency as soon as possible. Whilst this seems like common sense because of the volatility of the digital market, this process contradicts the purpose of obtaining a Grant of Representation.

13.31 Other advisors recommend personal representatives transfer the digital assets to a new wallet which is only accessible by the personal representatives. This however poses the risks that multiple people have access to a wallet which could contain significant value, and if private keys are lost or accessed by the incorrect people, the value could be lost too. Where the personal representatives are at fault for losing those private keys, beneficiaries of an estate will have a personal claim against the personal representatives. Personal representatives are therefore going to be under a lot of pressure to keep these decentralised assets secure.

13.32 In real life, a grant of representation demonstrates that personal representatives have a legal right and authority to deal with a deceased person's estate. At present, unless the deceased held their digital assets through a custodian, there is no requirement to demonstrate that you have the legal authority to access and distribute those digital assets. Custodians are not as common as their real-life comparison (investment advisors), and therefore each custodian has their own requirements. Some may want to see just a death certificate; some may want a grant of representation. It is worth the deceased, if they are able to before death, finding out this information and leaving guidance for their personal representatives.

13.33 Where personal representatives are able to access and value digital assets after death, they will need to declare these to HMRC. If inheritance tax is due on the estate, it should be paid in its entirety within six months of the end of the month when the deceased died unless an instalment option is available. At present, inheritance tax on digital assets does not qualify for the instalment-based provision and therefore if there is an estate which has a nominal value in real life, yet is affluent in the digital world, within six months of the death significant sums will need to be realised from the digital world to pay for inheritance tax due. This will be easily done if the personal representatives have immediate access to those assets without the need for a grant of representation. However, if a custodian is involved and they require a grant of representation, the personal representatives may find themselves either having to seek an inheritance tax loan, a grant on credit or facing late payment penalties and interest from HMRC where they cannot pay the inheritance tax due. It is therefore very much the case that there is significant development required in order for the current inheritance tax regime to be brought up to date with the concept of the digital world.

13.34 Where personal representatives are aware of value in the metaverse or other digital environments but have no access to such assets, it is recommended that HMRC are still notified of the existence of said digital assets. HMRC allow for personal representatives to declare some values in Form IHT400 as estimates, which whilst this environment and circumstance evolves, would be advisable to offer protection to personal representatives. Although it is acknowledged that if you cannot access an asset, you cannot possibly apply an estimated value to it, merely notifying HMRC that there was a digital personality that may have had value, provides an insurance for the personal representatives when they sign their statement of truth for the inheritance tax declaration.

13.35 Whilst there is no way to trace these assets at the moment, it may be the case in the future that personal representatives will need to demonstrate they have made all attempts to try and locate them which could include instructing experts to search electronic devices for passwords and private keys in a deceased's property. It is also likely that personal representatives will require indemnities from beneficiaries or seek to take out insurance for missed assets and liabilities to protect themselves from claims by disgruntled beneficiaries. Although the likelihood of insurance of this type being available now is slim, it may be something which develops in the future.

TRUSTS

13.36 Trusts are legal entities in the UK, like individuals. Within the English and Welsh legal system trusts are registerable (providing they do not fall within an excluded category), they are required to pay taxes if circumstances arise resulting in a taxable event, and they have the ultimate aim of being created to benefit beneficiaries. With the metaverse, if something is possible in real life, it is understood to be possible in the metaverse and therefore it is highly likely trusts will exist in the metaverse, and real-life trusts will have interests in the metaverse.

13.37 As trusts are not accepted universally, different metaverse environments will most likely take different approaches to them depending on who the service provider is and their original source. At present, it is possible to envisage that trusts could be established in real life and then part or all of their trust fund could be held in the metaverse. Where those trusts are required to be registered on HMRC's Trust Registration Service (TRS), there is hope that there will be a potential record of metaverse-based assets declared on the TRS. This will, however, only apply to taxable trusts on the basis of the current registration requirements. Access to those assets will be the responsibility of the trustees and, as with personal representatives, they need to be aware of their duties and responsibilities to the beneficiaries of the trust and ensure all wallets are secure from unwanted invaders.

13.38 Trustees of trusts governed by English and Welsh law have wide investment powers as set out in the Trustee Acts 1925 and 2000, unless restricted or amended by a trust document. Where trustee powers are provided by the legislation, it would be hard to understand how they would be upholding their duties to beneficiaries by investing in an emerging market like the metaverse. It is understood that a metaverse environment could be closed down with immediate effect by the service provider and therefore, if trustees voluntarily invest in that kind of market, it would be reasonable to expect beneficiaries to bring claims for potential loss against them if the value of the trust was lost due to a metaverse environment being closed down.

COURT OF PROTECTION

13.39 The Court of Protection is a UK government court which was created by the Mental Capacity Act 2005. The Court of Protection plays a huge part in the overall picture of estate planning for individuals. Individuals commonly lose mental capacity whether this be on a permanent or short-term basis. When individuals lose mental capacity on a permanent basis it is common for attorneys or deputies to be appointed to step in and manage an individual's affairs for them.

13.40 As with the role of personal representatives, if an attorney for property and financial affairs or a deputy appointed to make similar decisions, fall responsible for someone with a personality and wealth in the metaverse, they take on the control of that digital life. Professional attorneys and deputies will need to be particularly careful if they do find themselves in control of a personality in the metaverse to ensure the wealth, reputation and value is preserved for the benefit of the patient or donor.

13.41 The process of gaining access to digital assets in the metaverse is going to be similar to that of personal representatives gaining access to a deceased's estate. Private client practitioners should be encouraging their clients to insert express provisions in their Lasting Powers of Attorney for property and financial affairs decisions to deal with access to their metaverse stored assets and value. As with all jurisdictions in real life, there are different approaches to mental capacity. It is therefore not guaranteed that custodians and service providers of a metaverse will accept the service of a Court of Protection order for deputyship or Lasting Power of Attorney for property and financial affairs, as authority for an individual to take over the control of someone's metaverse personality.

WHAT NEXT?

13.42 The metaverse is still very new and developing. At present, in England and Wales, whilst there is development towards 'a thing' being property in law, we must take the view that on the whole interests in that property will be controlled by real-life people. The metaverse is a digital environment and the concept of it being controlled externally somewhat contradicts the decentralised identity it has.

13.43 As the metaverse becomes increasingly popular and people start to spend more of their time living in the decentralised environment, it is reasonable to expect that people will have to start estate planning in both their real life and their digital life. There is already talk of smart contract estate planning arising which leads one to perhaps expect the ability to create a metaverse based will being on the horizon. Like a real-life individual can make a will in various countries, it makes sense for them to eventually be able to do the same in the metaverse.

13.44 Whilst the ability to estate plan inside the metaverse does not exist, private client practitioners should continue to attempt to control the planning from an external position. As practitioners in this area, we should be encouraging our clients to educate their successors on the world they live their secondary life in, create secure inventories of ways to access their digital wallets and express their hopes and wishes for the succession of their digital life.

13.45 We should also bear in mind that whilst a metaverse is controlled by a service provider on their terms of service, there is the risk that if the concept does not take off commercially for that service provider, they could shut it down. Clients therefore need to be aware that whilst they think they have wealth, reputation and value in the metaverse, this is at the ultimate control of the metaverse service provider and the succession and ability to plan around it, falls down to the small print they engaged with when creating a login to that digital space.

CONCLUSION

13.46 This chapter considers estate planning in the metaverse. The key takeaway points are:

- Concern must be had as to how wealth generated in the metaverse can be passed on to the next generation.
- The metaverse is not as regulated yet to properly deal with digital assets on death, as we are in real life.
- The challenge with advising clients on estate planning for its digital assets is it is difficult to value the assets and the asset may be difficult (or even impossible) to access on death.
- Lifetime gifting of digital assets is one possible option. Some digital assets, however, cannot be transferred.
- It is good practice to include an express digital assets clause in a will to cover metaverse assets.
- Intended reform under the Property (Digital Assets etc) Bill will provide much needed clarity that digital assets are capable of being disposed of via a will and are property for the sake of intestacy rules.
- Self-executing contracts like smart contracts will pose difficulties when dealing with assets in the metaverse on death.
- Inheritance tax on digital assets does not qualify for the instalment-based provision. This is likely to have a real-world implication in respect of the need to liquidate digital assets on death.
- Trusts will be possible in the metaverse, but not all jurisdictions recognise trusts. This is an issue given the cross-border element of the metaverse.
- There should be express provisions in Lasting Powers of Attorney for property and in financial affairs decisions to deal with access to metaverse stored assets and value.

Chapter 14

Protection against harm in the metaverse

'Harnessing the power of the metaverse for good is important for unlocking a future for the public, industry and governments from across the globe but with any new technology comes an exploitative risk, similar to the introduction of the internet in 1991. It is vital that the UK is a digitally safe country and that this transformative technology is used for the right purpose.'

Carol Vorderman MA (Cantab), MBE, Honorary Fellow of the Institution of Engineering and Technology

14.01 It is vital that potential harms in the metaverse are correctly identified so that adequate protection can be put in place. Harm in the metaverse can take many forms, it is not just the harm caused by criminals but also includes the potential harms that can be caused as a result of the technology itself and use of the technology. Users of the metaverse are also at risk of harms caused by a breach of their human rights as set out in **Chapter 4**, privacy and data protection issues as discussed in **Chapter 6**, financial harms as explored in **Chapter 7** as well as harms caused by deep fakes influencing their decision making. This chapter not only delves into some of those harms but looks at what can be done to try and mitigate them.

14.02 In 2023 the Global Online Safety Survey[1] carried out by Microsoft showed that 67% of users had experienced some risk of harm online. This was most prevalent at 18–19 years old and showed the highest risk was in respect of misinformation which represented 50% of all risk. Most children are experiencing some form of online harm.[2] This is not going to stop in the metaverse; if anything it is likely to increase as there is an increased digital presence.

14.03 There is certainly a dark side to the metaverse, a side which has the potential to be used as a weapon; whether that be a weapon of war or terror or just being used by other types of criminals. As users increasingly rely on the technology of the metaverse to carry out their day-to-day life, this opens them up to vulnerability to cyber-attacks as well as exposure to propaganda and untruths.

1 https://www.microsoft.com/en-us/DigitalSafety/research/global-online-safety-survey.

2 In 2020 80% of children between the ages of 12 -15 reported instances of online harms – https://hansard.parliament.uk/commons/2022-04-19/debates/F88B42D3-BFC4-4612-B166-8D2C15FA3E4E/OnlineSafetyBill.

14.04 REPHRAIN[3] have seven active projects on different harms in the metaverse ranging from data protection to child abuse.[4] Minderoo Centre for Technology and Democracy[5] highlights the issue that AI can rapidly expand within the metaverse, and in turn this will amplify the harm it can cause.[6] A considerable amount of sensitive data will be contained in the metaverse and both that and users are at risk of manipulation. The DRCF in its December 2023 immersive Technologies Foresight Paper has identified that harms in the metaverse are likely to take both a traditional guise but also may cause new types of harm.[7] The Australian eSafety Commissioner considered that the metaverse should be built with safety in mind and steps taken to fundamentally prevent harm.[8]

14.05 Once a harm is categorised as a crime then steps can be taken to protect users through real-life punishment. Where the threshold is not reached and the harm is not categorised as a criminal offence then there are opportunities to put in place technological restrictions. Europol, however, raises concern over the effectiveness of censorship.[9] Consideration has to be had over what are suitable punishments in the metaverse and what can be done to protect users against war and other serious atrocities.

14.06 Metaverse proponents do recognise the potential for harm in the metaverse. Metaverse Safety Week organised by XRSI is held annually in early December.[10] The intention of this week is to draw attention to harm caused in the metaverse and the need for responsible development of the metaverse using technological solutions to protect users. They identify that the risk is not just to individuals but to society generally. They emphasise in their Metaverse Safety Week Charter the need to ensure that there are 'humans in the loop', 'societies in the loop' and 'connected ecosystems''[11]

CRIME IN THE METAVERSE

14.07 The European Citizens' Panel on Virtual World believes that there are three different types of crimes in the metaverse: those which are the same as in

3 The National Research Centre on Privacy, Harm Reduction and Adversarial Influence Online which is a UK collaboration of leading academics, industry experts, and regulators.
4 https://bpb-eu-w2.wpmucdn.com/blogs.bristol.ac.uk/dist/1/670/files/2023/05/REPHRAIN-White-Paper-Metaverse-and-Web-3.pdf.
5 A team of academics from the University of Cambridge.
6 https://www.mctd.ac.uk/wp-content/uploads/2023/07/MCTD-SecuringTheMetaverse-Report-WEB-1.pdf.
7 https://www.drcf.org.uk/__data/assets/pdf_file/0027/273195/DRCF-Immersive-Technologies-Foresight-Paper.pdf.
8 https://www.esafety.gov.au/newsroom/blogs/will-peril-outweigh-promise-metaverse.
9 https://www.europol.europa.eu/cms/sites/default/files/documents/Policing%20in%20the%20metaverse%20-%20what%20law%20enforcement%20needs%20to%20know.pdf.
10 https://metaversesafetyweek.org/about/.
11 https://metaversesafetyweek.org/wp-content/uploads/2023/12/MSW-Charter-by-XRSI.pdf.

real life; those which are offensive in the metaverse only; and the need to protect oneself in the metaverse.[12]

14.08 There is the need to identify what should be categorised as sufficiently serious to warrant being a crime and set international standards in the metaverse.[13] This is especially important considering the cross-border element of the metaverse. In real life there is not one uniform international penal code – different countries and even different states in the USA have categorised different actions as criminal. There is the need for some acts, especially, in the metaverse to universally be categorised as criminal regardless of where the perpetrator is located or the victim may be based. There is also the need for an effective extradition process to bring perpetrators to justice.

14.09 Bearing in mind the aim of the Metaverse is to extend reality, there is – in theory – no limit to the conduct that may play out on its platforms. New technology means new methods of attack for the nefarious user, either by using new technology to commit any number of criminal offences, including fraud, money laundering and bribery as well as non-financial crimes such as harassment, sexual offences (eg grooming), identity fraud, data protection and IP offences, or engage in conduct which may not be so easily categorised so as to constitute a new form of offending conduct (which may not in itself constitute an offence per se), native to the Metaverse.

14.10 The World Economic Forum has highlighted that there have been numerous situations where atrocities have been replicated online using VR such as the Christchurch Mosque shooting from 2019 which have appeared a number of times on Roblox.[14] It identifies that the underlying technology may actually present more of a risk of harm, especially with the development of haptic gloves to allow for a more tactile experience in the metaverse which is very invasive should this be misused.

STALKING AND HARASSMENT

14.11 The offences of stalking and harassment are obvious offences which will apply in the metaverse.[15] The traditional elements of the offences will be made out regardless of whether it is carried out in real life or in the metaverse, the latter will likely be termed 'cyber stalking' but are the same offences. What will need to be made out is that the victim has suffered a 'substantial adverse effect' which a jury would have to be persuaded is made out should the effects be caused in the metaverse only.

12 https://citizens.ec.europa.eu/document/download/5d55a9e4-a0f2-4974-b01b-a8382eb6cb4d_en?filename=ECP%20on%20Virtual%20Worlds_Final%20Report.pdf.

13 This is discussed by Yilmaz in https://dergipark.org.tr/en/download/article-file/3660505.

14 https://www.weforum.org/agenda/2022/01/metaverse-risks-challenges-digital-safety/.

15 Under the Protection from Harassment Act 1997.

14.12 We would expect to see the scope of restraining orders and stalking protection orders, as well as non-molestation orders, increased to cover the metaverse in the future. Those practising in this area should ensure that such orders cover the metaverse and the nature of interactions in the metaverse.

CYBERFLASHING

14.13 Cyberflashing was introduced as a criminal offence on 31 January 2024 following the 2021 report by the Law Commission, where it considered that given the advancements in technology the communications offences were out of date. The Online Safety Act 2023, s 187 introduced the Sexual Offences Act 2003, s 66A, which is considered as a communication offence. It carries a maximum sentence of two years.

14.14 The offence requires:

1) A person intentionally sends or gives a picture of someone's genitals;
2) That person
   a. intends another person to see the genitals and cause alarm, distress or humiliation; or
   b. sends or gives the picture for sexual gratification and is reckless as to whether the other person will be caused alarm, distress or humiliation.

14.15 In March 2024 the first cyberflashing perpetrator was sentenced to 52 weeks' imprisonment.[16]

14.16 There is the risk of cyberflashing in the metaverse. Whilst at this stage most interactions in the metaverse will be carried out by avatars this is likely to evolve as the metaverse itself matures.

EPILEPSY TROLLING

14.17 Epilepsy trolling was introduced under the Online Safety Act 2023, s 183. This offence is known as 'Zach's law' and criminalises the sending and/or showing of flashing images with the intention of harming someone with epilepsy. The maximum sentence is five years. Despite this offence being used to target any form of digital use it will also apply in, and seek to protect, the metaverse.

14.18 This offence starts the path to protecting the misuse of technology against underlying conditions. This is a pioneering offence and the first in the world to criminalise this behaviour. It shows that technology can be deliberately used to trigger conditions and therefore become weaponised. In the metaverse it

16 https://www.cps.gov.uk/east-england/news/prison-sentence-first-cyberflashing-case.

is likely that those with conditions such as epilepsy will be triggered via the VR so where this is intensified or deliberately used to cause harm then these new offences are welcome.

ENCOURAGING SELF-HARM

14.19 The Online Safety Act 2023, s 184 prohibits encouraging or assisting serious self-harm of another person. It is not necessary for there to be one individual victim nor for there to actually be any serious self-harm suffered. All that is required is that there is a communication whether in person, via electronic means or showing someone the communication. Communications via the metaverse would fall under this provision. The offence carries a maximum sentence of five years' imprisonment.

14.20 The platforms themselves would be excluded from the offence under the Online Safety Act 2023, s 184(10).

FAKE NEWS AND OTHER COMMUNICATION OFFENCES

14.21 The Online Safety Act 2023 introduced a number of communication offences all of which would be relevant in the metaverse including sending false communications,[17] sending threatening communications[18] and sharing intimate photographs or film.[19] Should offences take place in the metaverse then it would qualify as 'sending a message'. The Crown Prosecution Authority note that there are often jurisdiction issues with these offences and it necessary to show a substantial connection to England and Wales.[20] This may present an issue with the metaverse where it may be difficult to evidence that there is a substantial connection to the UK.

14.22 The Online Safety Act 2023, s 179 creates an offence where someone sends a message knowing that it is false and intends the message to cause psychological or physical harm.

14.23 The Communications Act 2003, s 127(1) provides for an offence where someone sends a message which is grossly offensive, indecent, obscene or menacing. The Communications Act 2003, s 127(2), as amended by the Online Safety Act 2023, has retained the offence where a person causes annoyance, inconvenience or unnecessary anxiety by persistently making use of public communication network. This would apply in the metaverse.

17 Online Services Act 2023, s 179.
18 Online Services Act 2023, s 181.
19 Online Services Act 2023, s 188 creating Sexual Offences Act 2003, s 66B(1)–(4).
20 https://www.cps.gov.uk/legal-guidance/communications-offences#:~:text=An%20offence%20of%20sending%20photographs, Section%20187%20OSA%202023%5D).

FRAUD, THEFT AND SUBSEQUENT MONEY LAUNDERING

14.24 The potential for fraud, theft and other offences of dishonesty to be committed in – or assisted by the capabilities of – the metaverse is generally accepted as being vast. These offences might include virtual asset and identity theft, account hacking and social engineering scams including phishing, impersonation scams or honeytrap scams.

Fraud

14.25 In most common law jurisdictions internationally, actions considered fraudulent can attract both civil and criminal liability. The elements of the criminal offences are extremely broadly drafted, with the key elements being:

a dishonesty; and

b the intention to make a gain (or cause loss, or to expose another to a risk of loss).

14.26 There are three types of fraud offence in the UK, including fraud by failing to disclose information and fraud by abuse of position. However, perhaps the broadest – in the sense that it can apply to a variety of different and behaviours – is the third: fraud by false representation, committed when a person:

a dishonestly makes a false representation; and

b Intends by making the representation:

  i. To make a gain for himself or another, or

  ii. To cause loss to another or to expose another to a risk of loss.

14.27 The UK offence of fraud may be engaged in a variety of scenarios, as long as the above elements are present. This approach contrasts with that taken in the US, where defendants may be indicted on a number of different kinds of specific types of fraud. Each are federal offences, and include:

a. Wire fraud (which criminalises the use of interstate electronic communications, in furtherance of a scheme devised to defraud another);[21]

b. Credit card fraud;

c. Financial institution fraud;

d. Identification fraud

14.28 The US federal offence of wire fraud is examined further below, in the context of the other more UK-centric examples.

21 https://www.justice.gov/archives/jm/criminal-resource-manual-941-18-usc-1343-elements-wire-fraud.

14.29 Wherever it is being investigated or prosecuted, typically, it is the mental elements of intent and dishonesty that law enforcement agencies may struggle to prove, bearing in mind that nefarious actors do not routinely create paper trails that document that they are acting dishonestly, nor that they are aware that what they are representing to their customer or counterparty is in any way untrue or misleading.

14.30 In those circumstances, law enforcement agencies rely on circumstantial evidence and in many cases expert opinions, seeking to leverage irresistible inferences that a statement relied upon by a victim was obviously false – even if there is no direct evidence of the same – and that it was dishonestly made. In the metaverse the investigation and prosecution of such conduct is unlikely to be any different, albeit that the subject matter may well be far more complex and technologically involved.

14.31 The below scenarios and analysis, which are based on the more 'traditional' (yet sophisticated) fraud typologies, seek to illustrate how such conduct might occur in a metaverse context.

Investment fraud

14.32 'Typical' investment-based frauds can take many forms and can involve a range of underlying products or assets which may not exist or are in fact worthless, for example:

> **Wine investment fraud,** where investors are deceived into purchasing overvalued or non-existing wines with the promise of significant returns, often by individuals using cold-calling and high-pressure sales tactics, fake companies and documents.
>
> **Carbon credit fraud,** using similar tactics, investors are persuaded to purchase 'Carbon Credits' – a certificate or permit representing the right to emit one tonne of carbon dioxide (CO_2)[22] – which they may not be able to sell on.
>
> **Art-based Fraud,** similarly, investors may be induced into buying art which does not exist, or is in fact a forgery or 'dupe' of a genuine piece.
>
> **Land banking**, a situation involving companies dividing land into smaller plots to sell to investors, with the expectation it will rise in value once it is available for development. However, the land is often in areas of natural beauty or historical interest, with little chance of it being built on[23] and therefore realising any profit for those investors.

14.33 While many of these scams could in theory occur on or may seek to utilise the metaverse, the two that may have the most significant application to the topic of this book are **Art-based Fraud** and **Land banking**.

22 https://www.fca.org.uk/consumers/carbon-credit-trading-scams#:~:text=If%20you're%20worried%20about, your%20 details %20to%20other%20criminals.

23 https://www.fca.org.uk/consumers/land-banking-investment-scams.

Land banking

14.34 Virtual land in the metaverse is already big business, with a number of multinational corporate entities, including banks, having acquired virtual land on established platforms, some creating virtual versions of their traditional bricks and mortar businesses. The sale of land in the metaverse is also becoming more mainstream, with land available for purchase to consumers from common platforms or from owners themselves.

14.35 However, in contrast to real property, metaverse based real estate exists only on the relevant platform, with proof of ownership provided by a blockchain-based Non Fungible Token (NFT), a unique digital asset connected to a specific digital record and recorded on the blockchain. In this case, the relevant asset is the parcel of land in the relevant platform.

14.36 Notwithstanding the potential security benefits offered by shared ledger technology, the process of buying land in the metaverse (like all purchasing processes) is open to abuse, as bad actors seek to leverage its complexities, and the 'hype' surrounding it.

14.37 In the metaverse, the nefarious user may seek to exploit the process of buying land in the metaverse to commit land-based fraud. This could occur in a number of different ways, including:

a *Metaverse Agent A* claims to have acquired for sale multiple plots of virtual land (which do not exist), either on established platforms (which provides credibility, with limited risk that potential investors will check) or in a compromised (or 'Evil Twin') metaverse environment or platform, which can be deactivated by the owner or administrator at any time (it should be noted that the same can be said of legitimate platforms, which is a key risk for users and 'investors' to consider).

b *New Metaverse Platform B* is a new virtual marketplace for the trade of NFTs relating to all forms of underlying digital assets including art, land and smart contracts. Upon inception, the platform already lists a number of NFTs and digital assets for sale, all of which appear legitimate but do not exist.

c *Metaverse Company C* uses direct and high-pressure sale tactics to target and persuade individual investors to invest relatively small amounts of money in order to purchase shares in or sole ownership of virtual land, underpinned by NFTs, 'copies' of which can be provided – to the potentially unsophisticated prospective investor – by more traditional methods.

Analysis

14.38 In each of these cases, the requisite elements of the UK offence of fraud are made out variously by the following:

a The offer to sell, or invitation to invest constitutes the representation.

b That representation is false, owing to the fact that the underlying assets do not exist or are worth significantly less.

c The representation is dishonestly made (or would be dishonest by the standards of ordinarily and decent people), bearing in mind the circumstances in which it was made.

d The intention of Agent A, Platform B or Company C is to persuade the victim to part with funds, thereby causing them a loss and securing a gain for themselves.

Art

14.39 Perhaps one of the most well-known use cases for NFTs is digital art and collectibles. Notwithstanding a general decline in sales between 2021 and 2022, it is assessed that sales of 'Art NFTs' and 'Collectible NFTs' still amounted in 2023 to $1.2 billion and $6.3 billion, respectively.[24]

14.40 Concerns that the market is susceptible to fraud have existed for several years. For example, in January 2022 it was reported that 'DeviantArt' had begun monitoring the blockchain for suspected copies of art, the originals of which belonged to artists that were part of its online community.[25] Part of the concern relates to the ability of anyone to 'mint' a digital file – which could in theory include one that has already been created by someone else – into a new NFT before offering it for sale on a platform.

DIGITAL ASSET 'THEFT'

14.41 International definitions of theft are broadly consistent with the UK offence, which came into being by virtue of the Theft Act 1968,s 1, which states that 'a person is guilty of theft if he dishonestly appropriates property belonging to another with the intention of permanently depriving the other of it; and 'thief' and 'steal' shall be construed accordingly.'[26]

14.42 The risk that digital assets could be stolen exists in the same way (but is not necessarily the same level) as the risk that fiat currency may be stolen from your bank account. A bad actor that seeks to steal another's NFT one day before selling it, probably utilising social engineering techniques such as 'phishing', and then causes the unauthorised transfer funds from the same individual's current

24 The Art Basel & UBS Art Market Report 2024, section 1.4. https://theartmarket.artbasel.com/download/The-Art-Basel-and-UBS-Art-Market-Report-2024.pdf

25 https://www.theguardian.com/global/2022/jan/29/huge-mess-of-theft-artists-sound-alarm-theft-nfts-proliferates.

26 Theft Act 1987, s 1.

account the next day can be expected to be prosecuted for similar offences in respect of both scenarios.

14.43 In respect of the latter, an individual charged having engaged in such conduct in England and Wales may face an indictment that reads as follows:

> **Count 1**
>
> **Statement of Offence**
>
> Unauthorised access to computer material with intent to commit or facilitate commission of further offences, contrary to the Computer Misuse Act 1990, s 2.
>
> **Particulars of Offence**
>
> Person A, on [DATE] caused a computer to perform a function to secure access to data held in another computer, namely by causing an unidentified computer to obtain access to data held in a crypto wallet belonging to Person B, with intent to commit or facilitate the commission of further offences.
>
> **Count 2**
>
> **Statement of Offence**
>
> Theft, contrary to the Theft Act 1968, s 1.
>
> **Particulars of Offence**
>
> Person A, on [DATE] stole a non-fungible token belonging to Person B.

14.44 If – as envisaged – the defendant successfully sells the stolen NFT to an unsuspecting purchaser, they could equally face proceeds of crime related charges, which seek to criminalise the possession, conversion and transfer of 'criminal property, defined as property that 'constitutes a person's benefit from criminal conduct',[27] whether or not the NFT is sold for fiat currency, cryptocurrency, a combination, or something completely unrelated. In those circumstances, the 'property' is the proceeds of the sale or the item acquired in exchange.

BCI TECHNOLOGY

14.45 BCI enables the identification of a user's innermost thoughts. Whilst the idea of intent is a cornerstone of the *mens rea* in most offences to date courts have had to rely on a combination of many different forms of evidence to be able to establish this element of an offence; with BCI technology the intention of someone's mind is enacted via the BCI, and therefore there can be little scope to dissect the idea of intent. Instead, the question becomes whether the person would have actually acted on the intent had it not been caused by the BCI technology. We do not yet know if this would be sufficient to break the chain of causation.

27 Proceeds of Crime Act 2002 contains a number of offences, under Part 7 ('Money Laundering'). See also s 340 for the definitions of both 'criminal conduct' and criminal property'.

UN CYBERCRIME TREATY

14.46 Since 2021 the United Nations had been negotiating the 'Cybercrime Treaty'.[28] There had been considerable disagreement during the negotiations of the proposed Treaty, which is reflective of the complexities of the area. The Ad Hoc Committee to Elaborate a Comprehensive International Convention on Countering the Use of information and Communications Technologies for Criminal Purposes scheduled for the end of January 2024 was suspended due to the lack of consensus. A draft resolution was, however, agreed in August 2024 and the UN General Assembly adopted the Treaty on 24 December 2024. It will enter into force 90 days after being ratified by the 40th signatory. The convention, hailed as a landmark convention,[29] includes:

1 The statement that the member states are 'determined to deny safe haven to those who engage in cybercrime by prosecuting these crimes wherever they occur';[30]

2 A commitment to collect, preserve and share evidence digitally;[31]

3 Respect for sovereignty of the other states;[32]

4 Requiring states to establish criminal offences:

   a of intentionally accessing information and communications technology systems without a right to do so;[33]

   b of illegally intercepting communication data and interfering with electronic data;[34]

   c of misuse of devices or passwords to commit one of the other offences;[35]

   d related to IT related theft, fraud and forgery;[36]

   e related to the creation, distribution, accessing, broadcasting etc of material concerning child sex abuse or child exploitation, and grooming[37];

   f commonly known as 'revenge porn';[38] and

   g money laundering / proceeds of crime offences.[39]

28 The ad hoc intergovernmental international convention on countering the use of information and communications technologies for criminal purpose was created under UN Resolution 74/247.

29 https://www.unode.org/unode/en/press/releases/2024/December/un-general-assembly-adopts-landmark-convention-on-cybercrime.html.

30 Preamble – https://documents.un.org/doc/undoc/gen/n24/372/04/pdf/n2437204.pdf.

31 Article 3(b).

32 Article 5.

33 Article 7.

34 Articles 8 and 9.

35 Article 11.

36 Articles 12 and 13.

37 Articles 14 and 15.

38 Article 16.

39 Article 17.

BUDAPEST CONVENTION

14.47 The Budapest Convention is properly titled the Convention on Cybercrime ETS No 185. It came into force in July 2004 and was the first international treaty on cybercrimes. The Treaty sought to address the dark side of emerging technologies. It acknowledges that cybercrimes transcend traditional borders, harmonisation of cybercriminal offences is necessary and there is the need to balance human rights with the protection of citizens.

MALABO CONVENTION

14.48 Despite being adopted in 2014 the Malabo Convention only came into effect for the African Union in 2023 after being ratified by Mauritania, the 15th state to ratify it and therefore reaching the requisite threshold to become binding. The Treaty sets to create a framework for cybercrimes, data protection and cyber security for the African Union.

TERRORISM IN THE METAVERSE

14.49 Terrorism is a significant threat in the metaverse.[40] Counter-terrorist organisations are however already considering what steps are required now to prevent terrorism and extremism in the metaverse. Over the course of 2021 and 2022 the UN Office of Counter-Terrorism held events on 'Safeguarding the Metaverse: Countering Terrorism and Preventing Violent Extremism in Digital Space'.[41] Around 1000 people attended the events. Europol identify that the metaverse has the risk for being used by terrorists for propaganda, to recruit others, to train other terrorists and even to virtually create virtual spaces which depict terrorist ideals.[42]

14.50 The United Nations Office of Counter-Terrorism considers that the immersive nature of the metaverse will make it a target for terrorists looking to recruit and spread propaganda. Further the use of digital currency makes the metaverse attractive for terrorists since it enables terrorists to hide the source of funds. Digital twins and real life replicated infrastructure are vulnerable to terrorists, either attacking them directly or using them for training for real-life attacks. Many stakeholders are already working together to try and build suitable

40 Weimann and Dimant discuss the different ways in which terrorists may use the metaverse as 'radicalisation, recruitment, training, fundraising and the coordination of attacks' The Metaverse and Terrorism: Threats and Challenges, Perspectives on Terrorism, Issue XVII volume 2 June 2023 – https://pt.icct.nl/sites/default/files/2023-06/PT%20-%20Vol%20XVII%2C%20Issue%20II%20-%20June%202023%2027.06%20final.pdf#page=115.

41 https://www.un.org/counterterrorism/events/safeguarding-metaverse-countering-terrorism-and-preventing-violent-extremism-digital-space.

42 https://www.europol.europa.eu/cms/sites/default/files/documents/Policing%20in%20the%20metaverse%20-%20what%20 law%20enforcement%20needs%20to%20know.pdf.

safeguards to protect the metaverse.[43] This includes a cooperation between both the private and public sectors.[44] It is generally agreed that action should be taken from the outset to try and protect the metaverse from terrorism and ensure that there is effective monitoring deployed.

14.51 Under the EU Terrorism Content Online Regulation 2021[45] any terrorist content has to be removed within an hour of its discovery online. This would apply to content which is disseminated via the metaverse. The Regulation enables authorities within the EU to order any applicable hosting providers to remove infringing content.

14.52 Tech against Terrorism, which was created by the United Nations in 2016, is a collaboration between a number of Government bodies, including the UK, and private organisations addressing the terrorist threats online.[46] They operate as a not for profit and will cover the threat posed by the metaverse. Tech against Terrorism both acts as an advisory body as well as taking action against threats of terrorism.

WAR IN THE METAVERSE

14.53 The military are moving into what is being termed by some the 'Battleverse'.[47] The metaverse is being used to train the military[48] but cognitive warfare, dubbed as 'cyberwarfare' is already taking place following the invasion of Ukraine by Russia. Whilst the metaverse may become a battlefield upon which action takes place, legal commentators consider that care should be taken to avoid calling this 'warfare' since to fall under the terms of the Geneva Convention it seems that this must be an armed conflict in the more traditional sense.[49] That said, the commentary on the Conventions themselves recognise that both 'armed conflict' and 'war' are vague terms.

43 https://www.un.org/counterterrorism/events/safeguarding-metaverse-countering-terrorism-and-preventing-violent-extremism-digital-space.

44 Weinmann et al, 'The Metaverse and Terrorism: Threats and Challenges' Perspectives on Terrorism, Issue XVII v2 (2023).

45 Regulation (EU) 2021/784 of the European Parliament and of the Council of 29 April 2021 on addressing the dissemination of terrorist content online.

46 https://transparency.techagainstterrorism.org/#about.

47 Baughman discusses the fact that China was discussing the idea of military use metaverses from 2021 in 'Enter the Battleverse: China's Metaverse War' Military Cyber Affairs, Volume 5, Issue 1 HammerCon 2022 Special Edition (2022) https://digitalcommons.usf.edu/cgi/viewcontent.cgi?article=1083&context=mca.

48 The Royal Navy are using the metaverse for training – https://www.royalnavy.mod.uk/news/2024/may/09/20240509-royal-navy-sails-into-the-metaverse-with-virtual-reality-training.

49 M. Marsili. 'Guerre a la Carte: Cyber, Information, Cognitive Warfare and the Metaverse' ACIG, vol 2, no 1, 2023 – https://www.acigjournal.com/pdf-184299-105057?filename=Guerre%20a%20la%20Carte_%20Cyber_.pdf.

14.54 This is not to say that the metaverse would not be used as a weapon of war. The metaverse is at considerable risk of being used to spread disinformation and with the rise of the industrial metaverse there is a considerable risk of denial-of-service attacks resulting from cyber-attacks via the metaverse. All the while the military use any part of the metaverse for tactical training it is exposed to hacking.

14.55 The International Committee of the Red Cross consider that International Humanitarian Law would apply when cyber-attacks happen as part of an armed conflict.[50] The cyber-attack is effectively used as a weapon of an existing war, with the same analogy as when nuclear weapons were first considered. This means under International Humanitarian Law there should not be direct attacks on civilians and they should be properly protected. The cyber-attack would have to meet the definition of an 'attack' under International Humanitarian Law, however, the International Committee of the Red Cross consider that this threshold could be met by a cyber-attack, particularly if this was targeting key infrastructure, such as would be the case if a digital twin of, say, an energy system was targeted.

14.56 Just as the weapons are changing to include technology such as the metaverse, so to should the laws of war. The Hague Conventions and the Geneva Conventions are the backbone of the international rules of war. These conventions however were not implemented with the metaverse in mind. The Hague Conventions were adopted in 1899 and 1907, the Geneva Conventions, and their Protocols between 1864 and 2005.

14.57 The Tallinn Manual is a non-binding framework dealing with issues relating to cyberwarfare. Tallinn 2.0 is currently in place; however, it is expected that Tallinn 3.0 will be in place by 2026. Under the rules one country is prohibited from undertaking cyber operations that would violate the sovereignty of another country.[51] Under the Tallinn Manual it is recognised that human rights law does apply.[52]

14.58 In 2023 the UK joined forces with other countries to participate in the Tallinn Mechanism to help defend critical infrastructure in Ukraine from cyber-attack from Russia.[53] This demonstrates international appetite to protect digital infrastructure vulnerable to attack as part of a war, which is likely to continue in the metaverse and in particular the industrial metaverse.

50 https://www.icrc.org/sites/default/files/document/file_list/icrc_ihl-and-cyber-operations-during-armed-conflicts.pdf.

51 Rule 4.

52 Jensen 'The Tallinn Manual 2.0:Highlights and insights' Georgetown Journal of International Law (2017).

53 https://www.gov.uk/government/news/uk-and-partners-form-the-tallinn-mechanism-for-cyber-security.

CYBERBULLYING

14.59 Cyberbullying happens everywhere online, including in the metaverse. Cyberbullying itself has a devastating effect on its victims. There are calls for both greater parental involvement in the protection against cyberbullying in the metaverse where the victims are often children, as well as legislative reform.[54]

14.60 First, it is important to be able to identify that cyberbullying is taking place before it can be addressed. There are many different forms of cyberbullying in the metaverse, from sending abusive messages to posting embarrassing information, to spreading 'fake news'. Steps are being taken to create tools to identify, monitor and prevent cyberbullying.[55] Technology itself therefore is helping to create a solution to cyberbullying with self-monitoring and then action being taken to mute, block or filter certain behaviour and harm. Technological controls then automatically report infringing behaviour.

GRIEFING

14.61 In gaming 'griefing' is the terms used when a player deliberately does something to annoy the other players. The Council of Europe identify 'griefing' as a form of misconduct.[56] Depending on the actual behaviour it may be a criminal offence, such as repeated action may meet the threshold for harassment. In almost all cases the behaviour exhibited in 'griefing' will fall foul of platform terms.

DEFAMATION

14.62 Lemley and Volokh[57] consider that it is possible to defame an avatar and damage its reputation. In England and Wales the tort of defamation falls under the Defamation Act 2013. Whilst it is possible for a statement made in the metaverse to qualify as defamation, one of the key issues is whether the statement is being made in respect of the avatar or the underlying person. The Defamation Act 2013, s 1 requires that there must be a serious harm to the reputation of the claimant. If the statement is made only as against an avatar and does not relate to the individual user themselves then it is unlikely to meet this requirement on strict interpretation. There are questions over whether someone has defamed

54 Upadhyay et al, Cyberbullying in the Metaverse: A Prescriptive Perception on Global Information Systems for User Protection, Journal of Global Information Management, Volume 31 • Issue 1 (2023).

55 Upadhyay et al, Cyberbullying in the Metaverse: A Prescriptive Perception on Global Information Systems for User Protection, Journal of Global Information Management, Volume 31 • Issue 1 (2023).

56 https://rm.coe.int/the-metaverse-impact-on-and-its-impact-on-human-rights-the-rule-of-law/1680ae6bce.

57 Lemley and Volokh, University of Pennsylvania Law Review, April 2018, V.166, No 5.

another person when the statement relates only to something which is capable of having an impact on their avatar in the metaverse. As the distinction between real life and the metaverse blur, and more of real life move into the metaverse, this should be revisited.

14.63 Legal commentators, albeit based on US Law, consider that real life courts should deal with defamation in the metaverse and that judges should interpret any ambiguity in the legislation so to safeguard people, and their virtual reputations, against such harms.[58] In the UK we expect to see a similar position with the common law determining in the context of the metaverse what is meant by 'serious harm to the reputation of the claimant'.[59] There are arguments that either the avatar is effectively the property of the user (or their intellectual property) which is being damaged as a result of the defamation, or that the avatar is effectively the alter-ego of the user (in the same way as a company and its shareholders), or the avatar is the technological extension of the user.[60]

14.64 Whilst some legal commentators seek to equate defamation in the metaverse with defamation on social media, it is not possible to use the same rules since some conversations in the metaverse may be intended to be private unlike on social media.[61]

14.65 The metaverse will provide anonymity for those who want to defame others using the metaverse. In such circumstances attention should be had to the case of *Blackledge v Persons Unknown*[62] which concerned defamatory statements made by anonymous persons via an online blog. In his Judgment Saini J made clear that where someone refuses to disclose its identity and there is ongoing grave defamatory allegations being made then it is appropriate to grant an injunction restraining the publication and then utilise section 13 of the Defamation Act 2013, s 13 to compel the website operator to take down the infringing material.

14.66 The Defamation Act 2013, s 13 states:

> 'Where a court gives judgment for the claimant in an action for defamation the court may order—
>
> (a) the operator of a website on which the defamatory statement is posted to remove the statement, or
>
> (b) any person who was not the author, editor or publisher of the defamatory statement to stop distributing, selling or exhibiting material containing the statement.'

58 Bettina M. Chin, Regulating Your Second Life: Defamation in Virtual Worlds, 72 Brook. L. Rev. (2007). Available at: https://brooklynworks.brooklaw.edu/blr/vol72/iss4/4.

59 Defamation Act 2013, s 1(1).

60 Bettina M. Chin, Regulating Your Second Life: Defamation in Virtual Worlds, 72 Brook. L. Rev. (2007). Available at: https://brooklynworks.brooklaw.edu/blr/vol72/iss4/4.

61 https://nickclegg.medium.com/making-the-metaverse-what-it-is-how-it-will-be-built-and-why-it-matters-3710f7570b04.

62 [2021] EWHC 1994 (QB).

14.67 In the metaverse there may be some argument in respect of the Defamation Act 2013, s 13 since the metaverse is not a 'website'. This is likely to be symptomatic of the changes in technology since 2013. Protection was afforded to operators of websites under the Defamation Act 2013 on the basis that they should not be responsible for infringing material posted without their knowledge. Further the definitions of 'author', 'editor' and 'publisher' are based on the Defamation Act 1996 and do not provide for the different roles in the metaverse. Accordingly, this is an area where it would be prudent for legislators to take affirmative action to extend the provisions to avoid any form of doubt that the metaverse would not be caught under these provisions.

PERSONAL INJURY

14.68 There is a risk of injury when using VR equipment. As discussed in previous chapters there are concerns over the potential health impact on the user of VR. There are significant mental health risks in respect of the metaverse, including risk of addiction.[63]

SAFEGUARDS

14.69 In 2022 the Institution of Engineering and Technology[64] prepared a detailed report considering risks known to arise as a result of XR. Not only did it consider the potential crimes which may be perpetrated in the metaverse but it also addressed the issues which may be caused as a result of the use of XR such as personal injury and damage caused by using VR headsets and issues relating to over use of VR and perceptions of reality. They believe that it is necessary for the metaverse to install safety features that go beyond those that have to be activated by the individual users. It cannot be appropriate for the only technological controls in place to require activation by users. This would require the user to have to identify that a harm is being committed against them, which may not be immediately apparent, especially for children or those with disabilities. The Institution of Engineering and Technology identified that many children were unsupervised in the metaverse which presented challenges when dealing with any online harms they may experience. Furthermore, in most cases it is difficult for parents, or indeed anyone, to effectively monitor someone's experience in the metaverse since most of the time people do not project or share their screen but instead it can only be viewed by the user.

14.70 The World Economic Forum[65] highlights that one of the main issues with the way that harm in the metaverse is currently dealt with is that it is reactive as opposed to trying to prevent infringing behaviour. They believe that it would

63 https://www.telefonica.com/en/communication-room/blog/main-risks-and-benefits-of-metaverse-on-mental-health/.
64 https://www.theiet.org/media/9836/safeguarding-the-metaverse.pdf.
65 https://www.weforum.org/agenda/2022/01/metaverse-risks-challenges-digital-safety/.

be more effective if the harms were not attractive and that positive behaviour was instead incentivised.

14.71 There are many different ways to deal with harms in the metaverse. This should be a combination of real-life laws, cybercrimes and sanctions in the metaverse, and technological solutions to prevent the occurrence of the harm. Whilst the metaverse is effectively in private ownership it is likely that harm will continue to be dealt with through technological restriction and contractual provisions.

CHILDREN

14.72 There is a heightened risk of harm towards children in the metaverse. Some harm is traditional harms which children are exposed to generally online, but there are also novel risks of the metaverse given the immersive nature of the metaverse.[66] The Center for Countering Digital Hate published 'Horizon Worlds Exposed' in which it identified that children were being exposed to adult content on Meta's Horizon Worlds and were easily able to access the adult only metaverse 'Mature Worlds'.[67] The World Economic Forum highlights that the use of depersonalised avatars in the metaverse may intensify issues of body dysmorphia, which is already a concern for children's interactions on online.[68] The Internet Matters organisation has considered how the metaverse should be built in such a way as to safeguard children.[69] The voices of children and their protection in the metaverse should not be forgotten. One overarching concern is the lack of education about and awareness of the metaverse, especially for parents. One of the fundamental ways that children can be protected from harm in the metaverse is by educating their caregivers on the concerns and risks relating to the metaverse. There are many benefits to children embracing the metaverse but this should be done responsibility. As part of Safer Internet Day 2024 the Virtual Reality Risk Against Children project released a series of videos aimed at helping children stay safe in the metaverse.[70] UNICEF considers that the technology itself should be designed to protect children.[71]

14.73 Age restrictions should be appropriately implemented in the metaverse. There is the opportunity, especially using ZKP and smart contracts to embed technological restrictions which prevent access to certain material such as self-

66 This was considered by the United Nations Interregional Crime and Justice Research Institute in their 2022 report – https://unicri.it/Publication/Gaming-and-the%20Metaverse.

67 https://counterhate.com/wp-content/uploads/2023/03/Horizon-Worlds-Exposed_CCDH_0323.pdf.

68 https://www3.weforum.org/docs/WEF_Metaverse_Identity_Defining_the_Self_in_a_Blended_Reality_2024.pdf.

69 https://www.internetmatters.org/wp-content/uploads/2023/01/Internet-Matters-Metaverse-Report-Jan-2023.pdf.

70 https://uel.ac.uk/about-uel/news/2024/february/teaching-children-how-be-safe-metaverse.

71 https://www.unicef.org/innocenti/stories/what-happens-children-when-physical-and-virtual-worlds-merge.

harm, suicide and sexual content. It is not effective, however to simply exclude children from spaces where adjustments could be made to give proper safeguards. Exclusion has been known not to work both in real life and online; children and young people will find effective work arounds to access spaces where they should not be, whether in real life or in the metaverse. More needs to be done to implement solutions which require proof of some form of adult supervision. The system itself could require a parent's fingerprint for example remain on a device for the duration of the time that the child is in the metaverse. In addition, access may be denied to certain content without a supervisory VR headset being connected. The supervisory VR headset could monitor and view everything seen by the user and could enact technological controls such as personal boundaries or reporting certain events or turning off the users VR headset if necessary. It would be akin to a driving schools vehicle, a dual controlled VR experience for children.

14.74 One of the issues with online experiences, which would be intensified in the metaverse is monitoring what another user has experienced online. Sufficient technological advancements are required to assist parents to effectively monitor use of the metaverse by the children.

14.75 The Internet Matters organisation[72] believes that in order to achieve a metaverse suitable for children there is a need for effective collaborations between all stakeholders. LEGO and Epic Games have partnered to develop a child-friendly metaverse.[73] The Internet Matters organisation considers that the metaverse should:

1 Ensure everyone has accountability for the safeguarding of children and young people. This should be embedded within effective legislation;

2 Have effective time-limits in place to restrict the amount of time that children can spend online and in the metaverse. They reference safeguards that have been implemented online such as with YouTube and TikTok.

3 Limit the ability of children to engage in commercial interactions in the metaverse.

4 Have effective controls in place where children can move between different platforms to ensure that restrictions remain in place for each platform.

5 Try and address the digital divide.

14.76 The Internet Matters organisation[74] highlights that the risk to children is not only in respect of exposure to crimes in the metaverse but also health concerns including obesity risks from lack of physical activity and immersive advertising.

72 https://www.internetmatters.org/wp-content/uploads/2023/01/Internet-Matters-Metaverse-Report-Jan-2023.pdf.

73 https://www.lego.com/en-us/aboutus/news/2022/april/the-lego-group-and-epic-games-team-up-to-build-a-place-for-kids-to-play-in-the-metaverse?locale=en-us.

74 https://www.internetmatters.org/wp-content/uploads/2023/01/Internet-Matters-Metaverse-Report-Jan-2023.pdf.

OFCOM Children's Online Safety Code

14.77 Utilising its powers under the Online Safety Act 2023 OFCOM published its first draft code in May 2024 as part of a consultation phase. It is perhaps most telling that the first code is aimed at protection of children in the digital environment. Whilst there remain some questions over whether all parts of the metaverse and digital interactions will fall under the Act[75] it is still prudent for all platforms which enable children to access their environments to comply with both the Act and the Code. The Act and Code do not only apply to large providers but also to anyone who provides online services. This means that the Act and Code would be applicable to anyone who is providing services within the metaverse environment.

14.78 The Act requires risk assessments for any services which may be accessed by children. The measures that should be implemented are then based on this assessment.

EU

14.79 The European Parliament has prioritised the protection of children in virtual worlds in both resolution 2022/2198 (INI)[76] and resolution 2023/2062 (INI).[77] The European Parliament has issued a fact-sheet 'protecting children in virtual worlds (ie the metaverse)' in which they confirm that funding has been provided by the European Commission on specific uses of the metaverse for children, such as in education. It confirms that the EU have implemented framework regulations which will protect children in the metaverse such as the Digital Services Act and GDPR but noted that no legislation has yet been adopted, although suggested, on preventing online child abuse.

US Online Safety Act

14.80 The Kids Online Safety Act is currently being considered in the United States. The draft bill seeks to establish an extensive framework at the federal level to protect children from harm online. This law would, once implemented, cover the metaverse and the different current metaverse platforms. The law is likely to have provisions that enable parents to monitor and control their children online usage, as well as creating a duty of care for the platforms.

75 See chapter 3 and the issue with the exclusion of aural communications.

76 European Parliament resolution of 17 January 2024 on virtual worlds – opportunities, risks and policy implications for the single market.

77 European Parliament resolution of 17 January 2024 on policy implications of the development of virtual worlds – civil, company, commercial and intellectual property law issues.

TECHNOLOGICAL SOLUTIONS

14.81 There are a number of technological solutions which seek to try and protect users from harm in the metaverse. These include:

1 Personal Boundaries in Meta.

2 Safety bubbles.

3 Global Information systems monitoring interactions such as on social media and user behaviours.[78]

4 Filtering systems which prevents access to certain content.[79]

5 In-built education and training on harms.

6 Virus protection and cyber-security.

14.82 The Personal Boundary was introduced by Meta in 2022. This enables users to effectively build a force field around their avatar. This is still an agile feature for Meta and continues to be evolved.[80] The Personal Boundary technologically stops other avatars from breaching the perimeter. This shows one way that safeguards can be built in the metaverse to not only protect against harm but also to make other users feel more comfortable. It is a proactive measure, rather than a user only being able to respond to harm it has suffered.

14.83 The World Economic Forum advocates the creation of 'ecosystems of trust' with technological in-built safeguards.[81] Users would be technologically prevented from infringing regulation within this ecosystem to keep its users safe. The hardware and software would be designed to prevent infringement. The Forum notes that currently the platforms implement moderation as the barrier to safeguard against harm, however this is not a practical solution as the metaverse expands.

REPORTING CRIMES

14.84 Reporting crime and harm in the metaverse needs to be properly considered and effective provisions implemented within the technology. This is not least because of the cross-border nature of the crimes, the difficulties in identifying the perpetrators and the rules of the different platforms. Whilst the different platforms have built in some form of ability to report violations, critics consider that these are not properly equipped to deal with the potential magnitude

78 Upadhyay et al, Cyberbullying in the Metaverse: A Prescriptive Perception on Global Information Systems for User Protection, Journal of Global Information Management, Volume 31, Issue 1 (2023).

79 Upadhyay et al, Cyberbullying in the Metaverse: A Prescriptive Perception on Global Information Systems for User Protection, Journal of Global Information Management, Volume 31,Issue 1 (2023).

80 https://about.fb.com/news/2022/02/personal-boundary-horizon/#:~:text=How%20It%20Works,there%20is%20no%20haptic%20feedback.

81 https://www.weforum.org/agenda/2022/01/metaverse-risks-challenges-digital-safety/.

of the problem as the metaverse expands, since they are often too complex and inconsistent.[82] This again relates back to the difficulties the metaverse experiences in general in seeking to rely on private law principles to deal with issues (such as crime and punishment) which should properly be dealt with by government organisations and public bodies and therefore instead be subject to public law controls where consideration is much more about principles of reasonableness and creating a fair system.

14.85 Any technological solution must be balanced against a user's human rights. Too prohibitive and the metaverse becomes effectively under authoritarian rule, which is not desirable either in real life or in the metaverse. Whilst the platforms are still privately owned, run and governed, questions have to be raised over who is making decisions on sanctions and controls. It is prudent to combine both traditional protections with technological solutions.

PUNISHMENT IN THE METAVERSE

14.86 Given the metaverse blurs the distinction between real life and virtual reality, where the harm being committed transcends real-life criminal laws then the user should face real-life consequences and sanctions. There is scope, however, for using the metaverse as a form of virtual punishment. Such punishment may be financial, such as a fine, or cyber-prison.

14.87 Scholars have for a long time considered the purpose of punishment. This again comes into the forefront in respect of the metaverse. Many academics group together the different purposes of punishment as either utilitarian or non-utilitarian.[83] Creators of the metaverse need to consider what purpose they seek to achieve with punishment in the metaverse.

14.88 The utilitarian purpose looks at the impact of punishment on the offender and others who witnessing the punishment of the offender. These look at the idea of rehabilitation and deterrence. To act as a deterrent however, the punishment in the metaverse will need to be sufficient and to get the optimal impact, it should be done in public. To rehabilitate an offender in the metaverse there needs to be consideration of how a user can learn from any harm they cause. It is possible with technological intervention to assess whether a user has learnt from any punishment carried out in the metaverse.

14.89 The focus in respect of the non-utilitarian purpose of punishment is on retribution and justice. The object is to look at the concept of what is fair punishment for the offence and how blameworthy the individual should be

82 https://pacscenter.stanford.edu/wp-content/uploads/2022/08/We-Need-a-911-for-the-Metaverse——The-Information.pdf.

83 Richard Frase, Punishment Purposes, 58 Stan. L. Rev 67 (2005) – https://scholarship.law.umn.edu/faculty_articles/543.

considered, based on the nature of the harm. In the metaverse consideration has to be had as to how much the harm impacts on the user in real life. Is it just to punish someone in real life for a virtual harm which impacts on the user in the metaverse or does the punishment need to be carried out in the metaverse?

CONCLUSION

14.90 This chapter considers protection against harm in the metaverse. The key takeaway points are:

- Harm in the metaverse can take many forms. This is not only criminal harm but also civil harm and war. The metaverse as a virtual world has many of the real-life risks as well as specific risks which exist because of the technology and its vulnerability to misuse.
- Where the harm is categorised as a crime then steps can be taken to bring the perpetrator to justice, either in real life or via the metaverse.
- Many real-life crimes will occur in the metaverse. These include stalking and harassment, fraud, theft, money laundering,
- New crimes which relate more to digital interactions will occur in the metaverse. These include cyber-flashing, epilepsy trolling, encouraging self-harm and fake news,
- Traditional gaming harms such as cyberbullying and 'griefing' will occur in the metaverse. With the evolution of society it may be necessary to categorise these as civil harms with tortious liability.
- The UN Cybercrime Treaty will go some way to establishing a framework for dealing with cyber-crimes and criminals.
- The metaverse has the risk of being used both as a weapon by terrorists and a weapon of war. International humanitarian law would apply when cyber-attacks happen as part of an armed conflict.
- Avatars can be defamed in the metaverse. It is likely, however, that this defamation will be against the individual user and not the avatar.
- There is the risk of personal injury through the use of VR, which includes addiction.
- There is a significant risk of harm to children in the metaverse. Safeguards should be built into the technology to protect children and parents should be properly educated on harms in the metaverse.
- OFCOM has released its Children's Online Safety Code under the Online Safety Act 2023. This is the first code under Online Safety Act 2023 and it is perhaps telling it is designed to protect children.
- Punishment for harms committed in the metaverse could take place in real life or in the metaverse. The metaverse will need to determine what the purpose of punishment is in the metaverse.

Chapter 15

Enforcement and investigations in the metaverse

'The rise of powerful technologies such as the Metaverse is making the criminal landscape increasingly complex and transnational, posing new challenges for law enforcement.'

Jürgen Stock, INTERPOL Secretary General

15.01 The metaverse is already firmly in the minds of law enforcement agencies. In 2022 Europol Innovation Lab held an event in the metaverse for law enforcement bodies and released its 'Policing in the metaverse: what law enforcement needs to know'.[1] In 2022 Interpol introduced its metaverse division[2] and Metaverse Expert Group. In 2024 Interpol released its White Paper on the 'Metaverse: A Law Enforcement Perspective' under which it considered that from an enforcement agency perspective there are both benefit and threats of using the metaverse as well as the opportunity to use it as part of an investigation.

15.02 Law enforcement agencies have over time always sought to use new and developing technologies when detecting, investigating and prosecuting criminal offences or regulatory breaches. In part, these uses are a response to the increasingly complex and data-driven world we live in. A good example of technology-assisted crime detection, which seeks to leverage the wealth of data available and being collected for regulatory and non-regulatory purposes, is the UK Financial Conduct Authority's use of Suspicious Transaction Order Reports (or STORs)[3] and wider market data in order to produce metrics of market cleanliness, abnormal and potentially abnormal trading volumes.

15.03 In 1988, in Leicester, United Kingdom, Colin Pitchfork became the first person to be convicted and imprisoned for murder using 'DNA profiling'. Since then, the UK's National DNA Database has grown to include DNA samples of over 6.5 million people and although prosecutions are rarely based on DNA

1 https://www.europol.europa.eu/cms/sites/default/files/documents/Policing%20in%20the%20metaverse%20-%20what%20law%20enforcement%20needs%20to%20know.pdf.

2 https://www.interpol.int/en/News-and-Events/News/2022/INTERPOL-launches-first-global-police-Metaverse.

3 Suspicious Transaction Order Reports (STORs) are reports required to be submitted by market participants subject to the UK Market Abuse Regulation (MAR) to the FCA in respect of any transactions that could constitute insider dealing or market manipulation.

evidence alone, UK government figures suggest that in 2021/2022, the chance that a DNA profile collected at a crime scene would match a profile stored on the database was 64.8%.[4] Broadly, DNA profiling technology, involves the extraction of DNA to reveal a 'sequence' of bars (the 'profile'), is not the only example of how those detecting, investigating and prosecuting crime across the globe have both adopted and taken advantage of technological advancement to assist their work. GPS and 'cell site' technology, facial recognition capabilities, biometric testing and digital forensics are all key weapons in the armoury of the modern law enforcement officer. Bearing in mind its flexibility and potentially limitless capabilities, the metaverse stands to join this list in the near future.

15.04 Although some states have been more bullish than others, on an international basis, governments have sought to respond to technological advances by: (a) affording the authorities the capability to investigate offences without concern for potentially outdated and inflexible legislation; and (b) providing frameworks for individuals and corporate entities to be penalised in ways which take into account their technological abilities.

15.05 Despite providing great benefits for law enforcement agencies, technological advancements – including the metaverse – also represent their biggest global challenge. Digitally held or 'cloud-based' information and documents are more difficult to seize, interrogate and interpret; app-based banking and seamless payment processes means criminal-obtained property is more difficult to trace; and an ever-increasing suite of data-enabled hardware means new techniques are required to interrogate, analyse and present digital evidence. Mr Cristea of Romania told the Parliamentary Assembly of the Council of Europe that one of the key concerns of the metaverse is the risk of it being used as a surveillance tool.[5]

15.06 As well as being adopted by law enforcement agencies, multinational corporates are highly likely to want to leverage the benefits of the metaverse. As well as engaging corporate liability in respect of the activities they conduct on the platform, many – in the UK and elsewhere – will be subject to stringent regulatory regimes, meaning the scope of conduct which gives rise to an increased risk that breaches of these regimes may occur.

Technology and criminal investigations

15.07 In this chapter, we explore the opportunities and challenges in the context of key aspects of the metaverse and the evolution of law enforcement as a whole.

4 https://www.gov.uk/government/publications/forensic-information-databases-annual-report-2021-to-2022/forensic-information-databases-annual-report-2021-to-2022-accessible-version.

5 https://rm.coe.int/-risks-and-opportunities-of-the-metaverse/1680ace8c1.

THE METAVERSE: ENFORCEMENT CHALLENGES AND OPPORTUNITIES

Challenges

Gaps in societal knowledge and policy

15.08 Governments, regulators and practitioners have long recognised the need – particularly where prosecutions and court proceedings in general are concerned – to consider how best to adapt criminal justice systems and legal frameworks in order to cater for societal developments.

15.09 Typically where new issues arise which have no obviously applicable legal framework the Law Commission will get involved. The Commission works by producing consultations and reports, many of which have considered matters of direct relevance to the metaverse, including:

1 **Smart Contracts**[6] – A project which sought to build on the issues identified by the 'Legal Statement on crypto assets and smart contracts' issued by the UK Jurisdiction Taskforce, on the application of UK and 'private international' law to smart contracts.

2 **Digital Assets**[7] – a project which in June 2023 reported broadly on the impact the advent of digital assets has on the law of personal property. In February 2024, the Law Commission presented a draft bill[8] which seeks to introduce a third category of personal property rights into UK law, which would codify an emerging trend of case-law[9] by ensuring that 'things' which are neither a 'thing in possession' nor a 'thing in action' nevertheless constitute an object of personal property.

3 **De-centralised Autonomous Organisations**[10] – a call for evidence which considers, *inter alia*, the extent to which DAOs may be subject to the UK's broad and ever developing anti-money laundering regime.[11] This would create obligations for a number of more traditional regulated businesses, enforceable by a range of supervisory authorities[12] including HMRC and the FCA, concluding[13] that DAOs must assess their own individual position,

6 https://s3-eu-west-2.amazonaws.com/cloud-platform-e218f50a4812967ba1215eaecede923f/uploads/sites/30/2021/11/Smart-legal-contracts-accessible.pdf.

7 Law Commission, 'Digital Assets'.

8 Draft legislation, put to parliament with a recommendation that it be debated and adopted.

9 In *AA v Persons Unknown* [2019] EWHC 3556 (Comm), Mr Justice Bryan followed the decision in the earlier Singapore courts in *B2C2 Limited v Quoine PTC Limited*, that cryptoassets are property because they are '*definable, identifiable by third parties, capable in their nature of assumption by third parties, and having some degree of permanence*' and therefore meet Lord Wilberforce's classic definition of property in *National Provincial Bank v Ainsworth* [1965] 1 AC 1175.

10 Law Commission, 'Decentralised Autonomous Organisations (DAOs): Call for evidence', November 2022.

11 Principally, under the Money Laundering, Terrorist Financing and Transfer of Funds (Information on the Payer) Regulations 2017 (**'the MLRs'**).

12 See section 7 and Schedule 1 of the MLRs.

13 Ibid, 8, paragraph 6.18-6.31.

the services they provide and the extent to which they may be subject to the regime.

4 **Reform of the Communications Offences**[14] – A project which led to the recommendation that new offences ought to be implemented in the UK, including so-called 'cyber-flashing', now an offence under the Sexual Offences Act 2003 and which criminalises the sending or giving of any photograph or file of any person's genitals to another person if done: (a) with the intention that the other person will see the genitals and be caused alarm, distress or humiliation; or (b) for the purpose of obtaining sexual gratification, being reckless as to whether the other person will be caused alarm, distress or humiliation.[15] 'Photograph or film' includes images, whether made or altered by computer graphics or in any other way, which appears to be a photograph or film. This offence is considered in more detail in **Chapter 14**.

15.10 While these recent projects may be those most relevant to the topics considered in this book, they form only a very small part of the Law Commission's work.

15.11 While these projects focus on how the law may require modification, others have made robust – and in some case radical – suggestions as to how the courts that hear criminal cases ought to be modified for certain types of cases, recognising that the subject matter of those cases may be more complex than others. In the UK, this has occurred as far back as 1986, when the 'Fraud Trials Committee Report'[16] made a number of recommendations as to how cases involving serious fraud ought to be litigated, including the suggestion that complex cases should be heard by a specialist 'Fraud Trials Tribunal', borne out of a concern expressed by witnesses to the Committee that 'many jurors are almost certainly out of their depth in complex fraud cases'.[17] This recommendation later became a statutory provision, but was repealed without coming into force. The issue nevertheless remains a live one today, with the concept of 'trial by jury' under an almost constant flow of scrutiny.[18]

CRYPTO-COURTS?

15.12 Whether or not one agrees with Lord Roskill's 1986 conclusions, in many ways, the advent of the metaverse – and other related technological advancements – both as means to commit criminal offences and as platforms for doing so, may present similar challenges. For example, it is conceivable – and may in fact be inevitable – that juries will in the very near future be required not

14 https://lawcom.gov.uk/project/reform-of-the-communications-offences/.
15 Sexual Offences Act 2003, s 66A.
16 Also known as the Roskill Report.
17 Roskill report, paragraph 8.29.
18 See for example, 'Reforming the criminal justice system: juryless trials', Law Society Gazette, 25 June 2023.

only to follow a judge's directions on the relevant legal standards, but they will also be required to comprehend a myriad of concepts including the blockchain, NFTs, cryptocurrency and digital assets, avatars, deFi, DAOs, as well as the 'metaverse' itself.

15.13 This will present significant challenges for both prosecution and defence lawyers, seeking adequately to explain their respective cases to a jury in clear and simple terms. It may be the cases where this becomes necessary the court will have to rely on expert witnesses to define these concepts and to explain them to juries. However, in some cases – most notably, in a UK carbon credit-related fraud trial – the 'expert-led' approach has been shown to carry significant risks, as those seeking to act in such a capacity have been revealed not to possess adequate qualifications or experience, resulting in the collapse of high profile prosecutions.[19] There is therefore a need for lawyers to keep abreast of these new technologies to be able to both understand their client's position and to be able to advance this in court.

FORENSICS AND INVESTIGATIVE METHODS

15.14 The increased prevalence of the metaverse, its platforms and related technologies means that it will become a rich source of information, data and – ultimately – evidence. Law enforcement authorities will need to consider how best to harness, access and interrogate this data. The extent to which this data may be secured or obtained via some of the traditional 'information gathering' powers is considered below. However, whether those powers will provide an appropriate legal framework or if new legislation is required, law enforcement agencies will need to 'up-skill' themselves in order to approach investigations appropriately. In considering how users may be able to contact the police in the metaverse, there may be the need for some form of technological API interface.[20]

15.15 The key challenges already faced by law enforcement agencies include the practicalities of accessing, verifying and then presenting digital evidence, all the while bearing in mind that continuity must be secured in order to safeguard evidential integrity.

ACCESS AND VERIFICATION

15.16 Digital forensics tools have been refined and standardised over time to interrogate traditional mobile devices including mobile phones, laptops and tablets. In the future, these tools will have to be developed so as to be in a position to interrogate a wider range of end-point devices, including virtual reality (VR)

19 https://www.independent.co.uk/news/uk/crime/carbon-credits-fraud-trial-collapses-andrew-ager-expert-witness-a8935921. html.

20 https://www.europol.europa.eu/cms/sites/default/files/documents/Policing%20in%20the%20metaverse%20-%20what%20law%20enforcement%20needs%20to%20know.pdf.

headsets, and augmented reality (AR) glasses, noting that such devices may have the capability to store a range of data including biometrics, user profiles, application data and more.

15.17 Evidence to be gathered by law enforcement is in some ways already limited to what can be accessed on endpoint devices. The shift towards decentralisation and data distribution means accessing a single device may not allow a law enforcement officer to gather a complete picture in relation to any given scenario. To an extent, this problem already exists in relation to more traditional techniques and evidential data-sets, meaning that such evidence is very often used to create inferences which support a particular case theory. The use of cell site technology, for example, allows law enforcement to assert with relative accuracy, the geographical location of a mobile device when it made or received a phone call or text message or when it connected to the internet. Such an exercise is carried out by reference to call data records (CDRs) which must be obtained from the network provider for the phone of interest.

15.18 What cell-site technology cannot tell you is:

a The precise location of the mobile device;

b The identity of the person using that device; or

c In the case of telephone calls, what it being discussed.

15.19 Decentralisation may mean that similar problems are faced by those charged with investigating metaverse based crimes, who may not be in a position to determine the full extent of a user's interaction with other users, a platform or platforms, if the data is held in a cloud-based or other decentralised way. The dynamic nature of metaverse-based platforms and environments may also mean that data will need to be preserved with speed, or agencies risk losing evidence. In addition agencies may also find a reluctance from platform owners to engage with some investigations as platforms seek to balance protection against harm against the rights and privacy of its users. This will be made more complex with the fact that users are likely to be spread out globally and data is likely to be highly encrypted. As discussed below it is going to be challenging for those investigating offences to gain access to data, encryption keys and devices, especially where these are outside of the jurisdiction.

15.20 Europol confirm that it expects the difficulties of trying to ascertain the location of someone to intensify in the metaverse especially as its use increases.[21]

15.21 This will require significant knowledge, and potentially an increased reliance on experts (see above), in order to define, extract and interpret relevant data.

21 https://www.europol.europa.eu/cms/sites/default/files/documents/Policing%20in%20the%20metaverse%20-%20what%20law%20enforcement%20needs%20to%20know.pdf.

PRESENTING

15.22 Complex criminal cases often involve subjects and themes which are highly technical, and the challenge of seeking to ensure that juries and tribunals in general understand them is well-trodden ground (see above in relation to fraud trials and criminal trials more generally). Significant effort goes into such cases, with prosecting authorities likely to need to rely increasingly on the use of in-court technology and the presentation of evidence in graphic form, in order to ensure that juries can understand the evidence that they are hearing. At least in the near term it is expected that prosecuting authorities are going have an uphill battle to try and move away from the perception of the public that the metaverse is just an extension of video-gaming and show the real-life impact of crimes that have been committed.

INFORMATION GATHERING POWERS

15.23 Having considered the practical difficulties of evidence gathering in metaverse based cases, we must also consider the application – and adequacy – of the current legal frameworks on gathering evidence for regulatory, criminal and other investigations. This section seeks to do this by reference to a handful of well-known – and some less well-known – information gathering powers.

15.24 Many of these powers have been subject to significant judicial scrutiny over a number of years, as their flexibility has been continually tested against an everchanging and increasingly globalised world. The metaverse, its platforms and underlying technologies, will serve only to fuel further scrutiny, as law enforcement agencies look to compel the production of data held only in the metaverse, seize digital metaverse-based assets, search metaverse platforms and worlds and actively police the metaverse.

15.25 As with digital forensics, the principal issue may not be in identifying what material is required or – subject to the potential for it to be held in a decentralised way – where it is. It is more likely to relate to having mechanisms in place to access that material, so that a complete picture may be obtained. With this in mind, in this section we do not seek to consider all aspects of potentially relevant information gathering powers, but rather the extent to which they may be used to gather information held on metaverse platforms and – if so – what they say about access to that material.

THE POLICE AND CRIMINAL EVIDENCE ACT 1984

15.26 The Police and Criminal Evidence Act 1984 (or 'PACE'), is the principal source of the powers afforded to UK police forces to secure evidence, by means – for example – of 'stop and search' powers, or via formal applications to secure warrants to search premises or to compel a party to produce specific material.

15.27 Various of the powers contained within PACE are already used for the seizure of 'endpoint' electronic devices, including additional powers, such as those contained within the Criminal Justice and Police Act 2001 which allow police officers that are lawfully on any premises to seize anything which they have reasonable grounds to believe contains something for which they are authorised to search, even in circumstances where that thing is comprised in something which they are not authorised to seize.

15.28 ***Scenario 1*** below illustrates where this might be relevant.

15.29 ***Scenario 1***

1. Police Officer A is in attendance, along with investigators from the UK Serious Fraud Office ('SFO'),[22] to execute a warrant issued to search the home address of Suspect B, pursuant to the Criminal Justice Act 1987, s 2(4) and (5).[23]
2. Suspect B is under investigation by the SFO due to their suspected involvement in an extensive phishing scam, resulting in thousands of customers of a well-known crypto-exchange and wallet provider having lost their digital assets.
3. The Warrant authorises the seizure of '…any documents relating to Suspect B's personal bank accounts and assets, crypto-wallets and any documents indicating his connection to or ability to access to the relevant crypto exchange'.
4. When on the premises, Police Officer A seizes a number of hard copy folders with labels indicating that they relate to Suspect B's digital asset holdings. In addition, Police Officer A seizes two mobile phones, a laptop, a tablet and a VR headset on the basis that he has reasonable grounds to believe that the devices may contain documents of the same description as those set out in the Warrant.

15.30 In such circumstances, the Criminal Justice and Police Act 2001 authorises the examination of the property, as soon as reasonably practicable, to ascertain the extent to which it contains property which:

a the person seizing it had power to search when he made the seizure but is not property the return of which is required by s 54;

22 The Serious Fraud Office will often act with the assistance of the Police, as the warrant issued under Section 2 of the Criminal Justice Act 1987 requires execution / supervision by a 'constable'.

23 Section 2(5) authorises a judge in the magistrates' court to issue a warrant to enter premises, search for and take copies of documents where satisfied that there are reasonable grounds for believing (i)a person has failed to comply with an obligation under this section to produce them; (ii)it is not practicable to serve a notice under in relation to them; or (iii)the service of such a notice in relation to them might seriously prejudice the investigation; and (b)that they are on premises specified in the information,

b that it is property the retention of which is authorised by s 56; or

c that it is something which, in all the circumstances, it will not be reasonably practicable, following the examination, to separate from property falling within paragraph (a) or (b).

15.31 Criminal Justice and Police Act 2001, s 56 in effect provides a catch all, allowing officers to retain property which is:

a obtained in consequence of the commission of an offence; and

b necessary to be retained in order to prevent its being concealed, lost, damaged, altered or destroyed.

OR

c evidence in relation to any offence; and

d necessary to be retained in order to prevent its being concealed, lost, altered or destroyed.

15.32 It should be noted that the powers of seizure and retention may also be used in a range of scenarios, involving the broad range of search and seizure powers available to UK law enforcement.

The Criminal Justice Act 1987, s 2 – the production of documents

15.33 The Criminal Justice Act 1987, s 2 authorises the Director of the SFO, by notice in writing, to 'require the person whose affairs are to be investigated ("the person under investigation") or any other person whom he has reason to believe has relevant information to answer questions or otherwise furnish information with respect to any matter relevant to the investigation at a specified place and either at a specified time or forthwith'.[24]

15.34 It also authorises the SFO, by notice in writing, to 'require the person under investigation or any other person to produce at such place as may be specified in the notice and either forthwith or at such time as may be so specified, any specified documents which appear to the Director to relate to any matter relevant to the investigation or any documents of a specified description'.

Judicial scrutiny

15.35 The SFO's s 2 powers have been subject to particular judicial scrutiny and commentary in recent years, including in circumstances which have some significance to the particular issues covered in this chapter.

24 Criminal Justice Act 1987, s 2(3).

15.36 On 5 February 2021, the UK Supreme Court in *R (on the application of KBR, Inc) (Appellant) v Director of the Serious Fraud Office (Respondent)* ruled that s 2 does not permit the SFO to compel a foreign company to produce documents held abroad.[25] The Supreme Court was required to rule on what were relatively narrow issues which were approached as such. However, the judgment being appealed[26] contained significant mention of the 'modern phenomenon' of the internet and cloud-based storage, as well as the wider policy challenges presented by investigating serious and complex fraud in a today's world. In that judgment, LJ Gross stated:

> 'It is scarcely credible that a UK company could resist an otherwise lawful s.2(3) notice on the ground that the documents in question were held on a server out of the jurisdiction.
>
> The policy underlying s.2(3) required the section to have some extraterritorial application in 1987; and the same policy can and should permit s.2(3) to apply where technological developments have further illustrated the necessity for a degree of extraterritorial application.'

15.37 In *KBR*, it was agreed that if the addressee of a notice issued under s 2 had been a British-registered company, it would have authorised the service of a notice to produce documents held abroad by *that* company. However, bearing in mind this agreement, there was no further analysis required on the extent to which that British company may not have been in a position to produce the relevant documents, because they were in fact 'held on a server out of the jurisdiction'.

15.38 But what if the documents or information required a UK company to produce data held in equal parts in the following way:

a locally, on a local server or endpoint device;

b abroad, on an overseas server; and

c decentralised, using blockchain technology.

15.39 Further analysis on the decision and its reference to the approach adopted in the US is below.

Applications in the metaverse

15.40 Bearing in mind that the volume of the VR headset market in the UK is expected to reach 1.45 million by 2028,[27] investigations will increasingly involve the seizure and examination of such devices (in circumstances similar to those in ***Scenario 1***, for example) to identify evidence. There are already some significant

25 [2021] UKSC 2.

26 Ibid, 23, [2018] EWHC 2368 (Admin).

27 https://www.statista.com/outlook/cmo/consumer-electronics/gaming-equipment/vr-headsets/united-kingdom#volume.

suggestions that criminal investigations are producing evidence that these types of devices are being used to commit criminal offences, including sexual offences against children.[28]

15.41 While these laws provide UK law enforcement with the ability to seize various types of hardware, including VR headsets and AR glasses, similar issues will apply when considering the limits of end-point forensics (see above) and agencies will need to upskill in order to ensure they have the ability to secure data from these pieces of hardware and be able to extract and use this evidence for the purpose of proceedings. However, once those skills are acquired and robust methods are in place, we may in the future see cases where evidence is presented as having been secured from VR headsets. This may be presented either as data or text based extracted code or, probably the more compelling, replaying the data in VR to the tribunal or jury in a similar approach to CCTV evidence.

15.42 Should those skills not be developed – which is unlikely – it may fall to other powers to be used to secure the production of material held in the metaverse.

PACE, s 20

15.43 While in practice it is rarely used, mention should be made of PACE, s 20, which expressly provides that each the powers of search and seizure contained within it includes a 'power to require any information stored in any electronic form contained in a computer and accessible from the premises to be produced in a form in which it can be taken away and in which it is visible and legible or from which it can readily be produced in a visible and legible form'.[29]

A US PERSPECTIVE

15.44 In 1986 the *Stored Communications Act* ('the SCA 1986') was passed by Congress. The reach of this legislation when data is held outside of the US was however, unclear until 2018.

15.45 The leading case on this area is *Microsoft v US*.[30] Microsoft was initially held in contempt of court for failing to produce details of email accounts which were stored on servers in Ireland. Microsoft successfully appealed against the orders of the United States District Court for the Southern District of New York and then the US Government obtained leave to appeal to the Supreme Court. Before the Supreme Court were able to rule however, on 23 March 2018 the Clarifying Lawful Overseas Use of Data Act (CLOUD Act), came into force,

28 https://www.bbc.co.uk/news/uk-64734308.
29 PACE, s 20.
30 829 F 3d 197 (2d Cir. 2016).

amending the SCA 1986. This legislation specifically allows for extraterritorial application.

15.46 The *Microsoft* litigation is of interest in a number of respects. First, as a reminder of the state of technology in 1986/87. Secondly, for the ruling of the Court of Appeals, Second Circuit against the extraterritorial application of the SCA 1986. Thirdly, for the fact that the US Supreme Court was prepared to entertain the case. Fourthly, because the US chose a legislative solution to put the matter beyond doubt. Given the questions *KBR* still raises in respect of extraterritorial scope in the circumstances discussed above, legislative reform in this area would be welcome.

BARRIERS TO ENFORCEMENT

15.47 As well as the distinction as between the US-UK approaches as set out above in respect of data stored overseas (no amendments have been made to s 2 powers since the Supreme Court judgment), there are serious issues that will be faced by law enforcement once metaverse-related crime becomes the norm. The courts are likely to find themselves routinely having to address issues where data is held in different territories. In addition, there may be ongoing or connected crimes committed over multiple different platforms, which may involve having to request data from a number of different third parties, based in multiple jurisdictions with data held globally and encrypted. To request, analyse and consider this data alone will be a considerable, and expensive, task. This is likely to be the main barrier to enforcement and investigations in the metaverse; its cost.

A TECHNOLOGICAL SOLUTION

15.48 Given the barriers to traditional enforcement and investigations in the metaverse it is conceivable that a technological solution may be more effective at enforcement in the metaverse. Through the use of smart contract technology in particular the owners of the different metaverse platforms could work with legal experts to implement both effective enforcement mechanisms as well as enhanced investigative tools. The benefit of blockchain technology specifically is that it records all interactions on the blockchain itself. This would be a valuable data tool for investigators. In addition, the software itself could capture, akin to CCTV, specifically pre-programmed events and make these available to the authorities to review or be able to identify and extract the relevant data upon a report being made to the relevant authorities within the metaverse. It would also be possible to automatically trigger a notification to the authorities via smart contract if a specific event happens in the metaverse. This does, however, rely on the support of the metaverse platforms who may be reluctant to assist given the potential impact this will have on its users' privacy.

POLICING

15.49 In its European Citizens panel on virtual worlds in 2023 the European Commission recommended the need for an international police force such as Europol to police the metaverse and emphasised the benefits in using artificial intelligence to support the police in this area.[31]

15.50 Interpol established a headquarters in the metaverse in October 2022 and released its White Paper 'Metaverse a law enforcement perspective'[32] in January 2024 under which it made a commitment to help other law enforcement agencies with guidance on how to police the metaverse and to try and create a coordinated response to this this threat.

Opportunities

15.51 Many of the opportunities the metaverse presents to law enforcement are rooted in the same capabilities that offer opportunities to the rest of the professional and non-professional world. The endless ability to build worlds and collaborate provides a myriad of ways to both augment and supplement investigations, prosecutions and enforcement in general – some more technical than others.

Training and collaboration

15.52 As well as using the metaverse for advanced crime scene and crisis simulation and immersive training, providing officers with realistic scenarios to practice their response to various situations, it also presents an opportunity for police forces and law enforcement in multiple jurisdictions to collaborate.

15.53 As highlighted above (see *KBR*), developments in technology coupled with exponential globalisation present one of the biggest challenges to criminal investigations and prosecutions. Gathering information through so-called Mutual Legal Assistance (MLA) is often slow. Meeting and sharing information seamlessly on metaverse platforms has the potential to reduce this logistical burden, although this will likely require 'up-front' international cooperation to ensure proper governance and legal frameworks.

Digital crime scene preservation

15.54 The metaverse allows for the digitisation of crime scenes, which can be used for investigation and evidence preservation.

31 https://citizens.ec.europa.eu/document/download/5d55a9e4-a0f2-4974-b01b-a8382eb6cb4d_en?filename=ECP%20on%20Virtual%20Worlds_Final%20Report.pdf.

32 https://www.interpol.int/content/download/20828/file/Metaverse%20-%20a%20law%20enforcement%20perspective.pdf.

Witness protection

15.55 Legal commentators[33] consider the metaverse could be used to encrypt the identity of witnesses affording heightened security protection which is likely to be useful in certain proceedings like organised crime.

Understanding cybercrime

15.56 By engaging with the metaverse, law enforcement can gain a better understanding of cybercrime and develop strategies to tackle emerging threats.

15.57 These opportunities can help law enforcement agencies adapt to the evolving digital landscape and enhance their capabilities in crime prevention and investigation.

CIVIL (OR QUASI-CRIMINAL) 'ENFORCEMENT'

15.58 Although this chapter focuses on the impact the metaverse may have on criminal and – by analogy – regulatory investigations, it should be noted that not all frauds, thefts and misconduct in general lead to such investigations and – ultimately – prosecutions. In some instances, criminal matters may conclude (or not be proceeded with) but ancillary 'civil' proceedings nevertheless continue, such as confiscation,[34] civil recovery or account or cash forfeiture proceedings, all under the Proceeds of Crime Act 2002.

15.59 In such cases, issues of true ownership, third party rights and interests often prevail and so it is helpful to consider how the metaverse and its underlying technologies may play a part in the same.

15.60 Broadly speaking, each of these areas may be resolved by or are instigated using methods similar to those that might be employed in the event that a civil order or judgment requires compliance by a losing defendant (often referred to as a 'judgment debtor'). These methods may include:

> *'Payment Orders' under the Proceeds of Crime Act 2002, s 67*
>
> A court (specifically, the magistrates' court) may make an order for funds held in bank or building society accounts to be paid into court. Such orders may also be made in respect of 'cryptoassets', held by a person in a wallet administered by a UK-connected cryptoasset service provider[35] with the added possibility that such

33 *Bertovskiy, L.V., Devyatkin, G.S. and Fedorov, A.R.,* (2024*). Interdisciplinary Aspects of the Introduction of Virtual Reality Technologies in Court Proceedings. Kutafin Law Review*, 11(1), pp. 124– 141, doi: 10.17803/2713-0533.2024.1.27.124-141

34 Confiscation will only ever follow a conviction, whereas civil recovery and cash or account seizure and forfeiture proceedings do not require a conviction to have occurred.

35 Proceeds of Crime Act 2002, s 67ZA.

assets could be 'destroyed' in the event that it is not 'reasonably practicable' to sell them or there are ' reasonable grounds to believe that the realisation of the cryptoassets would be contrary to the public interest, having regard in particular to how likely it is that the entry of the cryptoassets into general circulation would facilitate criminal conduct by any person'.

'cryptoassets' are broadly defined as 'a cryptographically secured digital representation of value or contractual rights that uses a form of distributed ledger technology and can be transferred, stored or traded electronically'.[36] In a circular issued in April 2024, the UK government confirmed that this broad definition is intended to 'encompass a range of different technologies in use such as non-fungible tokens (NFTs), which are cryptographic token versions of a particular asset and cannot be swapped directly for other NFTs and Stablecoins, which are cryptoassets whose value is pegged to specific government-issued fiat currencies'.'[37]

'Property Freezing Orders', as the pre-cursor to Civil Recovery Proceedings[38]

15.61 The High Court may make an order prohibiting any person whose property is specified in the order from dealing with the asset. Subject to negotiation and lengthy litigation, the ultimate aim of the applying enforcement agency will be to secure a 'recovery order', to vest the 'recoverable property in the 'trustee for civil recover',[39] whose role it is to give effect to the order by 'realising'[40] the property.

Seizure and forfeiture orders

15.62 The regime also includes 'standalone' powers available to a wide range of enforcement officers to seize cash, funds held in accounts, 'cryptoassets' (see above) and 'crypto wallets', as well as the ability to secure an order forfeiting those assets (or some or all of the assets held).

Civil recovery – outlook

15.63 There is a lower standard of proof that applies in respect of civil recovery, seizure and forfeiture proceedings in the UK, when compared with the burden of proving criminal charges against a defendant. Securing a freezing order only requires that the officer has 'reasonable grounds to suspect' that the property is recoverable (ie was obtained through unlawful conduct). Forfeiture requires that the court hearing the application is satisfied that the property is – on the balance of probabilities, rather than beyond a reasonable doubt – recoverable property.

36 Section 150A and – in relation to civil recovery, Section 303Z20, Proceeds of Crime Act 2002.
37 https://www.gov.uk/government/publications/circular-0042024-cryptoasset-confiscation-order-provisions/0042024-economic-crime-and-corporate-transparency-act-cryptoasset-confiscation-order-provisions#definitions
38 Such proceedings apply to '…any property (including cash) whether or not any proceedings have been brought for an offence in connection with the property', Proceeds of Crime Act 2002, s 240(2).
39 Proceeds of Crime Act 2002, s 266.
40 Proceeds of Crime Act 2002, s 267.

15.64 This has led to a perception that enforcement authorities will secure a greater benefit for a lower cost, by pursuing these civil orders, rather than pursuing complex and costly prosecutions. A healthy line of case law already demonstrates that there is significant appetite in the UK to freeze and recover/forfeit 'cryptoassets', under powers such as those summarised above.[41]

CONCLUSION

15.65 This chapter considers enforcement and investigations in the metaverse. The key takeaway points are:

- Interpol already has a presence in the metaverse. Policing the metaverse will be a challenge and we expect to see law enforcers take novel approaches with this new technology. The metaverse has significant potential for training and crime scene recreation.
- Law enforcement agencies and the courts will need to adapt to, and understand the new technology. In the early days this may not be easy since there are many novel concepts and names.
- There are considerable challenges for law enforcement when dealing with the metaverse. There is a gap in knowledge given the speed at which the technology is expanding.
- There are challenges for juries to comprehend many of the concepts relating to the metaverse and there will be the need to rely on expert evidence.
- There will be an extensive amount of data that may have to be collected in the metaverse as part of an investigation. Some of this data may be difficult to access, others will have limitations similar to cell-site data.
- Investigators will via PACE have the powers to seize and examine VR headsets and XR hardware to analyse it and extract evidence, likely via digital forensics.
- *R (on the application of KBR, Inc (Appellant) v Director of the Serious Fraud Office (Respondent)*[42] examined the ability of the SFO to compel the production of documents held abroad on overseas servers. In this case they were not compelled since they were not a British company and were based overseas. This is an unhelpful decision in light of the cross-border nature of the metaverse, where it would have aided the enforcement authority to have the production of documents compelled regardless of the location of those in possession of the same.
- A technological solution may be more suitable for enforcement in the metaverse.

41 *AA v Persons Unknown* [2019] EWHC 3556 (Comm); *Vorotyntseva v Money-4 Ltd (T/A Nebus.com)* [2018] 9 WLUK 501; *Danisz v (1) Persons Unknown (2) Huobi Global Ltd (Trading as –Huobi)* [2022] EWHC 280 (QB).

42 [2021] UKSC 2.

Chapter 16

Dispute resolution and the metaverse

> *'The virtual world is not the enemy. The pioneers invented a world they believed in, but the followers must follow that world whether they believe in it or not.'*
>
> Leos Carax, Film Director

16.01 This chapter considers the idea of civil dispute resolution in the metaverse. In the UK considerable resource is being put into building a new digital justice system to enable people to access digital resources and help early. Led by Sir Geoffry Vos, Master of the Rolls the pioneering system seeks to bring in the ability for people to access early resolution through services such as ACAS and the Financial Services Ombusdman.[1] This progressive move is hopefully the backbone of a fully digitalised court system and the hope that this will make it easier for disputes in the metaverse to be dealt with in the real-life court system and eventually be used to transition to Web3.

UNDERSTANDING DISPUTES IN THE METAVERSE

16.02 The types of disputes in the metaverse are unlikely to differ much from real-life disputes. Whilst the issues may be different, such as a virtual product or digital interaction, fundamentally there will be the same underlying nature of civil disputes that has existed for centuries – purported failed promises, misfeasance, poor behaviour, using something that you don't have the right to use, and lies. All litigation in the first instance depends on its facts. Legal practitioners will need to be able to understand those facts in the context of the metaverse, but translate these into the real life to be able to bring proceedings. In his March 2022 speech, the Master of the Rolls Sir Geoffrey Vos considered that with the rise in blockchain and other technologies we may not be required to determine the facts of a matter in the same way as we have to at this point.[2] It may be that instead the technology itself accurately records the truth.

16.03 The Business and Property Court has considered digital disputes and the considerable work that has been done to prepare for the expected onslaught of such cases.[3] It identifies some of the key issues in digital disputes are much

1 https://www.judiciary.uk/speech-by-the-master-of-the-rolls-driving-system-change-and-addressing-injustice/.
2 https://www.bailii.org/uk/other/speeches/2022/RDU16.pdf.
3 https://www.judiciary.uk/courts-and-tribunals/business-and-property-courts/commercial-court/the-work-of-the-commercial-court/digital-disputes/.

the same as traditional disputes, including emergency interim relief, service and enforcement.

16.04 One of the key complexities in respect of the metaverse is its cross-border nature. This is a complicating factor in any civil litigation both from determining the correct jurisdiction to enforcement.

EARLY RESOLUTION

Online Dispute Resolution

16.05 The EU enables online dispute resolution for consumers via its Online Dispute Resolution Platform. This type of dispute resolution process may prove a useful platform for smaller disputes in the metaverse to enable a swift and relatively low-cost form of resolution. With Online Dispute Resolution the process is entirely dealt with online. In the metaverse it may be appropriate that the process is conducted virtually. With Online Dispute Resolution a dispute resolution body is agreed between the parties from a list of approved dispute resolution bodies. These bodies are specialists for different industries, eg aviation, insurance, energy. Each body can set its own rules and processes. This combines the effectiveness of Online Dispute Resolution but the determination is being made by a suitable body, agreed between the parties. The bodies are not private companies and are not connected to the platforms themselves. This is important as the judicial decision-making is independent.

Digital Dispute Resolution

16.06 In 2021 the UK Jurisdiction Taskforce published its Digital Dispute Resolution Rules. The rules are intended to be used within smart contracts, embedded into digital assets and on the blockchain through reference to the rules[4] and have the stated purpose[5] to 'facilitate the rapid and cost-effective resolution of commercial disputes, particularly those involving novel digital technology such as cryptoassets, cryptocurrency, smart contracts, distributed ledger technology and fintech applications'.[6] The rules will therefore be used in some form in the metaverse if they are widely adopted, and they also have the potential to expand into use for virtual assets purchased in the metaverse.

16.07 Under the Rules[7] any dispute must be subjected to arbitration unless there is an automatic dispute resolution process.[8] Alternatively, disputes can

4 Rule 3.
5 Rule 1.
6 https://ukjt.lawtechuk.io.
7 Rule 5.
8 This facilitates alternative dispute resolution as discussed below under decentralised dispute resolution.

be determined by an expert if agreed.[9] The Rules deal with the procedure for commencing proceedings and an initial response to proceedings within three days which must include the identity of the parties and electronic contact details.[10] The Rules are deliberately flexible to enable the tribunal to set the rules once proceedings are initiated, however, the Rules are clear that determination can be made on paper and there is no absolute right to an oral hearing.

16.08 The main issue with the Rules, however, is that whilst they may be incorporated by reference into the digital asset it is unlikely that many, especially less sophisticated, users will be aware of the existence of such Rules. The agreement ascribed to the Rules may be contained within say the protocol of a smart contract or even coded into the digital asset itself.

16.09 The timeframes provided for under the Rules are much shorter than is usual in litigation with final determination being hoped for within 30 days of appointment of an arbitrator.[11] Whilst this is a positive step, more awareness is needed to bring the attention of normal users of such services to these measures. It is unclear how an arbitrator may rule if such a user seeks to try and avoid an arbitration hearing, given the express provision and by extension of the transfer of the asset its acceptance, of arbitration as binding dispute resolution. This means that users will in most cases be precluded from commencing civil litigation.

16.10 The guidance to the Rules expects that users will have to agree to the incorporation of the Rules in writing, however, given the nature of digital (and virtual assets) it is difficult to understand how this will be done and it is more like to be a technological method in the way that the Rules are notified and accepted much like terms and conditions in Web2 in real life

16.11 The Rules provide for anonymity and will publish only anonymised decisions. This is because the Rules will use arbitration as the accepted form of dispute resolution. Not everyone prefers arbitration to litigation. Should these Rules become commonplace for digital assets it does somewhat call into question whether such process will uphold one of the underlying purposes of justice, being that it should be seen to be done. Where dispute resolution is being purposely conducted in an anonymised fashion, with provisions being built into the code itself to compel such Rules there is a clear risk. Whilst the Rules are better than the uncertainty which exists without them, it is essential that clear safeguards are implemented and it remains under constant review to ensure they are not being misused and that arbitration is the most appropriate form of resolution in the circumstances.

16.12 Legal practitioners need to carefully check prior to commencing any civil litigation process whether the dispute has been subjected to arbitration by

9 Rule 5.
10 Rule 7.
11 Rule 12.

virtue of either the Digital Dispute Resolution Rules or under any other platform rules. If litigation is incorrectly commenced, they risk their client's claim being stayed and costs awarded under the Arbitration Act 1996.

ARBITRATION

16.13 As discussed in **Chapter 3** the UAE has established the Dubai International Arbitration Centre metaverse as a solution to deal with disputes in the metaverse. The platform enables parties to participate in the arbitration remotely from anywhere in the world.

16.14 Arbitration can be utilised in the metaverse and may be the most effective dispute resolution tool to deal with its cross-border nature. There is the ability through arbitration to pre-agree the seat of arbitration and the laws. This is typically reflected in the initial agreement between the parties. As discussed above the Digital Dispute Resolution Rules provides for arbitration as the effective form of dispute resolution.

16.15 Legal commentators have considered the effectiveness of arbitration in the resolution of disputes concerning digital assets[12]. They consider that this type of forum lends itself well to the decentralised nature of blockchain given it removes the involvement of a centralised court system and instead the parties are able to choose the key aspects of the way in which disputes are handled and resolved. Further in arbitration there is a larger degree of flexibility and an expert can be appointed in virtual assets or the metaverse to determine the matter. US Dispute resolution provider JAMS has created arbitration model clauses and Rules relating to disputes which arise out of smart contracts.[13]

MODERATION

16.16 Since the metaverse is currently based principally on private law principles much of the dispute resolution processes are based on moderation by the metaverse owners. As discussed earlier in the book these owners can then make final decisions over the sanction for a user. As the metaverse expands, and peoples are spending more time and money in the virtual world they will seek proper recourse if there is a dispute. As a result we expect to see litigation and ADR used more frequently in the metaverse. Critics of moderation as a form of dispute resolution express concern at the impact this has on freedom of expression. Further moderation tends to have little rights to appeal.

12 Chen, Joyce W., Dispute Resolution in the New Digital Era—Exploring Arbitration as a Suitable Mechanism to Resolve Disputes Over Crypto Assets (November 30, 2022). Contemporary Asia Arbitration Journal, Vol. 15, No. 2, pp. 255-282, November 2022, Available at SSRN: https://ssrn.com/abstract=4417688.

13 https://www.jamsadr.com/rules-smart-contracts.

DISPUTE RESOLUTION IN DECENTRALISED ENVIRONMENTS

16.17 Blockchain is capable of being used for decentralised dispute resolution (DDRS). Systems such as Kleros are being promoted as an effective dispute resolution for smaller disputes.[14] Effectively users participate in the dispute resolution by purchasing tokens and work effectively as a peer-to-peer jury. Those that participate, however, are also often rewarded in tokens. Those that promote the use of DDRS cite its ability to deal effectively with low value cross-border claims which will shape the new digital landscape.[15] It is likely that some cases would not be suitable for resolution in this way and would require a more traditional form of dispute resolution. It may well be likely that such DDRS systems evolve to incorporate the use of legal representatives assisting clients put forward the most compelling case albeit it is presented in this new forum and determined by peers. At this stage there is a distinct lack of uniformity in terms of the way in which disputes are dealt with both at the initial determination and later appeals. In England civil matters are typically considered and judged by professional judges who are experienced legal professionals. In America, however, trial by jury for certain civil matters is much more common-place and is protected under the constitution.

16.18 Critics of the use of smart contracts to resolve disputes, in a form of DDRS, raise concerns about the ability of such platforms to determine a significantly high volume of matters and their struggle to maintain any form of anonymity especially where the dispute is taken into real life and 'off-chain' (or outside of the issues which arise from within the blockchain environment).[16] They raise concerns over the inability of DDRS to be able to compel a party to provide evidence, but this is also the case in many civil cases in English courts where witnesses cannot be compelled to give evidence. Litigating via smart contract does remove the ability for oral arguments, to test the evidence by seeing and hearing the witnesses give their evidence.

CIVIL PROCEDURE AND THE METAVERSE

Pre-action

16.19 The first step in any civil proceedings is to consider the causes of action for which the potential defendants may be liable. In the context of the metaverse it is not just identifying the impact of the virtual landscape on the underlying cause of action, but as below identifying the details of the potential defendant, which itself can be challenging, and then determining the nature of the defendant

14 Zhuk, A. Applying blockchain to the modern legal system: Kleros as a decentralised dispute resolution system. *Int. Cybersecur. Law Rev.* **4**, 351–364 (2023). https://doi.org/10.1365/s43439-023-00086-x.

15 https://www.frontiersin.org/journals/blockchain/articles/10.3389/fbloc.2021.564551/full.

16 Buchwald, M. Smart Contract Dispute Resolution: The inescapable flaws of blockchain based arbitration *University of Pennsylvania Law Review Vol 168: 1369.*

especially if this is a DAO and deciding whether it has its own legal identity or not. Once this has been identified attention is turned to the Pre-Action Protocols.

16.20 The Online Procedure Rule Committee was established by the Judicial Review and Courts Act 2022 to create the rules for online court proceedings in the UK. Reflecting the changes in technology and the need for procedures to reflect the same the Justice Minister said:

> 'It is vital that digital court processes are governed by rules more suited to evolving technologies, and the creation of this committee secures the government's longstanding commitment to leading the way in making this a reality.'[17]

16.21 The Committee is not simply tasked with creating rules but instead will also establish the framework for the early tier systems as set out above. It is also expected that it will create the standards to govern online practices.[18]

Parties

16.22 As above it is not always immediately obvious who the correct parties will be in any litigation proceedings arising out of disputes in the metaverse. Often there is a veil of anonymity shielding the identity of the various parties. We also have the added complexities relating to DAOs. Prior to commencing any form of litigation arising out of a dispute in the metaverse it is going to be important to try and identify the respondents' identities. For a DAO it is important to understand the legal classification of the entity prior to commencing the litigation to identify the correct entity and applicable Civil Procedure Rules. In some DAOs there is a combination of both corporate persons (a limited company) and individuals, in such cases it is likely to be a complex exercise to establish where blame lies. It is likely that we will see those DAO with some form of legal wrapper try and assert some form of shielding from the corporate veil.

16.23 We have already seen in various cryptocurrency litigation that in certain situations a claim does not automatically fail simply because the identity of the respondent cannot be ascertained and instead we see various claims being brought against persons unknown. In contrast it is accepted however that the Claimant must be identified at least at the point of any claim being commenced[19].

16.24 Certain formalities in respect of the parties and their identification in the claim form depend on whether the defendant is a company, partnership, unincorporated association or individual. This is highly relevant in the context of a DAO given the unknowns in respect of their legal classification under English Law as discussed in **Chapter 8.** It is unlikely to be a straight-forward exercise

17 https://www.gov.uk/government/news/new-online-procedure-rule-committee-launched.

18 https://www.judiciary.uk/speech-by-the-master-of-the-rolls-driving-system-change-and-addressing-injustice/.

19 *Wright v Persons Unknown* [2022] EWHC2982.

to complete a claim form where the parties originate from conduct within the metaverse, especially where the interactions have been on a decentralised platform.

Service

16.25 As discussed in **Chapter 8** the court has already confirmed that service is permitted via NFT[20] and it is expected in the future this could extend to service of proceedings via VR given the Civil Procedural Rules has the necessary flexibility to enable service of a claim form by alternative means.[21] In *LCX AG v John Does* Nos. 1-25 (2022) the New York Supreme Court permitted service via the airdropping of a token into the wallet of unknown defendants. It is important to note that permission is required to serve a claim via alternative means under rule 6.15 of the CPR. The 2024 case of *Tai Mo Shan Limited v Persons Unknown*[22] highlights the need for safeguards to be implemented with service via NFT. In this case the court considered the issue of the public nature of an NFT recorded on the blockchain and required specific passwords

Interim applications

16.26 The court has already permitted interim freezing injunctions in several cryptocurrency matters. Freezing injunctions have even been granted against unknown persons and attached to the crypto-wallet.[23] It is likely that where there is a serious risk that assets may be dissipated then an injunction will be granted by the court in the metaverse relating to virtual assets, given the risks in respect of digital assets generally. It is highly likely that a judge will seek to try and mitigate the risks associated with the lack of certainty over where users are based, their identity and enforcement issues by permitting such injunctions.

REMEDIES

Damages in the metaverse

16.27 Given the new frontier it may be difficult to determine the quantum of damages which would be appropriate to compensate for loss suffered in the metaverse. As in real life it will depend on the substantive cause of action being claimed.

20 Cases of *D'Aloia v Persons Unknown & Others* [2022] EWHC 1723 (Ch*) Osbourne v. Persons unknown and others* [2023] EWHC 39 (KB) and *Jones v Persons Unknown* [2022] EWHC 2543 (Comm).

21 CPR rule 6.3 and 6.15.

22 [2024] EWHC 1514 (Comm).

23 *AA v Persons Unknown* [2019] EWHC 3566 (Comm).

16.28 Damages for loss of opportunity may be available for certain claims, which given the advancements in the technology may be significant as the metaverse continues to grow. It may be hard to assess the diminution in value especially with regard to damage caused to virtual assets, and it is expected that expert evidence will be required. Damage cannot be claimed where it is too speculative, which is a current risk in the metaverse, but as this evolves then this should not be the case.

16.29 Consideration is needed in respect of damages where an item has been paid for in tokens or in cryptocurrency. Should the user be compensated in the same manner or in fiat currency? The date used to determine the value of the tokens or cryptocurrency is very important and can make a considerable difference in the valuation as discussed in the recent case of *Southgate v Adam Graham* [2024] EWHC 1692 (Ch). This case addressed how the court should deal with the substantial increase in value in the cryptocurrency Ethereum between the date of the loss and the date of the award, for which the claimant was deprived.

Equitable remedies

Specific performance

16.30 Where damages are not a suitable remedy for a dispute in the metaverse a user may be able to obtain the discretionary equitable relief of specific performance and compel the performance of something promised in the metaverse unless there is a bar to the remedy of specific performance. To obtain this remedy the user will need to show that what they are asking for is unique. This may be a limited-edition virtual asset, a digital service (such as attendance at an exclusive metaverse conference) or an exclusive NFT. The case of *Southgate v Adam Graham* [2024] EWHC 1692 (Ch) was actually about damages in lieu of specific performance, and the High Court found on appeal that damages should be assessed at the date of judgment, not the date of breach. This is important with new technologies such as the metaverse where the value of virtual goods and services fluctuates considerably.

16.31 The case of *Southgate v Adam Graham* [2024] EWHC 1692 (Ch) does not close the door completely on specific performance being available on cryptocurrency as a unique asset, but Mr Justice Trower does state:

> 'There is nothing special about a contract to transfer cryptocurrency by reason of the nature of the asset concerned. The usual rules will apply to the issue of whether it should be the subject of an order for specific performance'

Rescission

16.32 The remedy of rescission will be available in the metaverse as it would in real life. One issue for consideration however, is where some part of a contract in the metaverse has been performed and some benefit has been obtained by the user. Consideration has to be had as to whether the user can be restored back to their pre-contractual position. In the metaverse, given the ability for the fantastical the avatar may already look and act differently than it did prior to the contract.

Bailment

16.33 Issues relating to bailment should apply in the metaverse should a digital asset be wrongly transferred to an incorrect user. The statutory clarification that digital assets be recognised as a category of personal property will aid in such determination and the removal of any uncertainty over whether virtual property is property.[24]

Injunction

16.34 As above the courts have already allowed injunctive relief for digital assets and there is no reason why this would not apply in the metaverse.

Tracing in the metaverse

16.35 As discussed in **Chapter 8** the door has been left slightly open to impose a fiduciary duty on software developers. There will, however be other more traditional fiduciary relationships in the metaverse. Accordingly, the issue of tracing in the metaverse will be relevant. Tracing is a remedy which provides rights '*in rem*', meaning that the assets themselves can be traced irrespective of the solvency of the defendant. Given that the accepted position, at least with the proposed legal reforms, is that digital assets are property they should be capable of being traced. In the metaverse the actual tracing is not without complications. This is because it may be technologically difficult to trace the location of assets in the metaverse once transferred or compel information in respect of the same. Where transactions are, however recorded on the blockchain tracing should be much easier.

ENFORCEMENT

16.36 Traditional methods of enforcement of any legal judgment will be challenging in the metaverse. Whilst the Hague Convention on the Recognition and Enforcement of Foreign Judgments in Civil or Commercial Matters 2019, which has been ratified in the UK[25] and will come into effect within 12 months of ratifying the Convention, will go some way to try and help with the enforcement

24 As under the case of *Colonial Bank v Whinney* [1885] 30 ChD 261.

25 Under the Recognition and Enforcement of Judgments (2019 Hague Convention etc.) Regulations 2024.

of English Judgments there are still considerable challenges with enforcement in the metaverse. In many cases the location of the other party will not necessarily be readily identifiable in the metaverse. Dealings with the other party in the metaverse may be exclusively via an avatar, with little or no other way of contact. As discussed earlier in the book novel structures such as DAOs add to this complication.

Technological enforcement

16.37 The metaverse may, however, be better equipped to assist with the enforcement of judgments in alternative ways. It is possible that judgments can eventually be enforced automatically via smart contract.

16.38 It may be possible to affix judgment to an avatar and receive recompense for any sums earned by the avatar in the metaverse.

ALTERNATIVE DISPUTE RESOLUTION IN THE METAVERSE

ADR

16.39 The metaverse has the opportunity to be used for alternative dispute resolution. Mediation in the metaverse was explored by Watanabe et al in their paper ODR in the metaverse.[26] They highlight that the current iteration of avatars being used in the metaverse may not aid mediation, since they fail to properly reflect human characteristics, especially negative reactions. Not only therefore will the mediation be artificial, it is also likely to mask important body language indicators. There are, however, benefits to using the metaverse for dispute resolution, it aims to bridge the gap between real life in-person mediation and remote mediation. It is likely that it will not be that effective until the underlying technology has improved and the avatars are more humanistic with better facial expressions.

FUTURE OF DISPUTE RESOLUTION

16.40 The Master of the Rolls, Sir Geoffrey Vos in his 2022 lecture on 'The Future for Dispute Resolution: Horizon Scanning' highlights that in the next 20 years considerable changes and challenges are expected in the civil litigation landscape.[27] He considers that once transactions and interactions are recorded on the blockchain it is unlikely that civil litigation will have a focus on determining the factual position in any dispute. Instead the 'truth' will be reflected entirely in

26 https://inns.innsofcourt.org/media/196886/some-thoughts-on-mediation-in-the-metaverse.pdf.
27 https://www.judiciary.uk/wp-content/uploads/2022/03/MR-to-SCL-Sir-Brain-Neill-Lecture-2022-The-Future-for-Dispute-Resolution-Horizon-Scannings-.pdf.

the technology. This is perhaps a little optimistic, since any interactions outside of that being recorded on the chain will surely just seek to ignite factual disputes. It is, however, clear that the use of this technology (which purists of the metaverse seek to have underpinning the virtual world/Web3 interactions) will at least make some of these disputes unnecessary. He goes on to explain that he considers the use of AI to resolve simple conflicts will be deployed to speed up the process and reduce its costs.

CONCLUSION

16.41 This chapter considers dispute resolution in the metaverse. The key takeaway points are:

- Disputes in the metaverse are unlikely to differ much from real-life disputes. There may be references to new forms of technology but the types of disputes are likely to be broadly the same.
- Arbitration is considered to be an effective dispute resolution mechanism in the metaverse.
- Steps are being taken in the UK to try and implement a cost-effective solution for early resolution of small disputes. A new infrastructure is in the process of being created in the UK. Some learning should be taken from the EU Online Dispute Resolution Platform for trying to resolve small disputes in the metaverse. What is important, however, is that the platform owners should not be the final arbitrators of truth.
- The Digital Dispute Resolution Rules are designed to be compatible with smart contracts and digital assets. This would be relevant in the metaverse. Some consideration is still needed prior to the commencement of any civil litigation process to understand whether such rules have been incorporated or not. This is important since the rules use arbitration as the basis of any dispute resolution. Meaning, if litigation is commenced and the contract is subject to the Digital Dispute Resolution Rule the litigation will be stayed.
- Where civil litigation is commenced in the UK there will need to be compliance with the CPR. Whilst dispensation can be applied to pre-action matters it is likely that a judge will want to see at least some steps have been taken to try and bring the matter to the attention of the potential defendants.
- There are likely to be issues with identifying the other parties in the metaverse, and even if this is resolved it may not be that straightforward to ascertain the nature of the other parties, their real-life identity or contact details.
- Under the CPR there is suitable flexibility to deal with issues which may arise in respect of service. There is already established case law that NFTs can be used to serve a claim form. It is likely that this will be extended further to provide for service via VR in the metaverse, but thought would

have to go into how this would be evidenced. The permission of the court would be required for such service.

- Traditional forms of remedy will be available in the metaverse. Some care is needed where an asset is likely to have considerably fluctuated in value.
- Enforcement is likely to be difficult in the metaverse given the cross-border nature, however, the technology itself, in particular blockchain and smart contracts, can be used to record and enforce judgments,

Chapter 17

Legal practice and the metaverse

'Change is the law of life. And those who look only to the past or present are certain to miss the future'

John F Kennedy

17.01 Legal practitioners need to be ready to practise in the context of the metaverse. This does not necessarily mean that lawyers need to practise within the metaverse itself, nor do they all need to be able to prepare contracts on the blockchain taking effect via smart-contracts. They will, however, increasingly see a transition into a more digital world, where disputes will arise because of interactions in the metaverse, where contracts are formed in the metaverse and where real-life issues collide with the virtual. Legal practitioners need to be ready to address the unique challenges of the metaverse, but also to be able to extrapolate virtual interactions back into real life and the traditional justice system.

REGULATION

17.02 Legal practitioners will need to ensure that their behaviour in the metaverse complies with their professional regulatory obligations. Solicitors will need to ensure that their actions are in compliance with the SRA Code of Conduct and barristers will need to comply with the Bar Standards Board Handbook.

17.03 Legal practitioners will need to ensure that at all times they are acting in the best interests of their client and this will include consideration about whether using virtual world technology, whether for dispute resolution or to effect contracts is appropriate for that client and that matter. To be able to do this a legal practitioner needs to have a firm understanding of the implications of the metaverse and its use for their client.

17.04 Legal regulators are however, minded to innovate. The SRA have established SRA Innovate which is effectively a regulatory sandbox for innovation for those regulated by the SRA.

ACCESS TO JUSTICE

17.05 The metaverse affords new ways for people to access legal services. As the metaverse expands it means that users can engage and liaise with their solicitors virtually. This means that they do not need to leave their house to be able to reach out and get advice. It also potentially means that there is the ability for 24-hour access to legal assistance.

17.06 The use of the metaverse also means that lawyers will not need a physical office which should reduce their costs, which can be passed on to their clients. This new way of engaging with lawyers should also engage younger users to access legal services.

17.07 Given the issues raised in this book, having access to legal services directly in the metaverse would be positive. It would enable those using the metaverse to be able to obtain advice swiftly from professionals who have an understanding of this terrain.

LAW FIRMS IN THE METAVERSE

17.08 Under current SRA rules it would not be possible for a solicitor's firm to be entirely virtual and operate only in the metaverse, since the SRA Authorisation of Firms Rules requires that there is at 'least one practising address in the UK'. This does not mean that a firm cannot be virtual in some respects, provided there is at least one identifiable UK address. This is likely to be the physical location of where the real-life solicitor is practising.

17.09 The SRA Code of Conduct for Firms requires that there are 'effective governance structures, arrangements and systems in place'.[1] This may be more of a challenge in the metaverse given it is a new landscape. Careful consideration will be needed on confidentiality and security of documents where these are either being stored or accessed via the metaverse.

17.10 It is also likely to be harder to supervise staff who may be practising in the metaverse since it is likely to fall outside of existing case management systems. Any firm looking to expand into the metaverse will need to have effective systems to be able to monitor cases and properly record matters where this is being carried out in the metaverse.

MARKETING FOR LEGAL SERVICES IN THE METAVERSE AND REFERRAL FEES

17.11 Solicitors will remain subject to restrictions on unsolicited marketing approaches in the metaverse. In addition, any referral or introduction fee that may be made available via the metaverse (whether in fiat or in tokens or other consideration) will remain subject to restrictions under the SRA Code of Conduct

1 Rule 2.1.

and where applicable will be prohibited if they are banned referral fees in real life.[2]

CLIENT CARE IN THE METAVERSE

17.12 Where clients would like to engage with a legal professional in the metaverse it is important that proper consideration is had to regulatory requirements and best practice on client care.

17.13 Processes will need to be implemented to ensure that you can identify the client, especially if your only interaction is as avatars. The use of an avatar could result in a user concealing their true identity from you, resulting in you having difficulties undertaking proper conflict checks to comply with the SRA Code of Conduct.[3] You may therefore not really know from whom you are taking instructions, and who else may be able to hear your interactions. Identifying the client may also not necessarily be straightforward in the metaverse, especially if there are alternative business structures such as a DAO.

17.14 It is good practice to agree how you will be communicating with your client.[4] This is something that will need to be addressed clearly in the metaverse, and whether communication via avatars in the metaverse is sufficient. It is vital that lawyers comply with the Equality Act 2010 in respect of their communications with people with specific disabilities and suitable adjustments are made.

17.15 Key information regarding any case and the firm[5] should be provided to the client. This is usually done in writing. Information being made available in writing may not always be the most practical approach in the metaverse. Law firms will need to determine when it is appropriate to use innovative forms of technology to convey mandatory information[6] and other important details about any case and where more traditional forms of communication are appropriate. In the future, key information about costs and information on the case could be put on the blockchain as a permanent point of reference. Care would have to be had given the issues with data protection and the blockchain as discussed above. Perhaps more concerning is the issue with potentially recording privileged information on the blockchain.

2 Under the Legal Aid, Sentencing and Punishment of Offenders Act 2012, ss 56 – 60.

3 Rule 4.1 requires that you can only act on instructions from a client or someone authorised by a client, but in the metaverse such checks will be difficult as someone could access the VR headset and pose as your client – this is likely to pose problematic especially in family law matters.

4 https://www.lawsociety.org.uk/Topics/Client-care/Guides/Engaging-clients.

5 Such as regulation/ complaints processes/ ombudsman and challenges to a bill.

6 Such as that information required under Provision of Services Regulations 2009.

KNOW-YOUR-CLIENT AND AML

17.16 The metaverse raises novel practical issues for lawyers. One such area is around know-your-client checks and anti-money laundering considerations. Law firms will need to establish clear KYC and AML checks for clients operating in the metaverse. This should be reflected on their updated risk assessment.

17.17 The widespread use of DAO structures especially in blockchain related metaverses brings added complications. The dealing in crypto-assets will present further AML risks and considerations. The Law Commission considers that changes may be required to anti-money laundering regulations to deal with DAOs

TRANSPARENT PRICING

17.18 Those regulated by the SRA will need to ensure that they comply with the transparency rules and provide pricing information where they work in certain areas. The metaverse could be used effectively to provide such information in a new and innovative way. Where services are provided in the metaverse steps will need to be taken to consider how the pricing information can be displayed.

VULNERABLE CLIENTS

17.19 Should legal services be delivered via the metaverse, this may act as a barrier for certain vulnerable clients. Further consideration is needed where a client requires a carer. In the metaverse it will be difficult to see whether that client is being subjected to coercion or unfair pressure in real life since it is expected that the carer will be in the same room as the client and will be effectively shielded by the VR. In fact in certain circumstances, it may be that the lawyer is not even aware that there is a carer or potentially even other people in the same room as the client since all they will see is the client's avatar in the metaverse.

CYBER SECURITY AND INSURANCE

17.20 Cyber security is already a key area of risk for law firms and many have already recently suffered attacks. Moving into the metaverse may increase the risk of cyber-attacks depending on the platform being used and how this may be integrated into the main firm software. To effectively use the metaverse and transition legal services into the metaverse there will need to be a suitable level of integration with case management systems to enable efficient delivery of legal services.

CONFIDENTIALITY AND LEGAL PRIVILEGE IN THE METAVERSE

17.21 The principles of confidentiality and legal privilege underpin the trusted position between a regulated legal professional and their client. In the metaverse there are currently serious concerns around the level of confidentiality that can be afforded to any dialogue. Interactions in the metaverse will be recorded on the platform owner's systems. There is no certainty that such information will be treated as confidential. Further in the metaverse there is always the risk that any confidential conversation may be interrupted by a third party or even overheard (either in the metaverse or in real life). A solution is needed if the idea of legal practice in the metaverse is to be properly adopted. This could be a technological solution which enables protective bubbles where lawyers and their clients can have private conversation. Clarification would be needed that records held of conversations in the metaverse would be treated as confidential and not impact on privilege, much in the same way as with email now. Put simply, the metaverse would be a new way of interacting but not change these fundamental principles.

COURTS IN THE METAVERSE

17.22 In February 2023 Colombia held the first court hearing in the metaverse.[7] This shows that hearings can successfully take place in the metaverse and paves the way for future use of the metaverse for court hearings. The proceedings lasted two hours and there were no technical issues. The court followed legal conventions and complied with all legal obligations. Whilst this is clearly a progressive step there is the need to ensure that suitable security measures are implemented so that the correct avatars have the correct levels of permission to attend and participate properly. The longstanding maxim of Lord Hewart comes to mind:

> 'It is not merely of some importance but is of fundamental importance that justice should not only be done, but should manifestly and undoubtedly be seen to be done'[8]

17.23 If there are technological barriers which would impede the ability of the public to attend and bear witness at courts in the metaverse then this principle of justice is at risk of being lost. The metaverse court needs to be seen to be just, fair and following proper processes. In the UK there are strict court procedures and customs, such as bowing to the Royal Coats of Arms and witnesses would need to swear an oath or affirm before giving their evidence. Given this would technically be done by the avatars it is unclear at this stage whether this can all be complied with; however, the courts have been able to adapt to remote hearings relatively swiftly.

7 https://www.weforum.org/videos/colombia-just-held-a-court-hearing-in-the-metaverse/.

8 *R v. Sussex Justices ex parte McCarthy*, [1924] 1 KB 256.

17.24 Legal commentators[9] consider that the use of metaverse courts may speed up proceedings and the length of time it takes for a matter to come to court. In the UK the courts are already routinely listing court hearings via Microsoft Teams as a way to reduce costs and speed up delays. As part of their study into 'Are our courts fit for purpose' the Law Commission found that many solicitors found courts to have significant delays, over one third felt unsafe at court and over one quarter felt that courts were not fit for purpose.[10] There is the risk however, that courts in the metaverse may act as a barrier for vulnerable clients and further assistance may be required to help them with the same. In particular the Law Society in their 'Law under lockdown: the impact of Covid-19 measures on access to justice and vulnerable people'[11] raised concerns about the effectiveness of translators for remote hearings as well as the feeling of a loss of support that vulnerable people felt during a remote hearing when compared with a real-life hearing. These same issues will manifest in the metaverse. In fact, it may be more pronounced since in the metaverse the digital representations will be avatars whereas during the remote hearings at least the clients could see the real-life advocates. This may decrease once there are more realistic looking avatars.

EVIDENCE AND PROOF IN THE METAVERSE

17.25 The law of evidence concerns how facts are be determined by a court or tribunal. The metaverse presents a new set of factual constructs which in the first instance are going to have to fit into the traditional legal landscape. In Horizon Worlds data is made available only for a short time to users so that they can use it to complain to the platform, it is then deleted making it difficult for the user to enforce later.[12] Any evidence will be deleted from the user's device before the expiry of limitation periods and is apparently not stored on the Meta servers.

17.26 Given the global nature of the metaverse the underlying differences and approaches between the adversarial systems and inquisitorial systems will cause issues in the metaverse. This has a knock-on effect on evidence and proof. Common law countries typically use an adversarial system, seeking the 'truth' through a combative process with a 'winner' and 'loser' refereed by a judge. The inquisitorial system of civil law systems instead puts the emphasis on the judge as the arbitrator of truth and an active player in the pursuit of the truth. With common law systems it is likely to be easier to adapt current laws and regulations to apply to the new technology. As Lord Denning said 'the principles of the

9 *Bertovskiy, L.V., Devyatkin, G.S. and Fedorov, A.R.*, (2024). Interdisciplinary Aspects of the Introduction of Virtual Reality Technologies in Court Proceedings. Kutafin Law Review, 11(1), pp. 124– 141, doi: 10.17803/2713-0533.2024.1.27.124-141.

10 https://www.lawsociety.org.uk/Topics/Research/Are-our-courts-fit-for-purpose.

11 https://www.lawsociety.org.uk/Topics/Research/Law-under-lockdown-the-impact-of-Covid-19-measures-on-access-to-justice-and-vulnerable-people.

12 https://nickclegg.medium.com/making-the-metaverse-what-it-is-how-it-will-be-built-and-why-it-matters-3710f7570b04

lawyer should be modified when found to be unsuited to the times or discarded when found to work injustice'.[13] It may be time to look for alternative solutions, given the global reach of the metaverse.

LEGAL TRAINING IN THE METAVERSE

17.27 There are considerable opportunities for junior lawyers to train as lawyers in the metaverse. There is the scope for the metaverse to run mock court cases and virtual mock mediations, client interviewing and negotiations – where training and feedback can be provided in real time.[14] Further ongoing continuing professional development could also be offered and monitored in the metaverse.

WHAT NEXT?

17.28 The metaverse is ready to be explored. It is a new terrain with almost limitless potential. Never before have we had the opportunity to participate in the establishment of literally a new world, a new jurisdiction and a new form of reality. There are opportunities right now to help establish not only the legal framework of this land but the very principles of justice, the rule of law, democracy and human rights. It is no coincidence that throughout history industrial revolutions have caused changes in law.[15] It is exciting to see how the current digital revolution will change the law and legal practice.

13 Lord Denning, *The Discipline of Law*, (1979) Butterworths, London.

14 Andrea M. Seielstad, 'Enhancing the teaching of lawyering skills and perspectives through virtual world engagement' (2012) 7 U. Mass. L. Rev. 40 pp 40-108.

15 Simonyan in 'The Fourth Industrial Revolution and the New Path of Law' (2023) Bulletin of Yerevan University c: jurisprudence vol 14. No 2 (39) highlights that the First Industrial Revolution coincided amongst other new laws in the Napoleons Civil Code; the Second Industrial Revolution created labour laws.

Index

[*All references are to paragraph numbers*]

E

R